Civilian Jihad

Nonviolent Struggle, Democratization, and Governance in the Middle East

Edited by
Maria J. Stephan

palgrave
macmillan

First published in 2009 by
PALGRAVE MACMILLAN®
in the United States—a division of St. Martin's Press LLC,
175 Fifth Avenue, New York, NY 10010.

Where this book is distributed in the UK, Europe and the rest of the world,
this is by Palgrave Macmillan, a division of Macmillan Publishers Limited,
registered in England, company number 785998, of Houndmills,
Basingstoke, Hampshire RG21 6XS.

Palgrave Macmillan is the global academic imprint of the above
companies and has companies and representatives throughout the world.

Palgrave® and Macmillan® are registered trademarks in the United States,
the United Kingdom, Europe and other countries.

ISBN: 978–0–230–62140–4 (hardcover)
ISBN: 978–0–230–62141–1 (paperback)

Library of Congress Cataloging-in-Publication Data is available from the
Library of Congress.

A catalogue record of the book is available from the British Library.

Design by Newgen Imaging Systems (P) Ltd., Chennai, India.

First edition: December 2009

D 10 9 8 7 6 5 4 3

Printed in the United States of America.

*The views presented in this book do not reflect
those of the U.S. government*

Contents

(b)   Challenging Domestic Tyranny and Promoting Democratic Reform

(c)   Movements for Social and Political Rights

Illustrations

Table

Figures

Acknowledgments

I would like to thank my colleagues at the International Center on Nonviolent Conflict (ICNC), including Peter Ackerman, Jack DuVall, Shaazka Beyerle, Vanessa Ortiz, Hardy Merriman, Nicola Barrach, Andy Kostrub, and Kristen Kopko, for their great encouragement and help in bringing about the publication of Civilian Jihad. I would like to especially thank Hardy Merriman for his careful review of the chapters and thoughtful editorial suggestions. It has been tremendous pleasure working with all the authors; they have brought the story of civil resistance in the Middle East to life with their stories and cannot be thanked enough. To Robin Surratt, for her copyediting acumen and tremendous support throughout the process, I owe a debt of gratitude and then some. Mary E. King, who has been an outstanding mentor and booster throughout this process, deserves special recognition and thanks. Farideh Koohi-Kamali, Robyn Curtis, Allison McElgunn, and Maran Elancheran at Palgrave and Newgen Imaging Systems have been terrific partners in this endeavor, and I owe them many thanks. The Java House on 17th and Q Streets, NW (Washington, DC) afforded me a comfortable and stimulating space to write and edit; I am grateful to the staff for their support and good humor. Most importantly, to my parents and brother, whose support and encouragement have known no bounds, words cannot express my appreciation.

Introduction

Maria J. Stephan

Ordinary people across the Middle East, a region notorious for its many conflicts, have for decades fought for rights, freedoms, self-determination, and democracy without using violence. Khalid Kishtainy, an Iraqi intellectual, coined the term *civilian jihad* to describe a form of political struggle whose "weapons" include boycotts, strikes, protests, sit-downs, humor, and other acts of civil disobedience and nonviolent defiance.[1] Challenging the notion that the fight against tyranny and oppression is best left to guerillas, armed insurgents, or foreign actors, the essays and case studies that follow show how civil resistance, defined by scholars as the "widespread and sustained activities by ordinary civilians against a particular power, force, policy or regime"[2] can achieve remarkable results. *Civilian Jihad: Nonviolent Struggle, Democratization, and Governance in the Middle East* examines the past, present, and future of advancing justice, rights, and democracy without the use of violence in one of the most fascinating and geopolitically important areas of the world.

Groups worldwide have adopted civil resistance for a multitude of purposes: to resist colonialism; to challenge foreign invasion and occupation; to resist rigged elections, dictatorship, or military rule; to win minority rights; to fight corruption; and to eradicate institutionalized discrimination. Since the early twentieth century, struggles pitting unarmed civilians against historically entrenched economic and military opponents have produced dramatic results: the popular struggle led by the Hindu-Muslim tandem Mahatma Gandhi and Khan Abdul Ghaffar Khan against British colonialism on the Indian subcontinent (1930–1931); the nonviolent ouster of Chilean dictator Augusto Pinochet (1988); the dismantling of communist dictatorships in Eastern Europe (1989); the abolition of apartheid in South Africa (1990s); the overthrow of Western-backed dictators from the Philippines (1986) to Mali (1991); and the reversal of stolen or rigged elections in Serbia (2000), Georgia (2003), and Ukraine (2004–2005). Civil resistance has been and continues to be a propulsive, if still misunderstood, force for change around the world.

The study of civil resistance, notably in the context of nondemocratic societies, has expanded significantly since the scholar Gene Sharp wrote *The Politics of Nonviolent Action* in 1973.[3] Sharp's simple yet provocative assertion that political power is rooted in and dependent upon cooperation and obedience, and that this cooperation and obedience can be withdrawn, opened an avenue of analysis and thinking that has since been traveled by scholars from various academic disciplines. His theories and observations led social scientists, historians, regional studies experts, and strategic studies scholars to take a closer look at nonviolent direct action as a methodology of struggle.[4] The number of works dedicated to the study of popular nonviolent movements has grown as the number of successful campaigns of civil resistance around the world has increased.[5] *People Power and Protest since 1945*, a meticulously researched bibliography of nonviolent action compiled by April Carter, Howard Clark, and Michael Randle, reveals the breath and depth of scholarly examination of this phenomenon.[6]

Why a volume on civil resistance in the Middle East? In part, because the greater Middle East is not typically imagined as a place where civil resistance could take root, much less succeed.[7] The region has had no shortage of conventional wars, insurgencies, terrorist attacks, and other forms of political violence. It is well known that, based on ratings of political rights and civil liberties, the Middle East is the most autocratic region of the world.[8] *The Arab Human Development Report* (2002), a remarkably forthright document written by Arab intellectuals and civic leaders, concluded that the "freedom deficit" in Arab countries "undermines human development and is one of the most painful manifestations of lagging political development."[9] The intransigence of "full autocracies" and "liberalizing autocracies" (along with full and semi-authoritarianism),[10] the long history of colonialism and foreign interventionism in the region, oil-fuelled rentierism,[11] the 60-year-old Arab-Israeli conflict, nuclear weapons proliferation, and the spread of violent extremism help make the area "the most difficult region in the world for democracy."[12]

Although democratic deficiencies loom large in the Middle East, the democratic aspirations of the region's people loom even larger. Polls consistently reveal strong support for democracy among Middle Easterners even in the aftermath of the 2003 U.S.-led invasion and subsequent occupation of Iraq.[13] There also exists a growing realization that democratic development consists of more than toppling dictators and holding elections.[14] One finds a greater awareness that militarily driven democratization has profound limitations and can result in any number of tragic and unpredictable consequences. What continues to be missing from most scholarly and policy discussions about democratic development in the Middle East is the role of civilian-driven strategies in forging regional transformation. *Civilian Jihad* is an attempt to expand the debate on democratization and governance in the area to include these powerful but overlooked indigenous forces for change.

While experts debate the pros and cons of "go-slow" approaches versus rapid movement toward democracy and justice in the region—with autocrats and their supporters generally preferring the former—people's patience with the status quo appears to be wearing thin. The region's large, youthful populations, desperate for jobs and a political voice and less risk-averse than their parents, are increasingly clamoring for new, radically different systems of governance based on the will of the people. The role of youth, women, and moderate Islamist and nationalist movements in accelerating political change, above and beyond mere tweaks to the authoritarian status quo, constitutes a central theme of this volume. As this book goes to press, a "green movement" continues to unfold in Iran. Sparked by popular outrage over the declared victory of Mahmoud Ahmadinejad in the June 12, 2009 elections widely believed to have been rigged, the Iranian people have risen up to demand that their civil and political rights be respected. More than any time since Iran's 1979 Islamic revolution, the country's theocracy is being shaken to the core as nonviolent protestors, enduring severe repression, persist in their protests and erstwhile regime backers, including prominent religious figures, are switching to the opposition. The outcome of the green movement, described at the end of Chapter 20, could have a profound impact on the country, the region, and the world.

Civilian Jihad examines locally originated nonviolent campaigns as a force for change in the region. At the same time the role of external actors in this process cannot be overlooked. Efforts at external democracy promotion in the region, notably those led by the United States, appear to Middle Easterners and to many foreign observers as inconsistent and rife with double standards.[15] The 2003 invasion and occupation of Iraq, in part justified by the Bush administration on the grounds of spreading democracy in the region, has served in some ways to reinforce the influence of radicals in the region while offering the autocratic regimes a convenient excuse to brand dissent as foreign-inspired and to besmirch democratic reform.[16] Although the Barack Obama administration is winning accolades in the region and around the world for the young president's willingness to listen, reach out to enemies, and reengage multilateral partners, conflicting foreign and domestic policy priorities will continue to pose a serious challenge to U.S. support for democratic development in the region.

Even nonmilitary and arguably other helpful forms of democracy assistance—diplomatic and economic sanctions targeting regime elites, conditioning aid based on democratic performance, strengthening political parties, protecting human rights defenders, promoting independent media, providing training and assistance to nonviolent civic groups, and so on cannot substitute for locally-driven processes of democratic development in the region.[17] Few would dispute that democracy must be locally owned and operated to have a chance at long-term success. Indeed, empirical evidence supports this contention. A 2005 Freedom House study authored by Peter Ackerman and Adrian Karatnacky found that 50 out of 67 transitions from authoritarianism between 1972 and 2005, or more than 70 percent of them, were driven by bottom-up civic movements.[18] Top-down transitions, launched and led by elites, had comparatively little positive effect for freedom. Meanwhile, armed revolutions and insurgencies—ostensibly, functional alternatives to nonviolent civil resistance—fared extremely poorly in replacing authoritarianism with rights-respecting governments. An opposition's recourse to armed struggle, the report found, "is significantly less likely to produce sustainable freedom, in contrast to nonviolent opposition, which even in the face of state repression is far more likely to yield a democratic outcome."[19]

This situation necessarily raises the question of whether and to what extent structural conditions determine the outcomes of civic movements. Another recent quantitative study found that contrary to what one might assume, such factors as regime type, level of economic development, literacy rate, or fractionalization of society along ethnic, linguistic, and religious lines have not had a statistically significant impact on the ability of a civic movement to achieve success through civil resistance campaigns.[20] In other words, groups committed to the democratic, nonviolent transformation of authoritarian societies are not prisoners of preexisting political or environmental factors. The major implication of these findings is that the strategies and skills employed by nonviolent civic groups are as important, if not *more* important, than the conditions surrounding their struggle—a hopeful conclusion for nonviolent freedom fighters in the Middle East. The strong correlation between bottom-up civil resistance and democracy, furthermore, begs the following question: What is it about this method of struggle that makes it conducive to removing oppression?

The answer to this question gets to the core of how civil resistance "works" to shift power and effect change. By its very nature, civil resistance is highly participatory. Ordinary people of all kinds—young and old, rich and poor, men and women, farmers and factory workers, religionists and atheist—can become frontline fighters, as opposed to passive observers, as is often the case in armed struggles, which tend only to involve young, able-bodied males. Civil resistance offers participants hundreds of different tactics, ranging from relatively lower-risk symbolic protests and consumer boycotts to higher-risk demonstrations and sit-ins. The barriers to participation are low, and after regime repression, people can return to the "battlefield" quicker than in armed campaigns.[21] Readers will likely be impressed by the remarkably creative, albeit culturally specific tactics that civilian activists in the Middle East have devised to expose injustices, mobilize opposition, and put pressure on power-holders throughout the region. Anti-corruption hero contests, soccer stadium sit-ins, street theatre, rooftop chanting, jokes sent via SMS, "no taxation without representation" campaigns, parliamentary walk-outs, and the creation of a nonviolent "army" are only a few of the nonviolent tactics described in the book.

The process by which broad-based coalitions form over the course of nonviolent struggles also contributes to their success. In fact, *How Freedom Is Won* reports that "the presence of strong and cohesive civic coalitions is the most important of the factors examined in contributing to freedoms."[22] Strong civic movements that enjoin the active participation of many different sectors of society do not form automatically, nor are they maintained through coercive means, as is often the case in armed struggles.[23] The negotiations and deliberative dialogue involving different societal groups that lead to the formation of nonviolent coalitions, and the negotiations between oppositionists and regime supporters that often occur during nonviolent struggles, also help create the basis for democratic sustainability.[24]

Nonviolent struggles do not always succeed. The 1989 Chinese student-led protests in Tiananmen Square and the 1988 and 2007 Burmese uprisings against the military junta in Myanmar offer stark reminders that civil resistance sometimes falters or fails. As with armed uprisings, any number of factors can affect the likelihood of success or failure. This book does not shy away from discussing the shortcomings of civil resistance in the Middle East; just as much—if not more—can be learned from failure as from success. At the same time, it is important to point out that compared to armed campaigns civil resistance has been remarkably successful. A recent study of 323 violent and nonviolent resistance campaigns from 1900 to 2006 found that nonviolent campaigns have outperformed their armed counterparts by an almost 2:1 ratio, achieving success 51 percent of the time compared to a 26 percent success rate for armed insurgencies.[25]

As noted, and as the essays in this book highlight, nonviolent resistance campaigns are more likely than violent campaigns to attract mass participation, enhancing the legitimacy of the challenge group and making it more likely that the opponent's use of violent repression against members of the resistance will backfire.[26] The systematic withdrawal of consent and cooperation by large numbers of people undermines the opponent's social, political, economic, and even military sources of power, thereby raising the physical and economic costs of maintaining control.[27] The relative strategic effectiveness of civil resistance, compared with its violent alternatives, affords further rationale for studying its applications in the Middle East.

About This Book

A number of books have examined the philosophical and religious foundations of "nonviolence" while others have focused on negotiation, conflict resolution, and third party intervention in the region.[28] The focus of this book is different; *Civilian Jihad* describes how peoples throughout the Middle East have waged conflict using nonviolent, nonmilitary means—risking death but unwilling to take lives to achieve their objectives. The subject of nonviolent struggle in this part of the world has not received much attention in or outside the academy, with an exception being *Arab Nonviolent Political Struggle in the Middle East* (1990), an edited volume by Ralph E. Crow, Philip Grant, and Saad Eddin Ibrahim.[29] More recent works have focused on actors and agency in movements for rights and democracy in the Middle East.[30]

Civilian Jihad broadens and deepens these earlier works, discussing contemporary applications of civil resistance and exploring the relationship between civil resistance, democratic development, and governance. In addition to the significant number of case studies, a few of which may be new to readers (others have never been fully documented), the book offers a rich look at related topics, including Islamists' use of civil resistance, the use of humor and satire in nonviolent struggle, and the complex, double-edged nature of external support for local actors and movements. The multidisciplinary treatment of civil resistance in this volume should interest scholars, activists, and policymakers from diverse intellectual backgrounds. The contributors consist of political scientists, sociologists, historians, and regional studies experts. A few of the authors actively participated in the campaigns that they chronicle, affording readers an "insider's perspective" on some of the most significant and consequential nonviolent struggles in the Middle East.

A few of the issues addressed by the authors and contributors to this volume include the following:

- Where has civil resistance been used in the Middle East, by whom, and for what purposes? How effective has it been?
- What are the main challenges and obstacles faced by advocates and practitioners of civil resistance in the region? How have they been overcome?
- What roles have ideology, discourse, and rhetoric played in legitimizing and mobilizing popular resistance, violent and nonviolent?
- How have external actors, governmental and nongovernmental, influenced the trajectories and outcomes of civil resistance campaigns in the region?
- What lessons about strategic nonviolent action can be distilled from the cases discussed in this book? How does skillful civil resistance relate to democratic development?

Readers will discover a strong emphasis on human agency, skills, and strategy in the chapters that follow. Although Orientalist accounts of the region and its people would have us believe that the region's culture inherently makes the establishment of a stable indigenous democratic order impossible[31] (and successful civil resistance even more unthinkable) this book challenges that view. Middle Eastern activists and civic leaders have put life and limb on the line in struggles for freedom and self-determination, but their stories as told here are not an elegy to victimhood, but profiles of courageous resistance to oppression.

At the same time, the emphasis on agency in *Civilian Jihad* is not to the exclusion of structural factors and geostrategic realities. The scholarly and policy debates on the causes and consequences of the democratic deficit in the Middle East reveal the obstacles faced and the opportunities available to civic activists in the region. Understanding structural constraints is important to understanding possible trajectories of civil resistance and the prospect of this method of struggle being a force for political change in the region.[32] The roles played by political parties and elites and the institutional dynamics of democratic reform are also discussed. The volume, however, does not focus primarily on top-down, elite-driven processes of reform. Other experts on the Middle East and democratization have analyzed the "modernization approach,"[33] as well as other aspects of democratic transitions far more systematically.[34]

Analyses and Case Studies

The first part of the book covers the theoretical foundations of and interdisciplinary themes associated with civil resistance and its applications in the Middle East. In the opening overview chapter, Hardy Merriman defines civil resistance and related terminology and provides an analytical framework to understand why and how civil resistance works. Merriman discusses the relationship between power and obedience, surveys the six key sources of power over which nonviolent movements and their opponents compete, analyzes structural weaknesses in regimes that can be targeted by nonviolent movements, classifies different categories of nonviolent tactics, highlights key attributes of communications by nonviolent movements, and explains how the systematic application of nonviolent sanctions by large numbers of people can fundamentally shift power even in repressive contexts. In presenting the core strategic principles of civil resistance, Merriman also weaves in examples from the Middle East case studies that follow.

A number of misconceptions and red herrings bedevil the popular view of civil resistance, some of which are not uncommon in the Middle East. Ralph E. Crow and Philip Grant's chapter, originally published in *Arab Nonviolent Political Struggle in the Middle East,* highlights some of the central issues and controversies involving this approach in the region. These include the association of civil resistance with pacifism, weakness, or the mere renunciation of violence, the perception that nonviolent resistance is an imperialist stratagem or prevents legitimate self-defense, and the belief that only violence can mobilize global pressure against oppression or liberate the oppressed. Most of these ideas stem from fundamental misunderstandings about civil resistance. Correcting these misperceptions is crucial to waging an effective battle of ideas against those who advocate violence in challenging injustice and oppression in the Middle East.

Asef Bayat rebuts the oft-heard claim that Islam and democracy are incompatible. As Bayat writes, "the compatibility or incompatibility of Islam and democracy is not a matter of philosophical speculation, but of political struggle; it is not as much a matter of texts as a balance of power between those who want an authoritarian religion and those who desire a democratic version." He introduces the notion of "post-Islamism" and discusses how this ideology fuses religiosity with rights and challenges the hegemonic discourse of violence that has taken root in some (but not all) Islamic societies today. Bayat also examines the logic, conditions, and forces behind rendering the Islamic experience democratic or undemocratic by comparing the socioreligious movements in Iran and Egypt since the 1970s.

Humor and civil resistance often go hand in hand. Khalid Kishtainy discusses how political jokes and satire have been used as a "weapon" for denunciation, opposition, and resistance in the Middle East. For Kishtainy, political humor is a "a lower-risk, nonviolent channel for discussing injustice, defying foreign occupation, and challenging defunct precepts and misrule." He offers examples of how, historically, jokes have been used, mainly in Egypt but also in other Arab countries, to unify people and provide a sense of shared destiny, while inculcating a spirit of resistance. Readers should be forewarned that some of the jokes that Kishtainy recounts are unabashedly bawdy.

Mass-based Islamist groups and parties, those with grassroots support and religious legitimacy, have transformed the political landscape of the Middle East and continue to do so. As Shadi Hamid describes in his chapter on Islamists and nonviolent action, the largest of these groups, including Egypt's Muslim Brotherhood, Jordan's Islamic Action Front, and Morocco and Turkey's Justice and Development Parties, have taken violence off the table in entering the political mainstream. Although these groups have focused their efforts on building parallel structures and institutions, (a form of nonviolent intervention), they have also avoided the use of more confrontational forms of nonviolent direct action when dealing with their respective autocratic regimes. Hamid describes how strategic calculations made hitherto by Islamist groups, combined with a lack of external support for them, have influenced their views on civil resistance as a means of advancing their goals.

Rami Khouri elaborates on Islamists' recent turn to civil resistance by examining the powerful role played by religious discourse, leadership, and organization in popular struggles for basic rights and freedoms throughout the Middle East. Comparing the role of religion in the U.S. civil rights movement with the "Islamist awakening" in the Middle East, Khouri argues that the "single most pivotal element in both instances was the manner in which religious values and political activism naturally converge. Religion became a vehicle—the only one available—for political transformation." The author also contends that the popular yearning for freedom in the region has been thwarted by decades of U.S. and Western-backed interference and foreign occupation and calls for greater understanding of and solidarity with those fighting nonviolently for rights and dignity in the region.

Although indigenous movements have driven virtually every successful nonviolent campaign in the Middle East and elsewhere, external actors often play important supportive roles. Stephen Zunes and Saad Eddin Ibrahim, the latter a prominent Egyptian pro-democracy dissident, examine the double-edged nature of external support in a region whose history of colonialism, neocolonialism, and foreign occupation have made its inhabitants understandably suspicious of outside involvement. They review the positive and negative ways in which diaspora groups, Western governments, and nongovernmental organizations have influenced nonviolent opposition movements in the region. "Although any struggle against a repressive regime would normally welcome international solidarity," the authors conclude, "if the outside support is seen as coming from forces which are not believed to have the best interest of the country's people in mind, it can harm the chances of such a movement succeeding."

The second part of the volume consists of case studies. The first group of cases chronicle and analyze popular nonviolent struggles against colonial regimes and foreign occupations in the greater Middle East. Mohammed Raqib's contribution on the Khudai Khidmatgars (Servants of God) movement, first published in *Waging Nonviolent Struggle*,[35] offers a compelling example of nonviolent resistance in difficult circumstances. Khan Abdul Ghaffar Khan, a highly respected Pashtun, led thousands of Muslims Pashtuns, along with Hindus and Sikhs, in defiance against British rule in the North-West Frontier Province (along what is now the volatile border region between Pakistan and Afghanistan), by creating a nonviolent "army" whose soldiers wore red uniforms, underwent prolonged training, and pledged to defend their homeland without violence. The so-called Red Shirts organized tax revolts, boycotted foreign products, and refused any form of cooperation with the British colonial administration. The alliance between the Muslim Khudai Khidmatgars and the Hindu-led Indian National Congress, forged around a common strategy of civil resistance, played a pivotal role in ending British colonial rule.

The Druze population of Syria's Israeli-occupied Golan Heights turned to a different form of resistance to defend their community against forced assimilation by Israel. Fourteen years after capturing the Golan during the June 1967 war, Israel passed legislation in 1981 to effectively annex the territory, thereby forcing the Druze, a tightly knit minority sect known for its members' fierce independence and military prowess, to accept Israeli identification. Scott Kennedy describes how the Druze first petitioned for a reversal of the Knesset's action, and when that failed, they announced a campaign of total noncooperation. Druze laborers refused to work, crippling industry in northern Israel for several weeks. Those who took Israeli ID cards faced ostracism. When Israeli forces cordoned Druze villages, the Druze defied curfews, confronted armed Israeli soldiers, and persisted with acts of nonviolent defiance until the Israelis lifted the siege. The Golani Druze ultimately succeeded in preserving their Syrian national identity.

The first Palestinian intifada is one of the most impressive examples of civilian jihad in the Middle East. Launched in December 1987, the uprising was a popular rebellion against the Israeli occupation of the West Bank, Gaza Strip, and East Jerusalem. Mary King describes how the intifada grew out of more than two decades of local community organizing, the creation of diffuse centers of power in the occupied territories, and creative partnerships between Palestinian and Israeli activists starting in the early 1980s. The intifada's scope, intensity, mass participation, and relatively nonviolent character made it an exceptional event that permanently altered Palestinian society and transformed the Palestinians' relationship with Israel. King notes that the leadership of the Palestine Liberation Organization never fully understood the role of civil resistance in challenging the Israeli occupation, and after two years, the popular uprising turned violent only after the original advocates of nonviolent resistance in the territories had been arrested by Israel. The intifada led to the U.S. efforts that resulted in the 1991 international peace conference in Madrid and to Palestinian participation in Middle East peace talks. King concludes the chapter by describing the current Palestinian-led popular resistance against the separation barrier in the West Bank.

Salka Barca, a Western Saharan activist, and Stephen Zunes examine how the indigenous Sahrawi population of the Western Sahara uses nonviolent struggle to resist Morocco's long-standing occupation of this North African territory. Although Morocco has liberalized considerably since King Mohamed VI succeeded his father, King Hassan II, the Western Sahara, annexed illegally by Morocco in 1975, continues to be governed with severe repression. Following a period of armed struggle against Morocco by the nationalist Polisario Front, a cease-fire took effect in 1990. With negotiations over the future of the territory stalled, the indigenous Sahrawi population, now grossly outnumbered by Moroccan settlers, launched a nonviolent intifada for independence in 2005. The Sahrawis' nonviolent resistance campaign has included protests inside the occupied territory and in southern Morocco, with activists using Paltalk and other technologies to communicate and mobilize. Barca and Zunes analyze the unique features of this anti-occupation struggle while stressing the strategic imperative of extending the nonviolent battlefield inside Morocco and internationally.

In March 2005, following the assassination of former Prime Minister Rafiq al-Hariri, more than a million Muslims, Christians, and Druze from all parts of Lebanon descended on Martyrs' Square in Beirut for the largest and most dramatic nonviolent demonstration in that country's history. Together with Rudy Jaafar, we describe how a combination of sophisticated grassroots organizing, creative use of nonviolent methods and SMS text messaging, savvy public relations, and strong external pressure contributed to the ouster of a pro-Syrian prime minister, forced the withdrawal of Syrian forces from Lebanese territory, and paved the way to the freest and fairest elections in Lebanon's history. The popular uprising, which Lebanese refer to as their "independence intifada," achieved its objective of ending the de facto occupation, though it did not create structural changes in the Lebanese government, which meant that the country's dysfunctional sectarian and elite-dominated political system remained intact. The chapter analyzes the strengths and shortcomings of the Lebanese campaign, which produced some of the most stunning images in the history of nonviolent struggle.

The next set of case studies focuses on nonviolent struggles against authoritarianism. It is sometimes forgotten that the 1978–1979 Iranian Revolution, which dramatically altered the social, political, and geostrategic landscape of the Middle East, was achieved through a popular nonviolent uprising. Mohsen Sazegara, a member of Ayatollah Ruhollah Khomeini's inner circle during the revolution, and I describe how civil resistance toppled an unjust, 37-year-old government in less than 100 days. The Islamic revolution, led by the exiled Khomeini but carried out by Iranians living under the shah, was guided by an ambiguous ideology that mobilized groups from across Iran's religious and political spectrum to participate in mass anti-government protests, strikes that paralyzed the country's economy, and sustained noncooperation with the shah's repressive regime. The mosque-baazari network in Iran played a crucial role in organizing a popular resistance that systematically removed the shah's most important pillars of support and helped neutralize his security forces. The Iranian Revolution—which overthrew a secular regime through nonviolent means, yet paved the way for the installation of a theocratic regime that consolidated power in the hands of a few clerics—offers a paradox for scholars of civil resistance. The 2009 green movement, interestingly, has featured many of the same forms of nonviolent mass action that ultimately led to the shah's ouster.

Egypt, the most populous country in the Middle East, has witnessed a dramatic rise in civil resistance over the past few years. The Egyptian Kefaya (Enough) movement, founded in 2004, played a pivotal role in bringing civil resistance against the government of Hosni Mubarak into the political mainstream. Sherif Mansour describes how Kefaya united groups from across Egypt's political and ideological spectrum and organized street protests and other acts of civic defiance to highlight its demand for multiparty elections and an end to hereditary succession. Although the movement succumbed to internal divisions and lost momentum, Kefaya shattered a number of Egyptian taboos, activated young people, and led to the creation of spin-off movements, including an "April 6 movement" that has used Facebook and other technologies to unite students, workers, women, and opposition politicians in protests that put unprecedented pressure on the Mubarak regime. Mansour's chapter examines the achievements and weaknesses of Kefaya and reflects on the future of nonviolent struggle in Egypt.

The tiny, oil-rich state of Kuwait experienced a highly successful, albeit unheralded, victory for civil resistance in 2005. Faisal Alfahad and Hamad Albloshi convey how the Nabiha 5 movement succeeded—through effective communications and creative nonviolent resistance—in forcing the government to agree to reduce the number of electoral districts in Kuwait from 25 to 5. The reduction represented an important step in combating political corruption in the country. This Orange Movement, named after the color adopted by the opposition, mobilized a large number of young protestors, won over politicians as well as legislators from different parties, created splits in the royal family, and ultimately forced the government to accept their demand. The campaign featured mass protests, parliamentary sit-ins, and "blogger power" to achieve a significant victory for democracy in that country.

Civil resistance has also been used to achieve more limited, reformist goals in the Middle East. *Arba Imahot*, the Israeli Four Mothers movement, provides an interesting example of a civic campaign, led by women, which combined nonviolent direct action with effective coalition building to put pressure on the Israeli government to withdraw its troops from southern Lebanon in 2000. Tamar Hermann describes how the movement, founded by four kibbutzim women whose sons served in elite Israel Defense Forces units, gained popular support for its singular goal—Israel's unilateral withdrawal of its occupation forces from southern Lebanon—by using vigils, symbolic actions along the Israel-Lebanon border, and protests in front of the Defense Ministry to demonstrate popular support for withdrawal. The Four Mothers movement, which, Hermann notes, was careful to remain within the Israeli "national security consensus," formed alliances with influential political parties and won the backing of Israelis from across the country's ideological and political spectrum. Although the Four Mothers' precise role in the withdrawal from southern Lebanon is debated inside Israel, the movement showed how hypersensitive Israeli politicians can be about making foreign and security policies that might generate deeply negative public opinion.

In addition to pressuring foreign occupiers and ousting domestic autocrats, nonviolent resistance has also been used to advance good governance. Corruption, one of the most serious obstacles to democratic development in the Middle East and around the world, has led numerous communities to launch creative campaigns of civil resistance against it. Shaazka Beyerle describes how the 1997 Citizen Initiative for Constant Light mobilized the Turkish people in an anti-corruption campaign lasting six weeks. The campaign forged new alliances, employed a sophisticated publicity campaign, and focused on the strategic use of a low-risk, mass-action tactic—turning off the lights at the same time every night for one minute—to generate participation by people who might otherwise have sat on the sidelines. Beyerle notes that in the short term the campaign succeeded in breaking down fear and hopelessness about confronting corruption. Though not all of the campaign's objectives were achieved, the effort empowered citizens, forced the government to launch judicial investigations that resulted in guilty verdicts, and exposed crime syndicate figures and relationships.

Arwa Hassan examines how two related civic groups are cooperating in Egypt to harness public disgust over corruption into a broad-based, nonviolent campaign. Led by women, the civic initiative Shayfeencom—a clever combination of *shayfeen*, meaning "we see" and the add-on "com," a simple suffix that slightly changes the sense to "we see you" or "we are watching you"—became the driving force behind the creation of a larger initiative, Egyptians Against Corruption. In addition to disseminating leaflets, developing a "brand," and speaking out on Arab satellite stations independent of the Egyptian government, they are using the Internet and new mobile phone technology to provide ordinary Egyptians a platform from which to collectively make themselves heard. Shayfeen.com played an important role in collecting and publicizing evidence of voter fraud during the 2005 legislative elections, despite abuse and harassment endured by its members.

Organizers have also used civil resistance to advance women's rights in the Middle East and throughout the world. Fariba Davoudi Mohajer, Roya Tolouee, and Shaazka Beyerle discuss how Iranian women, who experienced a serious erosion of their rights following the Islamic revolution, have used creative forms of nonviolent direct action to mobilize support for gender equality under notoriously difficult conditions. In August 2006, Iranian women launched One Million Signatures, a national grassroots campaign with the goal of promoting gender equality and abolishing laws discriminating against women. The authors assert that the women's movement expanded the frontiers of civic action in Iran beyond its own vision of gender equality—and was a harbinger of the "green movement" of 2009.

Rola el-Husseini describes how Hizbullah's roles as a resistance organization and as a sociopolitical movement representing Lebanon's Shiite population explains its dual approach toward the concept of resistance. "Hizbullah's opposition to the government and other political actors has for the most part been nonviolent—despite a recent notable exception—while resistance to Israel continued to involve the use of violent force." Husseini discusses the ideological foundations of Hizbullah's conception of jihad and shows how the organization's notion of resistance has changed over time. Although its 2006 war with Israel may have strengthened Hizbullah regionally (and among certain groups within Lebanese society), the violent clashes that broke out between its militia and Lebanese pro-government supporters in 2008, she argues, has challenged the latter's credibility as a *national* Lebanese resistance organization.

* * *

As long as advocates of violent jihad possess a monopoly (or near monopoly) on the rhetoric of militancy in a part of the world where high levels of repression, low levels of freedom, and large and mostly disaffected youth populations desperately seek change, they will continue to capture the popular imagination. Only when alternative methods of waging struggle against the forces of oppression in the region are discussed and debated, and shown to produce results, will the allure of violence be lessened. That is the preoccupation of this book.

In a part of the world commonly associated with political violence, tyranny, foreign adventurism and fundamentalism, *Civilian Jihad* highlights a different, powerful means of expanding freedoms and promoting democratic development in the Middle East. I hope that readers will come away with a greater appreciation for the real and potential power of civil resistance in helping the peoples of the Middle East achieve self-government, rights, and justice.

Notes

1. Khalid Kishtainy, "Nonviolence and 'Civilian Jihad,'" Common Ground News Service—Middle East, June 6, 2002, www.commongroundnews.org/article.php?id=21078&lan=en&sid=0&sp=1. When used to describe active civil resistance, the term *nonviolence* can be confusing and problematic for reasons elaborated in the chapters by Hardy Merriman (chapter 1) and by Ralph Crow and Philip Grant (chapter 2).

2. Adam Roberts and Timothy Garten Ash, "Definition of Civil Resistance," in *Civil Resistance and Power Politics: The Experience of Nonviolent Action from Gandhi to the Present*, ed. Adam Roberts and Timothy Garten Ash (Oxford: Oxford University Press, 2009).

3. Gene Sharp, *The Politics of Nonviolent Action*, 3 vols. (Boston: Porter Sargent Publishers, 1973).

4. Sharp's study of the technique of nonviolent action should be distinguished from "nonviolence" as a philosophy or as a way of life encompassing personal behavior, thought, and social behavior. Although a few prominent leaders of civil resistance campaigns—among them Mahatma Gandhi, Khan Abdul Ghaffar Khan (discussed in Mohammad Raqib's chapter in this volume, chapter 8), and Martin Luther King, Jr.—espoused nonviolence as a way of life and emphasized the interconnectedness of principled nonviolence and pragmatic nonviolent action, it is nevertheless the case that most participants in nonviolent struggles have not been pacifists or shared principled views of nonviolence. *Civil Resistance* focuses on organized protest and resistance rather than the philosophy of nonviolence. For elaboration on these different approaches, see the chapters by Hardy Merriman and Ralph E. Crow and Philip Grant (chapters 1 and 2) in this volume.

5. Nonviolent resistance is the subject of numerous important works: Roberts and Garton Ash, *Civil Resistance and Power Politics*; Gene Sharp, ed., *Waging Nonviolent Struggle: 20th Century Practice and 21st Century Potential* (Boston: Porter Sargent, 2005); Sharp, *Politics of Nonviolent Action*; Peter Ackerman and Christopher Kruegler, *Strategic Nonviolent Conflict: The Dynamics of People Power in the Twentieth Century* (Westport, Conn.: Praeger, 1994); Peter Ackerman and Jack DuVall, *A Force More Powerful: A Century of Nonviolent Conflict* (New York: Macmillan, 2000); Peter Ackerman and Adrian Karatnacky, eds., *How Freedom Is Won: From Civic Mobilization to Durable Democracy* (Washington, DC: Freedom House, 2005); Kurt Schock, *Unarmed Insurrections: People Power Movements in Nondemocracies* (Minneapolis: University of Minnesota Press, 2005); Paul Wehr, Heidi Burgess, and Guy Burgess, eds., *Justice without Violence* (Boulder, CO: Lynne Rienner, 1994); Stephen Zunes, "Unarmed Insurrections against Authoritarian Governments in the Third World," *Third World Quarterly* 15, no. 3 (September 1994): 403–26; Stephen Zunes, Lester Kurtz, and Sarah Beth Asher, eds., *Nonviolent Social Movements: A Geographical Perspective* (Malden, MA: Blackwell, 1999); Vincent Boudreau, *Resisting Dictatorship: Repression and Protest in Southeast Asia* (New York: Cambridge University Press, 2004); Mary E. King, *A Quiet Revolution: The First Palestinian Intifada and Nonviolent Resistance* (New York: Nation Books, 2007); Souad Dajani, *Eyes without Country: Searching for a Palestinian Strategy of Liberation* (Philadelphia: Temple University Press, 1994); Maria J. Stephan, "Fighting for Statehood: The Role of Civilian-Based Resistance in the East Timorese, Palestinian, and Kosovo Albanian Self-Determination Struggles," *Fletcher Forum on World Affairs* 30, no. 2 (Summer 2006): 57–80.

6. April Carter, Howard Clark, and Michael Randle, *People Power and Protest since 1945: A Bibliography of Nonviolent Action* (London: Housmans Bookshop, 2006). An earlier, lengthier bibliography is Ronald M. McCarthy and Gene Sharp, *Nonviolent Action: A Research Guide* (New York: Garland, 1997).

7. For the purposes of this volume, the "greater Middle East" includes all the Arab world, Afghanistan, Iran, Israel, and Turkey. This geographic delineation was used by Saad E. Ibrahim, "Why Nonviolent Political Struggle in the Middle East?" *Arab Nonviolent Political Struggle in the Middle East*, ed. Ralph E. Crow, Philip Grant, and Saad E. Ibrahim (Boulder, CO: Lynne Rienner, 1990).

8. See Freedom House, *Freedom in the World Survey, 2007*, www.freedomhouse.org.

9. *The Arab Human Development Report, 2002* (New York: United Nations Development Program, 2002), 2.

10. "Liberal autocracies" temper authoritarianism with pluralism. Their leaders tolerate and even promote a degree of political openness in civil society, the press, and the electoral system, yet they maintain the upper hand through control of the security apparatus and the media and with economic clientalism. "Full autocracies" rely on the provision of jobs and economic benefits in exchange for political support, and use sheer force and intimidation to maintain their grip on power; they have no tolerance for political openness. See Daniel Brumberg, "Liberalization versus Democracy," in *Uncharted Journey: Promoting Democracy in the Middle East*, ed. Thomas Carothers and Marina Ottaway (Washington, DC: Carnegie Endowment for International Peace, 2005), 15–35. For further analysis of the different forms of authoritarianism in the region, see Oliver Schlumberger, *Debating Arab Authoritarianism: Dynamics and Durability in Nondemocratic Regimes* (Stanford, CA: Stanford University Press, 2007); Marina Ottaway, *Democracy Challenged: The Rise of Semiauthoritarianism* (Washington, DC: Carnegie Endowment for International Peace, 2003).

11. For a discussion of rentierism in the Middle East and on oil as a potential inhibitor of democracy, see Hazem Beblawi and Giacomo Luciani, eds., *The Rentier State: Nation, State, and Integration in the Arab World* (London: Croom Helm, 1987); Paul Collier and Anke Hoeffler, "Resource Rents, Governance, and Conflict," *Journal of Conflict Resolution* 49, no. 4 (2005): 625–33; Michael L. Ross, "Does Oil Hinder Democracy?" *World Politics*, no. 53 (April 2001): 325–61; Eva Bellin, "The Political-Economic Conundrum: The Affinity of Political and Economic Reform in the Middle East and North Africa," Carnegie Endowment for International Peace, Carnegie Paper no. 53, November 2004, www.carnegieendowment.org/publications/index. cfm?fa=view&id=16051.

12. Larry Diamond, *The Spirit of Democracy: The Struggle to Build Free Societies throughout the World* (New York: Times Books, 2008), 337. For further analyses of the democratic deficit in the Middle East, see Carothers and Ottaway, *Uncharted Journey*; Hassanein Tawfiq Ibrahim, "Social and Political Change in the Wake of the Oil Boom," *Arab Insight Report* (Fall 2008).

13. During 2006–2007, the Arab Barometer conducted face-to-face interviews with large and representative samples of citizens in seven Arab societies: Algeria, Jordan, Kuwait, Lebanon, Morocco, Palestine, and Yemen. A total of 8,555 men and women were interviewed. The surveys revealed strong support for democracy in the region. See www.arabbarometer.org. See also, Amaney Jamal and Mark Tessler, "Has the U.S. Poisoned Democracy?" *Arab Reform Bulletin*, October 2008.

14. For an insightful comparison of "liberal" and "illiberal" democracy, see Fareed Zakaria, *The Future of Freedom: Illiberal Democracy at Home and Abroad* (New York: W. W. Norton, 2003).

15. Carothers and Ottaway, *Uncharted Journey*.

16. See, for example, Daniel Brumberg, "Democracy and Security in the Middle East," *Democracy and Society* 4, no. 2 (Spring 2007): 12–14.

17. Stephen Zunes and Saad Eddin Ibrahim elaborate on these and other external actor roles in their chapter in this volume.

18. Ackerman and Karatnacky, *How Freedom Is Won*, 6.

19. Ibid., 8.

20. Eleanor Marchant and Arch Puddington, *Enabling Environments for Civic Movements and the Dynamics of Democratic Transition* (Washington, DC: Freedom House, 2008), 5.

21. See Erica Chenoweth and Maria J. Stephan, "Mobilization and Resistance: A Framework for Analysis," in Erica Chenoweth and Adria Lawrence, eds., *Rethinking Violence: State and Non-State Actors in Conflict* (Cambridge, MA.: MIT Press, forthcoming 2010).

22. Ackerman and Karatnacky, *How Freedom Is Won*, 7.

23. On how armed groups rely on coercive means to maintain societal "support," see Jeremy Weinstein, *Inside Rebellion: The Political Economy of Rebel Organization* (New York: Cambridge University Press, 2007).

24. Shifts in loyalty involving members of bureaucracies, security forces, professional groups, and other organizations and institutions that often occur during nonviolent struggles are important facets of civil resistance. See Hardy Merriman's chapter (chapter 1) in this volume.

25. See Maria J. Stephan and Erica Chenoweth, "Why Civil Resistance Works: The Strategic Logic of Nonviolent Conflict," *International Security* 33, no. 1 (Summer 2008): 7–44.

26. "Backfire" is a process or outcome that occurs when an action is counterproductive for the perpetrator. Brian Martin, who coined the term, elaborated on Gene Sharp's notion of "political ju-jitsu," whereby the opponent's violent repression of nonviolent resisters is turned to operate politically against the opponent, thereby weakening it vis-à-vis the nonviolent opposition. See Brian Martin, *Justice Ignited: The Dynamics of Backfire* (Lanham, MD: Rowman & Littlefield, 2007), 3.

27. See Chenoweth and Stephan, "Mobilization and Resistance."

28. See Karim Douglas Crow, *Islam–Peace–Nonviolence: A Select Biography* (Washington, DC: Nonviolence International, 1998), www.nonviolenceinternational. net/islambib_001.htm.

29. See Ralph E. Crow, Philip Grant, and Saad E. Ibrahim, eds. *Arab Nonviolent Political Struggle in the Middle East* (Boulder, CO: Lynne Rienner, 1990).

    This particular chapter, "Questions and Controversies about Nonviolent Struggle in the Middle East," written by Ralph E. Crow and Philip Grant, is reprinted in this volume (chapter 2).

30. See Robin Wright, *Dreams and Shadows: The Future of the Middle East* (Penguin Press, 2008); Joshua Muravchik, *The Next Founders: Voices of Democracy in the Middle East* (Encounter Books, 2009).

31. A few classic Orientalist works include Bernard Lewis, *What Went Wrong? The Clash between Islam and Modernity in the Middle East* (New York: Harper Perennial, 2003); Bernard Lewis, *The Middle East* (New York: Scribner, 1997; London: Phoenix, 1997); Raphael Patai, *The Arab Mind* (New York: Hatherleigh Press, 2007).

32. The best attempt thus far to bridge the structure-agency divide in the study of civil resistance is Schock, *Unarmed Insurrections.*

33. See Amy Hawthorne, "The New Reform Ferment," in Carothers and Ottoway, *Uncharted Journey*, 68–70; Michael McFaul and Tamara Cofman Wittes, "Morocco's Elections: The Limits of Limited Reform," *Journal of Democracy* 19, no. 1 (2008), 19–33.

34. For some of the most significant works on this subject, see Carothers and Ottoway, *Uncharted Journey*; Vali Nasr, "The Rise of Muslim Democrats," *Journal of Democracy* 16, no. 2 (2005): 13–27; Diamond, *Spirit of Democracy,* 263–91; Nathan Brown, Amr Hamzaway, and Marina Ottoway, "Islamist Movements and the Democratic Process in the Arab World: Exploring the Gray Zones," Carnegie Endowment for International Peace, Carnegie Paper no. 67, 2006; James Piscatori, *Islam, Islamists, and the Electoral Principle* (Leiden: ISIM, 2000); Mona el-Ghobasy, "The Metamorphasis of the Egyptian Muslim Brotherhood, *International Journal of Middle East Studies* 37 (August 2005): 373–95; Samer Shehata, "Egypt's Opposition Politics: A Fleeting Moment of Opportunity?" *Arab Reform Bulletin*, October 2004; Tamara Coffman Wittes, "Three Kinds of Movements," *Journal of Democracy* 19, no. 3 (2008): 7–12; Thomas Carothers, "The End of the Transition Paradigm," *Journal of Democracy* 13, no. 1 (2002): 5–21.

35. See note 4.

Part I

Overview

1

Theory and Dynamics of Nonviolent Action

Hardy Merriman

Nonviolent action is a technique of waging conflict. For centuries, diverse groups of people have used this technique and its wide array of methods—including boycotts, strikes, demonstrations, civil disobedience, and the establishment of alternative institutions—to fight for freedom, justice, rights, and equality. Groups engaged in nonviolent struggle, defined as the use of nonviolent action to wage a conflict, have been far more successful at achieving their objectives than is often recognized. This under-recognition is due in part to misunderstandings about how nonviolent action works. The notion that unarmed citizens can successfully overcome the challenges of contesting power from armed and well-financed opponents is baffling to many. Yet, as the cases in *Civil Resistance* and others throughout history attest, this is exactly what has happened in many parts of the world. To understand how nonviolent movements work, one must understand the theory and dynamics of nonviolent action.

A widely-accepted definition of nonviolent action is offered by Gene Sharp in *Waging Nonviolent Struggle*:

> [Nonviolent action is a] general technique of protest, resistance, and intervention without physical violence.... Such action may be conducted by (a) acts of omission—that is, the participants refuse to perform acts that they usually perform, are expected by custom to perform, or are required by law or regulation to perform; (b) acts of commission—that is, the participants perform acts that they usually do not perform, are not expected by custom to perform, or are forbidden by law or regulation from performing; or (c) a combination of both.[1]

Therefore, nonviolent action is by definition action that is not violent and that takes place outside the context of normal political, economic, or social behavior. In this regard, what qualifies as an act of nonviolent action is to some extent context specific. For example, wearing a certain color shirt or symbol may be within the confines of normal behavior (and therefore not nonviolent action) in one society but may be subversive and outside the realm of normalcy (and therefore nonviolent action) in another, where such a color or symbol is banned.[2]

Regardless of what is and is not considered normal political, economic, and social behavior in a given society, throughout history nonviolent action has often been used to complement and augment normal political, economic, and social behavior. For example, in a certain society a movement may use traditional (normal) methods of creating change—such as filing lawsuits, lobbying legislators, and participating in elections—but may also use forms of nonviolent action—such as strikes and protests—to gain additional leverage and increase their effectiveness.[3]

Nonviolent action is referred to by many names, including *civic defiance, civil resistance, political defiance,* and *people power*.[4] Some people also use the terms *nonviolence* or *passive resistance*, but they are not synonyms for nonviolent action. For many people, the term *nonviolence* carries a religious or ethical connotation, none of which is intrinsic to the use of nonviolent action. "Passive resistance" connotes resistance that is passive, but nonviolent action is powerful at times precisely because it can be actively and assertively disruptive.

Some misconceptions about nonviolent action arise from this confusion over terminology, whereby people assume that the technique has an inherent religious or ethical basis. Terminology that melds nonviolent action and religious or ethical nonviolence into one phenomenon may decrease the likelihood that nonviolent struggle will be adopted by certain groups. Although historically nonviolent action has been successfully practiced by individuals and groups committed to religious or ethical nonviolence, it has also been successfully practiced by individuals and groups who are not committed to religious or ethical nonviolence. Those who are not committed to religious or ethical nonviolence may be more likely to adopt nonviolent action if it is presented to them as a pragmatic and effective way of waging conflict, rather than as a religious or ethical creed to which people should convert.

Consent, Obedience, and Sources of Power

Nonviolent action is based on the insight that economic, social, political, and military power ultimately comes from the consent and obedience of the people in society. Simply put, if people do not obey, rulers cannot rule. Power therefore is not inherently fixed and stable, but rather is fragile and can shift according to people's willingness to consent to and obey a ruler.[5]

Rulers and nonviolent movements know this. Rulers depend ultimately on people to run the country, and nonviolent movements need people's support, or at least need them to stop obeying the ruler, in order to wield power. Therefore, conflicts between nonviolent movements and their opponents are contests. Each side has different actions and tactics that it can use in an attempt to shift people's loyalties and obedience patterns and gain power. In particular, there are six "sources of power" that rulers and nonviolent movements compete for and attempt to control. These influence people's loyalties and obedience patterns, and therefore power, in society.[6]

Legitimacy: Legitimacy is the quality that leads people to voluntarily accept and consent to an individual's or an organization's orders. It is a function of the degree to which people believe that an individual or an organization has the right and capability to rule. Legitimacy is one of the most important sources of power for a ruler or a nonviolent movement because it is often the least costly way to influence people's obedience patterns. For example, when people consider a ruler to be legitimate, they willingly give their consent and voluntarily obey that ruler, which means that the ruler does not need to expend additional resources to ensure continued obedience.

The legitimacy of an individual or organization can be increased through a variety of means, including by taking actions that are responsive to the concerns of people in a society, by holding formal titles, positions, and responsibilities (for example, president, general, judge, board of directors, and so on), and by being or appearing to be installed in power through some socially accepted means, such as elections. (Even if elections are fraudulent, they can provide the appearance of legitimacy, which is why so many authoritarian rulers hold them.)

Legitimacy ultimately, however, does not emanate from any formal position, actions, or procedures, but rather from the public's perception of whether an individual or organization represents their interests, has earned the right to rule, and is capable of ruling. Therefore, a nonviolent movement can sometimes gain more legitimacy than an official ruler of a country if the people in that country feel that the nonviolent movement is a viable alternative that represents their interests better and deserves to be in power more than the ruler's government does.

Human Resources: Human resources are the number of people that obey an individual or organization and the extent of these people's organization and cooperation. The more people that obey an individual or organization, and the more organized they are, the more these people can act collectively in ways that influence or coerce others to obey as well. Human resources are an essential source of power for rulers and for nonviolent movements.

Skills and Knowledge: Some human resources provide certain valuable skills and knowledge to an individual or organization. For example, to ensure that society continually functions according to a ruler's wishes, most rulers depend on the cooperation of people with skills in engineering, construction, manufacturing, mechanics, media and communications, computer programming, banking, tax collection, surveillance and other forms of intelligence gathering, legal procedures, policing, and interrogation techniques. If a nonviolent movement is able to gain the support of people with some of these skills and knowledge or is able to convince people with these skills and knowledge to deny them to the movement's opponent, the movement is able to gain power or deny power to the opponent.

Material Resources: Material resources include, but are not limited to, money, access to the financial system, physical infrastructure, access to raw materials, refining and manufacturing capabilities, and transportation and communications capabilities. Material resources help an individual or organization to maintain people's obedience in a myriad of ways, including by directly paying people (which is why some authoritarian governments choose to employ large segments of their population), by providing for people's needs (food, health, shelter, and so on), by enabling communication and transportation to organize human and material resources in society, and by enabling the publication and dissemination of messages through media that influence people's perceptions.

Cultural, Religious, and Ideological Factors: All societies indoctrinate people with certain cultural, religious, or ideological values. Depending on the society, examples of these values include deference of women to men, respect for elders, and the belief that the head of state is in some way backed by a higher religious power. If significantly engrained in people's consciousness, even patterns of buying and unquestioned loyalty to certain commercial products or brands fit into this category and influences behaviors in ways that directly or indirectly support certain individuals or organizations.

To increase people's obedience, rulers often use cultural, religious, or ideological values or symbols in ways that affirm their views and that make them seem like they are the protectors of these values and symbols. For example, a ruler may claim that an attack against him or her is an attack against the country as a whole. On the other hand, nonviolent movements may also emphasize cultural, religious, or ideological values and symbols—such as the national flag, religious, ethnic, historical iconography, or famous quotes, slogans or religious language—that resonate with people and that encourage people's self-identification with and participation in the movement.

Sanctions: Sanctions are the ability to impose punishments on those who disobey. They serve to enforce obedience by individuals and to deter potential disobedience by others. In the case of a regime, sanctions may be physically coercive and violent, such as arrests, beatings, and assassinations, or they may not involve physical violence, as in the cases of blackmail, loss of a job or educational opportunities, attacks on one's reputation, lawsuits, fines, and confiscation of property. Nonviolent movements may also develop a repertoire of sanctions—from strikes and boycotts that deprive their opponent of material resources, to protests and petitions that may reduce their opponent's legitimacy, to the ability to launch social boycotts and ostracism against corrupt government officials or abusive police or military officers.

In the case of a regime, however, relying on sanctions to enforce obedience and shift the behavior of individuals often has a high cost in terms of legitimacy and material resources. In most societies, the capacity of rulers to impose their will through sanctions would be overwhelmed if a moderate percentage of people disobeyed consistently and in an organized way. To prevent this from happening, rulers primarily use sanctions to deter disobedient behavior. It is the deterrent effect of sanctions that makes them powerful. For example, by expending the resources necessary to publicly sanction only a few individuals, a ruler can sometimes instill fear in a far greater number of individuals who will then obey.

These sources of power derive from people's loyalties and obedience patterns, and they are used by rulers to perpetuate people's loyalties and obedience to them even further. A nonviolent movement may, however, interrupt this process and shift people's loyalties and obedience patterns away from being supportive of a ruler. When this happens, the movement may gain legitimacy, human resources, material resources, skills and knowledge, and the ability to carry out sanctions while the ruler is denied these sources of power. Furthermore, as nonviolent movements begin to shift people's loyalties and obedience patterns, a self-reinforcing cycle may be created. For example, when a sufficient number of people choose to disobey a ruler, his or her ability to carry out sanctions, gain material resources, or use people's time, energy, or skills and knowledge to consolidate his or her rule will be diminished; this loss of power may lead to even more people in society choosing to disobey the ruler. If the nonviolent movement is successful, over the course of the struggle the balance of power in society continues to shift away from a concentration on the ruler and toward the nonviolent movement, which is often more decentralized because it relies on the voluntary participation and initiatives of thousands or millions of people.

Pillars of Support

Rulers and nonviolent movements know that power derives from people's loyalties and obedience patterns, and therefore they engage in a contest to shift these patterns. In this contest, however, it is not just the loyalties and obedience of isolated individuals that matter, but also the loyalties and obedience of individuals and groups who comprise organizations and institutions.

Organizations and institutions are loci of power in society because they concentrate and magnify the power of the individuals who work in them. Therefore they are an important focal point of nonviolent struggle, and successful nonviolent movements exert large amounts of effort on shifting their behavior. The organizations and institutions that support a nonviolent movement, or its opponent, are called pillars of support. Pillars of support provide a foundation for a nonviolent movement's, or an opponent's, economic, social, and political power, as well as an opponent's military power.

For example, in the case of an authoritarian state, some common pillars of support may include the military, paramilitaries, the police, the judiciary, civil servants, state-controlled media, corporations, certain religious groups and institutions, and the education system. A state may also have external pillars of support, such as multinational corporations or friendly governments that provide material assistance or technical expertise or serve as international trading partners.[7]

In the case of a nonviolent movement, a new movement may be so small that it initially has no backing from any major organizations. Over time, it may develop pillars of support, such as labor unions, university or secondary school students, teachers, academic and professional organizations, religious groups, and human rights, women's rights, or minority rights organizations. Furthermore, as the movement becomes more successful, some of its opponent's pillars of support may shift and begin to support the movement as well. Movements may also develop support from external organizations, though movements typically do not succeed if they depend predominantly on outside support for their continued viability.

Therefore, successful nonviolent movements take actions to strengthen and expand their own pillars of support and to undermine and shift the loyalties of their opponent's pillars of support. Not all pillars are equally important to any given opponent, but if enough withdraw their support from an opponent, or if a few of the most crucial ones do, the opponent becomes powerless and is no longer able to function. For this to happen, it is not necessary for an opponent's pillars of support to begin actively supporting the nonviolent movement, although some might. Sometimes, having several crucial pillars become neutral or simply reduce their existing support for the opponent will weaken the opponent sufficiently for the nonviolent movement to achieve victory.[8]

To determine how best to approach an opponent's pillars of support, nonviolent movements must determine how important each pillar is to the opponent's continued rule; how loyal members of each pillar are to the opponent; why members of each pillar are obedient to the opponent; and what divisions, if any, are present within each pillar or between different pillars of support.[9] Answers to these questions generally reveal that an opponent's pillars of support are not monolithic, but rather that each has its own interests, organizational culture, values, allegiances, and different reasons for supporting the opponent. Nonviolent movements can then perform actions that agitate or aggravate these differences and create splits and loyalty shifts among an opponent's pillars of support.

In addition, individual pillars may have divisions or "cracks" within them because of grievances or rivalries among their members; for example, top leadership, middle management, and workers within the same pillar are rarely completely unified. Using this information, successful nonviolent movements identify the points of least loyalty among the members of their opponent's pillars of support and attempt to shift the obedience of those members by targeting communications and tactics at them.

Mechanisms of Change

Gene Sharp identifies four processes that nonviolent movements use to cause individuals or groups (such as those that comprise pillars of support) to change their behavior. He refers to these processes as mechanisms of change.[10]

Conversion: Sometimes, because of a nonviolent movement's actions, an individual or group will come to better understand the perspective of the movement and change its views to agree with those of the movement. This is conversion. The individual or group decides that the movement is correct in doing what it is doing and changes its behavior as a result.

Conversion is more likely to occur with neutral parties or among members of the opponent's pillars of support who are not great beneficiaries of the opponent's rule and who do not feel directly threatened by a potential change of rulers. It rarely occurs among the leadership of the movement's opponent or with the opponent's closest supporters, who have the most vested in preserving the status quo.

Accommodation: In accommodation, an individual or group does not shift its views to agree with the nonviolent movement, but rather decides that the costs of continuing to oppose the movement are greater than the potential benefits from doing so. In essence, the individual or group does a cost-benefit analysis and decides that some sort of compromise or negotiation with the movement is in its best interest. For example, a corporation facing a well-organized boycott or strike may accommodate the demands of the boycotters or strikers, or a government facing mass disobedience over a certain policy may choose to change that policy.

Sometimes accommodations occur through negotiations with an opponent, such as in labor disputes. In these cases, there are a number of considerations that may influence the outcome. First, the relative power balance or imbalance between the two (or more) sides in the conflict may influence and be reflected in the terms of the negotiated compromise. Second, the greater the differential in the relative power balance or imbalance between the sides in the conflict, the more likely it is that breaches and poor enforcement of the compromise agreement will occur. Third, if a compromise agreement is negotiated between two sides of equal power, breaches and poor enforcement can become more likely if at some point in the future the balance of power shifts and begins to favor one side over the other. Fourth, negotiations and some compromises may lead to splits among the supporters of a nonviolent movement or among the supporters of the nonviolent movement's opponent, and these splits can weaken the negotiating position of the movement or opponent even further. For example, one party in a negotiation may offer concessions that appeal only to a certain faction of supporters within the other party, and this can cause internal ruptures and weakness.[11]

Nonviolent Coercion: Sometimes a nonviolent movement is able to wield such power that it can impose its will on an opponent or an opponent's pillar of support. This is nonviolent coercion. In this case, the opponent or opponent's pillar of support is forced to meet a movement's demands because failure to do so would result in a complete loss of its power through withdrawal of obedience by its members or supporters.

In some cases, nonviolent coercion of an opponent may enable a movement to achieve all of its objectives. In other cases, however, nonviolent coercion of an opponent is only successful if it is followed by a plan for what happens after the opponent is coerced. For example, if a movement aims to transform an authoritarian government into a democratic government, the movement may be able to nonviolently coerce its opponent to yield power, but to achieve its objective—democracy—the movement must also have a plan in place for how to manage and legitimize the transition to a new power holder. In such a case, if a movement applies coercive pressure to its opponent but does not have a plan for what to do next, it increases the likelihood that nonviolent coercion will devolve into disintegration.

Disintegration: In disintegration, an opponent's pillars of support dissolve uncontrollably beneath it, and order in society may break down. This is not necessarily a desirable outcome for a nonviolent movement. For example, if an authoritarian ruler's power collapses quickly, it can lead to confusion, and the resulting power vacuum, if not quickly filled by a new group sympathetic to the movement taking power, can create an opportunity for some members of the armed forces that may not be sympathetic to the movement to launch a coup under the justification of restoring order.

Several or all four of these mechanisms of change may be simultaneously operative on different groups during a nonviolent struggle. In fact, different mechanisms may be operative even within a single pillar of support. Take for example the pillar of support of the military. The soldiers on the street may be the most prone to the mechanism of conversion. They have the most contact with members of the movement and thus can be targeted with tactics and communications designed to make them question their loyalties. They may also be from a relatively similar sociopolitical or socioeconomic background as the members of the movement that they encounter. They may even know people, such as their children, spouse, extended family members, friends, or acquaintances, who are sympathetic to the movement or may actually be part of the movement. In addition, they are often the least well-paid and have the most dangerous and physically exhausting work of any members of the military. All of these variables may influence the likelihood that they will convert to supporting the movement.

Mid-level military officers may be more likely to accommodate the movement. They frequently have less contact with people in the movement, and are often greater beneficiaries of the status quo than are the soldiers on the street.[12] They may not necessarily be profiting greatly from the existing system, however, and although they may not agree with the movement on all issues, they may decide that the cost of continuing to oppose the movement is excessively high.

The military's upper echelon, such as generals, often have the most invested in the existing system of power and therefore often bear the greatest cost if the system changes. In some cases, nonviolent coercion may be necessary for some of them to shift their behavior.[13]

Tactics of Nonviolent Action

In order to create shifts among pillars of support and to activate different mechanisms of change, movements must take specific actions. Tactics are the actions that members of movements take to strengthen the movement or to influence or weaken the movement's opponent. There is a multitude of ways for people to nonviolently disobey or create new behaviors in any given society, and hence there are a wide variety of tactics available to nonviolent movements.

In 1973 Gene Sharp identified and catalogued 198 different nonviolent tactics that have been used historically by nonviolent movements.[14] Since that time, many other tactics have been created as well.[15] This multitude of tactics can be classified in a variety of different ways. Sharp developed the most common classification schema, which consists of three classes of nonviolent tactics.[16]

Nonviolent Protest and Persuasion: These tactics consist of verbal, written, or symbolic acts of protest against the status quo or attempts to persuade people to support the movement. Examples of protest and persuasion tactics include petitions, rallies, sending letters, distributing literature, displaying symbols, singing songs, street theater, vigils, public statements, SMS messages, and creating new Web sites.[17]

Protest and persuasion tactics communicate that the nonviolent movement is in favor of or against something, the degree of opposition or support, and sometimes how widespread that opposition or support is.[18] Because these tactics do not involve substantial shifts in people's behavior patterns, movements relying only on protest and persuasion tactics often are not able to create change against a strong and entrenched opponent. Protest and persuasion tactics can, however, be important in mobilizing a movement, undermining the loyalties of some of the opponent's supporters, and shifting third parties to support the movement or to oppose the opponent.

Noncooperation: Noncooperation tactics shift people's behavior patterns so that they deny their obedience and cooperation to an opponent or an opponent's pillar of support. There are a wide variety of noncooperation tactics, which can be classified into three forms: social noncooperation, economic noncooperation, and political noncooperation. Examples include the following:

- *social noncooperation*: ostracism, withdrawal from events, social disobedience, avoidance, suspension of social activities (for example, sports, festivals, and so on.)
- *economic noncooperation*: consumer boycotts, retail boycotts, secondary boycotts, strikes (limited, slowdown, general), walk-outs, sick-ins, staying at home, refusal to pay rent, withdrawal of bank deposits, refusal to pay taxes
- *political noncooperation*: resignations, withdrawal from or refusal to participate in government institutions or programs,[19] withholding information from the government

Noncooperation tactics can be quite powerful because they disrupt people's obedience patterns and therefore alter the flow of power from the people to the ruler. Generally speaking, the more people that participate in acts of noncooperation, the more powerful their impact. Some noncooperation tactics, such as general strikes and consumer boycotts, may even depend on the participation of broad and diverse groups—that is, men and women, young people and older people, minority groups—to be effective. Some noncooperation tactics, such as a consumer boycott, also enable participation by broad and diverse groups in society because they can be relatively low-risk while still having a significant impact on the opponent.

Nonviolent Intervention: Nonviolent intervention tactics directly disrupt the ability of the opponent to function. The movement takes actions that intervene in the status quo to block some societal function from taking place or to replace some societal function with a new one, as in the case of creating parallel institutions.[20] Examples of nonviolent intervention include various acts of civil disobedience, sit-ins, blockading buildings or streets, and the creation of parallel institutions.[21]

Because many nonviolent intervention tactics are directly disruptive and confrontational, they usually carry a higher level of risk than other nonviolent tactics. They also often require a high amount of discipline by those who participate in them. Despite their risk and the discipline that may be required, some nonviolent intervention tactics have the advantage of being effective even if only relatively few people participate in them. For example, a well-publicized sit-in by a few well-respected people can have a major impact in a struggle.

Sharp's classification of tactics is based on the action that members of the movement are taking; that is, protesting in various forms, not cooperating, or intervening. There are, however, numerous other ways and other criteria by which nonviolent tactics can be classified, and different classifications yield different emphases. For example, in *Unarmed Insurrections,* sociologist Kurt Schock, citing the work of Robert J. Burrowes, classifies nonviolent tactics into two categories: methods (tactics) of concentration (in which people participate and act in relatively dense physical proximity to each other, such as in rallies and protests) and methods (tactics) of dispersion (in which people participate and act in a decentralized and widely diffuse way, as with consumer boycotts and stay-at-home strikes). These categorizations—based on the relative concentration or dispersion of activity and people—emphasize the issue of risk associated with various tactics, because methods of concentration tend to have a higher visibility and are easier for an opponent to repress than are methods of dispersion.[22]

Nonviolent tactics have also been divided according to the operational functions that they serve, and this form of classification emphasizes the desired impact of the actions. For example, tactics have been categorized as communication tactics (petitions, letters, displaying symbols, distributing literature), capacity-building tactics (community service projects), attack tactics (rallies, blockading buildings), and denying tactics (boycotts and strikes).[23]

Communications

Some form of communication accompanies almost all nonviolent tactics. For example, rallies, petitions, and acts of civil disobedience rarely take place without a movement communicating why it is taking action and what its objectives are. When done effectively, these communications can significantly increase the power of a movement's nonviolent tactics. Therefore, designing communications is an important function of nonviolent movements, and a movement's skill at formulating and communicating messages to various audiences can be a critical variable in determining its success.

The content of the messages that accompany a movement's tactics are diverse and depend on the movement's objectives with regard to different audiences. For example, movements communicate with their supporters to get them to mobilize, to donate their time and resources, to take risks, and to make sacrifices. Movements communicate with neutral and uncommitted groups as a way to obtain their support, expand the movement, and build mass participation. Movements also communicate with their opponent's supporters to shift their loyalties.

The diversity of communications in nonviolent movements is tremendous. The subtleties and nuances of communications extend beyond the scope of this chapter, but three common themes (upon which there are many variations) regarding the content of communications of successful nonviolent movements are as follows:

Emphasis on Common Values and Interests: A primary way for nonviolent move ments to increase their strength is by gaining new supporters. People are more likely to support a movement and participate if they feel that the movement shares their values and interests. Therefore, effective nonviolent movements emphasize their shared values and interests in their communications with different audiences.

An Inclusive Vision: Nonviolent movements often require the support of diverse groups and pillars of support in order to achieve their objectives. However, different audiences have different aspirations, and therefore successful nonviolent movements work to develop and communicate a vision that is inclusive of the aspirations of different groups in society. Movements that are able to interweave these aspirations into an inclusive, unifying vision are more likely to achieve mass participation and to undermine the loyalties of its opponent's supporters. The more inclusive a movement's vision is, the more people it can attract, and the more likely those people are to participate and take action on the movement's behalf.[24]

Avoidance of Threats: Nonviolent movements reduce their opponent's power by eroding the loyalties of their opponent's supporters, particularly the members of the opponent's pillars of support. In order for the opponent's supporters to shift loyalties, however, they must feel that the achievement of the movement's objectives does not threaten them. Therefore, successful nonviolent movements generally avoid directing threatening communications at their opponent's supporters.[25] Threatening communications increase the opponent's supporters' fear of the movement, which often makes them more loyal to the opponent and therefore more likely to fight against the movement. By avoiding the use of threatening language when addressing their opponent's supporters, nonviolent movements are more likely to be able to co-opt their loyalties.

Conclusion

Nonviolent action is a powerful and complex technique of waging struggle. It is based on the view that power comes from the people in society, and that if people shift their loyalties and obedience patterns, power in society will shift as well.

Nonviolent movements compete with their opponents to shift people's loyalties and obedience patterns. When movements are successful at this, they may gain legitimacy, human resources, skills and knowledge, material resources, and the ability to perform sanctions while the opponent may experience reduced capacity in those areas.

The potential for people to exert power is often increased significantly if they are organized into organizations and institutions. Organizations and institutions that support a nonviolent movement, or its opponent, are called pillars of support. Successful nonviolent movements often target actions at its opponent's pillars of support in order to gain their support and to reduce their support for the movement's opponent.

Nonviolent movements create change through several different processes, ranging from conversion, to accommodation, to coercion, to disintegration. During a nonviolent struggle, each of these processes may be operative at the same time on different groups and individuals within the struggle.

In the contest for people's loyalties and obedience, nonviolent movements use tactics. Tactics can be classified in a variety of ways, such as according to the actions that people perform during the tactics (protest and persuasion, noncooperation, intervention), the density of people carrying out the tactics (concentration and dispersion), and the operational function of the tactics (communicating, capacity building, attacking or denying). Because there are a wide variety of ways for people to shift existing obedience patterns, there is a large number and a wide breadth of nonviolent tactics. New tactics continue to be created as new struggles occur.

In compliment to their tactics, nonviolent movements also use communications to appeal to people for their support and to undermine their loyalties to the movement's opponent. Successful movements target their communications at a variety of audiences, including their own supporters, uncommitted or neutral groups, and their opponent's supporters. Three characteristics that often accompany the communications of successful movements are an emphasis of common values and interests, an inclusive vision, and an avoidance of threats.

Notes

1. Gene Sharp, *Waging Nonviolent Struggle: 20th Century Practice and 21st Century Potential* (Boston: Porter Sargent, 2005), 547.
2. In a similar vein, in many societies, women may freely attend football (soccer) matches, but in Iran, women are forbidden from doing so. Thus, women finding a way to enter a stadium and attend a football match during the World Cup qualifying rounds in 2006 constituted an act of nonviolent action.
3. There are numerous examples of using nonviolent action to augment normal political processes. For example, in 2006 in Kuwait, the Orange Movement used nonviolent action in conjunction with the legislative process and political coalition building to pressure the government into adopting an electoral redistricting plan that it favored. In 2005 in Egypt, the Kefaya movement used the presidential election as a focal point of nonviolent action; first the movement planned to support several candidates, but when none were forthcoming, it called for a boycott. Nonviolent action has also been used in conjunction with lawsuits, such as by the anticorruption groups shayfeen.com and Egyptians Against Corruption; through this approach they elicited the Egyptian government's acknowledgment of its obligations under the United Nations Convention Against Corruption in 2007.
4. The term *civic defiance* carries the connotation of nonviolent action used for political purposes. See Sharp, *Waging Nonviolent Struggle*, 543. The term *civil resistance* tends to be used more in Europe than in the United States and connotes a sustained campaign of nonviolent action. See Adam Roberts, "Civil Resistance and Power Politics: The Questions" (paper presented to the "Conference on Civil Resistance and Power Politics," St. Antony's College, Oxford, March 15–18, 2007). The term *political defiance* was devised by Robert L. Helvey and connotes nonviolent action used to fight a dictatorship. The term *people power* began to be widely used as a way to describe the 1986 nonviolent revolution in the Philippines that ended the Marcos regime.
5. The degree to which a population in a nonviolent movement provides power to its opponent will vary depending on the particular struggle. For example, in some circumstances the population in a nonviolent movement comprises the majority of the society from which the opponent derives its power. In these instances, the nonviolent movement is capable, by itself, of applying coercive leverage to the opponent through withdrawal of obedience. In other cases, such as in some struggles by minorities and in some

self-determination and anti-occupation struggles, the population in a nonviolent movement may not comprise the majority of the society from which the opponent derives its
power. In these cases, nonviolent movements often must find ways to "expand the nonviolent battlefield" by appealing to and expanding their movement to include members
of the larger population upon which the opponent's power depends.

6. These six sources of power were first outlined in Gene Sharp, *The Politics of Nonviolent
   Action: Part One: Power and Struggle* (Boston: Porter Sargent, 1973), 11–12. The list
   here renames and elaborates on some of the sources of power that Sharp identified.

7. When a state has powerful external pillars of support, a movement must sometimes
   "expand the nonviolent battlefield" to include an international component, such as
   support by allied international NGOs, external governments, or foreign populations, to
   their struggle in order to exert pressure on these external pillars. For a discussion of the
   role of expanding the nonviolent battlefield in nonviolent struggle, see Maria Stephan,
   "Fighting for Statehood: The Role of Civilian-based Resistance in the East Timorese,
   Palestinian and Kosovo Albanian Self-Determination Movements," *Fletcher Forum for
   World Affairs* 30, no. 2 (Summer 2006).

8. Examples of this occurred in Serbia (2000) and Ukraine (2004). In both cases, state security forces—the army and the police—did not openly support the nonviolent movement
   but instead chose to execute orders less efficiently, a demonstration of their decreased
   loyalty to the state. At key points in the struggle, they became neutral by simply ignoring orders to carry out repression against members of the nonviolent movement.

9. Common reasons for obedience include fear, self-interest, consent, psychological identification with the ruler, and lack of confidence. For a more detailed analysis of reasons for obedience, see Srdja Popovic, Slobodan Djinovic, Andrej Milivojevic, Hardy
   Merriman, and Ivan Marovic, *CANVAS Core Curriculum: A Guide to Effective
   Nonviolent Struggle* (Belgrade: Centre for Applied Nonviolent Action and Strategies,
   2008), 46–50.

10. This list elaborates on Sharp's description of each mechanism of change. Sharp, *Waging
    Nonviolent Struggle*, 45–47.

11. This list of variables influencing the outcome of negotiated agreements between non-
    violent movements and their opponents is not meant to be comprehensive, but rather
    illustrative of some of the issues at play in such negotiations.

12. Successful nonviolent movements often try to break through the insulation of military
    officers and police leadership by developing lines of communication with them. The
    ability of a movement to understand and respond to the concerns of the military and
    police leadership can be highly important in influencing the behavior of these influ-
    ential actors and can at times lead to defections among officers if the officers feel that
    the movement represents a legitimate and better alternative to the existing system of
    government.

13. This is a hypothetical example. Different cases will yield different patterns of mecha-
    nisms of change in societies. For example, in some struggles, such as Ukraine (2004),
    some high-ranking military officers accommodated or possibly even converted to sup-
    porting the movement. See Anika Locke Binnendijk and Ivan Marovic, "Power and
    Persuasion: Nonviolent Strategies to Influence State Security Forces in Sebia (2000) and
    Ukraine (2004)," *Communist and Post-Communist Studies* 39 (2006): 411–29.

14. Sharp uses the term *methods of nonviolent action*, but I use the term *tactics of nonvio-
    lent action*. Their meanings, however, are the same. The list and description of Sharp's
    198 methods of nonviolent action are found in Sharp, *The Politics of Nonviolent
    Action: Part Two: The Methods of Nonviolent Action* (Boston: Porter Sargent, 1973).

15. New tactics are often developed through human ingenuity in response to new move-
    ment capabilities and evolving circumstances in a nonviolent struggle. There is often
    a co-evolution between a movement using a tactic, the movement's opponent learning
    how to respond to the tactic, and the movement then developing a new tactic in order

to maintain the initiative in the conflict and to keep their opponent off balance. In addition, new tactics may be developed around new technologies, such as the Internet and cell phones. Examples of new tactics using these technologies include sending mass SMS messages and establishing Web sites, social networks, blogs, and listservs that defy government restrictions.

16. Sharp, *Part Two: The Methods of Nonviolent Action.*

17. As mentioned earlier, what qualifies as an act of nonviolent action is context specific, therefore what qualifies as an act of nonviolent protest and persuasion is also context specific. For example, in a state such as Egypt or Iran, where some rallies are illegal, holding a rally may not simply be a protest and persuasion tactic, but may also be an act of civil disobedience, which some would argue belongs under the category of nonviolent intervention because the movement is intervening in a way that directly disrupts the status quo.

18. Sharp, *Waging Nonviolent Struggle*, 51.

19. An example is when the Druze in the Golan Heights refused to accept Israeli identification documents in the early 1980s.

20. The creation of parallel institutions has been widely used in diverse movements across the Middle East, from Hizbullah and the Muslim Brotherhood's establishment of social service networks in Lebanon and Egypt, respectively, to the Khudai Khidmatgar's establishment of alternative educational programs in the North-West Frontier Province in the 1930s in British-occupied India.

21. Sharp refers to civil disobedience as an act of political noncooperation, whereas I classify it as an act of nonviolent intervention.

22. Kurt Schock, *Unarmed Insurrections: People Power Movements in Nondemocracies* (Minneapolis: University of Minnesota Press, 2005), 51–52.

23. This classification of tactics is used in "A Force More Powerful: The Game of Nonviolent Strategy," a training simulation game produced by York Zimmerman, Inc., International Center on Nonviolent Conflict, and Breakaway Ltd., 2006.

24. An example of an inclusive vision is the call that some movements, such as the anti-apartheid struggle in South Africa, make for "national reconciliation" after the struggle is over. This vision articulates that there is a place for different groups in the movement that enables the movement to garner support because it offers hope to those who may have supported the opponent, but also offers some degree of redress for those who suffered under the opponent.

25. Some movements, however, do nonviolently threaten their opponent's supporters, but attempt to do so in a way that does not invoke fear in the majority of them. For example, some movements will threaten that certain key individuals (i.e., major human rights abusers or highly corrupt officials) will be held accountable for certain actions (i.e., ordering the abuse of political prisoners), but the movement makes these threats without threatening a larger group (e.g., a movement may say that it is not against the police as a whole, but that it is against the way a particular police chief is using the police, or it is not against everyone in a certain government bureaucracy, but rather it is against a particular bureaucrat that is the most corrupt and abusive to the movement's members).

2

Questions and Controversies about Nonviolent Political Struggle in the Middle East

Ralph E. Crow and Philip Grant

Arab Objections to a General Strategy of Nonviolent Political Struggle

In the Arab world, much skepticism and suspicion accompany any suggestion that nonviolent political struggle be employed to combat injustice and oppression. Nonviolent resisters often are seen as pacifists or principled persons, so opposed to the use of force, they would permit the continuation of widespread suffering rather than resort to violent resistance. This critique equates nonviolent struggle with conflict management, or the use of techniques of negotiation and compromise designed more to avoid the spread and intensification of violence than to attack the causes underlying it. It assumes nonviolent struggle is a passive, not active, form of struggle, a weapon of the weak rather than that of the strong.

Nonviolent Struggle Prevents Legitimate Self-Defense

Such assumptions about nonviolent struggle prompt Arab critics to associate adoption of the strategy with policies similar to the Israeli demand that Palestinians formally renounce violence before they will be permitted to negotiate for the return of territories illegally occupied by Israel after the 1967 war. This association of weakness with nonviolent resistance leads to the belief that the adoption of nonviolent struggle would prevent Arab people from effectively protecting themselves against aggression. Discussion of nonviolent struggle is interpreted as symptomatic of Arab defeat and Israeli victory.

Nonviolent Struggle Is an Imperialist Stratagem

Similarly, efforts to diffuse knowledge of nonviolent struggle among the Arabs are sometimes seen as attempts by former colonial and imperialist powers to deflect the revolutionary potential of the Arab people. This position often leads to the belief that engaging in nonviolent struggle would deprive the Arabs of their right to wage wars of national liberation to throw off the last shackles of their colonial legacy. Arabs view hostility to wars of liberation as a culturally convenient denial of their past importance to Europeans. Arab critics point out that the liberation of many Western nations illustrated the sentiments of nationalists like Italy's Giuseppe Mazzini, who wrote: "Insurrection—by means of guerrilla bands—is the true method of all nations desirous of emancipating themselves from a foreign yoke.... It forms the military education of the people and consecrates every foot of the native soil by memory of some warlike deed."[1]

Nonviolent Resistance Is Not Found in Arab History

The entire subject of nonviolent struggle is sometimes regarded as an ideology imported from the West or East Asia, rather than a way of thought and action indigenous to Arab culture and consistent with the ethos of Islam. Since many Arabs think of their tradition as valuing chivalry, courage, and the open confrontation of opponents, they wonder how a system of resistance that rejects the use of arms can be considered part of their heritage. Arab critics equate nonviolent struggle as more appropriate to African Americans or Indian Hindus rather than a strategy of resistance natural to their own people.

Violent Struggle Is Necessary to Establish Dignity and Strength among the Oppressed

Arab skeptics of nonviolent struggle in the Middle East often claim violent struggle is necessary for the psychological health of the oppressed. They believe centuries of colonization and occupation by militarily superior non-Arab powers have rendered Arab nations incapable of thinking they can equal the power and status of their former rulers. Western and Israeli political hegemony in the Middle East is interpreted as the consequence of centuries of indoctrination into the myth of inherent European strength and endemic Arab weakness. Despite the tremendous financial influence of the Arabs in the international economy, the psychological effect of growing up impotent and humiliated in a postcolonial world dominated by Western military establishments is devastating to the personalities of Arab children. Only through violent struggle can this syndrome of weakness be broken. Militarization is the great equalizer through which Arabs can regain the dignity, pride, and self-respect necessary to compete in the global arena.

This view is especially attractive to the Arab young who interpret Israel's continuing expansion as a new stage in the colonization of the Arab world by Western and other non-Islamic powers. Many Arabs are convinced the Palestinians must engage the Israelis militarily to dispel the legend of foreign invincibility. Palestinians are continually urged to emulate the Lebanese Hizbullah, who successfully organized the effort to evict the Israeli army from Lebanon after the invasions of 1982 and 2005.

Nonviolent Struggle Is Inefficient

Arab critics of nonviolent struggle also argue that violent resistance is the most efficient way to attain political goals. While nonviolent political struggle requires extraordinary training and discipline from large numbers of people, the results are frequently problematic. Violent responses by elite groups to end mass suffering at the hands of a brutal regime are considered more admirable and effective. Arabs often celebrate Nasser's quick coup d'état in 1952, or refer to the sudden 1974 Turkish intervention in Cyprus, as examples of this policy.

Violent Struggle Can Mobilize World Opinion against Oppression

Arabs frequently think that violent resistance is the most effective way to attract world attention to injustice in the Middle East. They point out how the world was on the verge of forgetting the Palestinian problem before the execution of a series of violent acts by the Palestine Liberation Organization (PLO), and the deployment of suicide bombers by Hamas. Only the commission of political assassinations, kidnappings, bombings, and hijackings has forced the international community to tale seriously the Palestinian demand of a homeland.

Arab Arguments against a Strategy of Nonviolent Struggle in the Occupied Territories

Lack of Common Bonds between Palestinians and Israelis Makes Nonviolent Struggle Pointless

Arab critics of nonviolent struggle in the occupied territories think racial and cultural barriers between Palestinians and Israelis are unbridgeable. The conviction that God favors Jews makes impossible Israeli recognition of the legitimacy of any Palestinian claims to an equal and independent state. Moreover, as the "chosen people" doctrine conditions Israelis to believe the territory now jointly inhabited by Israelis and Palestinians is God's gift to the Jews, the property rights of Palestinians will be continually violated in order to force them to emigrate. Arabs routinely claim nonviolent struggle will merely provide a pretext for Israeli authorities to incarcerate or deport all Palestinian resisters, and expropriate their land.

Uniqueness of Palestinian Culture an Insurmountable Barrier to Nonviolent Struggle

Opponents of nonviolent resistance in the occupied territories also emphasize that Palestinian culture has few elements similar to those in other nations in which nonviolent struggle has proven effective. Most glaring is the absence of a strong tradition of popular participation in political decision making. The lack of strong democracy in the occupied territories has only worsened under the Israeli refusal to grant Palestinians an autonomous and self-sufficient state. Arab critics complain that without a politically activated and experienced citizenry, the mass support needed for the practice of nonviolent techniques of struggle cannot emerge.

Arabs also argue that Palestinian culture has no heritage of compromise and negotiation sufficiently institutionalized to peaceably settle the many disagreements plaguing Palestinian society. Without a well-organized popular front to support nonviolent campaigns, the Israelis will find it too easy to employ the time-honored stratagem of divide and rule to defeat nonviolent challenges to the occupation. In the face of Israeli provocation, factional Palestinian conflicts easily could be fanned into violent outbreaks, destroying any chance for the consensus necessary to anchor an effective nonviolent movement. According to some Arab observers, claims of leadership in Palestinian society today depend upon how many armed resisters a person commands. The charge has even been made that the gun is the primary means by which Palestinians resolve disagreements with each other.

Nonviolent Struggle Is Not Within the Islamic Tradition

Arab critics of nonviolent resistance also argue that nonviolent Palestinian responses to the Israeli occupation are unworkable because of the role played by *jihad*, or holy war, within the Islamic tradition. All sects of Islam accept the legitimacy of conducting a violent defense against attacks on the religion of Islam. With the growth and intensification of Jewish fundamentalism, coupled with menacing moves by extremists to violate Islamic shrines and seize Palestinian land, the entire administrative system set up under the Israelis is tantamount to an attack on Islam. In the face of such a massive assault on their religion, appeals to organize a nonviolent movement of resistance would prove incomprehensible to most Palestinian Muslims.

Nonviolent Struggle Is Inconsistent with Big Power Interests

A final objection to nonviolent political struggle within the occupied territories holds that because the Big Power interests are deeply embedded in the Arab-Israeli conflict, no lasting solutions can emerge without their consent and participation. If the Palestinians try to liberate themselves through a nonviolent struggle, the United States, the European Union, Russia, China, and other international actors, will intervene directly, or through their regional proxies, to prevent any possibility of success. The Big Powers will not allow any future independent Palestinian state to threaten their economic and political hegemony over the Middle East. The people of the occupied territories must await their freedom until the Big Players conclude an agreement to end Israeli rule under terms that serve their own national interests.

Arab Arguments in Support of a General Strategy of Nonviolent Political Struggle

Nonviolent Resistance Is an Effective Weapon against the Status Quo

Arab supporters of nonviolent political struggle in the Middle East are adamant in insisting they are calling for an effective, active response to injustice. They point to past examples of nonviolent resistance that movingly illustrate a willingness among the participants to risk injury or death to end oppression. Such struggles have been waged in countries of widely varying social, economic, and political circumstances. Cited examples demonstrate the common aim of changing a policy or a regime that violates widely accepted canons of fairness and freedom. The claim that those who urge such nonviolent resistance are apologists for imperialism and reaction ignores that some of the most successful nonviolent movements, as well as those containing a strong component of nonviolence, arose as a direct challenge to imperialism (Egypt 1922, Iraq 1948) and colonialism (Pakistan 1930) as well as internal repression (Iran 1979, Sudan 1985).

Nonviolent Political Struggle Is Not Pacifism

Advocates of nonviolent resistance draw an important distinction between nonviolent struggle and pacifism. They emphasize that popular confusion of the pacifist movement with doctrines such as appeasement, has commonly connected the meaning of passive resistance with peace at any price. In the Arab world, pacifists are accused of abandoning both a concern with redressing social grievances, and a commitment to changing unjust social structures in favor of discussion, negotiation, and compromise. Supporters of Arab nonviolent political struggle are adamant in denying all assertions that nonviolent methods in any way contribute to tolerating oppression, or perpetuating any existing system of injustice.

The purpose of nonviolent political struggle is to mobilize, not paralyze, oppressed and disempowered people. The choice of nonviolent methods is made out of a collective conviction that only these means can ensure political change will be truly remedial rather than temporary and superficial. Nonviolent Arab activists believe that if their kind of struggle can be integrated into an Arab nation's political culture, future conflicts will be conducted in a manner that reflects the innate capacity of all people to collectively determine their future destiny, while ensuring the worth and dignity of all members of the community.

Nonviolent Struggle Is More Appropriate to Long-term Solutions to Injustice than Violent Responses

Although advocates of nonviolent struggle are as concerned with effectiveness as are proponents of armed struggle, they more radically question the relationship between means and ends in politics. They ask if violent means can truly transform a violently oppressive system of exploitation. Although the question is not strictly empirical, and assumes moral and metaphysical presuppositions about human nature and the nature of cause and effect in the social world, proponents of nonviolent struggle still use factual evidence they consider relevant to bolster their arguments.

Most obvious is the extensive evidence assembled by anthropologists and sociologists showing that use of violent means in political struggle eventually results in a culture of violence. Nonviolent responses to the political, social, and personal controversies of life are gradually ignored and finally forgotten. Violence becomes institutionalized as the social groupings of society lose the capacity for nonviolent interaction at the most elementary level, like decision making within the family or church. A shift to a culture of violence strikes at the very heart of the concept of community, usually defined as a body of individuals who decide disputes through methods that avoid violence. In the Middle East a series of military coups and political assassinations has created a climate in which peaceful transfers of power are increasingly rare. In Lebanon especially, the practice of violence has so eroded the moral energies of the people that the political skills necessary to reconstruct the social fabric of the country have to be rediscovered through long years of trial and error. Violent means have seriously eroded the mutual trust and respect the different Lebanese communities and religious sects need to coexist harmoniously.

Proponents of a general theory of nonviolent struggle wish to transform cultures of conflict to make them more amenable to truly political solutions. They argue that tolerance and civility are critical to the mutual search for and pursuit of common goals within a civil society. Ever since the religious struggles between Islam and Christianity, Catholicism and Protestantism, political philosophers in the West have argued that violence in politics is bound up with the pride of self-righteousness—a refusal to recognize the possibility of error in one's own beliefs about truth, especially religious truth. Consequently, anyone holding opinions contrary to established orthodoxy is characterized as willfully in error and less than human. Advocates of nonviolent action think that unless such doctrinal tendencies and psychological weaknesses are addressed, violence will recur whenever a serious disagreement erupts within a political community.

In the Arab-Israeli conflict, for example, it is obvious that each side believes it alone possesses the full truth about the causes of the conditions in which the parties now find themselves. Arab critics insist that in instances of oppression like the Israeli occupation, Palestinians are more likely to see the situation more clearly than the Israelis. But possessing more of the truth might be the very thing that has hindered serious consideration of nonviolent struggle by the Palestinians. The illusion of absolute truth creates an inability to understand that the Israelis can in any way be justified in their actions. A continuance of the occupation is therefore attributed to a kind of absolute evil that must be violently confronted if it is to end.

This perspective can also explain the increasing use of violence by Israel since its founding in 1948. The full truth of the causes and consequences of the Holocaust provides an irresistible tendency toward self-righteous thinking by most Israelis. The never again assumption that lurks behind much Israeli political thinking causes any conflict with the Jewish state, legitimate or not, to be interpreted apocalyptically.

Proponents of nonviolent struggle like Abdul Ghaffar Khan and Martin Luther King, Jr. shared Gandhi's conviction that nonviolent action followed from the realization that no one side in a political struggle has a monopoly on the truth. Awareness that the truth they possessed was always relative to what they might attain required them to confront their opponents in a way that would allow both sides to correct their ideas and their image of the other party. Nonviolent struggle was embraced as a method capable of changing objective social conditions, subjective conceptions, and internal perceptions through a many-sided and evolving dialectic between theory and practice. Through the emergence of a new political ethic, the rules of political engagement could be permanently re-written. In any society in which a predominance of violent force has convinced the authorities they need not listen to the common people, nonviolent struggle is the last chance of carrying on a true dialogue between equals about critically needed change.

Other supporters of nonviolent political struggle hold a narrower but no less ambitious focus. They think nonviolent struggle rests upon a social power more potent than any that can be brought against it. Once the citizens of an oppressed society realize that by not participating in the daily round of social activities they can bring to heel even the mightiest of tyrants, this will permanently change the political formula upon which government rests. Such an exercise of popular power is not dependent upon any change in values or perception by the usurping authority. A nation's political culture can thus be transformed through instilling into the people an awareness of their immense potential in preventing future abuse at the hands of their rulers or even would-be invaders. After such a display of popular will, it would be only a matter of time before this mobilized social power exercised effective scrutiny and control over all public affairs within the community.

In the occupied territories, advocates of Gandhi's approach point out that without a change in the mutual perceptions of Palestinians and Israelis, any withdrawal to pre-1967 borders would not be accompanied by any lessening of tensions. With neither side having changed its basic understanding of the other, there might be separation or independence but not peace for a future Palestinian state. Continuing Israeli and Palestinian recriminations would prompt unending attempts to interfere and sabotage the well-being of the other side. The current impasse over Gaza is an example.

By contrast, those who base nonviolent struggle upon the concept of social power feel that a nonviolent mobilization of popular will against the occupation will so convince the Israelis of the futility of armed force that they will have no choice but to stop interfering in Palestinian affairs. Ignorant and prejudiced Israeli perceptions of the Palestinian people would prove irrelevant in the face of a realistic appraisal of the invincibility of nonviolent Palestinian power. Only if the Palestinians resorted to violent acts in the future would the Israelis accept the risk of violent retaliation.

Nonviolent Struggle Evokes Sympathy and Support for Just Causes

Supporters of nonviolent action also challenge the contention that violence is useful in attracting world attention to inequities and injustices long ignored. Is it the case, they ask, that the world's concern for Palestinians has increased as a result of daring acts of violence? Or is it more likely that hijackings, suicide bombings and assassinations have focused public attention on the violence committed by Palestinians rather than on Israeli injustice?

Another argument by nonviolent proponents is that violent acts have created a backlash in world opinion against the Arabs by reinforcing conventional stereotypes of them as uncontrollably volatile and irrational. Moreover, the killings of travelers and civilians by Arab assassination teams are said to have caused countries that have long sought better relations with Arab governments to unite with nations traditionally unfriendly to the Arab world in an alliance of mutual defense against the threat of terrorism. In parliamentary nations especially, the negative publicity of violent acts against civilians has drastically limited the flexibility of foreign-policy makers who otherwise might have been inclined to support Arab causes more vigorously.

Conversely, the voluntary acceptance of suffering by nonviolent resisters can do much to win worldwide support for their cause. The history of nonviolent struggle is replete with examples of public outpourings of sympathy for the goals of nonviolent resisters after reports and photographs of unmerited suffering have been circulated by word of mouth or the press (Pakistan 1930, Iraq 1948). It is generally acknowledged that television coverage of police dogs being set loose on black civil rights marchers in Alabama during the 1960s was a critical factor in gaining white allies in the African American struggle for full U.S. citizenship. Today the violence inflicted upon nonviolent African resisters in Zimbabwe and Nigeria has so swung world opinion in favor of the protesters that press censorship has been rigidly imposed in an attempt to stem the tide. This cannot, however, silence the grapevine, which can spread the news perhaps faster than can the press.

Nonviolent Struggle Is the Surest Way to Build Psychological Strength

Defenders of a policy of nonviolent political resistance do not deny that violence can act as a regenerating force on the personalities of a people who believe themselves too weak to fight oppression. Even Gandhi wrote that violent resistance to injustice was better than doing nothing. But proponents of nonviolent struggle also point out that the use of violence can cripple the personality of the perpetrator, giving rise to guilt, self-hatred, and insanity. In fact, through treating Algerian independence fighters during their war against the French, physicians became aware of the debilitating effects of violence on the personality. More recently, the high incidence of drug use and desertion among the militias of Lebanon has been attributed to decades of continual warfare. In the 1980–1987 Gulf War, the Iraqi army was plagued by constant problems with morale, while the Iranians had to resort to a kind of religious mesmerism to keep their troops motivated. Furthermore, Western nations are only now coming to terms with the emotional destructiveness of violent wars. Long after withdrawing from Vietnam, and as recently as the 1990 War with Iraq, and the current wars in Afghanistan and Iraq, the United States must today confront the incalculable psychological damage inflicted on its own highly-trained combatants.

Effective nonviolent resistance generates psychological benefits among the oppressed as great as those produced by violent struggle, but without the negative side effects. Participants in nonviolent resistance movements in nations as diverse as Indonesia, the Philippines, Pakistan, Sudan, and the United States, have testified how courage and confidence resulted from successfully confronting the agents of oppressive systems without resorting to the use of violence. Advocates of nonviolent resistance claim that nonviolent means rather than guns are the great equalizer that allows the common citizen to compete successfully with military force. Moreover, nonviolent resistance demonstrates to the people the meaning of a truly democratic system of defense. Conventional opponents, on the other hand, must rely on a specially trained elite to do their fighting for them.

Nonviolent Struggle Is the Weapon of the Strong, Not the Weak

Nonviolent resisters win their battles through courage, commitment, and the subtle potency of nonviolent methods of struggle. By contending that political power is subservient to social power, the nonviolent resister seeks to redefine the terms "strong" and "weak." Traditionally, politicians in the Middle East and the West have assumed that power flows from the top downward, the difference between authoritarian and democratic regimes stemming solely from the extent to which those at the bottom can somehow condition the policies and actions of those at the top. Theorists of nonviolent struggle, on the other hand, emphasize that political power is wholly "a by-product of social activity and the complex web of human relationships, as expressed through a variety of groupings, from the family upward."[2] The nonviolent resister tries to tap the latent potential of this immense force through popular education. In the case of societies whose institutions have been irremediably corrupted by misuse of power, a nonviolent movement will attempt to introduce new standards of social behavior and build new institutions.

Proponents of nonviolent struggle claim its acceptance and use by the citizenry can alter the social contract that implicitly exists between rulers and ruled. With skill and experience in the art of opposing injustice without weapons, the people can tame any dictator or usurper, and render illegitimate any unjust edict, law, or administrative practice. A realization by the people of their true political potential makes the ideal of popular sovereignty more than a convenient fiction, rendering obsolete Rousseau's observation that in representative democracies the people are only free while they are voting.

Oppressors Fear Nonviolent Struggle More Than Violent Resistance

The immense strength of nonviolent struggle is revealed in the desperate measures taken by authoritarian regimes to suppress it. Part of the reason for such a response is the arrogance of unjust rulers in assuming that a monopoly of superiority of violent force is sufficient to keep them in power. Because the nature of social power is misunderstood, tyrants customarily assume the main challenges to their rule will come from violent struggle. When confronted by nonviolent resistance, conventional attempts to suppress it are inappropriate, appearing at best clumsy and comical, and at worst genocidal. In the United States, for example, the white establishment in the South was much more comfortable fighting a violent black civil rights movement because the whites had an overwhelming superiority in conventional force. When women and children were firebombed while holding prayer vigils, however, the rottenness of the existing system was plainly exposed for all to see. Even the white power structure became demoralized at witnessing the brutal measures taken by its own supporters against unarmed demonstrators.

Arab Arguments for Nonviolent Struggle in the Occupied Territories

All Unjust Systems Are Vulnerable to Nonviolent Struggle

Those who recommend nonviolent resistance in the occupied territories believe that Israeli power rests upon a social base as surely as did British power before the partition of 1947. If the Palestinians were to engage in a strategically directed series of marches, boycotts, strikes, and work stoppages, nonviolent proponents think these could prove as threatening to Israeli authority as similar actions were to the British in the 1930s.

Nonviolent Resistance Can Bridge the Gap between Oppressors and the Oppressed

Besides uniting a divided community, the universal reach of nonviolent struggle allows its proponents to claim it alone can bridge the enormous social distance between Israelis and Palestinians. In most instances of imperialism and colonialism, the oppressors justified their domination by arguing that the oppressed were somehow inherently inferior. Nonviolent movements have succeeded in overcoming this barrier by appealing to that common core of humanity within each official or soldier of the oppressive regime. The willingness of unarmed, ordinary people to die for their beliefs can be extremely effective in breaking through psychological and social barriers constructed by prejudice and propaganda.

Nonviolent Struggle Can Educate the Oppressor

Some advocates of nonviolent struggle think that the willingness of the oppressed to suffer voluntarily forces their opponents to question fundamentally the rationale behind their oppression. These nonviolent advocates believe that the way to lessen social distance is to address its deep unconscious root. Since social systems of injustice are strengthened by fear and insecurity, an appeal to reason and conscience by nonviolent resisters is not enough to convince agents of an oppressive regime that they are acting in error. Nonviolent resistance can weaken fear and insecurity by demonstrating to participants in a regime of injustice that those resisting their oppression will not harm them. Once this underlying fear is allayed, assumptions about inherent superiority that have previously separated oppressor and oppressed may no longer be believed with the same conviction, opening opportunities for constructive dialogue between the two sides.

Nonviolent Struggle Can Overcome the "Chosen People" Doctrine

This same moral power released through nonviolent action can be used to challenge barriers between oppressors and oppressed constructed through doctrines of the chosen people variety. Proponents of nonviolent struggle point out that although most doctrines of alleged racial or cultural superiority rest upon some appeal to abstractions like God, history, reason, and natural law, this has never deterred subjugated peoples from successfully challenging these false doctrines through nonviolent campaigns. Gandhi's opponents in South Africa and India were as racist as any other imperialist power, yet they eventually succumbed to nonviolent demands for an extension of human rights in South Africa, and for independence in India. What makes the situation in Palestine somewhat different is the belief that a particular piece of ground has been given by God exclusively to the Jews, although apparently not all of them accept this doctrine literally because the majority of Jews live outside Israel.

Some Arab nonviolent proponents think the chosen people doctrine can even be used to engage the Israelis in a unique moral dialogue. Because the belief in being chosen requires Jews to adopt a high moral posture, it seems a perfect avenue upon which a nonviolent Palestinian movement could travel. Furthermore, the Jewish fear of genocide inherited from the pogroms and World War II, makes the Israelis extremely sensitive to moral condemnation for inflicting violence on nonviolent protesters. Advocates of nonviolent struggle in the occupied territories emphasize that violent Palestinian acts will serve only to remind the Jews of the persecution they suffered at the hands of the Nazis, whereas nonviolent resistance offers no excuse to continue the occupation on grounds of fending off extermination.

The Concept of Jihad Can Mean Inner Struggle

In response to the charge that Jewish threats to Islam will make the concept of jihad the basis for Palestinian resistance against the Israelis, supporters of nonviolent resistance reply that the well-educated Palestinian community is more likely to include nonviolent political struggle in discussions of the meaning of jihad than more fundamentalist Muslims. The term itself has many connotations for the educated Muslim, not the least of which is an inner struggle of striving against one's own weaknesses in living up to the commandments of God. As in other religions, Islam puts strict limits on acceptable violence. The life of the Prophet was one in which the qualities of mercy and forgiveness of enemies were continually stressed, while revenge was constantly condemned. In one of the Hadiths, the Prophet says the best jihad *is hejira* (flight) and the best hejira is to flee from evil to good.

Nonviolent Struggle Can Develop Social and Economic Strength and International Autonomy

Arab advocates of nonviolent resistance also recommend that the social divisions within the Palestinian community as well as between Israelis and Palestinians, can be lessened by a constructive program in which free, egalitarian social and economic institutions would be started in embryo to underpin the burgeoning nonviolent movement. These NGOs could serve as training camps where people could learn the skills necessary to become self-reliant guardians of their political rights and social responsibilities. Such a program would also initiate economic activities designed to develop the resources of the occupied territories in ways that would benefit the local inhabitants rather than foreign governments and transnational corporations. Moreover, self-sufficient economic institutions would guarantee that a liberated Palestine would not be vulnerable to economic blackmail by its more industrially developed neighbors. The Israelis in turn would be assured that an autonomous Palestine would not become an economic hostage of a regional power hostile to Israel.

A self-sustaining economic program also might demonstrate to the Palestinians they need not depend upon superpower politics for economic and military aid in establishing their own state. Many new nations become economically dependent upon outside powers through an underdevelopment of human resources, an over-development of imported technology, and an enormous indebtedness incurred through arms purchases. Once the Palestinians become aware of their capacity to regenerate indigenous institutions and build new ones, these usual patterns of destructive dependency could be avoided. Moreover, reliance on a nonviolent system of defense against outside aggression could save the new nation billions of dollars, while allowing public resources to provide for the satisfying of basic needs.

Critical Questions Concerning Nonviolent Struggle in the Middle East

Can Nonviolent Struggle Be Both a Creed and a Policy?

The preceding arguments in support of nonviolent political struggle in the Middle East contain a mix of pragmatic and moral considerations. Between these two spheres of emphasis lies a question central to the character of nonviolence. Is it a policy or a creed? As a policy, nonviolent struggle rests upon the assumption that only it accurately recognizes the nature of social power. The policy approach maintains that nonviolent struggle can release political energy metaphorically comparable to that of nuclear power in the physical world. In principle, it cannot be withstood. Nonviolent resistance as a creed, on the other hand, rests on a belief akin to what the Muslim saints Nuri, Raqqam, and Bayazid called the divine love of God, or complete compassion and unselfishness toward all creatures. Gandhi and Abdul Ghaffar Khan referred to this idea as *soul force*, something Saint Paul and Martin Luther King, Jr., termed *agape*. The claims made for the power of nonviolent struggle as a creed are as great as those advanced for the method as a policy. Gandhi believed that because the basis of all life was truth, reflected in the natural world through uniform patterns and polarities we call laws of nature, any attempt by men and women to live for truth would be supported by the complete intelligence of the universe, God.

Leading the Nonviolent Struggle

The distinction between nonviolent struggle as a policy and a creed also extends to the theory of nonviolent leadership. Those advocating the policy approach believe that education in the techniques and tactics of nonviolent struggle will equip the masses with the weapons they need to become fully empowered citizens of a strongly democratic nation. Directing this education would be teachers experienced in the full range of nonviolent methods revealed through knowledge of past struggles and the political principles they demonstrate. A thorough dissemination of such knowledge would prompt leaders to spontaneously emerge to put the strategy and tactics into practice. The replacement of killed, imprisoned, or deported leaders would follow naturally as understanding of the principles of nonviolent struggle became more widespread, and others stepped forward to fill their shoes.

Proponents of nonviolent struggle as a creed suggest that something more than mere education is required of the leaders of a nonviolent movement. They must be the shock troops of the resistance, specially trained in the ethical principles of a nonviolent way of life. With this knowledge and commitment, they can lead through the power of example, inspiring the people with the courage and confidence needed to face police batons and bayonets. Such leaders would have vowed to completely identify with the people, in a Maoist sense, and at the same time live like secular monks, as George Eugene Sorel and Gandhi understood. Totally devoted to the success of the resistance, this vanguard would generate new leaders as others sought to emulate their unflagging dedication.

Supporters of nonviolent struggle as a creed argue that this conception of leadership in a nonviolent movement is the most realistic because it accounts for the irrational in human nature. Most human beings fear death and will not risk their lives against the guns of an armed oppressor. To ask people to fight without the seeming security offered by weapons requires more than education in the strategy and tactics of nonviolent combat. It is necessary to inspire the people through the actions of those not afraid to die in pursuit of a just cause. The personal sacrifices they have made for the movement will arouse in others the moral strength to multiply and risk their lives in turn.

The distinction between nonviolent political struggle as a policy and a creed need not be absolute in practice. As some writers have pointed out, the concept of nonviolent struggle is great enough to accommodate many interpretations. What seems critical is some agreement on a minimal set of criteria about the meaning of nonviolent action in order to offer a basis for an overall strategy. If some people within the movement wish to adopt nonviolent struggle as a creed, this should not dissuade others from joining the cause. Similarly, if some are attracted to resist nonviolently because of its practical advantages, this should not interfere with the more ethical concerns of fellow resisters. More worrisome is the chance that some resisters might abandon nonviolent struggle when it seemed expedient, thereby threatening the overall success of the movement. Proponents of nonviolent struggle as a creed maintain that this possibility would be reduced as more resisters adopted the nonviolent ethic. Pledges, vows, and internal policing could then be used to reinforce self-discipline.

Conclusion

Whatever one's perspective on the merits of nonviolent struggle in the Middle East, it can hardly be denied that much more attention should be given to it. Case studies assembled in a variety of books have shown nonviolent responses to the abuse of power by rulers and invaders are a time-honored part of the history and politics of the Middle East. Proponents of nonviolent political struggle emphasize these efforts are active attempts at fighting oppression; not acquiescence to social evils. What is much less common in world history, however, is an organized nonviolent campaign to change the distribution of all forms of power within a nation or between nation-states. Advocates of nonviolent action claim this is possible in every part of the world, including the Middle East. This confidence still awaits confirmation in a region that has known little peace in the past one hundred years.

Notes

This chapter is based on the chapter of the same title from *Arab Nonviolent Political Struggle in the Middle East* (Boulder, CO: Lynne Rienner, 1990). The chapter has only been updated and modified slightly.

1. Quoted in Michael Howard, *War and the Liberal Conscience* (New Brunswick, NJ: Rutgers University Press, 1986), 49–50.
2. Raghavan Iyer, *The Moral and Political Thought of Mahatma Gandhi* (Santa Barbara, CA: Concord Grove Press, 1983).

3

No Silence, No Violence: A Post-Islamist Trajectory

Asef Bayat

The debate about a "democratic deficit" in the Middle East is nothing new.[1] The excessive attention paid to the argument that Islam hinders democratic reform is, however, notable. Because of Islam's emphasis on God's sovereignty and its patriarchal disposition, some observers view it as essentially incompatible with democracy. According to them, Islam's supposed lacking in the concepts of citizenship, freedom, and tolerance encourages believers to embrace coercion, violence, and jihad.[2] Thus Islam is seen as a "world in which human life doesn't have the same value as it does in the West, in which freedom, democracy, openness and creativity are alien."[3] Such views have been encouraged by homegrown Islamists who in the name of their religion suspiciously look upon democracy as a "foreign construct," suspend popular will in favor of their concept of God's sovereignty, and commit violence in the name of jihad.

Although other Muslims assert that God has granted sovereignty to humans to govern themselves, that Islamic justice values life—killing one person equals killing the whole of humanity—and that their religion forbids discrimination based on class, race, or gender,[4] the debate has become bogged down in textual and philosophical arguments, with little effort exerted in trying to understand the politics of religious affiliation and how in practice Muslims perceive their religion in relation to democratic ideas. The issue should not be Islam's compatibility with democracy, but how and under what conditions Muslims can interpret Islam to embrace a democratic ethos.

Nothing intrinsic to Islam, or to any other religion, makes it inherently democratic or undemocratic, peaceful or violent. What matters are the ways in which the faithful perceive, articulate, and live through their faiths: some practice their religion in exclusive, authoritarian, and violent ways, while others take from it a commitment to tolerance, peace, equality, and pluralism. Irrespective of how religious beliefs and experiences relate to supernatural reality, in the end "religion is expressed by means of human ideas, symbols, feelings, practices, and organizations."[5] In a sense, religious injunctions are nothing but our understanding of them; they are what we make them. Some 50 years ago, many social scientists believed Christianity and democracy to be incompatible, but today the most deep-rooted democracies are located in predominately Christian nations, despite flirtations with fascism associated with the Church.[6]

Religions are not fixed and well-defined entities. Rather, they are understood, imagined, and constructed by the faithful in diverse ways. Why individuals and groups perceive and present the same scriptures differently is an intriguing and complex sociological matter that depends largely on individual believers' and groups' differing biographies, social positions, and interests. The compatibility or incompatibility of Islam and democracy is not a matter of philosophical speculation, but of political struggle; it is not so much a matter of texts as a balance of power between those who want an authoritarian religion and those who desire a democratic version. Islamism and post-Islamism tell the story of these two forces.

With so much focus on "fundamentalist Islamists" and jihadi trends that draw on puritanical, exclusivist, and hostile interpretations of Islamic doctrine, little attention is being paid to the ethics and experiences of "post-Islamism"—that is, nonviolent social movements that aim to bridge the gap between Islam and democracy in Muslim societies. These movements face numerous obstacles but also stand to gain from opportunities in envisioning a post-Islamist democracy in the Middle East through nonviolent action.

Post-Islamism

Is post-Islamism a discursive break from Islamism or does it represent only one particular version of Islamist politics? Does it point to the historical end of Islamism? It is argued here that post-Islamism signifies a crucial shift in Islamic politics, without implying the death knell of Islamism. Emerging from the anomalies of Islamist politics prevalent since the early 1990s, post-Islamism represents an effort to fuse religiosity and rights, faith and freedom, Islam and liberty. It seeks to turn the underlying principles of Islamism on their head by emphasizing rights instead of duties, plurality in place of a singular authoritative voice, historicity rather than fixed scripture, ambiguity in place of certainty, and the future instead of the past. It strives to marry Islam with individual choice and freedom, democracy, and modernity (which post-Islamists stress) to achieve what some call an alternative modernity.[7] Its advocates hope to reverse the discourse of violence so ingrained in the ideologies and practices of some (but not all) Islamist trends today, in order to dial back the current association of Islam with violence. Post-Islamism is expressed in acknowledging secular exigencies, in freedom from rigidity, and in breaking down the belief in a monopoly of religious truth. In short, whereas the fusion of religion and responsibility mark Islamism, post-Islamism emphasizes religiosity and rights.

Whether the practice of Islam corresponds to democratic ideas depends primarily on whether and how advocates of Islamism or those of post-Islamism succeed in establishing hegemony in a society and state. The history of socioreligious movements in Iran and Egypt since the 1970s offers fertile ground for examining the logic, conditions, and forces behind rendering Islam democratic or undemocratic. In Iran, the 1979 revolution and establishment of an Islamic state set the stage for the rise of post-Islamist ideas and movements that aimed to transcend Islamism in society and governance.[8] The end of the war with Iraq (in 1988), the death of Ayatollah Khomeini (in 1989), and the program of postwar reconstruction under President Ali Akbar Hashemi Rafsanjani marked Iran's turning point toward post-Islamism.

This movement was expressed in various social practices and ideas, including in urban management, attitudes and policies toward women and women's rights, theological perspectives, and social and intellectual trends and movements. Youths, students, women, religious intellectuals, as well as large numbers of state employees, among others, called for democracy, individual rights, tolerance, and gender equality, but they refused to altogether discard their religious sensibilities. Daily resistance and struggle by ordinary people led religious thinkers, spiritual elites, and political actors toward a crucial paradigmatic shift. Scores of Islamist revolutionaries renounced their earlier ideas on exclusivism—that is, the idea that their model is the only model, or their truth is the only truth, but accommodating different ideas, models, and so on—revolutionary violence, and religion as ideology and politics, and lamented the danger of the religious state to religion as well as to the state. Scores of opponents from without and within Iran called for secularization of the state, but at the same time stressed upholding the religious ethics of Iranian society. The reformist government of President Mohamed Khatami (1997–2004) represented the political aspect of this societal trend.

Despite inroads in early 2000, Iran's post-Islamism failed ultimately to fully democratize the Islamic republic. Its project of "political reform," which for a time looked poised to become an indigenous model of democratic reformation in the Islamic Middle East, was thwarted by the reformists' own blunders and by the coercive power of Iran's ruling clerics. Undermined and unable to neutralize the conservative backlash politically, the reform camp also failed to confront it by popular force, via labor strikes, nonviolent civil disobedience, and civic disruptions. Unlike authoritarian states that rely on coercion, a movement's power lies in its social base, the collective strength of its grassroots. Societal force—built and sustained through education, organization, institutionalization, and mobilization—can pressure the state into reform and resist state repression, and it can also ensure a movement's continuity. Iran's reform movement failed, however, to develop such a social base.

The Iranian reform movement remained a middle-class entity entangled in a modernist strategy, which relied heavily on the transformation of public space, advocating "rational dialogue," democratic values, tolerance, and rule of law. Though noble and necessary goals, the strategies and efforts to realize them were not enough to overcome the state's coercive force. Partly as a reaction to the prevailing populist politics of the clerics and nonclerical revolutionaries of earlier periods, especially the 1980s, post-Islamists did little to organize the popular classes, especially the poor and the working people, who were interested in concrete and immediate issues, such as price rise, housing shortage, joblessness, and so on. In fact, economics mattered little in the post-Islamist Iranian literature. Although the post-Islamist movement in Iran failed to dislodge the Islamists, it was able to undermine the moral and political legitimacy of Islamism, which for more than two decades had subjugated the majority of Iranians in the name of religion. The movement popularized the discourses of democracy and political (if not social) pluralism to a degree never before realized in Iran (at least not since the time of Prime Minister Mohammed Mossadegh in the early 1950s) or any other area of the Islamic Middle East, with the exception of Turkey. Post-Islamists in Iran demonstrated that one simultaneously can be a Muslim and a democrat and that democratic ideals can take root in a Muslim society.

Egypt, however, experienced a different trajectory. By the early 1990s, an Islamist movement using *da'wa* and associational work commanded large segments of civil society and had begun moving to claim space in state institutions.

This pervasive movement espoused a conservative moral vision, populist language, and a patriarchal disposition and advocated adherence to scripture. Although it has thus far failed to dislodge Egypt's secular regime, the movement has left an enduring mark on the Egyptian people and the state by successfully embedding an "Islamic mode" in society. Taking heed of the Islamists' inroads, major actors in Egyptian society—including the intelligentsia, nouveau riche, al-Azhar (the institution of the establishment Islam), and ruling elites—converged around the language of nativism and a conservative religious moral ethos and used them to severely marginalize critical voices, innovative religious thought, and demands for genuine democratic reform. Threatened by an expanding Islamism, the authoritarian state appropriated aspects of conservative religiosity and nationalist sentiment (cultivated by the ongoing Arab-Israeli conflict) to style a Gramscian "passive revolution."[9] This revolution was essentially a managed Islamic restoration in which the state, the original target of change, succeeded in remaining completely in charge.[10] Although in 2005 Kefaya, a nascent democracy movement offered the prospect of change in the political arena, the Egyptian power structure remained authoritarian, religious thought stagnant and exclusive, and the political class nativist. Little in Egypt resembled Iran's post-Islamist trajectory.

Since the 1990s, Islamism and post-Islamism have unfolded simultaneously in the Muslim world. On the one hand, social and political conditions globally and locally in individual countries have continued to generate a desire for religious and moral politics, especially in those nations yet to experience Islamism. Anti-Islamic sentiment in the West following the September 11 al-Qaida attacks against the United States in 2001 and the George W. Bush administration's subsequent "war on terror" have reinforced a profound feeling of insecurity as well as outrage among Muslims who sense that Islam and Muslims are under an intense onslaught. These attitudes have increased the appeal of religiosity and nativism such that Islamic parties—including in Algeria, Bahrain, Morocco, Pakistan, and Turkey—have had considerable success in national elections since 2002 while emphasizing among other elements of their platforms opposition to U.S. policy in Afghanistan, Iraq, and the broader Middle East in general.

Nonetheless, against this backdrop of intensifying religious sentiment in the Muslim world, a new post-Islamist trend continues to try to emerge, attempting to accommodate aspects of democratization, pluralism, women's rights, youth concerns, and social development with adherence to religion. For example, Hizbullah has transcended its initial exclusivist platform, set out in the 1980s, calling for an Islamic state in Lebanon. Over the years, Hizbullah's leaders adapted to the pluralistic political reality of Lebanese society, and the organization has since come to act increasingly like a traditional Lebanese, confessional political party.[11] In Egypt, Hizb al-Wasat, a breakaway faction of the Muslim Brotherhood, dissociated itself in the late 1990s from the violent strategy of Gama'a al-Islamiya (which in 1997 would renounce violence unilaterally and opt for peaceful activities) as well as the authoritarian disposition of the Muslim Brothers. Hizb al-Wasat privileged modern democracy over Islamic *shura*—the Quranic notion of "consultation" in public affairs that some Islamists see as an adequate alternative to democracy—embraced pluralism in religion, and welcomed gender mixing and ideological tendencies. In fact, the primary ideologue of the party, Rafiq Habib, has been a Coptic Christian.

Leaders of the Moroccan religious movement Adl wal-Ehsan (Justice and Benevolence) do not claim an exclusive understanding of Islam, and they rely on interpretation and historicizing and embrace flexibility and ambiguity. They reject imposing *sharia* and the *hijab* on Muslims and endorse human rights, pluralism, democracy, and separation of powers.[12] More so than Adl wal-Ehsan, however, Morocco's Justice and Development Party has spearheaded post-Islamism by participating in multiparty electoral competition. Turkey has smoothly and rapidly transcended the Islamism of the Virtue and Welfare parties by embracing the self-conscious, post-Islamist trend expressed by the Justice and Development Party (AKP) that advocates a pious society within a secular democratic state. Even in strongly conservative Saudi Arabia, a post-Wahhabi trend primarily among intellectuals has been attempting to compromise with democracy through "liberal Islam."[13] Yet, with the exception of the Turkish AKP party, none of these movements have assumed governmental power, which would ultimately require them to make a determination of how and to what extent they would be willing or able to forge democratic governance.

Egypt's Islamist movement failed to fully "Islamize" the Egyptian state, and Iran's post-Islamism could not democratize the Islamic Republic, largely because both movements encountered stiff opposition from their respective power elites. The political impasse in these countries has been less a function of religion per se than of structural impediments and the longtime vested interests of the ruling elites. A discursive shift alone is clearly insufficient to cause real institutional transformation. Movements need in addition to win political power. To what extent can social movement mobilization bring about political and structural change? To what extent can states accommodate the aspirations and goals of adversarial social movements? How much can social movements alter, without resorting to violence, the political status quo in the Middle East, a region with authoritarian regimes of both secular and religious dispositions, exclusivist Islamist opposition, and foreign interference?

Social Movements and Political Change

Successful social movements are sustained, multifaceted processes of agency and change, with ebbs and flows and enduring "forward linkages" that can revitalize popular mobilization when opportunities arise.[14] The most common goal of social movements is to pressure authorities, or opponents, into fulfilling social or political demands. These movements attempt to accomplish their goals through mobilization, threatened disruptions, or fomenting uncertainty in the opponent's ranks.[15] For instance, the Islamist campaign in Egypt compelled the government to restrict liberal publications, persecute authors, and prohibit films. Even if social movements are not engaged in a political campaign, they may still be involved in what Alberto Melucci calls "cultural production."[16] The very existence of a social movement is in itself change, because it involves creating new social formations, groups, networks, and relationships. Its "animating effects," by enforcing and unveiling alternative relations and institutions, enhance the cultural production of different value systems, norms, behaviors, symbols, and discourse. This process of building power relies in part on producing alternative ways of being and doing things. Post-Islamist movements represent a vivid example of this phenomenon, using the media, publications, associations, education, fashion, lifestyle, and new discourse to bring about moral and intellectual changes in civil society en route to political reform.

Social movements may induce change also by discretely operating on institutional fault lines between the state and civil society. For example, in the early 1990s,

Egyptian Islamists succeeded in penetrating the state education system, influencing policymakers, teachers, and above all a generation of students through their activities at teacher training colleges. State-appointed, Islamist judges enforced Islamic law, punishing secularists while ruling in favor of Islamic-oriented legal suits. Even the police and the military were not immune to Islamist infiltration. Social movements, if they are accommodated by an incumbent regime, may be able to capture segments of governmental power through routine electoral means. The cases of Turkey's ruling AKP and Iran's reform government under Khatami represent two recent such examples.

One of the great challenges for a social movement is retaining its original mission and goals, core constituencies, organizational culture, and character while exerting governmental power or at the least effecting power shifts or policy changes. Although sharing state power may enable a movement to turn some of its ideas into public policy, a failure to do so, even if such failure is the result of the opponent's actions, can undermine its base of support in society, thus weakening it. Social movements therefore need to move beyond solely discursive struggles for a democratic polity by connecting substantively with diverse constituencies and consolidating their organizational and institutional foundations in society. Not only can a solid organizational social base compel an opponent to undertake political reform, as occurred in Mexico in the 1990s, in Lebanon in 2005, and in Kuwait in 2008,[17] it might even pave the way for a political agreement between the democracy movement and the state, as took place in Chile and Spain. Such a foundation can also protect movements from repression and annihilation and ensure continuity and revival after a downturn. The Egyptian Muslim Brotherhood is a pertinent example. The movement, founded in the late 1920s, has endured for decades, through ebbs and flows, primarily as a result of its deep-seated associational work in civil society and to its kinship networks.

The Art of Presence

Reform of authoritarian states usually requires a distinctly laborious struggle by the citizens of those states, the significance and difficulties of which one cannot discount. Civic mobilization, however, remains indispensable to meaningful and sustained democratic reform of the state. A shift in a society's sensibilities remains a precondition for democratic transformation.

Social change might occur partly as the unintended outcome of structural processes, such as migration, urbanization, demographic shifts, or a rise in literacy. It may also result from the exchange of ideas, information, and models. Regardless, the most crucial element for democratic reform is an active citizenry, that is, the sustained involvement of individuals, groups, and movements in available social, political, and economic spaces—institutional and informal, collective and individual—where they assert their rights and fulfill their responsibilities as citizens and members of whatever communities. It is in such spaces that alternative ideas, norms, practices, and politics are produced. The aptitude and audacity associated with an active citizenry come together in the "art of presence," the skill and stamina against all odds to assert the collective will by circumventing or transforming constraints, utilizing what is possible, and discovering new spaces within which to be heard, seen, and felt.[18]

Muslim citizens will not be able to spearhead a democratic shift unless they master the art of presence. Authoritarian regimes may be able to repress organized movements or collective resistance, but they are limited when it comes to stifling the everyday life of an entire society. It is important to recognize that campaigns of nonviolent resistance can adjust and adapt their strategies and tactics to maintain steady pressure on the opponent and to raise the cost of repression. Indeed, the art of presence is made more powerful and robust when civilian groups apply strategic thinking for undertaking daily acts of resistance. Although structural constraints and state-sponsored repression pose challenges to effective nonviolent resistance, strategic planning can greatly empower groups to recognize and exploit opportunities by tying acts of resistance to specific sociopolitical goals.

Beyond serving as a precondition for sustaining democratic reform, changes in a society's sensibilities through an active citizenry can induce and compel change by an authoritarian state. In this regard, the strategy requires that diverse social groups generate change in their immediate domain: children at home and at school, students in college, teachers in classrooms, workers in factories, athletes in stadiums, artists in galleries, intellectuals in the media, women at home, and as public actors. Not only must citizens make themselves heard, giving voice to their demands and broadcasting violations against them, they must also take responsibility for excelling at what they do. An authoritarian regime should not be the reason cited for failing to produce excellent novels, brilliant handicrafts, math champions, world-class athletes, dedicated teachers, a film industry, and so on. Excellence is power; it is identity.

With the art of presence, a society, through the daily activities of its citizens, can rejuvenate itself by affirming values that reject the authoritarian leader and opposition elites with the ultimate goal of having the state and its supporters adapt its collective sensibilities. Citizens engaged in the art of presence have the power to subvert authoritarian rule, because the state usually does not govern as an externality to society; rather, it remains dominant by weaving its own logic of power—through norms, institutions, as well as coercion—into the fabric of society. Challenging the state's norms, institutions, and logic of power is likely to subvert "governmentality," that is, its ability to govern.[19]

In Muslim societies, women's struggles to challenge patriarchy in their day-to-day interactions are enormously critical because patriarchy is embedded in the perception and practice of the authoritarian religious polity. The patriarchy may initially only tolerate the public presence of women, but changed circumstances may also alter societal attitudes. For instance, females who overtake males numerically and academically in college increase their chances of becoming directors or managers; in such cases, men are compelled to accept, if not internalize, these women's authority in the workplace. This alone would represent a significant shift in a society's norms and balance of power.

The focus here on the art of presence, or an active citizenry, is not intended to downplay the significance of organization and concerted collective endeavors for change or action by individual citizens; in fact, an active citizenry is likely to embrace and facilitate organized collective action. Yet it is crucial to recognize that authoritarian rule routinely impedes collective action and organized movements, so it is unrealistic to expect a civil society to sustain a constant high level of vigor, vitality, and collective struggle. Society, after all, consists of ordinary people, who at times get tired, are demoralized, or become disheartened. Activism—taking extraordinary action to produce social change—is the stuff of activists, people who energize collective sentiments when the opportunity allows. A well-planned strategy of nonviolent resistance entails managing expectations, avoiding exhaustion by participants, and balancing constructive work with more confrontational and defiant activities. The point is not to reiterate the political significance of social movements in bringing about political change or to ignore the necessity of under-cutting the coercive power of the state. Rather, it is to acknowledge the social spaces in which citizens live, where they conduct the practices of ordinary, every-day life, because it is here, through the art of presence, that an active citizenry can influence established political elites and retool state institutions, introducing into them their sensibilities.

Conclusion

A refashioning of the state may result not only from an active citizenry, individual initiative, or education, but more pervasively from the long-term impact of social movement activism. Through cultural production—establishing new social facts on the ground, that is, modes of thinking, behaving, being, and doing—movements can acclimate states to new or different ways of conducting affairs. For instance, to maintain legitimacy, the Egyptian government had to concede to some (albeit con-servative) codes, methods, and institutions that resident proponents of Islamism preferred. In a similar way, the Islamic regime in Iran moved to recognize and min-imally to act upon the popular desire for secularization, a democratic polity, and civil liberties that the country's social movements had helped to articulate. Further, that the AKP in Turkey has often bowed to that nation's secular democracy is nei-ther a sign of deception nor simply a fear of a military backlash. Instead, it is a position that has been nurtured and shaped by the secular democratic sensibilities of Turkey's religious and secular citizens. Such responses by government are indica-tors of the "socialization of the state," a laborious process of society influencing the state through the establishment of different lifestyles and new modes of think-ing, being, and doing. It requires conditioning the state and its supporters to the broader society's sensibilities, ideals, and expectations. Socialization of the state is in effect "governmentality" in reverse. It can serve as a crucial venue through which citizens cultivate and compel democratic reform of an authoritarian state.[20]

Whenever and wherever religion is a key element in the popular ethos, there is no alternative to mobilizing consensus around a liberatory interpretation of reli-gion. In nations with a Muslim majority, the primary goal must be to generate the intellectual and social mobilization necessary to adequately challenge authoritar-ian regimes, whether religious or secular, and the "fundamentalist" opposition. Such movements stand a chance to democratize religious discourse and authori-tarian states that often benefit from the orthodox presentation of religion. In the Middle East, initiatives for sustained democratic reform must originate with the region's indigenous movements, which would then determine if and how interna-tional assistance should be deployed. International support may be productive only if it is initiated and managed, that is, its process and consequences controlled by the indigenous democracy movements in the region. Otherwise, painstaking reform efforts in the area will yield little outcome if democracy is preached and pushed by foreign forces, and even less if imposed through coercion and conquest.

Notes

1.   This chapter draws heavily on Asef Bayat, *Making Islam Democratic: Social Movements and the Post-Islamist Turn* (Palo Alto, CA: Stanford University Press, 2007). For fuller

elaboration of the arguments and issues raised here, and for extensive historical and empirical narratives, please refer to that volume.

2. See, for instance, Robert Spencer, *Religion of Peace? Why Christianity Is and Islam Isn't* (Washington, DC: Regnery, 2007). A number of influential scholars and policy-makers in the United States, including Eliot Cohen of Johns Hopkins University and Kenneth Adelman of the Defense Department advisory policy board suggest that Islam is essentially intolerant, expansionist, and violent. Some evangelical Protestants have declared Islam an "evil" religion. See William Pfaff, *International Herald Tribune*, December 5, 2002.

3. Benny Morris, Israel's foremost revisionist historian, quoted in Joel Beinin, "No More Tears: Benny Morris and the Road from Liberal Zionism," *Middle East Report* (Spring 2004): 40.

4. See Bayat, *Making Islam Democratic*, 71–97.

5. James Beckford, *Social Theory and Religion* (Cambridge: Cambridge University Press, 2003), 2.

6. Some influential commentators on World Wars I and II concluded that Catholicism and democracy were not particularly compatible. See S. Lipset, K. Seong, and J. C. Torres, "Social Requisites of Democracy," *International Social Science Journal* 13, no. 6 (May 1993): 29.

7. Modernity is a complex issue, but here it is understood in terms of a social existence in which the individual and reason are the central players, creating a societal arrangement associated with rationality, specialization, urban life, industry, individuality, and so on, with all of their attendant opportunities and problems. It is a social existence that is particularly self-reflexive; it is constantly critical of almost everything. These features distinguish modern from premodern life. "Alternative modernity" is understood in terms of an alternative to Western modernity, which is usually associated with secularism, and implies that modernity can go together with religion. Secularism is meant not in terms of the separation of religion from the state, but in terms of the eroding role and significance of religion in society.

8. The practice or idea of Islamism is a prerequisite for post-Islamism, which is a reflexive project that thinks about, reflects on, and critiques Islamism and then transcends it. This distinguishes the notion of "post-Islamism" from ideas and practices that might have existed before the rise of Islamist movements and states.

9. A Gramscian "passive revolution" describes the way in which a social movement that aims to dislodge the ruling class and ruling system (capitalism) gets co-opted in the logic of the system such that although some demands of the movement are met, it becomes part of the system without causing fundamental change.

10. Islamism had come to sweep the secular state aside, but the state, instead of fighting Islam and Islamism, reinstated and reinforced religious/Islamic sensibilities in society.

11. See Rola al-Husseini's chapter in this volume (chapter 16).

12. On the basis of discussions with two young leaders of the movement, Rabat, Morocco, January 30, 2006.

13. See Stephane Lacroix, "Between Islamists and Liberals: Saudi Arabia's New 'Islamo-Liberal' Reformists," *Middle East Journal* 58, no. 3 (Summer 2004): 345–65.

14. Forward linkages are the ongoing effects of a movement after it has ceased to exist.

15. Sidney Tarrow, *Power in Movement: Collective Action, Social Movements and Politics* (Cambridge: Cambridge University Press, 1994).

16. Alberto Melucci, *Nomads of the Present* (Cambridge: Cambridge University Press, 1989), 60. Melucci's "cultural production" is roughly what Sztompka terms "latent change"—change that is not readily visible or immediately obvious (as is making new laws or policies). Rather, it is piecemeal, gradual, and cumulative. "Cultural production" refers to social movements' effect on creating (often without intention) new ways

of seeing, behaving, and doing things or new codes, symbols, and language, and so on. See Piotr Sztompka, *Sociology of Social Change* (Oxford: Blackwell, 1999).

17. In Mexico, the democracy movement—composed of students, peasants, and workers' organizations—sustained a prolonged campaign that forced the state to undertake democratic reform in the 1990s. See Jorge Cadena-Roa, "State Pacts, Elites, and Social Movement in Mexico's Transition to Democracy," *State, Parties, and Social Movements*, ed. Jack Goldstone, 107–43 (Cambridge: Cambridge University Press, 2003). On events in Lebanon, see, Rudy Jaafar and Maria J. Stephan's chapter in this volume (chapter 12) and concerning Kuwait, see Hamad Albloshi and Faisal Alfahad's chapter in this volume (chapter 15).

18. For details see, Bayat, *Making Islam Democratic*, 200–205.

19. Foucault describes "governmentality" in terms of the state devising mechanisms, methods, and ideas through which citizens govern themselves in accordance with the interests of those who govern. See M. Foucault, *Power* (New York: New Press, 1994).

20. See Bayat, *Making Islam Democratic*, 204–5.

4

Humor and Resistance in the Arab World and Greater Middle East

Khalid Kishtainy

To the politically minded, jokes and satire represent weapons that can be used to denounce, oppose, and resist. George Orwell, the author of *Animal Farm*, said that every joke is a small revolution. A number of Arab commentators, including the Egyptian writer Kamil al-Shinnawi, consider the joke a "devastating secret weapon." Egyptians have used it against their "invaders and occupiers"; Shinnawi demurred to President Gamal Abdel Nasser by omitting "and their rulers."[1] Shinnawi's perspective has been more than reinforced by his compatriot Adil Hammuda, author of *How Egyptians Satirize Their Rulers: The Political Joke.*[2]

Many modern Arab thinkers adhere to the classical Arab notion—espoused by al-Jahiz, probably the most distinguished medieval humorist—that humor is instructive and constructive. Aristotle influenced Arab philosophers in this regard, as he did in other areas, through his commentary on the educational benefits of comedy in exposing and addressing problems and issues. Over the centuries, Arab humorists have often justified their works as acts of piety. Thus, in the 1920s, Michael Tays, an Iraqi, launched the magazine *Kannas al-Shawari* (The road sweeper), asserting his intent to take his broom to the streets of Baghdad to rid it of anyone committing an act injurious to smell or taste.[3]

The peoples of the Middle East have long been obsessed with poetry, making it an easy and relatively safe but powerful medium through which their spokespeople could express dissenting opinions, a trick to which Thomas Hardy also resorted in his later years. Humor, second only to poetry in popularity among Middle Easterners, is even more pliable for venting unpopular or defiant ideas. Once a person laughs, he becomes more relaxed and tends to be more forgiving and indulgent. It was Freud who drew attention to the fact that humor diverts the tendency toward violence and aggression. Furthermore, people often forget what they read, but a joke, like a verse or a song, sticks more easily in the mind. It is repeated to friends and kinsmen, and they, in turn, do the same. Middle Eastern Web sites and blogs have become saturated with political jokes, cartoons, and satirical material borrowed from each other freely and frequently and circulated among friends by email.[4] Humor has become a handy, cheap, and nonviolent means of information and communication for the opposition, helped liberally by the Internet.

It is rather easy to pinpoint the effects of violent means of change, as they are direct, immediate, and physical. It is difficult, however, to gauge the exact effect of humor on the social and political changes of any country or the overthrow of tyranny. Such events are always the result of so many interacting factors that there is hardly any room for hair-splitting attempts to assess individual contributions separately. The means of nonviolent action, and especially humor, often influence the course of history gradually and surreptitiously. There is no record of a regime falling because of a joke, but there is hardly any such event occurring without being preceded by a rich harvest of political jokes and satirical literature. They are invariably the true expression of the masses and the conscience of their leaders. Encouragement of the development and widespread use of political humor and satirical literature should be an essential part of any strategy of civil resistance. This is a task that has been made easier with the development of the Internet and other technical means of mass communication, so widely spread throughout the Middle East and the Third World in general. It is therefore incumbent on nonviolent movements to identify themselves through this popular technology. Translating foreign humor also helps to sharpen the native wit and provide ready material for adaptation and recycling. Of note, many of the political jokes in the Middle East are borrowings from Western sources.

Iranian satirists offer a good example of the ease with which humor can be used to attack authority. The clergy—the ayatollahs, hujjatullahs, and the rest of the mullahs—have become sacred cows that must never be touched. Yet Iranians found the means—through humor—to attack them. Most of these jokes can be found at "Jokestan," a Persian-joke Web site.[5] According to one joke, a mullah became so fat that his doctor urged him to lose weight. The doctor was amazed to find that the mullah had managed to lose 10 kilograms in two days. The mullah lost the weight by shaving off his beard. Another joke dared strike at the holiest of them all, Ayatollah Ruhollah Khomeini: The government allowed people to apply for immigration visas, so a long queue formed outside the Swedish consulate. Soon after, the queue disappeared and everybody went home happily—as soon as they saw the ayatollah coming to join the line.

Smut and sex are also frequently elements in Middle Eastern humor. For example, the Iranians, in their feud with Egypt after the peace treaty with Israel, related that President Anwar Sadat had left his house one day completely naked. His guards stopped him and said, "Sir, you have forgotten to put on your clothes." Sadat replied, "Yes, I want the Egyptian people to see that I have nothing to hide."

Egypt continues to be recognized today as the center of satire and political humor in the Arab world. Its journalists began laying the foundation for this claim as early as the mid-nineteenth century, when Ya'qub Sannu' published the anti-British and antiestablishment satirical newspaper *Abu Naddara Zarqa* (The one with the blue spectacles). As a result, Sannu' suffered physical attacks and ultimately exile to France, from where he continued to publish and smuggle his newspaper into Egypt. A host of humorous publications by other journalists followed, culminating in the 1920s with the celebrated Lebanese magazine *Ros al-Yusif.* The satirist press gave rise to many gifted cartoonists, such as the Egyptian Rakha, whose clever innuendoes, expressions, and jibes entertained readers throughout the Arab world in the 1930s and 1940s and inspired scores of artists and writers. Over the years, the use of humor in the Middle East has, indeed, proven to be instructive and constructive.

An Invasion of Humor

In the nineteenth century, some of Shakespeare's and Molière's works and other borrowings from the West were translated into Arabic and staged in Egypt and Syria. They attained a certain popularity among the educated elite and inspired native theater on a small scale, prompting the emergence of a few notable playwrights, among them Tawfiq al-Hakim, and other theater professionals. Comedy proved to be the most popular format.

The primary themes in literature, theater, and humor centered on social criticism and political defiance. The former followed the Aristotelian recipe of reform through the exposure of deficits. Feudalism, polygamy, oppression of women, inequality, corruption, and nepotism were frequent targets of commentators. Over time, political issues grew in popularity, largely in response to foreign rule and native dictatorship. A wealth of jokes circulated about the Ottoman Turks, mainly concerning the corruption and stupidity of their *qadis* (judges), *walis* (governors), and *effendis*.[6] France's occupation of Egypt under Napoleon also lent itself to popular humor.

One amusing anecdote about the British mandate for Iraq has been passed along as a true story, rather than as a joke: The Kurds were pressing the British administration to grant independence to Kurdistan, so Colonel Wilson sent an officer to negotiate with Shaykh Mahmud al-Hafid, the Kurdish leader. The officer informed him that Her Majesty's government would look favorably upon such a project and would install Shaykh Mahmud as the king of Kurdistan provided that he agree to act only with the approval of the British high commissioner. Shaykh Mahmud requested a couple of days to think things over. After careful deliberation, he notified the British that his followers preferred that Wilson become the king of Kurdistan and that he, Shaykh Mahmud, become high commissioner, reflecting Kurdish notions of where real power resided. More recently, Iraqi dramatists have attacked the U.S. occupation of their country. In 2007 the Soho Theatre in London staged *Baghdad Wedding*, an antiwar comedy by Hassan Abdulrazzak.

In nineteenth-century Egypt, resistance to occupation assumed a xenophobic form—against the *khawajas* (foreigners), for which Greek traders suffered the most, rather than the real occupiers, the British. On another level, however, the khawajas symbolized the country. In the humor magazine *Tankit wa al-Tabkit* (Joking and censure), the journalist Abdullah al-Dayim related the story of a night watchman who spotted a thief: "Hey! Who's there? Come down here!" shouted the watchman brandishing his gun. The thief replied, "A khawaja." The watchman walked away, meekly saying to him, "Oh, I beg your pardon. I mistook you for an Egyptian." The joke was an obvious attack on the so-called Mixed Court, which dealt with cases involving foreigners. The regular courts had no power to try alien subjects or to resolve cases involving them. Abolishing these courts became a national cause.

Arab humorists reserved most of their rhetorical gunpowder for their native oppressors and despots. Resistance to dictatorship reached its zenith during Nasser's regime, especially after the 1967 war with Israel. All Arabs attributed their humiliating defeat to corruption, immorality, inefficiency, ignorance, and stupidity. Adil Hammuda dealt with this subject and its reflection through humor in *The Political Joke*. Field Marshal Abd al-Hakim Amir, the Egyptian chief of staff, generated more than his share of jokes. In one, he complained to a visitor that his deputy was utterly stupid. "I'll show you," he said, calling for the officer and asking him to find out whether he, Amir was at home. The officer took a car and returned after a couple of hours. He reported to his boss, "No. They told me you were not there." Amir then turns to his visitor and says, "What did I tell you? My deputy is stupid. He didn't need to go that far. We have a telephone. He could have rang and found out whether I was there."

Nasser was not corrupt, but the corruption in state bureaucracy offered little respite for the country. As one story goes, a woman had had enough of her husband, who was an enthusiastic supporter of Nasser. She asked him what they had gained from Nasser's socialist program. The man decided to put this question to the Egyptian leader to satisfy his wife. Nasser received the husband in his office, and after hearing the man's question, told him to look out of the window and tell him what he saw. The man did so and described to Nasser the wonderful gardens, palaces, and fine streets in his range of view. :There," said the president, "Go tell your wife. Ten more years with my socialism and the whole of Egypt will be so." The man returned home and directed his wife to look through the window and tell him what she saw. She noted the derelict hovels surrounding them, swampy puddles, and children in rags. "There," the man said, "ten more years with Nasser's socialism and the whole of Egypt will be like that."

The Free Officers' Revolution in Egypt inspired other disgruntled military men across the Arab world—including in Algeria, Iraq, Syria, and Yemen—to stage similar coups d'état. This development gave rise to privileged officer classes, which ran roughshod over their countries and oppressed their populations. The wits in local cafés took note: In one inspired yarn, a young man accidentally rests his foot of the foot of a fellow passenger in a tram. The passenger suffers silently until he can no longer endure the pain.

"Excuse me, Sir," he says to the young man, "Are you an officer in the army?"
"No, I am not."
"Are you married to the daughter of an officer in the army?"
"No, not at all."
"Do you have a relative who is an officer in the army?"
"No, never."
The aggrieved man then lands a punch to the face of the young man and kicks him in his groin. "Then how dare you stand on my foot all this time!"

The fiasco of the 1967 war inspired Ahmad Fu'ad Najm, a vernacular poet, and Shaykh Imam, a blind singer and 'ud player, to form a duet. Together they created satirical songs castigating the Nasser government. In one popular piece, they ridiculed the army and its officers, "Oh, how lovely, the return of our officers from the firing line!" Their songs became a hit throughout the Arab world, a state of affairs that deeply concerned Nasser.

Egypt was probably the only country in the world with a special unit in its intelligence service assigned to monitor political jokes and report daily to the president about them. Egyptians used jokes to devastating effect, in the eyes of Nasser, destroying morale not just among the officer corps but also spreading nihilism through the broader population, eroding their confidence as well as that of their sons, the average soldier. The situation was such that Nasser at one point felt the need to step in. He addressed the National Assembly: "I know the Egyptian people. This is a nation seven thousand years old. They defeated and destroyed all invaders, from Qambiz to Napoleon. Then they sat and laughed at them.... This is a people who love to joke. I think this is a privilege, for it implies philosophizing over all matters. But if our enemies come and exploit this nature to achieve their own aims, we must be vigilant. Every one of us must be vigilant."

The call went out: "Enough is enough." Shaykh Imam stopped singing "Oh, how lovely, the return of our officers from the firing line." The notable journalist Anis Mansur later wrote that these jokes were not directed at the military, but at Nasser himself and his regime. Regardless, these musings appeared clearly to express the people's resentment toward the arrogance and corruption of the officer class, which constituted the backbone of the regime.

One joke focused on the security apparatus of a corrupt regime went as follows: Soon after arriving in Cairo on a flight from Sinai, a young lieutenant was seen running after a bus. Just managing to haul himself aboard, he stumbled and fell into the lap of an old woman. "Oh, sonny," said she to him, "Still running [from the front]?" There were no similar or equivalent jokes about the Israelis, so many Arab observers concluded that such jokes were manufactured by Israeli intelligence and fed to the populace to destroy what was left of Arab morale and convince them of the futility of seeking revenge or defying Israeli diktat.

The absence of anti-Israeli jokes is even more noticeable in Palestinian humor and satire. The Palestinians instead have tended to reserve their wit for their own leaders and their decisions. One humorist was brave enough to question the efficacy of suicide bombers: In his tale, a young man goes to Hamas to volunteer for a suicide mission. He receives an explosive belt, a revolver, and a cell phone. He then enters Israel, where he sees four soldiers sitting on a bench. He rings his handlers, and they tell him to move on; there aren't enough targets. He then comes across a group of people at a bus stop. He calls his handlers. No, they say, still not enough. He next enters a cinema and makes the call. "I am in a cinema packed with Israelis." The handler says, "Ok. Say your prayer and do it." The young man says his prayer, takes out his revolver, and shoots himself in the head.

Adil al-Usta, in his analysis of Palestinian literature, cites a few verses aimed at Arab rulers—described by the Iraqi poet Mudhaffar al-Nawwab in a famous poem as "sons of a whore"—including one by Ibrahim Tuqan:

> You are the faithful patriots,
> The ones who bear the burden of our cause,
> You who work for it silently,
> Bless your strong arms.
> One statement from you is equal to a whole army,
> With all its attack weaponry.
> One meeting you hold restores
> Our old glory and all the conquests of the Umayyads.
> The salvation of our country is just round the corner.
> Its purple days are at hand.
> We don't forget your favors,
> But we have one desire in our hearts.
> We still have a portion left of our country.
> Please do retire, before we lose what is left!

The Language of Humor: Origins, Art, and Essence

Under dictatorial rule, be it foreign or native, Arab satirists have had to be content with expressing themselves through word of mouth, often in whispers at home or discreetly in cafes, clubs, and other public spaces. In Egypt, exchange of the latest jokes became a national preoccupation and form of social entertainment. As an Englishman might start a conversation by asking his friends for a football or cricket score, an Egyptian would ask his friends about the latest joke they had heard. In troubled times, which too often was the norm, the jokes would invariably concern the politics of the hour. Today it is still common for bursts of laughter to rumble through Cairo's coffeehouses, accompanied by momentary pauses from puffing on water pipes.

Yet, when my book *Arab Political Humor* was published in 1985, the *Times* (London) included it among the 10 most bizarre titles of the year.[7] To them, apparently, the Arabs had no sense of humor, an opinion shared, no doubt, by many people in the West. Of course, humor, in its Anglo-Saxon conception, is alien to most other peoples, including the French, who are often puzzled by it. The Arabs, likewise, have their own sense of "humor." For some, the difficulty with Arab humor is its indulgence in language. An Arab student probably spends more time learning Arabic grammar, poetry, rhetoric, and figures of speech than he or she does studying science or math. The Arabic language permeates all artistic and cultural activities, from architecture to music and theology, not merely as a form of communication, but as an art form or structure in and of itself. Most Arab jokes and humorous anecdotes build upon the language, relying on word play, which makes them difficult to translate and to be appreciated by non-Arabic speakers.

In addition, the Quran and the sayings of the Prophet Muhammad constitute a large part of any Arab gentleman's education. All students, including non-Muslims, must learn extensive passages of the Quran by heart. Cultured wits and humorists have, over the centuries, made extensive use of hyperbole in invoking these sacred texts. The resultant jokes and gibes are lost entirely on those who have no knowledge of the originals.

Most people do not know the meaning, if any, of their names. Not so with the Arabs. Practically every proper noun in Arabic means something: "Nasser" is victory giver; "Mansur," victorious; "Adil," just; "Khalid," immortal, and so on. It takes little effort on the part of any wit worth his salt to make the names of ministers and prime ministers sound ridiculous through wordplay. It is a simple and primitive form of satire, but an effective one. The renowned poet Mahdi al-Jawahiri famously satirized the pious Iraqi president Abd al-Salam Arif—servant of peace and knowledgeable—in stinging verse:

> Oh, Servant of War and Enemy of Peace,
> The disgrace of all who pray, fast and pay *zakat*.[8]

As nomadic peoples, Bedouin Arabs came over the ages to look with contempt upon craftsmen and on manual labor, which they viewed as "urban." This attitude later carried over into settled environments. Public figures possessing a surname denoting a craft or manual work—such as Haddad (blacksmith), Najjar (carpenter), Khayyat (tailor), and so on—often faced harsh treatment from political opponents. Poor Abd al-Rihman al-Bazzaz (cloth maker), the late prime minister of Iraq, suffered through every election because of his name. Nasser was the son of a postman. Baghdad Radio mocked Nasser and ridiculed his lineage by incessantly playing the song "al-Postagia Ishtaku" (The postman complained). Again, a crude kind of humor, but popular and effective.

The wandering life of Arabian nomads also left no space for certain types of arts and activities associated with settled life, such as theater, sculpture, painting, or architecture. Nomads and Bedouins by necessity traveled lightly, and their art forms, for example, poetry—*diwan al-Arab* (the annals of the Arabs)—developed because of and from this lifestyle. Poetry is still the most popular form of artistic and literary activity among Arabs. *Al-hija'* (satire), one of its primary forms, was used to expose or challenge rulers, including the Prophet Muhammad. Arab verse's approach to rhythm and rhyme to create repetitive magic and its traditions that developed over time made it an effective weapon of attack. Poets used these elements in expressing political opposition to foreign occupiers as well as to national or tribal authorities. For instance, in Iraq, Maaruf al-Risafi in the 1930s and 1940s and Jawahiri from the 1930s to the 1960s created a wealth of such poetry, though alas, another branch of resistance humor that does not translate well.

The scarcity of such resources as food and water in the desert led to various forms of population control. Emphasis on female virginity and chastity evolved as a controlling mechanism in this environment. Thus wayward wives, daughters, or sisters were for men a fate worse than death. The actual or supposed infidelity of a politician's or a ruler's female kin became fertile ground for satirists. This underground humor was the kind whispered between and among friends. There exists a rich harvest of generally known caustic and amusing verses that are rarely printed. Among the latter is a verse by the satirist poet Bayram al-Tunisi questioning the virginity of Queen Nazily, King Faruq's mother, on her wedding day:

> The goose had her neck cut before the celebration,
> The road was opened before the regulation,
> And when the disgraced came for her wedding jubilation,
> Silence, said I, do let girls cover up their shame.

With this poem on everybody's lips, the royal court could no longer tolerate the rebellious poet. Henchmen dutifully delivered a frightful beating, but Tunisi, insufficiently intimidated, went on to compose another poem, in which he attacked Nazily's husband, King Fuad, as a mere stooge of British imperialism:

> The English, O Fuad brought you and seated you
> To play on the throne the role of kings.
> And let you wreak havoc on your father's nation,
> Where can they find a fool and a rogue the like of you?

Beaten again, Tunisi was then sent into exile. He lived initially in France before eventually returning to Tunisia, his original home.

The very nature of sexual satire restricted its transmission to intimate conversations among close friends. An obsession with pride in male virility and thus sex, induced humorists to attack rulers by insinuating impotence on their part. Thus evolved an amusing juxtaposition of the ruler's wife as a nymphomaniac wedded to an impotent man. Napoleon, who refused to sleep with fat Egyptian women—considered by ordinary Egyptians to be the most desirable—became the target of jokes about his lack of virility and the effete nature of his troops. The French occupation of Egypt led to the development of an interesting expression of patriotism through sexuality. Ali Kaka, a doll with a monstrous penis, became a symbol of Egyptian "manhood," defying French domination. The dolls were popular gifts among Egyptians, and pastry shops produced Ali Kaka cakes for children. After a few months of this satirical sexual prelude, Egyptians rose up in a bloody revolt.

What's Old Is New Again

Like other nations in the so-called Third World, Middle Eastern countries became depositories for the import from Europe of all that theoretically symbolized high culture and civilized living. Theater, discussed above, was the first cultural borrowing, introducing intellectuals and cultured elites to new forms of Western humor, including farce and comedy. In retrospect, Arab classical humorists were somewhat hampered by the absence of theater in Arabic arts, for it is in the theater that an artist learns how to give dialogue its bite, the timing and finish that arouses the spirit of mirth in the listener or reader. The arrival of theater helped improve this situation.

Ros al-Yusif—the successful magazine named after Lebanese actress Rose al-Yusif, who started it—provided Mustafa Amin and other young humorists a forum for creating, polishing, and deploying witty dialogue. Arab artists were thrilled by the Western genre of cartoon and caricature and emulated what they saw. In addition, satirical monologues sang on radio or as a form of cabaret grew in popularity. The Iraqi Aziz Ali excelled in the area, exposing social evils and challenging British domination of his country. Writers and artists went on a shopping spree in European humor markets, emerging with a new genre of polished jokes and situation comedy employing wit, intellect, and highbrow dialogue.

In more recent years, the theater world has witnessed the development of a new breed of satirical plays in Syria pioneered and championed by the partnership of Durayd Lahham and Muhammad al-Maghut. Their *October Village* (1974) is a black comedy, or a comic lament, on losing the Golan Heights to Israel. "Cheerio, my country" is a series of funny and critical sketches about Syrian and Arab society. Through poignant satire, Lahham and Maghut poke fun at the failure of Arab unity, depicted by a divided village and a divided pub where the frontier, drawn by Britain and France, cuts through the premises, creating a farcical situation. Their work serves up sharp indictments with its witty dialogue.

One institution sorely overlooked by Arab humor is parliament, which in most places is sometimes brought to life via verbal clashes, offering representatives the opportunity to exhibit sharpened tongues and excel in the use of words and repartee. In Arab states with national assemblies, dictatorship and fear of the consequences of speaking out have inhibited the development of talented parliamentary interlocution, the rise of a Sheridan or a Churchill, and political literature. Moreover, religious, tribal, and conventional constraints in general have hampered the free expression of controversial ideas and styles. Frustrated humorists often express their lament over this situation. Risafi took on the suppression of free expression in one of his famous poems written in the 1930s:

> Speak not, O people,
> For talking is prohibited.
> Sleep and never wake up,
> Only the sleeping prosper.
> Regress from all things
> Which beckons to progress
> Give up trying to understand,
> Better for you not to.
> Hold on to your ignorance.
> It is evil to learn.
> Laugh when you suffer injustice.

Be merry and never complain.
Thank them when they insult you
And smile when they strike you!
If they say your honey is bitter,
Say "just like colocynth."
If they say your day is night,
Say "And how dark."
If they say your puddle is a torrent,
Say "And flowing fast."
And if they say, "O people,
Your country will be partitioned,"
Praise them, thank them,
Swing and sing!

Jokes may be local, but they are often the child of globalization. Arab wits who enjoy access to Western political humor recycle exceptional European jokes, reworking them to apply to their personal situations. A German joke about Hitler and Goebbels was adapted to incorporate and Field Marshal Amir: The Egyptian president saw his commander in chief sitting, depressed. "Why so glum?" Nasser asked. Amir grumbled about a lack of recognition. "Your pictures are everywhere," Amir said to Nasser, "but no one hangs my picture." The president promised to remedy the situation by ordering the production of stamps bearing Amir's portrait. Days later, Nasser found Amir in the same black mood. "What's the use of putting me on stamps that don't stick?" Amir asked. "Why don't they stick?" Nasser obtained one of them, licked it, and stuck it on a piece of paper. "There. It stuck. Why do you say they don't stick?" "Yes, of course they stick if you lick the gummy side. But the people don't do that. They spit on my picture and try to stick it that way." Months later in the 1960s, I heard the same joke in Iraq but featuring Gen. Abdul Karim Kasim and Col. Fadhil Mahdawi.

In the interest of full disclosure, I must admit to having recycled jokes in my daily satirical column in *al-Sharq al-Awsat* (London). Indeed, I have called on my readers to indulge in this nonviolent method of resistance, recycling political jokes and anecdotes by applying them to their own circumstances. One of my favorites is adapted from a Russia joke and involves former Iraqi leader Saddam Hussein. It gained widespread popularity and was even acknowledged in the National Assembly of Kuwait: The occasion was a sham election to rubber-stamp Hussein's presidency. A woman asked her husband, "Where have you been?" He told her that he had gone to cast his vote and had marked "No" on the ballot. His wife was furious. "You stupid idiot, saying 'No' to Saddam! They will soon be after you. They will take us both. They will hang you upside down and rape me in front of you and give us both a frightful beating. You ignorant sod! Go, hurry up and tell them that you were confused and made a mistake." Frightened, the man rushed to the polling station. He apologized for his mistake and said that he wanted to correct it. "Oh, don't worry my dear man!" said the poll worker. "We knew you were confused and made a mistake. As soon as you left, we corrected it. We changed your vote to 'Yes.'"

Any number of Arab writers could recycle this joke and apply it to their own country's sham elections. Humor is a collective harvest, sewn in one place, replanted, and nurtured in another place, adopted and retold by many. It is a product free to all, void of copyright, royalties, or patents. Humorists and comedians constantly borrow from each other. Nonviolent mujahidin and advocates of civilian jihad should learn how to use this wealth of material, the inheritance of the entire family of man.

Jokes do not only help in exposing evil and injustice but they often also produce direct, positive results, as demonstrated by Nasser. On many occasions, he revised a policy or issued new orders in response to a mere joke. His biographers reported that he was quite upset when he heard a comedian relate in a theater the story of a man going to Alexandria: A conductor asked the man why he going there? He replied that he had heard that there was rice in a shop there. After a short while, the conductor stopped the bus so the man could get off. "But this isn't Alexandria! This is Tanta," he protested (100 miles south of Alexandria). "Yes, but that is where the queue begins!" The joke supposedly so upset Nasser that he could not sleep that night. The next morning, he ordered the minister of supplies to obtain rice from whatever source was available. This joke was more effective than all the articles published on the shortage.

Laughing Together

There is currently a great demand in the Arab world for humorist publications. The public misses such old magazine and comic sheets as *Habazbuz* in Iraq and al-*Ba'kuka* in Egypt, which were entirely dedicated to humor and cartoons. The present atmosphere of religious extremism, terrorism, rampant suspicion, and political instability unfortunately make the task of the humorist not only difficult, but risky as well. It is upsetting and disheartening to spend a day racking ones brain to write an article only to have an editor throw it in the rubbish bin for fear of repercussions. Worse still, is having it published and the following day receiving an ominous message in which the caller threatens, "We'll cut your throat like a sheep."

Yet, humor is more pertinent now than at any other time in the Middle East. For me, it has offered refuge in political debates when opponents have gone out of their way to insult and taunt me. One casual joke can make an opponent laugh, transforming him into my new best friend; it can ease tension in an entire hall, which then becomes a friendly and inviting place. People you laugh at, Henri Bergson pointed out, don't reply to your joke with force. Our bodies refuse to react with violence when our faces and our throats are engaged in laughter. When was a man ever seen using violence while laughing?

Humor is most required in a nation's darkest hours, for it is at such times that people begin to lose faith in themselves, submit to despair, and descend into melancholy and depression. Life appears to be meaningless, and the homeland feels like a spider's web. People lose contact with fellow citizens and eventually come to accept their solitude. The will to stand together and resist is thus destroyed. Humor is the best remedy for such ills. Laughter lifts one from melancholy and lethargy; a political joke told by another reconnects citizen with citizen. Both are no longer alone. There are others who share my thoughts; we have shared suffering and hopes. Laughter is a collective fraternity. One doesn't laugh alone. We need others to laugh with us, just as we need someone to laugh at. It is this collective spirit that has helped the Jews maintain their identity and survive some three thousand years. "Jewish jokes" helped them endure rabbinical oppression as well as gentile persecution. Some Jewish jokes, however, have been used to dehumanize and perpetuate stereotypes about Jews.

The oral tradition of jokes helps foil the efforts of oppressors and security apparatuses to censor. As a nonviolent tool, jokes can be used to spread knowledge, provide instruction, and encourage defiance. The merry side of a joke can help in bringing about recognition, appreciation, and even conversion on the part of their oppressor or its supporters. It can make him them feel the extent of his oppression, the resentment of the oppressed, and the state of the oppressed people's civilization and mind. Again, Nasser's monitoring of jokes and his pride in their exercise is telling. Haven't Egyptians laughed at all their oppressors? Surely, Nasser must have entertained the thought that they would laugh at him just as well in life and in death.

Despite records indicating the use of humor and jesting in early Islam, including by the companions of the Prophet, strident Islamists today frown upon any semblance of humor. To them, laughter is sinful and demeaning to a Muslim, especially Muslim women. This stand comports with their adoration of the sword. Although Nasser tolerated the jokes about him and against his government, many other Muslim rulers—Saddam Hussein comes to mind—have reacted in a hostile manner to such jokes. There is no record of anyone being punished by Nasser on this score. He was wise, not simply because he realized that he could not gag 40 million laughing Egyptians, but it seems also that he recognized that creating and telling jokes was a peaceful way for a people suffering to channel their sorrows, anger, frustrations, and fears.

Philosophers like Spencer and Freud argued that laughter is an outlet for releasing pent-up emotions. It is advantageous to rulers to allow the free flow of jokes. Political humor is a lower-risk, nonviolent channel for discussing injustice, defying foreign occupation, and challenging defunct precepts and misrule. It can also help in strengthening a collective sense of national unity, identity, and destiny, and through laughter, offer momentary pleasure where there is suffering. In the face of the current wave of international terrorism, tribal and sectarian bloodletting, and violence, the encouragement of meaningful humor should be considered as part of the repertoire of any nonviolent activist, and is one of the best and cheapest nonviolent means for tackling today's problems.

Notes

1. In these words, Shinnawi might have been referring just as well to the sadistic Qaragush, who ruled Egypt in the middle ages with the stick and the sword. Jokes and satirical anecdotes about him still circulate and are often recycled.
2. Adil Hammuda, *How Egyptians Satirize Their Rulers: The Political Joke* (in Arabic) (Cairo: Dar al-Sfinks lil-'iba'ah wa al-Nashr, 1990).
3. Within a few months, an attempt was made on Tays' life, and he abandoned his broom and brought his journalistic career to a close.
4. See, for example, my blog at www.kishtainiat.blogspot.com.
5. *Jokestan* is the largest Persian-joke site. The jokes are contributed by people living in Iran and Persians around the world. See www.jokestan.com.
6. I know of only one joke about the Ottoman sultan himself, yet according to a common proverb, "Despite all his pomp, the sultan is insulted behind his back."
7. Khalid Kishtainy, *Arab Political Humor* (London: Quartet Books, 1986).
8. For some, this might be an instance in which the word play and hence the humor may not accompany the translation from the Arabic.

5

Islamists and Nonviolent Action

Shadi Hamid

What is remarkable about the Middle East is not that the political opposition has so often resorted to violence in the face of repression, but that it has not. This contradicts the more common portrayals of the region as being exceptionally prone to violent conflict. It is true that a disproportionate amount of terrorist activity worldwide can be traced to the region. According to the RAND-MIPT Terrorism Incident Database, 42 percent of claimed attacks between May 2003 and December 2006 originated in the Middle East.[1] This, however, is not the most useful prism through which to interpret the political changes under way in the region.

Terrorist groups, such as al-Qaeda and its offshoots, Egyptian Islamic Jihad, or the Islamic Armed Group in Algeria, have received a great degree of attention, and rightly so. While these are, and always will be, relatively small organizations, they enjoy outsized influence, in part because they provoke disproportionate responses from both Western powers and Arab regimes. If, however, one is interested in questions of systemic political change, extremist groups are not particularly consequential. They neither have the capability nor the popular backing to challenge existing power structures in Middle Eastern countries. It is more worthwhile to focus on mass-based Islamist groups and parties with grassroots support and religious legitimacy. These organizations—such as Egypt's Muslim Brotherhood, Jordan's Islamic Action Front (IAF),[2] and Morocco's Justice and Development Party (PJD)—are not fringe entities. Rather, they are part of the political mainstream, despite regime efforts to delegitimize them.

In Egypt and Jordan, Islamists are currently the largest opposition force in their respective parliaments, while in Morocco the PJD is the second-largest party in parliament. These, and most other mainstream Islamist groups in the region, have long renounced violence. They have made a strategic, or some would argue merely tactical, decision to use only nonviolent methods to advance their political interests. This raises three critical questions: Why have Islamist groups like the Muslim Brotherhood taken violent methods off the table? To what extent have they employed nonviolent action—defined by Hardy Merriman as activity taking place "outside the context of normal political, economic, or social behavior"—such as strikes, protests, boycotts, and, more generally, civil disobedience?[3] To what extent have these efforts been effective and why? These three questions are obviously related but not in the way one might expect.

The Interplay between Repression and Violence

Although Islamist groups enjoy parliamentary representation in Egypt, Jordan, Morocco, and elsewhere, this does not necessarily mean that they have been beneficiaries of increased regime tolerance and openness. Despite a growing literature on democratic reform in the Middle East, the role of political parties, and the rise of Arab civil society, the long-term outlook remains bleak.[4] According to the Freedom House index of political rights and civil liberties, Egypt today is more repressive, less free, and less democratic than it was in 1976, when controlled multiparty elections were first introduced under President Anwar al-Sadat.[5] Table 5.1 presents averaged Freedom House scores for particular time periods in Egypt. Parliamentary elections in 1984, 1988, 1991, 1996, 2000, and 2006 were selected as demarcations since a government's conduct just before and during elections is generally a good indicator of whether the years following will be marked by greater openness, or more likely, the opposite. Here, one can see that the trend toward a more restrictive and repressive political system has been remarkably consistent over the 30-year period in question. With the exception of a slight improvement from 1976–1984 to 1985–1987, each electoral period was marked by a decline in at least one of the two categories.[6]

The overall trend in Jordan is similarly negative. After the democratic "thaw" of 1989 to 1992, the monarchy reasserted its grip on power in 1993, marking the start of a long, gradual authoritarian retrenchment that continues to this day. As the 2006 Freedom House country report explains, "In 1989, the Hashemite Kingdom of Jordan launched the Arab world's most promising experiment in political liberalization and reform. A well-educated professional class, a history of political participation, and a cooperative Islamist movement all gave Jordan a comparative advantage in expanding rights and inclusion. Today, unfortunately, the country has reversed course."[7] Freedom House scores confirm this shift. An impressive rating of three in 1992 and fours for the remainder of the decade have given way to ratings of five and even six in the 2000s.

Table 5.1   Political rights and civil liberties in Egypt, 1976–2007

	Political Rights	Civil Liberties
1976–1984	4.875	4.625
1985–1987	4.66	4
1988–1990	5	4
1991–1995	5.6	5.8
1996–2000	6	5.6
2001–2005	6	5.6
2006–2007	6	5

Notes:
1 = best possible score
7 = worst possible score

Source: Freedom House Index, 1976–2007

From the standpoint of the Islamist opposition, the decision to work within such a restrictive political structure—one that appears to be closing rather than opening—is somewhat vexing. It can be explained, however, as a "participation-moderation tradeoff." Islamists agree to abide by the rules of the game and forego revolutionary designs against the regime. In return, they are promised a stake in the system, including the right to form legal parties, participate in elections, and otherwise be recognized as legitimate political actors. Implicit in the tradeoff is the opposition's long-term view toward increased political gains and the prospect of holding executive power at the local or national level.[8]

On the part of the state, this is a prudent course of action. Bringing Islamist parties into the political process is one way to wed them to an elaborate structure of institutional constraints and restrictions. Under the watchful eye of the state, Islamists can be effectively manipulated and controlled. Islamist parties are aware of these dangers when they opt into the system, but they are also cognizant of the potential benefits, which include less repression, the legal imprimatur of the state, and greater political access.

The "tradeoff" only works if Islamists believe that participation will lead to improvement on these key indicators, even if slow and tortured. However, in Egypt, the situation of the Muslim Brotherhood vis-à-vis the state has not only failed to improve but has deteriorated markedly. The promise of future gains has proven illusory. In exchange for committing to the rules of the game, the Brotherhood has been met with more repression, exclusion, and, most recently, what appears to be a concerted regime effort to irrevocably damage the group's organizational capabilities. In late 2006, authorities seized millions of dollars in assets and arrested some of the group's top financiers, including Deputy General Guide Khairat al-Shater, referring them to a military court on charges of belonging to a banned group and distributing unauthorized literature. Mass arrests of Brotherhood activists have become routine, with more than 800 being detained in the lead-up to 2008 municipal elections. Perhaps most problematic, the regime had pushed through a constitutional amendment to ban religiously oriented parties in March 2007.[9] It is, according to many observers, the worst period of anti-Islamist repression since the 1960s.[10]

Under these conditions, one might expect the Brotherhood to reconsider its commitment to respect the "rules of the game," which it had, in the first place, no real part in establishing. Moreover, a loss of faith in the efficacy of political participation could lead to a reconsideration of extra-legal, perhaps even violent, methods of contestation. The Egyptian Muslim Brotherhood and the Islamic Action Front in Jordan have not, however, altered their positions on the necessity of nonviolent political approaches. They have instead unequivocally wedded themselves to a nonviolent program for change under the precise circumstances in which one might expect them to waver. This alone should be enough to dispel the notion that politics in the Middle East is characterized by an overeager resort to arms.

For the same reasons that the groups in question have taken violence off the table, they have also been remarkably cautious in adopting more aggressive nonviolent tactics, including recourse to mass civil disobedience. Any actions that could be perceived as excessively confrontational toward the regime have generally been avoided. Organized nonviolent resistance is often of a "highly disruptive nature,"[11] and mainstream Islamists have shown little interest in causing any significant disruption to the overall economic or political structure in their respective countries.

Explaining Nonconfrontational Strategies

Two variables—one external and one internal—help to explain why mass-based Islamist groups and parties have steered away from confrontational approaches of either a violent or nonviolent nature. First, the international context today is particularly limiting for Islamists. In devising strategies against authoritarian regimes, Islamist groups are essentially fighting on two fronts. They cannot focus solely on their relationship with the regime; they must also keep in mind that Western players are watching closely. Most Arab dictatorships, including in Algeria, Bahrain, Egypt, Jordan, Kuwait, Morocco, Qatar, Saudi Arabia, Tunisia, and the United Arab Emirates, are supported and funded by the United States as well as European Union countries. Egypt, for instance, is the second-largest recipient of U.S. aid at around $1.7 billion annually, while Jordan is the second-largest per capita recipient. In light of the United States' active involvement in the region, Islamists know that gaining power will remain unlikely, if not impossible, without American encouragement, or at the very least, neutrality. The Algerian debacle of 1991–1992 is an instructive example, and one that Islamists have not forgotten, of how Western powers can block the legitimate election of Islamist parties. In this case, France and the United States effectively backed the military's decision to cancel elections after Islamists seemed poised for victory.[12]

On the other hand, Islamist politicians and strategists readily admit that U.S. pressure on Arab autocrats during the short-lived "Arab spring" of 2004–2005 was critical in opening up political space for the opposition, even if it did not last. President George W. Bush's strong pro-democracy rhetoric and mention of Egypt in his 2005 State of the Union address, coupled with Secretary of State Condoleezza Rice's cancellation of a March 2005 trip to Cairo in protest of liberal opposition leader Ayman Nour's detention, emboldened the secular and Islamist opposition alike. Muslim Brotherhood general guide Mahdi Akef, known for inflammatory anti-American comments, admitted in August 2006 that the Bush administration's pressure on the Mubarak regime had had a positive effect on Egyptian reform.[13] Abdel Menem Abul Futouh, a member of the group's Guidance Bureau, confirmed this impression, stating that "everyone knows it.... We benefited, everyone benefited, and the Egyptian people benefited."[14]

As Islamist groups continue to mature politically, they have devoted more attention to their relationship with the United States and other Western actors. In 2006 the Egyptian Brotherhood launched an internal initiative under the name "Re-Introducing the Brotherhood to the West," in which it identified misconceptions from both sides and suggested steps for addressing them.[15] The group has launched an official English-language Web site, www.ikhwanweb.com, published numerous op-eds in Western publications, and established informal links with U.S. officials, researchers, and representatives of nongovernmental organizations (NGOs).

To quell concerns regarding their perceived (and real) animosity toward Israel, some Islamist leaders have begun clarifying their views on the matter and even reaching out to Jewish American audiences. Abul Futouh has said that he would be willing to accept a two-state solution with "full sovereignty for a Palestinian state and full sovereignty for an Israeli state."[16] Esam el-Erian and Ibrahim el-Houdaiby, both prominent members of the group's reformist wing, have penned op-eds in the *Forward*, the largest Jewish newspaper in the United States.[17] Even as an organization, the Muslim Brotherhood, in its 2004 reform initiative, affirmed its "respect of international laws and treaties," which is the code Islamists often use to talk about the Camp David accords of 1979.[18]

The success of such charm offensives depends on many things, including reassuring Western audiences that Islamists will not consider violence or other "destabilizing" actions even under the very conditions where aggressive anti-regime measures would be most expected. In this context, "confrontational" actions, even if they are nonviolent and to legitimate ends, are perceived with worry by Western nations, which tend to conflate confrontation with radicalism, and radicalism with violence, when, in fact, it is of course conceivable, as has been the case in other regions, that confrontation can be a means for advancing a peaceful, pro-democracy agenda.

The second factor that helps explain Islamist caution is less straightforward and requires an understanding of how Islamist groups conceive of their strategic ends. The goal of virtually all mass-based parties is to advocate vote-maximizing policies in order to win elections, or alternately, to win elections in order to implement preferred policies.[19] Whether acting according to the traditional model of party competition (where winning elections is an end)[20] or Donald Wittman's "alternative competitive" and "restricted competition" models (where winning is a means),[21] political parties generally seek to win elections and assume executive power. The raison d'être of Islamists is different in that they do not necessarily need to rule in order to fulfill their primary objective—the Islamization of society, understood as the promotion of a sociopolitical environment more conducive to the fulfillment of Islamic ideals and behavior. This, in and of itself, is fairly unique. Contrast for example, the experience of socialists in Western Europe. Society there could be made "socialist" only if socialist parties were in power—and not really even then.[22]

Most mass-based Islamist parties, however, are not parties in the traditional sense. They are political wings of religious social movements or at least remain in some way tied to them through informal links and overlapping memberships. The Islamic Action Front is the political arm of the Jordanian Muslim Brotherhood,[23] while Morocco's Justice and Development Party remains closely linked to the Movement for Unity and Reform (MUR). Meanwhile, the Muslim Brotherhood in Egypt, although it sometimes acts like a party, is not a party. It is first and foremost a religious movement, or *gama'a*, meaning "society."[24] Certainly, it participates in elections and fields candidates for positions in local and national bodies as well as in trade syndicates and universities (although because of the technical ban on their group, Brotherhood members must run as independents). As of 2009, it held 88 of 453 seats in parliament, easily making it the largest opposition bloc. However, its electoral activities are just one facet—albeit the one most visible to Western observers—of the group's wide-ranging work. The Brotherhood like its counterparts in Jordan, Kuwait, and Morocco, operates as a kind of state-within-a-state, with its own set of parallel institutions, including schools, hospitals, banks, businesses, mosques, foundations, day care centers, thrift shops, social clubs, facilities for the disabled, detoxification centers, and boy scout troops. Millions depend on this vast social infrastructure for everything from access to jobs to affordable health care and from small grants for opening businesses to financial support to get married.

In short, the Brotherhood's strictly political concerns, such as preparing for parliamentary elections, are just one component in the group's diverse universe of activities. A traditional political party acts in the party's interest, usually which involves calculations of how to increase representation in elected bodies. A social movement, or a subsection of a social movement, acts in the *movement*'s interests, which sometimes diverge from those of the political wing. An example of this is when the Islamic Action Front announced its intention in 1997 to contest that year's national elections with "maximum momentum."[25] It went so far as to hold party primaries to select candidates before the Muslim Brotherhood pressured it to reverse course and announce a boycott.

The Strategic Need for Self-Preservation

Through social service provision, Islamists spread their message, gain new recruits, and mobilize activists. Their grassroots support and popularity among Islamists and non-Islamists alike stems from their attention to the needs of constituents at the local level. This is the Islamist lifeline.[26]

If Islamist parties are viewed more as states-within-states, rather than as parties, the instinct for organizational self-preservation becomes more obvious. Above all else, a state must preserve itself and stay functioning in order to serve its constituents, who depend on it for their livelihood. In this respect, Islamist groups bear some resemblance to what Roberto Michel calls "subversive parties," which are interested not only in replacing the current order but also in transforming it. The subversive party "organizes the *framework* of the social revolution. For this reason it continually endeavors to strengthen its positions, to extend its bureaucratic mechanism, to store up its energies and it funds."[27]

Ironically, the "revolutionary" component of the party's activities leads it to seek accommodation with the state, as has been the case in Egypt, Jordan, Morocco, Turkey, and other countries. Its vast organizational infrastructure can operate effectively only with the tacit approval and grudging tolerance of state authorities. The party must therefore tread carefully to avoid provoking the regime's wrath, as the costs of a crackdown are severe. The threat of repression, rather than actual repression, hangs over it like a sword of Damocles, profoundly affecting the group's calculations. This brings to mind Marion Boulby's observation that the nonconfrontational and relatively apolitical attitude of the Jordanian Muslim Brotherhood, during the period of martial law when parties were banned, was a product of its "eagerness to retain legal status at whatever cost,"[28] presumably so it could continue, unhampered, its social service and educational activities.

In especially repressive contexts, such as Egypt's, where Islamist groups are unable to secure legal accommodation with the regime, they will do whatever they can to minimize the extent of repression by absorbing blows and avoiding further escalation. In an effort to paint government crackdowns as disproportionate and unjustified, Islamists will become even more adamant about not resorting to violence precisely as the level of repression increases. This solidifies their nonviolent credentials in the eyes of observers, including other opposition parties whose support they need to avoid further repression and stave off political isolation. It also demonstrates to Western countries that Islamist parties, contrary to popular perception, have made a strategic, rather than a tactical, decision to forgo violence, even in the most trying circumstances.

As a result, the Egyptian Muslim Brotherhood has been decidedly nonconfrontational, even in response to particularly damaging regime measures. It has gone to great pains to avoid giving the regime any pretext for launching a full-scale effort to destroy the organization. Although the group is outlawed, and its explicitly political efforts are suppressed, the regime has tended to avoid directly attacking its social infrastructure. A full-scale attack would be extremely costly domestically and internationally. First, dismantling the Islamist social infrastructure would mean depriving millions of jobs, health care, welfare support, and other services. Most Arab regimes, even if they wanted to, are not in a position to fill such a gap. Second, the "eradication" option would likely provoke a violent response from fringe groups or unaffiliated individuals sympathetic to the Brotherhood. On the international side, Egypt and other pro-Western Arab regimes know how much they can get away with, and they are not likely uninterested in testing the limits of international tolerance.

For its part, the Brotherhood has been intent on maintaining this "truce," or at the very least preventing a Syria-like situation in which Islamists were driven completely underground and any organizational presence erased. In this, they have not wavered. It helps that the Brotherhood and other Islamist groups, perhaps more than their secular counterparts, are able to effectively uphold a policy of nonconfrontation since their grassroots "base" tends to be deferential to the leadership. This is for a variety of reasons, including a culture of discipline and "obedience" in low-to-mid-level Brotherhood ranks, largely a result of relative ideological homogeneity and what Robert Leiken and Steven Brooke call a "painstaking educational program."[29] In addition, organizational discipline is a necessary requisite for survival amidst decades of sustained government repression.

In short, because Islamist movements have been, to varying degrees, either neutralized (as in Egypt) or subsumed by existing regimes (as in Jordan and Morocco), their recourse to many of the more aggressive nonviolent methods described by Hardy Merriman has been circumscribed.[30] Any mass civilian action against the regime would be interpreted as an "escalation," thereby provoking a harsh and potentially debilitating response from the ruling establishment. In these circumstances, nonviolent action is seen as contrary to the movement's strategic interests.

Once a group is accepted into the political system as part of a "democratic bargain," the arrangement develops its own logic. In Morocco, where the PJD sees itself as a loyal opposition working in tandem with, rather than against, the monarchy, civil disobedience or other methods of direct action are particularly difficult to justify. If anything, the PJD has attempted to reassure the regime that it is not in any way fundamentally opposed to the interests of the ruling elite. It is not a surprise, nor an accident, that the newly elected secretary-general of the PJD, Abdelilah Benkirane, is a staunch defender of the monarchy and its prerogatives.

International Costs and Benefits of Nonviolent Action

I have argued that international factors provide incentives for Islamists to avoid not only violence but also confrontational *nonviolent* approaches. The opposite is often the case. Maria Stephan and Erica Chenoweth cite the role of international actors as a factor (albeit not the most critical) that may contribute to the success of nonviolent campaigns: "Externally, the international community is more likely to denounce and sanction states for repressing nonviolent campaigns than it is violent campaigns."[31] The regime's use of excessive force against nonviolent groups can be critical to the latter's success, resulting in "sympathy and a possible increase in legitimacy" as well as political and financial support from the international community.[32]

International outrage is fueled, at least in part, by U.S. and European outrage. Yet, the United States has only rarely expressed outrage or opposition to the repressive practices of authoritarian allies in the Middle East. Repression is understood to be part of the bargain: In exchange for respecting and furthering the United States' national security interests in the region—such as combating terrorism, supporting Israeli-Palestinian peace efforts, and isolating such adversaries as Iran—autocratic regimes are allowed a free hand to deal with domestic "problems" as they see fit. France and Spain have had similar policies in North Africa. That the victims of repression have tended to be Islamists makes the decision easier for Western powers, which, fear the prospect of religiously oriented groups coming to power through free elections.

International Responses to Islamist-led Nonviolent Campaigns

In assessing the success rate of nonviolent action, Stephan and Chenoweth use as their unit of analysis a "campaign," defined as "a series of observable, continuous tactics in pursuit of a political objective. . . . Usually campaigns have recognizable beginning and end points, as well as distinct events through their history."[33] Based on this definition, let us consider some recent Islamist-led campaigns to investigate the nature of international responses. As noted earlier, international condemnation of regime repression during such campaigns appears to be positively correlated with the success of nonviolent action.

During the last 20 years, there have not been any instances of anti-Islamist repression in the Arab world that have elicited significant international outrage. This is despite the fact that regimes tend to use more repressive methods against Islamist groups than they do against secular ones. Four major nonviolent campaigns provide cogent examples of this phenomenon: the efforts of the Islamic Salvation Front (FIS) in Algeria to pressure the government to reform electoral laws in advance of the 1991 parliamentary elections; the FIS's restrained, and nonviolent, response to the military's cancellation of election results; the Islamic Action Front's campaign, along with other civil society groups, to protect the independence of Jordan's powerful professional associations; and the Egyptian Muslim Brotherhood's efforts in 2006–2007 to support judicial independence. Examples from the post–Cold War period were chosen, since one might expect that, freed from geopolitical maneuvering with the Soviet Union, the United States and other Western powers would be more likely to evoke "international outrage" in response to either violent repression against nonviolent actors, or more "legalistic" repression designed to restrict and marginalize opposition groups.

The Islamic Salvation Front, 1991–1992: In March 1991, the Algerian government proposed a new electoral law that aimed to limit Islamist gains in national elections scheduled for that year. The law would increase the number of parliamentary seats from 295 to 542, with the extra seats being disproportionately allocated to areas where the ruling National Liberation Front (FLN) had performed well in local elections the year before.[34] In response, the FIS held a press conference during which it outlined several key demands, including revision or withdrawal of the proposed law.

When the government failed to address its concerns, the FIS launched a general strike on May 25, 1991. The military eventually intervened, using force to disperse crowds in Algiers, the capital. After the government of President Chadli Benjedid relented and issued guarantees that elections would be free and fair, it quickly reversed course and launched a massive campaign against the FIS, arresting thousands, including Abbasi Madani and Ali Belhadj, the organization's top two leaders. The government banned the party's two newspapers as well. The episode marked the army's reentry into the political sphere after having adopted a lower profile due to its role in the October 1988 riots, during which hundreds of protestors were killed and many more injured.[35] This time, however, the United States and Algeria's European allies did not object to the military's increasingly aggressive posture. Domestic secular opposition to the government's measures was also muted, in contrast to the fairly united front against the military's 1988 intervention. The difference, this time, was that the target was an Islamist party, which secular parties in Algeria and external actors viewed as a threat.

The FIS's efforts to change the electoral law failed, and the party emerged from the battle weaker, and, in the absence of Madani and Belhadj's leadership, more internally divided than ever. Regardless, the FIS still managed to perform surprisingly well in the first round of elections in December 1991, winning 47 percent of the vote and looking likely to secure more than two-thirds of total parliamentary seats.[36] Before the second round, set to take place on January 16, 1992, the military took action, forcing President Benjedid to resign and canceling the election results. For the next few weeks, it rounded up tens of thousands of FIS members and sent them to desert prison camps. On 4 March, the party was formally dissolved.

During this two-month period, contrary to what many observers had expected, the FIS acted with considerable restraint. It refused to resort to violence and called on supporters to avoid provoking the regime.[37] Again, despite this being an obvious case of an autocratic regime brutalizing a nonviolent, and legal, opposition party, it elicited little, if any, perceptible outrage on the part of the international community.[38] France sided with the Algerian military. The United States appeared to tacitly support the intervention. As one State Department official commented, "by not saying or doing anything, the Bush administration supported the Algerian government by default."[39] Secretary of State James Baker explained later that "generally speaking, when you support democracy, you take what democracy gives you.... We didn't live with it in Algeria because we felt that the radical fundamentalists' views were so adverse to what we believe in and what we support, and to what we understood the national interests of the United States to be."[40]

It is interesting to note that one factor that encouraged, rather than dissuaded, the military in its decision to destroy the opposition was its fear of foreign involvement. Instead of worrying that intervention might lead to international condemnation, the army worried that if it allowed the democratic process to continue, and the Islamists assumed power, severe international repercussions would follow. As Michael Willis explains, "there were considerable fears for the already highly fragile condition of the country's economy. Fear of the FIS coming to power threatened to further deepen the nation's colossal debt (estimated at $25 billion in December 1991) through capital flight and the cancelling by foreign petrol companies of agreements aimed at increasing exploitation of Algeria's oil and gas resources."[41] The case of Algeria shows that fear of international condemnation, which tends to benefit nonviolent actors in their struggle against repressive regimes, can work in almost the exact opposite way in the Middle Eastern context, making incumbent regimes more likely to resort to repression than they otherwise would be.

The Islamic Action Front and the Professional Associations Crisis, 2005: Jordan's professional associations, mostly led by members of the Muslim Brotherhood and Islamic Action Front, had become the center of opposition to the regime's pro-West foreign policy orientation. Hoping to further solidify its relationship with the United States and other Western nations, the government found the associations' emboldened opposition to normalization of relations with Israel increasingly intolerable. In early 2005, Interior Minister Samir Habashneh launched a sustained campaign against the associations, demanding that they "completely halt" all political activities.[42] Meanwhile, Amman governor Abdul Karim Malahmeh declared that "any kind of event, gathering or meeting, save for weddings, should obtain prior approval."[43] In March, Prime Minister Faisal al-Fayez presented a new draft professional associations law to parliament, with the aim of significantly restricting the political activities of the associations. Habashneh explained that the law was intended to eliminate the "prevalence of one current"—meaning Islamists—within the associations.[44]

The associations, along with other sectors of civil society—including human rights organizations, prominent individual activists, and leftist and nationalist parties—launched a coordinated effort against the government measure. Several peaceful protests were organized. On four separate occasions, "security officials physically intimidated protesters, shut down sit-ins, and even tore down posters at the associations' headquarters."[45] Prominent individuals refused to toe the government line, using the weapon of noncooperation to signal their opposition. Hussein Majali, for instance, resigned his post as president of the Jordanian Bar Association.[46]

The regime's increasingly aggressive tactics, and the general closing of political space during this time, provoked little international condemnation. The United States, Jordan's closest Western ally, failed to make even one public statement concerning the professional associations crisis. The lack of even perfunctory outrage demonstrated to Jordanian leaders that, despite the Bush administration's "freedom agenda," repression of a legal opposition party would, again, bear little international cost. After the associations crisis, the government's attack on the Islamist opposition intensified,[47] culminating in the 2007 parliamentary elections, which many observers consider the least free and fair in Jordan's history. As Asher Susser explains, "In 2007 the rigging system was double-tiered. In the municipal elections it was classic Glubb style, with the busing of soldiers...being a key mechanism. As for the parliamentary elections, as befitting the globalized economy of the postmodern early twenty-first century, the rigging was outsourced by the government to the private sector. Men of means bought the votes, hired the buses, and had the ballot boxes stuffed in time, as the government essentially turned a blind eye."[48]

The Egyptian Muslim Brotherhood's Campaign in Support of Judicial Independence, 2006–2007: After the 2005 parliamentary elections in Egypt, two judges, Hisham al-Bastawisi and Mahmoud al-Mekki, publicly criticized the government for unabashed vote rigging, cataloguing various irregularities and listing, by name, prominent judges who were involved in electoral fraud. Nearly overnight, Bastawisi and Mekki became opposition heroes, pioneering, as one commentator called it, "a moral revolt of the Egyptian judiciary."[49]

The government condemned the two judges and sent them before a disciplinary council. The campaign in solidarity with Bastawisi and Mekki and in support of judicial independence intensified in April 2006 and continued through June. The Muslim Brotherhood as well as secular groups, including Kefaya, organized a series of protests and rallies. Urged on by the opposition, spontaneous protests spread across Cairo. In a period of three weeks, between 24 April and 18 May, authorities arrested 700 protestors. Hundreds were beaten and harassed by security forces. Independent Egyptian observers described central Cairo as being "under occupation."[50]

The Muslim Brotherhood, as it often is, was the most powerful force fueling opposition to the government. In one high-profile action, Brotherhood members of parliament staged a "stand-in" on 18 May outside parliament, remaining silent and "wearing black sashes across their chests that read 'The People's Representatives with Egypt's Judges.' "[51] The group also paid the highest price, with Samer Shehata and Joshua Stacher estimating that out of the 700 or so people arrested, 85 percent were from the Brotherhood.[52] To make matters worse, the government continued to retaliate even after the protests subsided, with Human Rights Watch reporting the detention of around 800 Brotherhood members in subsequent months.[53]

Although the two judges in question were not dismissed from the bench, they were reprimanded by the disciplinary court. Either way, their careers as judges were effectively halted. The broader issue here, however, is the state of Egypt's judiciary. Rather than address the opposition's concerns, the regime decided on a course of action that further undermined judicial institutions. It stripped the Judges' Club of financial assistance and withdrew staff support, which is usually provided by the Ministry of Interior. More problematic, the ruling National Democratic Party forced through a series of constitutional amendments that effectively ended independent judicial oversight of elections, one of the only remaining checks on the regime's electoral manipulations. The amendment to Article 88, formally passed in a March 2007 referendum, shifts the role of election oversight from the judiciary to a supervisory committee. As Amr Hamzawy notes, "it is expected that [this] committee will be subject to the regime and the president."[54]

Once again, international outrage was minimal and consisted of the usual expressions of concern from the United States and others. But even here, the U.S. message was far from clear. State Department spokesman Sean McCormack, in an May 11, 2006 briefing, noted "our serious concern" at the repression of protestors, but then cast the Brotherhood, the primary organizer of the protests, as an illegal organization "that is not allowed to be." He then affirmed that "the Egyptian Constitution says that…there should not be any political parties that are based on religion."[55]

Conclusion

As these examples demonstrate, nonviolent action and civil resistance, when employed by Islamist groups, has not been particularly effective in the Middle Eastern context. This can be explained, at least in part, by the fact that international condemnation—often a key condition for the success of nonviolent campaigns—tends to be lacking when Islamists are involved. In fact, it appears that, to the extent that international factors affect the calculations of political actors, the effect is to make the Islamist opposition less willing to engage in confrontational nonviolent action and Arab regimes more willing to repress nonviolent action. This is the reverse of what one would normally expect. More quantitative data is needed to further identify the causal mechanisms involved, but a preliminary analysis seems to suggest that nonviolent Islamist groups and parties in the Middle East will continue to fight an uphill battle in devising effective strategies against regime incumbents.

Despite the fact that nonviolent action has, in the sense described above, failed, there remains a strategic logic to nonviolent participation within the normal confines of electoral politics, even if such a process is far from free or fair. One bright spot, albeit a rare one, is the desire of mainstream Islamists to demonstrate to international audiences, particularly the United States, their commitment to non-violent methods, even in increasingly repressive contexts. As for nonviolent action outside the normal electoral context, however, mainstream Islamist groups, in light of past experiences, will remain unwilling to launch sustained nonviolent campaigns unless they are convinced they will elicit some degree of international support, or perhaps they would do so if they detected real weakness or divisions within government ranks. So far, this has not been the case.

Notes

1. Dalia Dassa Kaye, Frederic Wehrey, Audra K. Grant, Dale Stahl et al., *More Freedom, Less Terror? Liberalization and Political Violence in the Arab World* (Arlington, VA: RAND, 2008), 20, www.rand.org/pubs/monographs/2008/RAND_MG772.pdf.
2. The IAF, while technically financially and administratively separate from the Jordanian Muslim Brotherhood, is in effect the Brotherhood's political arm.
3. Hardy Merriman, "Theory and Dynamics of Nonviolent Action," in *Civilian Jihad: Nonviolent Struggle, Democratization, and Governance in the Middle East*, ed. Maria J. Stephan (New York: Palgrave, 2009): 31–50.
4. See, for example, Jillian Schwedler, *Faith in Moderation: Islamist Parties in Jordan and Yemen* (Cambridge: Cambridge University Press, 2006); Mona el-Ghobashy, "The Metamorphosis of the Egyptian Muslim Brothers," *International Journal of Middle East Studies* 37 (August 2005): 373–95; Vali Nasr, "The Rise of Muslim Democracy," *Journal of Democracy* 16 (April 2005): 13–27; Daniel Brumberg, "The Trap of Liberalized Autocracy," *Journal of Democracy* 13 (October 2002): 56–68; Carrie Rosefsky Wickham, *Mobilizing Islam: Religion, Activism and Political Change in Egypt* (New York: Columbia University Press, 2002); and James Piscatori, *Islam, Islamists, and the Electoral Principle in the Middle East* (Leiden: ISIM, 2000), www.isim.nl/files/paper_piscatori.pdf; Augustus Richard Norton, *Civil Society in the Middle East*, 2 vols. (New York: Brill, 1994, 1996).
5. Freedom House, Annual Survey of Freedom Country Scores, 1972 to 2007, www.freedomhouse.org/template.cfm?page=15.
6. Freedom House explains in the methodology section of Freedom in the World, 2008 that the political rights score includes measures on "electoral process," "political pluralism and participation," and "functioning of government." The civil liberties score includes measures of "freedom of expression and belief," "associational and organizational rights," and "rule of law." For more on the methodology used, see Raymond D. Gastil, "The Comparative Survey of Freedom: Experiences and Suggestions," in *On Measuring Democracy: Its Consequences and Concomitants*, ed. Alex Inkeles (New Brunswick, NJ: Transaction, 1991), 21–46.
7. Freedom in the World—Jordan (2006), http://freedomhouse.org/inc/content/pubs/fiw/inc_country_detail.cfm?year=2006&country=6989&pf.
8. As Huntington explains, "A central compromise in most cases of democratization was what might be termed 'the democratic bargain,' the trade-off between participation and moderation. Implicitly or explicitly in the negotiating processes leading to democratization, the scope of participation was broadened and more political figures and groups gained the opportunity to compete for power and to win power on the implicit or explicit understanding that they would be moderate in their tactics and policies." Samuel Huntington, *The Third Wave: Democratization in the Late Twentieth Century* (Norman: University of Oklahoma Press, 1991), 169.
9. For more on regime measures against the Muslim Brotherhood and other opposition groups, see "Country Backgrounder Series: Egypt," Project on Middle East Democracy, 2008, http://pomed.org/docs/Egypt_Backgrounder.pdf.

10. International Crisis Group, "Egypt's Muslim Brothers: Confrontation or Integration?" June 18, 2008, 9, www.crisisgroup.org/home/index.cfm?id=5487&l=5.
11. Maria J. Stephan and Erica Chenoweth, "Why Civil Works: The Strategic Logic of Nonviolent Conflict," *International Security* 33 (Summer 2008): 10.
12. For more on the Bush administration's response to the Algerian crisis, see Fawaz Gerges, *America and Political Islam: Clash of Cultures or Clash of Interests* (Cambridge: Cambridge University Press, 1999), 74–78.
13. Mahdi Akef, interview with author, Cairo, Egypt, August 2006.
14. Abdel Menem Abul Futouh, interview with author, Cairo, Egypt, August 2006.
15. "Re-introducing the Brotherhood to the West." internal Muslim Brotherhood document, 2006.
16. Futouh, interview with author, Amman, Jordan, August 2006, originally quoted in Shadi Hamid, "Parting the Veil," *Democracy: A Journal of Ideas* (Summer 2007): 47.
17. Esam el-Erian, "Egypt's Muslim Brotherhood Belongs on the Ballot, Not Behind Bars," *Forward*, April 3, 2008; and Ibrahim El Houdaiby, "The Muslim Brotherhood Will Stand Up for All Egyptians," *Forward*, September 26, 2007.
18. "Mubadira al-Ikhwan al-Muslimun houl Mabadi' al-Islah fi Misr" (The initiative of the Muslim Brotherhood regarding principles of reform in Egypt), March 2004, 13.
19. "Mass-based" refers to those parties that have broad, diverse constituencies with the ability to win pluralities or majorities in free and fair elections. This is in contrast to single-issue or single-constituency parties.
20. The traditional model is best exemplified in Anthony Downs, *An Economic Theory of Democracy* (New York: Harper & Row, 1957).
21. Donald A. Wittman, "Parties as Utility Maximizers," *American Political Science Review* 67 (June 1973): 495.
22. See Adam Przeworski and John Sprague, *Paper Stones: A History of Electoral Socialism* (Chicago: University of Chicago Press, 1986). Although socialist parties often won large pluralities in numerous Western European contexts, they failed to "remake" society as they had originally intended.
23. The vast majority of IAF leaders are members of the Jordanian Muslim Brotherhood. For example, as of October 2008, five of the seven members in the IAF executive office were Muslim Brothers, while in the 2003–2007 parliament, 15 of 17 IAF MPs were Brothers.
24. The official name of the group is the Society of the Muslim Brotherhood.
25. *Jordan Times*, May 8, 1997.
26. The "non-political" activities of Islamist groups continue to grow in importance in light of recent developments in the region. The grassroots activists of groups like the Egyptian and Jordanian Brotherhood tend to be more concerned with the social, educational, and preaching components of the organization's work. In the past, they have tended to defer to the leadership's sometimes controversial political initiatives. However, this has begun to change. In recent years, the Islamist "base" has grown increasingly frustrated that considerable effort has been expended on electoral politics but with little to show for it. There is also a sense among more conservative elements that the leadership is preoccupied with demonstrating "moderation" on democracy, pluralism, and women's rights at the expense of core principles. This internal pressure helps explain why Islamist groups are devoting more effort to internal concerns, such as increasing recruitment, emphasizing organizational unity, and strengthening social infrastructure. In 2008 the Egyptian and Jordanian Brotherhoods as well as Morocco's Justice and Development Party held internal elections. In all three cases, the trends associated with prioritizing social, educational, and internal organizational concerns defeated the more politically oriented "reformists."
27. Robert Michels, *A Sociological Study of the Oligarchical Tendencies of Modern Democracy* (New York: Free Press, 1962), 335.

28. Marion Boulby, "The Ideology and Social Base of the Jordanian Muslim Brotherhood: 1945–1993" (PhD diss., University of Toronto, 1996), 97.

29. Robert Leiken and Steven Brooke, "The Moderate Muslim Brotherhood," *Foreign Affairs*, March/April 2007.

30. Merriman, "Theory and Dynamics of Nonviolent Action."

31. Stephan and Chenoweth, "Why Civil Resistance Works," 12. [*Note*: In the authors' unpublished manuscript, they cite data indicating that external support is more useful for violent insurgencies than for nonviolent insurgencies.]

32. Ibid., 15.

33. Ibid., 16.

34. Michael Willis, *The Islamist Challenge in Algeria: A Political History* (Reading, Pa.: Ithaca Press, 1996), 172.

35. Ibid., 183.

36. John L. Esposito and John O. Voll, *Islam and Democracy* (New York: Oxford University Press, 1996), 164, 166.

37. Willis, *The Islamist Challenge in Algeria*, 252–54.

38. The noteworthy exceptions were Iran and Sudan.

39. Gerges, *America and Political Islam*, 75.

40. "James Baker Looks Back at the Middle East," *Middle East Quarterly* 1 (September 1994), www.meforum.org/article/233.

41. Willis, *Islamist Challenge in Algeria*, 245.

42. *Jordan Times*, January 18, 2005.

43. *Jordan Times*, March 6, 2005.

44. *Jordan Times*, March 7, 2005.

45. "Country Report—Jordan," Freedom House, 2006; Stephen Glain, "Letter from Jordan," *Nation*, May 30, 2005.

46. Glain, "Letter from Jordan."

47. Regime measures against the Islamist movement during this period include the arrest and imprisonment of two prominent IAF members of parliament in July 2006, the forced dissolution of the board of the Islamic Center Society, the largest Brotherhood-run NGO, and the massive fraud of the 2007 municipal elections, which led the IAF to withdraw its candidates at the last minute.

48. Asher Susser, "Jordan: Preserving Domestic Order in a Setting of Regional Turmoil," Crown Center for Middle East Studies, Brandeis University, Middle East Brief no. 27, March 2008, 6. For a Jordanian account of government interference and fraud, see Yaser Abu Hilala, "The Answer to Difficult Questions," *al-Ghad*, August 5, 2007.

49. Tarek Osman, "Egypt's Phantom Messiah," *OpenDemocracy*, November 7, 2006, www.opendemocracy.net/democracy-protest/egypt_massiah_3729.jsp.

50. Samer Shehata and Joshua Stacher, "The Brotherhood Goes to Parliament," *Middle East Report* (Fall 2006): www.merip.org/mer/mer240/shehata_stacher.html.

51. Ibid.

52. Ibid.

53. "Egypt: Muslim Brotherhood Detainees Face Military Tribunals," *Human Rights Watch*, February 14, 2007.

54. Amr Hamzawy, "Egypt's Controversial Constitutional Amendments: Political Motivations and Implications," Carnegie Endowment for International Peace, Web commentary, March 23, 2007.

55. State Department, Daily Press Briefing, May 11, 2006.

6

Free at Last! Free at Last! Allahu Akbar, We Are Free at Last! Parallels between Modern Arab and Islamic Activism and the U.S. Civil Rights Movement

Rami G. Khouri

From the perspective of ordinary men and women and faith-based political groups throughout the Arab world, the citizen activism, resistance, defiance, and religious-based leadership of Islamist movements that have challenged the prevailing Middle Eastern order echo many of the sentiments that drove the U.S. civil rights movement two generations ago. Israeli, Arab, and U.S. and other Western leaders view the Islamist mass movements across the region as a serious threat that must be fought, isolated, and contained. Nevertheless, the Islamists continue to gain strength, in some cases assuming a share of power, through elections (as in Egypt, Lebanon, Palestine, and Turkey) and revolution (as in Iran).

I have long studied and admired the U.S. civil rights movement. I was fortunate to have experienced firsthand the climactic years of the movement in the 1960s, when I was a high school and university student in the United States. As an adult in the Arab world for the past four decades, I have lived through and witnessed a different kind of struggle for freedom, dignity, equality, and opportunity by Arabs, Muslims, and others across the region. In this latter struggle, the sentiments of ordinary citizens throughout the Middle East profoundly mirror the desires of African Americans in the 1950s and 1960s.

In Atlanta, Birmingham, Greensboro, Memphis, Selma, and many other places, African Americans challenged oppressive and racist political, economic, and social orders. They braved arrest, beatings, and possible death in refusing to back down in their struggle for equal rights in the face of angry crowds, police brutality, fire hoses, and police dogs turned on them, as well as many other indignities and dangers. Individually and collectively, African Americans chose not to participate in their degradation and their dehumanizing subjugation. Instead, they peacefully challenged their country and communities to respect their rights as fellow citizens and human beings.

The conditions for Arabs and Muslims in the Middle East today do not correspond exactly with those of African Americans in the United States, and the tactics they use sometimes vary because of these differing circumstances. That said, however, the underlying sentiments and motivations among Arabs are the same: a desire to assert their humanity and demand recognition of their civic rights from their government. To achieve this, they are willing to brave death, in order to affirm life; to fight powerful overlords, in order to overcome their own powerlessness and vulnerability, and to stand up and risk repression, rather than remain on their knees.

Islamist Movements and Trends

In recent years in the Middle East, Iran turned to revolution to overthrow the shah's repressive regime, while Turkey's Islamist leaders used the ballot box to ultimately take power after the military ruling elite had repeatedly deprived them of political legitimacy. The truly mass movements that have prevailed throughout the Middle East in the past generation have been and continue to be Islamist in nature, using religion as a motivating, legitimizing, and mobilizing force. In this they mirror some of the core attributes of the civil rights movement, which was spearheaded by religious leaders who used houses of worship, overwhelmingly churches, as critical organizational points, much as mosques have been crucial for the growth of Islamist movements.

The use of nonviolent action and resistance was one of the reasons for the success of the civil rights movement. The Islamist movements in the Middle East also have been predominantly nonviolent, except where they have acted as liberation movements fighting against foreign military occupation, for example, Hizbullah in south Lebanon, Hamas in Gaza, and some nationalist-Islamists in Iraq and Afghanistan. Some movements, including Hizbullah and Hamas, that have used violence or terrorism against military occupations, also for the most part have adopted nonviolent strategies in their domestic contexts. The exception has been their taking up arms as a last resort in what they viewed as self-defense when they felt their participation in the political process under threat by opponents, as happened in Palestine in 2007 and in Lebanon in early 2008. Violent Salafi movements, such as al-Qaida, tend to receive a disproportionate amount of media coverage and political attention because of the dramatic and gruesome nature of some of their attacks, but they represent only a small, fringe element among modern Islamist movements.

It is important to disaggregate the different kinds of Islamist movements and appreciate the variety among them. The broad movement of "political Islam" has settled down into three general trends that can be distinguished by their actions and approaches. One trend is the al-Qaida-style "terror-warriors" who see themselves as fighting to defend the Islamic nation from foreign aggression and domestic apostates; they constitute the smallest but most dangerous group, which provokes strong military responses by Arab, Asian, and Western governments alike. Another trend comprises Iran and allied, predominantly Shiite Arab movements in Bahrain, Iraq, and Lebanon. They focus on self-empowerment, redressing their subjugation to Sunni Muslims, and resisting what they claim are the predatory, and "hegemonic," aims of the United States and Israel. The largest trend, in terms of popular support, consists of predominantly Sunni mainstream Islamists and includes Hamas, the Muslim Brotherhood, the Justice and Development Parties of Turkey and Morocco and others like them, which increasingly engage in electoral democratic politics at the local and national levels.

The variety of Islamist political groups reflects a broad range of goals and tactics, usually spurred initially by local and national issues, rather than any regional or international struggle. They are evolving, rather than static, movements, constantly responding to domestic pressures and opportunities as well as to external stimuli. Like other political organizations, they are accountable to their core constituencies, which they depend upon for survival and success. Their motivations overlap in a few crucial areas, but their operational and strategic goals usually differ. Most of these movements engage in domestic elections, usually seeking seats in national parliaments, even when they know that their actual capacity to influence policy is limited. Other groups shun formal electoral politics and concentrate instead on neighborhood-level social activism, seeking instead to build an Islamic society from the bottom up. The "terror-warriors" are the likely exception to both types of participation.

The three Islamist trends and their political, social, and in some cases military manifestations are often conflated in much of the Western world into a single trend bent on violence and extremism. This perception stems from recent events and oftentimes media and official interpretations of them: Osama Bin Laden releases a threatening audio message or allied or copycat Salafi militants bomb an Egyptian tourist resort; Turkey's Islamist government confronts Kurdish militancy and separatism with military force; the Palestinians' elected government headed by Hamas is ostracized by Western powers and Israel, who label Hamas a terrorist organization; the Iranian government masters small-scale uranium enrichment which Western governments view as defiant and provocative; Hizbullah, an ally of Iran and Syria, flexes its muscles as the largest and best-organized political group in Lebanon and encounters calls for the dissolution of its armed wing or its incorporation into the national armed forces; the Muslim Brotherhood and similar movements in Egypt, Jordan, Morocco, and most other Arab countries explore how they can engage in democratic elections in order to share or control power but are met with being outlawed or emasculated.

The common denominator among all the Islamist trends is their shared sense of grievances against the three primary forces that they feel degrade their lives: autocratic Arab regimes that run security states usually dominated by a handful of members of a single family; the effect of Israeli policies on Arab societies through military attacks, occupation, and influence on U.S. policy in the region; and the military and political interference of the United States and other Western powers that harms the people in the region.

All Islamist strands have responded to these three principal grievances with a combination of three primary strategies: ideological defiance of the West, armed resistance against Israeli and U.S. occupation forces, and political challenges to Arab regimes. They part ways, however, when it comes to tactics and methods: al-Qaida attacks targets around the world; the Iranian and Shiite groups focus on empowering political resistance and defiance, often wrapped in revolutionary rhetoric; and Sunni and Shiite mainstream Islamists resist with force when faced with a foreign military occupation (Hamas in Palestine, Hizbullah in Lebanon) but more often concentrate on playing and winning the political game on the strength of their impressive numbers and organization (groups in Turkey and Egypt have made the most significant electoral gains to date).

In the Middle East and other predominantly Islamic lands, citizens who seek to become politically involved in changing their world have these three options before them. Two of them—Bin Ladenist terror and Iranian-led defiance—are being fought fiercely by the West and also by some governments and citizens. The third option, democratic electoral politics, is at a major crossroads with Islamist control in Turkey, the Hamas victory in Palestine, the role of Hizbullah in governing Lebanon, and the strength of the Muslim Brotherhood in Egypt.

Throughout the Middle East in the last 30 years, ordinary Arabs, Iranians, Turks, and others have mobilized to confront their governments, demanding a more equitable political and economic order and a system of governance in which they feel they have a voice so that they can enjoy their fair share of opportunity and wealth. They have used different approaches to break through the wall of government control, including elections, media campaigns, tribal and family associations, public demonstrations, human rights appeals, and political and civil society activism by women's groups, labor unions, and professional associations of lawyers, doctors, and engineers. People braved immense dangers in challenging powerful state police systems. Many died or were imprisoned or beaten, but they persisted in the struggle, because they no longer cared to endure life under the prevailing inequities and degrading and unacceptable abuses of power. In a number of instances, when all other means failed, large numbers turned as a last resort to religious-led and inspired political movements.

Religion, Values, and Rhetoric

The many and deep parallels between the Christian-led, nonviolent civil rights movement in the United States and the Islamist movements gaining power throughout the Middle East concern issues in two critical domains: the nature of the prevailing grievances endured by each citizenry and the role of religion in bringing about political change when existing institutions of governance failed to provide for such an opportunity. The single most pivotal element in both instances was the manner in which religious values and political activism naturally converge. Religion became a vehicle—the only one available—for political transformation. This is evident in the political vocabulary and themes in both movements.

Analyses of major texts and speeches from the civil rights movement and comparable passages from the contemporary Islamist movements reveal several common themes. Take for example Martin Luther King, Jr.'s April 1963 "Letter from a Birmingham Jail," his "I Have a Dream" speech from August 1963, and the Egyptian Muslim Brotherhood's reform policy statement from November 2007. These works, by different authors in very different circumstances, share two core elements: complaints against temporal stresses and a sense of drawing upon one's spiritual strength and conviction to change society, improve one's life, and regain one's humanity.

In these writings, King speaks to the themes that capture the totality of the civil rights movement. He mentions "poverty amidst prosperity," segregation and discrimination, the demand for justice and citizenship rights, "legitimate discontent" with roots in police brutality and life in the ghetto, and the feeling of suffering "exile in our own land" and "fighting a degenerating sense of nobodiness." He affirms the role of religion and the church in fighting the injustices that African Americans suffered, noting the urgency of the moment and the need to act rather than wallow in the valley of despair. "The yearning for freedom eventually manifests itself," he wrote. "Oppressed people cannot remain oppressed forever."

The same mix of fighting against oppression, demanding human and civil rights, and drawing on religious values as a guarantor of hope and change permeates the writings and speeches of Islamist leaders in the Middle East today. The Muslim Brotherhood in Egypt is the oldest and largest group of its kind; its ideas have influenced and inspired similar movements throughout the region for decades. Its November 2007 reform policy statement echoes the same themes that

King articulated a generation earlier on a distant continent. The Brotherhood's statement decries the pain of Arab dictatorships and oppression and champions the political, economic, and social rights of people deprived of their principal right to freedom. It speaks of citizens who endure atrocities and crimes of tyrants, the rights of people in their capacity as Muslims, citizens, and human beings, and police abuse and mass arrests.

The most common theme permeating the Muslim Brotherhood's rhetoric is the call for dignity and justice, which are presented as core Islamic values. The call for "freedom" is increasingly articulated in religious terms. Just as King reminded his compatriots that freedom was a promise made in the earliest days of nationhood, the Muslim Brothers cite Islamic forefathers for their emphasis on freedom from oppression. Reference is made to Omar Ibn al-Khattab, one of the earliest and most renowned Islamic caliphs, who asked, "How do you enslave people while their mothers gave birth to them free?"

The values and rhetoric of leaders in the U.S. civil rights movement and modern Islamist movements are routinely repeated in other contexts, reflecting populations that have risen up in protest after suffering oppression and injustice for decades or centuries. The Islamist movements have grown in size and strength, in some cases gaining official power, because like the civil rights movement they successfully harnessed the discontent of millions of their followers and channeled it nonviolently toward protests and challenges for transforming and sometimes even overturning the domestic political order. The Islamist movements have been successful for many of the same reasons that the civil rights movement triumphed:

- As indigenous movements, they have local credibility and do not reflect imported foreign ideologies.
- They build on the nature of religion as a source of hope and justice for people in situations of oppression and despair.
- Other movements and ideologies have been tried (and failed), and the existing political system is closed, so these movements are seen as a last resort for changing society.
- They provide social services, employment, and other assistance that meet people's daily needs.
- They provide a sense of unity and support against oppression and subjugation by one's own society or foreign powers and offer hope of liberation.
- They speak of redress for persistent historical grievances stretching back decades and sometimes centuries.
- They offer ordinary people a sense of empowerment, by combining improvements in personal lives with a sense of political power and change in society as a whole.
- They reduce or eliminate feelings of helplessness, marginalization, and vulnerability that have long plagued individuals and entire communities.
- They enable ordinary men, women, and children to assert their identities and to overcome feelings of being dominated by other, sometimes alien, cultures.
- They generate a sense of national or transnational solidarity, linking different communities with like-minded people in other regions or countries or of other persuasions.
- They use religious houses of worship and customs—sermons, prayers, celebrations—which are difficult for the state to control, as a way to create political space to organize people.

- Their emphasis on nonviolent domestic activism and resistance appeals to their constituents, especially in its sharp contrast to the heavy-handed tactics of the prevailing, often oppressive, power structure.

In the civil rights and Islamist movements, one can see that religion validates and empowers political action, mobilizes communities, legitimizes resistance, and gives hope, confidence, strength, and unity to citizens who otherwise feel intimidated by the more powerful ruling forces in their societies. It is not surprising, therefore, that men of religion emerged as leaders in both instances, using the rhetoric of faith to inspire mass movements that at heart seek political, national, and socioeconomic transformation, not theological affirmation. This is why King's proclamation "Free at last! Free at last! Thank God Almighty, we are free at last!" resonates so naturally with the modern Muslim's call of "Allahu Akbar" (God is Great). In both cases, temporal man beseeches the Almighty for divine succor and strength in order to live a life of freedom, justice, and dignity.

If a single common dynamic can be said to characterize the civil rights movement and the contemporary Islamist awakening, it is the end of mass docility—that is, millions of people simultaneously ending generations of lassitude and acquiescence and instead asserting their determination to replace the status quo with a more humane and equitable political, social, and economic order. They did and continue to do so, despite the risk of death and imprisonment, fortified by the powerful convergence of the conviction of their faith and the indomitable human will to live in freedom and dignity.

Although sharing motivating, mobilizing, and organizing principles, these two movements, separated by time, religion, culture, and geography, differ in other respects. The U.S. system of governance provided opportunities for political and judicial activism to end discrimination and segregation through legal challenges, but activists in the Middle East usually run into the brick wall of autocracies and security states. American religious leaders consistently preached nonviolence as a foundational ethic, but most Islamists who adhere to a similar philosophy make exceptions, such as when confronting foreign occupation, often pointing to the Prophet Muhammad's legacy of waging battle when that was the only way to redress injustices or protect Muslims.

Islamists in the Middle East and Americans also differ in their philosophies on the role of women, the status of minorities and adherents of other faiths, and the relationship between religious and political dictates. Some of these differences are deeply rooted in religious doctrine, while others are social traditions. Muslims themselves also differ on some key issues, such as whether to participate in elections that are obviously stage-managed by incumbent regimes, whether to make political alliances with Christian political parties, or whether to engage with the United States and other Western powers. Despite the differing politics, social cultures, and national contexts in the United States and in Islamic lands, recognizing similarities in what motivates individuals in both societies should be an important priority, if they are ever to reverse the trend of rising animosity, suspicion, fear, and occasionally violence that seems to define many relationships between them.

Bull Connor in the Middle East

In June 2005 at the American University in Cairo, U.S. Secretary of State Condoleezza Rice made a powerful case for the promotion of democracy and liberty throughout the Middle East. Her speech was all the more poignant because in calling for change in the Arab world, she alluded to the struggle for equality and freedom by African Americans in the United States. She speaks with authority on this issue, given her family's experiences in Birmingham, Alabama, a pivotal battleground in the U.S. civil rights movement.

Yet, I suspect that Rice's commitment to freedom for all people and her personal reference to growing up in Birmingham during the closing years of the civil rights movement lost some of their power because of her inability to appreciate the linkages between these two worlds that she tried to bring together—African Americans who only achieved full citizenship in her lifetime and an Arab world equally in need of radical changes. The terrible irony for her personally and for U.S. foreign policy generally is that something akin to the civil rights movement is already taking place in the Middle East, but in the eyes of many in the region, the United States seems to be on the wrong side of the equation of justice versus oppression.

Long-standing U.S. support for autocrats and dictators in the Middle East is one reason these governments have endured for so many decades. This legacy sparked a widespread awakening among average men and women, starting in the late 1970s, led by Islamist political movements in several countries. This awakening, like the U.S. civil rights movement, reflected a determination simultaneously to redress a number of grievances, including a denial of basic political and human rights, abuse of power by a top-heavy order ignoring the views and interests of ordinary citizens, social discrimination, economic marginalization, and, in the case of the Arabs, historical subjugation to foreign powers and interests.

Rice, in her Cairo speech, spelled out in impressive terms some of the criteria for democratic governance that the United States said it sought to promote in the Middle East. She cited free and fair elections, and "governments that protect certain basic rights for all their citizens—among these, the right to speak freely, to associate, to worship as you wish, to educate your children, boys and girls. And freedom from the midnight knock of the secret police." She also acknowledged two points regarding U.S. values and policies. The first point recognized the failure of the U.S. government to live up to its stated ideals. Rice noted that "the United States was born half free and half slave. And it was only in my lifetime that my government guaranteed the right to vote for all of its people. There was a time, not long ago, after all, when liberty was threatened by slavery. The moral worth of my ancestors, it was thought, should be valued by the demand of the market, not by the dignity of their souls. This practice was sustained through violence. But the crime of human slavery could not withstand the power of human liberty." The second point concerned U.S. policies that supported Arab autocrats for so many years. She acknowledged, "For 60 years, my country, the United States, pursued stability at the expense of democracy in this region here in the Middle East—and we achieved neither. Now, we are taking a different course. We are supporting the democratic aspirations of all people. Today, liberty is threatened by undemocratic governments. Some believe this is a permanent fact of history. But there are others who know better. These impatient patriots can be found in Baghdad and Beirut, in Riyadh and in Ramallah, in Amman and in Tehran and right here in Cairo."

Rice and her government, however, never confronted or resolved the doubts in Baghdad, Beirut, Riyadh, Ramallah, Amman, Tehran, and Cairo about crucial aspects of the U.S. policy of promoting freedom and democracy. The first doubt concerned whether Washington was motivated by a genuine appreciation of the Arab quest for human dignity and freedom or an expedient need to ring emotional rhetorical bells to camouflage the sound of trouble, and even failure, in Iraq and other traumatized lands that have been visited by U.S. armies and furies.

The second doubt concerned whether the United States would promote democracy, equality, and freedom consistently throughout the Middle East—including, for example, in Egypt, Israel, Libya, Palestine, and Tunisia—or only in selected countries where the process is somehow easier or politically less contentious. The third doubt was whether the United States would persist over the long haul, hand-in-hand with Arab democrats and freedom lovers, or only pursue these values as long as they serve current U.S. foreign policy interests.

Linked to this is a complex and troubling issue of responsibility for one's own actions. It is heartening that the secretary of state publicly admitted to the United States feeding and bolstering of Arab autocrats. Yet, it remains troubling that Washington feels that it can simply acknowledge culpability and error and then expect Arab nationals who have suffered the traumas of the cumulative impact of the 60 years of bad policy to change their attitudes toward the United States as instantaneously as the U.S. government says that it is changing its attitude toward the Arabs' condition and rights.

Six decades of Arab autocracy supported by the United States, the Soviet Union, and other Western powers has left deep scars, powerful distortions, and a great deal of political deviance and violence in Arab societies, which must travel a long, hard road on the return to normalcy. Six decades of poor governance have left the region riddled with killers and kidnappers, criminals and corrupt officials, beheading rooms, bomb-makers, child soldiers, massive peri-urban belts of unemployed men and women, hundreds of billions of dollars spirited abroad, and thousands of active and potential teenage suicide bombers.

Arabs will most likely escape these dire consequences in the same way that African Americans vanquished their two centuries of inhuman suffering—by demanding and agitating for their human and civil rights, by writing and applying laws that promote equality, by challenging oppression, confronting killers and racists, respecting the consent of the governed and the rights of majorities and minorities alike, speaking the truth, and not being afraid to stand up to police dogs or the police state. Arabs and Americans can gradually erase the debilitating consequences of six decades of failed policies by adopting a combination of consistency, perseverance, and equal treatment of all countries and peoples.

In this respect, the similarities between the forces that drove the civil rights movement and current Arab-Islamist activism are more than interesting historical parallels. They also suggest that Arabs, Americans, Iranians, Turks, and other interested parties could work together to bring about a new age of universal liberty, equality, and human dignity inspired by the heroism and ultimate triumph of the U.S. civil rights movement. The events of April 1963 in Birmingham, Alabama, ring especially relevant. The African Americans who sang hymns in the face of police dogs, fire hoses, racist wardens, and church bombers gave the world a master class in the power of persistent popular resistance in the struggle for human decency and universal values. Rice was right to invoke that lesson in addressing the challenge of freedom in the Arab world, though she may not have recognized that Arabs and Muslims fighting for their rights today are already motivated by the same spirit of fearless resistance and resolute determination that motivated African Americans who braved death and went to jail singing gospel songs.

During a subsequent visit to her hometown of Birmingham, Rice also spoke movingly of childhood friends killed in the bombing of the 16th Street Baptist Church by white racists in 1963. She framed her comments within the context of the major transformations in her life from a segregated childhood to success in academia to joining the world's top decision-makers. She cited her journey "as an example of a very American story." In Rice's youth, police chief Theophilus Eugene "Bull" Connor epitomized the racist mentality in Birmingham. He routinely unleashed baton-swinging deputies and vicious police dogs against nonviolent protestors demanding only that they be treated as human beings. The demonstrators prevailed, of course. The civil rights movement triumphed, laws were changed to end formal discrimination, and a generation later African Americans became secretaries of state and attained the highest U.S. office, the presidency. This trajectory affirms the simple truth about the unstoppable power of the individual and the collective quest for freedom and dignity. It pushes ordinary people to do extraordinary things, as happened in Birmingham when young children marched into Bull Connor's fire hoses and stood their ground against his police dogs. The spirit of Birmingham was about transcending fear and affirming humanity. It took exemplary courage, moral certitude, and discipline to stand firmly in the face of the violent, intemperate hatred and ignorance that Bull Connor represented.

I have watched that same spirit in action all around me in the Middle East during the past three decades. I have watched many courageous Arabs, Iranians, and Turks stand up to their own violent, intolerant governments or foreign military occupiers knowing that they might be killed, injured, or imprisoned, as many were. They resisted fearlessly, defying danger and intimidation, driven by the same passions that fueled the U.S. civil rights movement. In the eyes of most people in the Arab world, however, the United States has been the Bull Connor of our generation, the oppressor in our world that unleashes dogs against helpless civilians. That symbol became reality for a brief period in Iraq when the U.S. armed forces used police dogs to humiliate and terrorize prisoners at Abu Ghraib and other detention centers after the 2003 invasion that overthrew the Baathist regime led by Saddam Hussein. That image will persist for years, as did that of Bull Connor using dogs to degrade peaceful African American protestors in the early 1960s.

Of course, these are only symbols, not the full story. Bull Connor's dogs are long gone. Some of the abusive soldiers at Abu Ghraib were tried and sentenced, but symbols matter. They are not imagined evils; they reflect realities. They endure for generations, burning indelible images into hearts and minds. Although dogs are symbols of a broader policy and a larger reality, the images of them in Birmingham and Baghdad remain the most sharply etched in my mind. Many other images and symbols come to mind, as well. Young children killed. Old people degraded and humiliated. Bombs hurled among innocent civilians. Houses destroyed. Young men lynched. Families and communities seeking solace in their holy books and their shared God. Police units and armies using excessive force against schoolchildren or rock-throwing kids and throwing inspiring leaders in jail.

These struggles in the United States and the Arab-Islamic Middle East, a generation apart, represent credible, authentic, and historic mass movements that are also compelling for their universality. The spectacle of millions of Arabs and Muslims wedding their core faith values with a struggle for their political and civil rights brings that universality to life. When Condoleezza Rice was a child, Martin Luther King, Jr. wrote from the Birmingham jail, "I am cognizant of the interrelatedness of all communities and states. I cannot sit idly by in Atlanta and not be concerned about what happens in Birmingham. Injustice anywhere is a threat to justice everywhere. We are caught in an inescapable network of mutuality, tied in a single garment of destiny. Whatever affects one directly, affects all indirectly."

The Road Ahead

I stand in awe and humility before those who struggled for civil rights in the United States and in solidarity with those in the Arab world who muster the same spirit in their fight against oppression and foreign domination. More work and thought is needed by all of us to credibly connect these two worlds and eras in order to better appreciate the power of the millions of people who have and continue to risk their lives so that their children can experience the freedom and equality that they were denied.

It is important especially for Americans to grasp the connections between the forces that pushed ordinary men and women to do extraordinary things during the civil rights movement and similar forces that motivate men and women throughout the Middle East to seek a life of dignity, stability, and opportunity today. In fact, the broad struggle for rights and dignity across the Middle East may represent the latest in a series of great movements seeking change anchored in freedom and justice. Decolonization was a worldwide movement in the mid-twentieth century, followed by the U.S. civil rights movement, the antiapartheid movement in South Africa, and the liberation of the peoples of Eastern Europe and the Soviet Union.

Several different forces were at play in each of these great moments of liberation, including nationalism, sovereignty, occupation, democracy, religious identity, citizen and civil rights, political ideology, and dignity. These are distinct issues and apply to different degrees in individual situations. They are often easily confused; for instance, people singing hymns can be mistaken for religious fanatics when they are actually seeking civil rights nonviolently; a population that fights its occupier is viewed as practicing terrorism rather than seeking freedom. The religious dimension of a political act—such as one prefaced by the cry "Allahu Akbar"—often camouflages the true socioeconomic, political, nationalistic, or psychological motivation that drives people to act. Whenever mass movements are broadly couched in the public rhetoric of faith, they should be examined more closely to identify the true political or nationalistic forces that actually define them.

Most men and women who adhere to Islamist movements in the Middle East have persisted in their nonviolent struggle; only a handful here and there have drifted off to join the militants and terrorists. Islamist movements today have track records that young activists can examine when making their decision on whether to join them. Mainstream, peaceful political Islamism has only assumed controlling power democratically in Turkey, while sharing executive power in Lebanon and Palestine. Elsewhere, such as in Egypt, Bahrain, Kuwait, Morocco, Syria, and Tunisia, Islamism remains checked by local and foreign powers. It is not clear how young, frustrated Islamists will react if autocratic regimes thwart their nonviolent quest for democratic participation.

The civil rights movement and the current Arab-Islamist political wave confirm that many aggrieved people turn to religious politics and nonviolent resistance if the political system fails to provide them with an opportunity to resolve their grievances. For now, five of the six distinct and powerful brands of political activism and transnational identity that can be identified in the region are Islamist in nature: mainstream Sunni Islamism, represented by the Muslim Brotherhood and Hamas; militant and terrorist Sunni organizations, such as al-Qaida; secular Arab nationalists; anti-occupation military resistance groups that are often Islamist;

Iranian-Persian nationalist groups with a strong Islamist revolutionary core; and regional Shiite empowerment groups among Arabs and Iranians.

The Arab world and the broader Middle East have witnessed a dramatic expression of political self-assertion in recent years, most of it inspired by Islamism and manifested nonviolently. Militant resistance groups and a handful of small terror movements also vie for popular allegiance. For the first time in many decades, ordinary citizens in the Arab world have options to choose from in terms of political movements that express their thoughts and identities and respond to their needs. If nonviolent movements succeed in achieving their aims, this form of resistance is likely to persist and grow. If not, it is likely that more militant groups will dominate political and national scenes in the years ahead.

When looking at nonviolent Islamist groups, it becomes clear that beneath the veneer of religious rhetoric—the chants of "Allahu Akbar" and calls for *sharia*—lie real, long-standing grievances that have not been addressed by the prevailing political governance systems in the Middle East. After half a century of waiting passively, major segments of society in the Middle East have now decided to take matters into their own hands, just as African Americans and their partners in the civil rights movement did in the United States half a century ago.

7

External Actors and Nonviolent Struggles
in the Middle East

Stephen Zunes and Saad Eddin Ibrahim

The Middle East's history of colonialism, neocolonialism, and foreign occupation has created justified and unjustified suspicion toward most foreign intervention. This has resulted in the widespread acceptance of conspiracy theories by even well-educated segments of Middle Eastern societies and provided autocratic governments the opportunity to accuse almost any opposition movement of being an agent of foreign powers. In reality, although external actors have often played important supportive roles in past struggles, virtually every successful nonviolent action campaign in the Middle East has been primarily an indigenous movement. Although any struggle against a repressive regime would normally welcome international solidarity, if the outside support is seen as coming from forces that are not believed to have the best interest of the country's people in mind, it can harm the chances of such a movement succeeding. External support for nonviolent struggles today in the Middle East runs the risk of being a double-edged sword, but enhanced international mobility and communication make it likely that external actors will play an increasingly important role in the future.

Diaspora Communities

The Arab and Iranian diasporas have provided important support to nonviolent resistance movements for decades. Ayatollah Ruhollah Khomeini, while in exile in France in 1977, helped launch Iran's largely nonviolent uprising against the shah's regime through calls for strikes, boycotts, tax refusal, and other forms of noncooperation. Cassette tapes smuggled into the country gave inspiration and at times directives in support of the resistance.[1] Today, members of the large and generally well-educated Iranian exile community, through the Internet and in visits to their homeland provide encouragement to pro-democracy activists hoping to expand the use of nonviolent resistance against the Islamic regime. Taking advantage of freedoms afforded in Europe and North America and connections within Iran and among diaspora communities elsewhere, they have helped disseminate information about nonviolent resistance and offered solidarity to activists inside Iran. Satellite television and radio broadcasts presenting views normally not allowed by the government—such as exposés of official wrongdoing, news about political prisoners and opposition protests, and practical information about methods of strategic nonviolent action—have been beamed into the country. This became increasingly important during the crackdown following the June 12, 2009 presidential election as the diaspora community rallied to help facilitate communication on the rapidly unfolding events in the face of severe restrictions on the media within the country. To support the "green revolution" that continues to unfold inside Iran, a worldwide solidarity initiative called "Where Is My Vote" has organized protests, demonstrations, sit-ins, and a signature campaign to put pressure on the UN, the international media, and governments around the world "not to recognize the illegitimate authority of a government that does not have the support of its own people."[2]

At the same time, there are real limits to what can be accomplished from Los Angeles or other locations. In some cases, such efforts have been led by pro-Western elites who are often no more in touch with the pulse of their homeland than are government officials in Washington or London. In addition, although most exiles have tended to view U.S. policy toward Iran in recent years as counterproductive, some prominent individuals actively allied themselves with the George W. Bush administration and the neoconservatives. Some of these people accepted financial support from the U.S. government for their efforts, thereby damaging their credibility among activists in Iran who while strongly opposing their country's theocratic regime remained staunchly nationalistic. Given that some of these exiles were royalists who served under the repressive regime of the shah, a number of observers also questioned whether they were genuinely interested in democracy rather than a return to the status quo ante.

Exiles from autocratic Arab regimes, including Egypt, Libya, Saudi Arabia, and Syria, have acted similarly to Iranian exiles, using the Internet and other forms of communication to provide uncensored news of nefarious actions by the regime and opposition activities inside their countries of origin. In some cases, this has included information on strategic nonviolent action.[3] The large Palestinian diaspora has played a major role in the Palestinian struggle. The leadership of the first, and largely nonviolent, intifada (1987–1993) came from local committees and consisted primarily of a younger generation of Palestinians creating autonomous structures and networks, though many were affiliated with the major factions of the Palestine Liberation Organization (PLO). While initially the exiled PLO leadership in Tunis was sceptical about the largely nonviolent resistance unfolding in the occupied territories, the PLO and other Palestinian exiles provided crucial funding for the internal struggle and assisted in getting information to international solidarity networks and the media.

Exiled Palestinian businesspeople and scholars have long provided material and political support to ongoing nonviolent resistance efforts against the Israeli occupation as have Sahrawi exiles in support of the nonviolent resistance campaign against the Moroccan occupation of Western Sahara. These diaspora communities have taken advantage of the Internet to raise popular awareness of official repression by communicating through PalTalk and providing video of beatings of nonviolent demonstrators by occupation forces and other human rights abuses. Their activities have put pressure on foreign governments to protest abuses by the occupying governments.

In a similar vein, progressive Israeli activists—like their right-wing and centrist counterparts—have benefited from the political and financial support of Jews in Europe and North America. Such organizations as Jewish Voice for Peace,

Americans for Peace Now, Friends of Yesh Gvul, and others have provided backing, including participation by members in demonstrations and nonviolent direct action campaigns. Growing sympathy within the American Jewish community for Israeli progressives has led to the emergence of liberal Zionist groups such as J Street and Brit Tzedek v´Shalom to challenge long-standing U.S. policies toward Israel, notably on the issue of settlements. This has helped challenge the myth that the Jewish communities in foreign countries are monolithic in their support of Israeli government policies, making it easier for political leaders to voice their concerns about Israeli actions without being labeled as anti-Israel. Although perceived strategic interests remain the determining factor in on-going Western governmental support of autocratic Arab governments and of Israeli and Moroccan occupation forces, the pro-democracy and anti-occupation diaspora communities have contributed to the political debate within these countries by making continued support of their repressive allies more problematic in the future.

Foreign Governments

The history of foreign conquest, post-independence military interventions by Western powers, foreign-backed coups d'état, and other forms of interference have led to a fatalistic view among many Middle Easterners that has contributed to the relatively weak capacity of civil society organizations. Some Western-oriented liberals for a time had looked for a foreign "saviour" to advance their struggle for greater democracy in the region. U.S. President George W. Bush raised hopes when in November 2003 he announced a greater Middle East initiative to promote democratic freedoms in the area. Some took this as a sign that the United States would finally end its support for their dictatorial governments. The Bush administration, however, largely focused its attention on autocratic governments that opposed U.S. interests in the region, criticizing the human rights record of such countries as Syria and Iran and drawing attention to the plight of certain suppressed minorities, dissident organizations, and individuals, while continuing its diplomatic, economic, and military support of the pro-Western, dictatorial regimes of Egypt, Oman, Saudi Arabia, and Tunisia. As Thomas Carothers and Marina Ottaway observed, "[T]he United States has other important security-related and economic interests, such as cooperation on antiterrorism enforcement actions and ensuring secure access to oil. Such interests impel it to maintain close ties with many of the authoritarian regimes in the Middle East and be wary of the possibility of rapid or unpredictable political change."[4]

This double-standard has left most people in the region with a skeptical view of the United States and its commitment to democracy. Polls show that although the majority of Middle Easterners support greater democracy in their countries, there exists a decidedly negative attitude toward the Bush administration's stated goal of "democracy promotion." An average of only 19 percent say that such an effort has had a positive effect on their overall opinion of the United States, while 58 percent feel that it has had a negative effect.[5] The election of Barack Obama has led to a significantly greater openness within the Middle East for improved relations with the United States, though there is concern that the Obama administration's welcomed rejection of the neoconservative ideology and excessive militarism of its predecessor may be replaced by a return of realpolitik, or, at minimum, a reluctance to support popular pro-democracy struggles out of concern of being accused of interventionism.

Furthermore, the United States has in recent years also emphasized "economic freedom"—a neoliberal capitalist economic model that emphasizes open markets and free trade—as being at least as important as political freedom. It is noteworthy that in 2007 the Center for International Private Enterprise (CIPE) was by far the largest single Middle Eastern recipient of funding from the National Endowment for Democracy. In Egypt and Algeria, the two most populous Arab countries, CIPE received three times as much NED funding as did all Egyptian human rights, development, legal, and civil society organizations combined. Although liberalizing an economy from stifling state control can in many cases encourage political liberalization, the more extreme neoliberal model of the so-called Washington consensus has tended to further concentrate economic and political power in the hands of elites, particularly in authoritarian regimes. Often this results in crony capitalism, rather than a truly free market, which in turn weakens civil society rather than strengthens it.

France, Great Britain, and the United States have not historically supported democracy in the Middle East, preferring instead to back dictators open to accommodating Western economic and strategic interests. According to Harold Macmillan, who served as British prime minister in the late 1950s and early 1960s, it is "rather sad that circumstances compel us to support reactionary and really rather outmoded regimes because we know that the new forces, even if they begin with moderate opinions, always seem to drift into violent revolutionary and strongly anti-Western positions."[6] F. Gregory Gause III, an American specialist on Saudi Arabia, notes more bluntly, "The truth is, the more democratic the Saudis become, the less cooperative they will be with us. So why should we want that?"[7] As British journalist Robert Fisk states, "Far better to have a Mubarak or a King Abdullah or a King Fahd running the show than to let the Arabs vote for a real government that might oppose U.S. policies in the region."[8] Indeed, despite the November 2003 announcement by Bush concerning a shift in policy, U.S. aid to autocratic regimes in the greater Middle East subsequently increased during his administration and the early months of the Obama administration—despite some welcomed shifts regarding Iraq, Palestine, and Western Sahara—has not indicated a willingness to condition security assistance to an improvement on human rights.

Leading Arab democrats argued that conditional aid and putting teeth into expectations for minimal adherence to human rights standards in Arab countries would give heart to struggling democracy forces, but fears surrounding terrorism and Islamist political movements have dampened even the few occasional impulses of Western leaders to stand up to Arab dictators. Western democracies have not yet been willing to use their leverage in trade, aid, and technology to pressure Arab autocrats into opening their political systems and empowering pro-democracy movements, which they did with the regimes of Eastern Europe through the Helsinki Accord and other instruments. Since the 1980s, the U.S. government has launched some limited initiatives, such as the National Endowment for Democracy, to promote civil society efforts in a number of Middle Eastern and North African countries, but these have been largely restricted to institution-building primarily geared toward small, secular middle-class elements. Although some individuals who have been direct or indirect beneficiaries of NED's funding have later become part of large-scale nonviolent action campaigns, NED's emphasis on elite oppositionists rather than grassroots movements has often limited their effectiveness.

The U.S. invasion of Iraq was a major setback for nonviolent opposition movements and other indigenous pro-democracy actors in the Middle East. Codenamed Operation Iraqi Freedom by the United States, the invasion is widely seen in the region as an imperialist conquest. The Bush administration's rationalization of the invasion as an effort to promote democracy in the area has caused the expression "democracy promotion" to be associated with malevolent foreign influence.[9] Bush insisted that the invasion was not about oil or empire. Rather, he asserted, "I sent American troops to Iraq to make its people free,"[10] and "a free Iraq will also demonstrate to other countries in that region that national prosperity and dignity are found in representative government and free institutions."[11] The torture and abuse of prisoners in U.S.-run prisons, the large-scale killing of civilians in military operations, unilateral decrees under the occupying powers of the U.S.-led Coalition Provisional Authority privatizing much of the economy, initial U.S. opposition to direct elections, and other policies have led many in the Middle East to impugn American motives.[12] The chaos, sectarian violence, rise of extremist groups, and what some observers describe as ethnic cleansing unleashed following the invasion and occupation has not made Iraq much of a model for prosperity and dignity.

The U.S. large-scale and unconditional diplomatic, financial, and military support for Israel has hurt pro-democracy forces as well. While offering an exemplary democracy for its Jewish citizens, Israel continues to violate international humanitarian law with its policies toward Palestinians in the West Bank (including East Jerusalem), the Gaza Strip, and residents of Lebanon. This situation also raises questions regarding the sincerity of the U.S. pro-democracy rhetoric. For example, the support by the Bush administration and an overwhelming bipartisan majority of Congress for Israel's massive and devastating military assault on Lebanon's civilian infrastructure during summer 2006 severely so soon after the Cedar Revolution the previous year resulted in strengthening Hizbullah and other extremist movements and led many to question the sincerity of U.S. support for democracy in the Arab world. Such policies and actions made proponents of democracy look like deluded Western agents, which in turn hardened many Arabs against beleaguered democracy advocates in the region.

As noted, it is not unprecedented for autocratic regimes to accuse indigenous nonviolent action movements of being part of foreign conspiracies. The combination of unprecedented levels of U.S. and U.S.-backed military intervention in the Middle East and calls for "regime change" as a vehicle for democracy during the Bush administration also gave resonance to such accusations among the general population. Iranian dissident Akbar Atri notes that the Iranian government is "very sensitive. Everybody who is talking about an Orange Revolution or nonviolent action, they say '[O]kay, this is a CIA program.'"[13] While believing the United States and other Western governments should put human rights at the forefront of policy towards Iran and pressure the Iranian government to end its repression, they recognize that such direct support of opposition groups can be counterproductive.

In some cases involving U.S.-backed dictatorships, the pro-democracy rhetoric of the Bush administration may have contributed to something of a political opening for the opposition, but then the lack of sufficient follow through by the United States prevented any tangible progress. Pressure on Arab regimes by the Bush administration during the short-lived "Arab spring" of 2004–2005 was critical in opening political space for opposition voices, notably in Egypt.[14] In the case of Iran, however, support for pro-democracy opponents led to their being discredited. Given that the United States overthrew Iran's last democratic government in 1953 and supported the shah for a quarter-century afterward, any calls for freedom and democracy in Iran by the U.S. government are viewed as opportunistic, at best. Iranian dissident leader Akbar Ganji has refused invitations to the White House and to testify on Capitol Hill, preferring instead to meet with American human rights activists and left-wing intellectuals, such as Noam Chomsky of the Massachusetts Institute of Technology. As Ganji notes, "Any intervention by any foreign power would bring charges of conspiracy against us."[15]

While continuing to back repressive regimes in Saudi Arabia, Egypt, and other countries through security assistance, which has often been employed to suppress popular movements, Congress approved $75 million in funding (through the State Department) for various Iranian opposition groups in response to a White House request in 2006. At that time few Iranian groups were willing to accept such support from the U.S. government as a matter of principle or for fear of being exposed, which would not only subject them to arrest, but would discredit their movement.[16] More than two dozen Iranian American and human rights groups formally protested the program, arguing that "Iranian reformers believe democracy cannot be imported and must be based on indigenous institutions and values. Intended beneficiaries of the funding—human rights advocates, civil society activists, and others—uniformly denounce the program."[17] The Obama administration did not request a renewal of funding for this program, but has remained in active communication with some Iranian dissident organizations; he joined world leaders in condemning the violent attacks against nonviolent Iranians protestors challenging the June 12 election results. Given the ability of the Iranian regime to manipulate the strong nationalist sympathies among its people, it presents a difficult balancing act for leaders of Western nations with a history of intervention in the region, as Obama himself has acknowledged.

Some scholars have suggested a number of ways that foreign governments can help movements for human rights and democracy, in particular, by making security assistance and other government-to-government aid and materiel transfers conditional upon improvements in human rights and democratic reforms.[18] In response to the Egyptian government's closing of the Ibn Khaldun Center for Development Studies in 2003, along with the imprisonment of its director, Saad Eddin Ibrahim, and 27 colleagues, the U.S. Congress suspended supplementary economic aid to Egypt. This sanction was credited with the staff members' release and the reopening of the center.[19] European nations have combined carrots and sticks in their relations with Turkey, an aspiring EU member, in reducing repression and giving unprecedented political space for popular movements.

Comprehensive economic sanctions—such as those applied by the United States against Iran initially in 1979 and subsequently tightened and those imposed by the United Nations against Iraq—have tended to weaken the very elements in civil society that often have played the most significant role in challenging autocratic regimes. These sanctions serve to make populations even more dependent on a regime to meet their economic needs, hurt the middle and skilled working classes, which have historically taken the lead in many nonviolent struggles, and enable a regime to blame outsiders for its own economic mismanagement.[20] By contrast, sanctions which target government and military leaders—their overseas bank accounts, their ability to travel freely, and their means of suppressing the population—can, in certain contexts, make a positive difference.

Engaging in certain commercial, cultural, and intellectual exchanges with those living in countries under autocratic rule may sometimes allow for greater independence for entrepreneurs, intellectuals, and performing artists. Such interactions with civil society can provide leverage to promote greater respect for human rights and potentially cause splits within the regime and among its supporters between those who want a greater opening and those who want to maintain a more absolute level of control. Although placing sanctions on the export of certain technologies, materials, or capital in ways that weaken repressive state apparatuses can be an appropriate tool for pressuring a regime to lessen its repression, the current U.S. sanctions against Iran are so comprehensive as to make most of even these potentially useful forms of cooperation impossible.

Under certain circumstances, support by foreign governments through public and private diplomatic channels can be useful to human rights activists and members of the media. Foreign embassies, through their cultural sections, for example, offer opposition groups and others access to libraries and the Internet and space for gathering. Foreign governments might also facilitate meetings between members of local and national government and opposition groups, support free and fair elections, and fund nonpartisan trainings for political parties and civil society organizations.[21] Although repressive regimes have traditionally seen such foreign influence as violations of their national sovereignty, a case can be made that sovereignty is increasingly being defined in terms of the nation as a whole, not a particular regime; thus, an autocratic unrepresentative government would negate its claim of sovereign rights if intervention occurred on behalf of the majority of the population.[22]

Former Egyptian foreign minister and UN Secretary-General Boutros Boutros-Ghali, who has served as chair of a semiofficial human rights council in Egypt, asserts that the international community has a right to help and "interfere" in issues involving human rights and democracy.[23] The whims of international diplomacy, however, can sometimes make being dependent on foreign support problematic. For example, in 2004 Egyptian nonviolent activist Ayman al-Nour helped establish al-Ghad, a moderate-to-liberal political party, as a democratic alternative to Mubarak's ruling National Democratic Party. This effort initially appeared to generate sympathetic support from the United States. The Bush administration allowed Nour to meet with its ambassador to Egypt and with Secretary of State Condoleezza Rice the following year; Nour even received words of praise from Bush himself. The administration's support proved to be short-lived, however. The Egyptian government imprisoned Nour at the end of 2005 after he dared run against Mubarak in presidential elections that year, finishing a poor second in an election process riddled with fraud and for which no international monitoring was allowed. Nour went on a hunger strike to protest his imprisonment and the fraudulent electoral process. Visiting Egypt two months later, in February 2006, Rice did not publicly raise the issue of Nour's detention. Nour, however, released a statement from prison asserting that he was paying the price for the U.S failure to speak out in support of human rights and democracy. He noted, "[W]hat's happening to me now is a message to everybody."[24] The European parliament passed resolutions in support of Nour, and he was eventually released, but there was little apparent pressure on the Egyptian government by the United States—the supplier of more than $2 billion of aid annually to Egypt—to release Nour and other pro-democracy activists or to allow greater democratic freedoms.

Support for free independent media in autocratic Middle Eastern countries and indigenous-language broadcasts by the BBC, Voice of America, and other entities provide uncensored news and analysis that might be beneficial to nonviolent prodemocracy movements. This type of indirect support by foreign governments has won the praise of dissidents wary of direct foreign assistance to dissident groups themselves. Direct pressure from foreign governments can also at times be useful in reinforcing the demands of popular movements, such as during the 2005 Cedar Revolution to force Syrian forces from Lebanon, where pressure by the United States, France, and Saudi Arabia played an important complementary role. It is noteworthy that for more than a decade, international pressure for a Syrian with-drawal was unsuccessful, until massive, broad-based pressure by the Lebanese themselves brought it to the fore. In any case, until a movement embarks on a strat-egy of large-scale nonviolent action, there is little that foreign governments can do (short of military invasion or overthrow) on their own except to try to pressure a government to limit repression.

Large, bureaucratic governments accustomed to projecting political power through military force or diplomatic channels tend to have little understanding or appreciation of nonviolent action or any other kind of mass popular struggle or the complex internal political dynamics of a country necessary to create a broad-based coalition capable of ousting an incumbent, authoritarian government. This does not mean there cannot be some limited assistance through NGOs toward pro-democracy groups, including support for grassroots international solidarity efforts that may include capacity-building and related support, but this is on a very different level than traditional Western interventionism.

Nonviolent "people power" movements bring change through empowering pro-democratic majorities, unlike the regime changes promoted by foreign govern-ments during the colonial and much of the postcolonial period that tended to be violent seizures of power to install an undemocratic minority. The best hope for advancing freedom and democracy in the Middle East comes from civil society, not foreign governments that deserve neither credit nor blame for the growing use of nonviolent resistance movements in the region. The challenge for foreign gov-ernments, then, is to find ways which can help advance—or at least not retard or suppress—the growth of such civil society movements. *A Diplomat's Handbook for Democracy Development Support,* a project commissioned by the Community of Democracies and produced by the Council for a Community of Democracies, has responded to this challenge in a practical and useful way, by showing practical ways that democratic embassies and diplomats can assist human rights defenders and pro-democracy activists and movements.[25]

Every successful nonviolent insurrection has been a homegrown movement rooted in a realization by the masses that their rulers were illegitimate and that the political system was incapable of redressing injustice. No nonviolent insurrection or movement has succeeded without the backing of the majority of the popula-tion. Nonviolent revolutions, like successful armed revolutions, may take years or decades to develop as an organic process within the body politic of a given country. There is no standardized formula for a positive outcome that a foreign government or a foreign nongovernmental organization (NGO) can develop, because the his-tories, cultures, economics, and political alignments of each country are unique. Relevant factors include the history of state-society relations, the types and extent of repression used by the regime or those holding power, the presence of ethnic or sectarian divisions, and the regime's dependency relationships, which often influ-ence the tactical and strategic choices made by the opposition. Furthermore, no foreign government or NGO can recruit or mobilize the large numbers of ordi-nary civilians necessary to build a movement capable of effectively challenging the established political leadership, much less of toppling a government.

There have been a few cases in which support from foreign governments, usu-ally through NGOs and quasi-independent foundations, has been beneficial to nonviolent action campaigns. The limited Western financial support provided to pro-democracy movements in Serbia, Georgia, and Ukraine, for example, helped sustain them against serious challenges by the state apparatus. In the Middle East, although the history of foreign intervention and support for some of the region's worst dictatorships, has severely damaged the reputation of Western powers, given the serious challenges facing pro-democracy groups struggling against autocratic regimes, many activists will likely continue to look to the United States and other Western powers for, at a minimum, moral and diplomatic support. Western leaders who avoid messianic and self-righteous rhetoric when talking about democracy, who pursue policies that neither practice nor condone violations of international humanitarian law, and who communicate directly with and respect the wishes of nonviolent activists could help rectify the historically counterproductive policies that have for so long hurt the cause of democracy in the region. In his May 2009 speech in Cairo, Obama appeared to indicate an important rhetorical shift away from his predecessor in this regard, though many pro-democracy activists are waiting for more concrete changes in policy.

Nongovernmental Organizations

Foreign nongovernmental organizations, most of which reject direct or indirect government funding, provide a form of external support different from that of governments. Some of them sponsor workshops on the history and dynamics of nonviolent action for pro-democracy and anti-occupation activists, though this phenomenon has thus far been limited and fairly recent. Such groups as the Serbia-based Centre for Applied Nonviolent Action and Strategies (CANVAS), the U.S.-based Albert Einstein Institution and International Center on Nonviolent Conflict, and the transnational Nonviolence International have worked with pro-democracy and anti-occupation activists from Azerbaijan, Egypt, Georgia, Iran, Jordan, Palestine, Syria, and Western Sahara.

A number of governments, most notably Iran's, have postulated that these types of efforts are part of an attempt by the Central Intelligence Agency to instigate "soft coups." Some Western bloggers and other writers critical of the Bush administration and skeptical of U.S. intervention in the name of democracy accepted such assertions. These conspiracy theories were in turn picked up by some progressive Web sites and periodicals and even by members of the mainstream media, which repeated them as fact (or something approximating it).[26] Ironically, rather than being supporters of U.S. imperialism, a majority of North Americans and European activists involved in workshops in strategic nonviolent action and similar capacity-building efforts come from leftist and pacific traditions that are highly critical of U.S. policy in the Middle East and of U.S. interventionism in general. Virtually all such seminars and workshops follow at the direct request of opposition organizers themselves. None of these foreign groups seek out specific groups to assist; in fact, all of them generally follow a strict policy of not providing tailored advice to opposition groups.

The Open Society Institute (OSI), funded by the Hungarian American billionaire George Soros, has worked with independent media institutions as well as a number of civil society institutions in several Arab countries to help them develop their capacity and effectiveness. Some OSI programs have supported Israeli-Palestinian efforts at peace and reconciliation. Although none of these programs has been directly related to strategic nonviolent action, strengthening such efforts can be empowering for historically oppressed peoples and help lay the groundwork for those who may later choose to confront oppressive governments more directly. OSI has sponsored conferences, workshops, and field visits for Arab activists to Eastern European countries, where they meet with veterans of earlier nonviolent pro-democracy campaigns. Together they address various topics, such as ways to deflect police harassment and abuse, how to manage fear and intimidation, and what works (or does not) in challenging repressive regimes.

Another form of external NGO support is through third-party nonviolent intervention, which has been used with limited success in the Israeli-occupied Palestinian territories. Christian Peacemaker Teams (CPT) has provided an international presence and engaged in nonviolent intervention in the West Bank since 1992, primarily in the city of Hebron and the nearby village of al-Tuwani. Among its efforts have been physically intervening when Israeli forces invade Palestinian homes, providing accompaniment for Palestinian children facing violence from Israeli settlers while walking to school, monitoring the treatment of Palestinians at Israeli military checkpoints and roadblocks, visiting Palestinian families facing threats and harassment from Israeli settlers, accompanying Palestinian farmers and shepherds prone to attacks in their fields by Israeli settlers, joining Israeli peace groups replanting orchards and vineyards destroyed by Israeli troops and settlers, and joining Palestinian and Israeli activists in resisting construction of the separation barrier on West Bank territory.

The International Solidarity Movement (ISM) engages in similar work, though it has a more explicit anti-occupation political orientation. Its actions have included confronting Israeli armored vehicles and demolition equipment, removing Israeli roadblocks, participating in nonviolent anti-occupation demonstrations, escorting ambulances through Israeli checkpoints, assisting injured or disabled Palestinians in gaining access to medical care, and delivering food and water to families under house arrest or curfew restrictions.

Both CPT and ISM have tried to influence international media coverage, provide a sense of international solidarity for nonviolent anti-occupation activists, and educate the public in volunteers' home countries upon their return. Though such efforts have yet to have a discernable impact on the foreign policies of the volunteers' governments, they have contributed to the internal debate and have increased awareness of the human rights issues, particularly within the religious community.

CPT initiated a presence in Iraq in October 2002, six months prior to the U.S.-led invasion and occupation. For the next year and half, its members focused primarily on documenting detainee abuses and violations of Iraqis' legal and human rights by U.S. occupation forces in Baghdad. The deteriorating security situation led to an end of the program in Baghdad in 2006 following the kidnapping of four international volunteers, one of whom—American Tom Fox—was murdered. CPT then relocated its violence-reduction work to Sulaymaniya, in the Kurdish-controlled north.

The growth in transnational NGOs focusing on human rights and the ease of real time communications have led to an enhanced role by outside actors in support of nonviolent resistance struggles in the Middle East and elsewhere. Members of these groups are able to transmit video documentation of attacks on nonviolent protesters by security forces, dispatch communiqués documenting the arrest of prominent nonviolent activists, and issue calls for international solidarity.

As with any outside assistance, problems are almost inevitable without an adequate understanding of the political, social, and cultural context of a struggle. For example, during Lebanon's Cedar Revolution in 2005, the global advertising agency Saatchi & Saatchi offered to print stickers and posters in support of the popular nonviolent movement. Lebanese activists developed a few designs for the campaign, but Saatchi & Saatchi insisted on funding their own design, which involved a figure closely resembling the Statue of Liberty. Perceiving a need for what amounted to free advertising for their cause, the Lebanese reluctantly accepted the offer, thereby opening themselves up to claims of being puppets of the United States because of their use of a symbol so closely resembling an American icon.

The growth of pan-Islamic organizations, some of which stress human rights and nonviolent struggle and possess far more credibility in the Middle East than do Western NGOs, may offer an additional avenue through which external actors can play a role in promoting nonviolent civilian jihad. For example, there is a growing consensus within some movements, including the Jordanian-based Islamic Action Front, Yemen's Reformist Union, and Egypt's al-Wasat, that Islamist ideals can best be advanced nonviolently and through principles of democracy, human rights, and the rule of law.[27]

Conclusion

Writing in the *Independent* in 2005, Iranian human rights activist and 2003 Nobel Peace Prize winner Shirin Ebadi observed, "Respect for human rights in any country must spring forth through the will of the people and as part of a genuine democratic process. Such respect can never be imposed by foreign military might and coercion—an approach that abounds in contradictions." Observing that "[i]t is hard not to see America's focus on human rights in Iran as a cloak for its larger strategic interests," Ebadi insists that "the most effective way to promote human rights in Iran is to provide moral support and international recognition to independent human rights defenders."[28] It is important to recognize that because nonviolent movements for human rights and democracy are by nature indigenous, homegrown phenomena, they cannot be controlled by external actors. That being said, it is still essential to examine more thoroughly what role outside actors can play in support of nonviolent movements, or at a minimum, what they can do to avoid doing harm. Unfortunately, there has been little in the way of empirical study on this issue, but a few tentative hypotheses can be made.

One positive role that outside actors can play is that of setting an example. The success of nonviolent struggles for democracy or against occupation in non-Western countries—including the predominantly Muslim nations of Indonesia, the Maldives, Mali, and Pakistan—often provide inspiration to other grassroots pro-democracy groups. Well-targeted sanctions, in consultation with indigenous pro-democracy activists, can potentially weaken the ability of the state to engage in repression, whereas more general sanctions that primarily harm the population would be counterproductive.

Given the history of Western intervention in the Middle East and ongoing support by Western states for allied autocratic regimes, most overt support for pro-democracy movements in other autocratic regimes in the region run the risk of backfiring; such support is widely viewed as being based on advancing the narrow strategic or economic interests of the outside power rather than the principled backing of democracy. The potential propaganda value whipped up by a regime in attempting to link foreign governmental support to indigenous pro-democracy movements can be minimized if the support is backed by a broad array of governments, such as through an intergovernmental organization that also includes non-Western powers and is not provided unilaterally.

Support by foreign governments for media outlets independent of state control and other less intrusive forms of intervention—such as offering space for opposition groups to meet, facilitating meetings between members of a regime and the opposition, supporting free and fair elections, and funding nonpartisan training for political parties and civil society organizations—can produce positive results. Such efforts should be pursued only after extensive consultation with an array of indigenous activists and country experts.

In politically sensitive environments, reputable NGOs acting in concert and in solidarity with indigenous NGOs are likely to be more effective than governments when engaging in capacity-building efforts. Increasing the number of Middle Easterners capable of leading workshops in strategic nonviolent action could be particularly beneficial, as would making films and educational materials on strategic nonviolent action more widely available in local languages. Independent, outside facilitators have the potential to bring together various opposition factions that could then develop a strategy on their own. Groups and individuals in exile and in the diaspora also have the potential to exert a positive influence, but their support should focus on bolstering broadly inclusive pro-democracy efforts rather than particular factions.

Although developing a better understanding of how outside actors can support nonviolent struggles for democracy is critically important, it is also essential to recognize that the United States and other Western governments continue to pour billions of dollars of sophisticated armaments into the Middle East, provide repressive governments and occupying armies with financial assistance, and maintain large armed forces that have themselves engaged in human rights abuses. It should thus be acknowledged that the need for sustained strategic nonviolent action in the Middle East is no less important than the need for nonviolent action in the United States and other Western nations to oppose policies that help sustain the region's violent and undemocratic status quo.

People living in Western industrialized democracies have far greater freedom to organize nonviolent action campaigns than do those living under autocratic regimes or occupation armies in the Middle East. This places a particular responsibility on Westerners who profess to support pro-democratic movements in that part of the world. Should such campaigns be successful in shifting Western policies in a more genuinely pro-democratic direction, it could prove to be a worthy and inspirational model for courageous democrats in the Middle East.

Notes

1. See Mohsen Sazegara and Maria J. Stephan's chapter in this volume (chapter 13).
2. See http://www.whereismyvote.org/ [Accessed 30 July 2009].
3. DigiActive, an all-volunteer nongovernmental organization dedicated to helping grassroots activists around the world, uses the Internet and mobile phones to increase their impact. DigiActive developed a handbook for activists on the strategic use of Facebook, which was translated into Arabic and used by Egyptian activists from the April 6 movement. See www.digiactive.org. For an analysis of the use of digital technologies by Egyptian activists, see David Wolman, "Cairo Activists Use Facebook to Rattle Regime," *Wired Magazine*, October 20, 2008, www.wired.com/techbiz/startups/magazine/16–11/ff_facebookegypt. Also see Sherif Mansour's chapter in this volume (chapter 14).
4. Thomas Carothers and Marina Ottaway, *Uncharted Journey: Promoting Democracy in the Middle East* (Washington, DC: Carnegie Endowment for International Peace, 2005), 5.

5. Cited in David DeBartolo, "Perceptions of U.S. Democracy Promotion: Middle Eastern and American Views," Project on Middle East Democracy Report, Washington, DC, May 2008, http://pomed.org/perceptions-of-us-democracy-promotion.
6. Cited by Noam Chomsky, *World Orders Old and New* (New York: Columbia University Press, 1997), 198–200. The Macmillan quote is from his book *At the End of the Day* (New York: Harper and Row, 1973).
7. Charles M. Sennott, "Doubts are Cast on the Viability of Saudi Monarchy for Long Term," *Boston Globe*, March 5, 2002.
8. Ibid.
9. Although the congressional resolution authorizing the U.S. invasion is best known for justifying the attack on the grounds that the Iraqi government possessed "weapons of mass destruction" (which had actually been destroyed years before), it also includes clauses citing the need to overthrow the Iraqi regime, because of its record of internal repression, and replace it with a democratic government.
10. White House Press Office, "President Outlines Steps to Help Iraq Achieve Democracy and Freedom," speech at the U.S. Army War College, Carlisle, PA, May 24, 2004.
11. White House Press Office, presidential news conference, Washington, DC, July 30, 2003.
12. See Stephen Zunes, "The Failure of Democratization in Iraq," *Foreign Policy in Focus*, March 14, 2007, www.fpif.org/fpiftxt/4071.
13. Arlen Parsa, "Iranians Oppose US 'Pro-Democracy' Efforts," *Truthout*, January 24, 2007, www.truthout.org/article/arlen-parsa-iranians-oppose-us-pro-democracy-efforts.
14. See Shadi Hamid's chapter in this volume (chapter 5).
15. Parsa, "Iranians Oppose US 'Pro-Democracy' Efforts."
16. Ibid.
17. National Iranian American Council, "Joint Letter to Congress Requesting Scrapping of Flawed 'Democracy Funds,'" October 11, 2007.
18. See, for example, Larry Diamond, *The Spirit of Democracy: The Struggle to Build Free Societies throughout the World* (New York: Times Books, 2008), particularly the chapters "Promoting Democracy Effectively," 314–344, and "Can the Middle East Democratize," 263–289 263–89; See also Carothers and Ottaway, *Uncharted Journey*.
19. Subsequently, however, the center's director, and co-author of this chapter, was again arrested. He currently lives in exile.
20. See P. Wallersteen, *International Sanctions: Between War and Words* (Abingdon, Oxon: Routledge, 2005) ; Gary Clyde Hufbauer, Jeffrey J. Schott, and Kimberly Ann Elliott, *Economic Sanctions Reconsidered*, 3rd ed. (Washington, DC: Peterson Institute, 2007); Stephen Zunes, "Are Iraqi Sanctions Immoral?" *Foreign Service Journal*, February 1999.
21. See Community of Democracies, *A Diplomat's Handbook for Democracy Development Support*, www.diplomatshandbook.org.
22. See Peter Ackerman and Michael J. Glennon, "The Right Side of the Law," The American Interest Online, www.the-american-interest.com/ai2/article.cfm?Id=313&MId=15.
23. Hong Kong Human Rights Monitor, interview with Boutros Boutros-Ghali, 2004, www.hkhrm.org.hk/english/booklets/eng_bk2.html.
24. Christine Spolar, "Egypt Reformer Feels Iron Hand of the Law," *Chicago Tribune*, March 6, 2006.
25. See, *A Diplomat's Handbook for Democracy Development Support* (Council for a Community of Democracies, 2008). *Note*: The Handbook is a "live" document whose case studies and tool kit are periodically updated by governmental and nongovernmental sources and experts. See www.diplomatshandbook.org.
26. See, for example, Guy Dinmore, "Bush Enters Debate on Freedom in Iran," *Financial Times, March 30, 2006;* Mark MacKinnon, *The New Cold War: Revolutions, Rigged*

Elections and Pipeline Politics in the Former Soviet Union (Toronto: Random House Canada, 2007).

27. See, for example, Amr Hamzawy, "The Key to Arab Reform: Moderate Islamists," Policy Brief 40, Carnegie Endowment for International Peace, August 2005.

28. Shirin Ebadi, "Attacking Iran Would Bring Disaster, Not Freedom," *Independent* (London), February 19, 2005

Part II

Case Studies

(a)

Challenging Foreign Occupation and Fighting for Self-Determination

8

The Muslim Pashtun Movement of the North-West Frontier of India, 1930–1934

Mohammad Raqib

After a violent and tumultuous history, the Pashtuns of the North-West Frontier Province (NWFP) of British India adopted nonviolent struggle to resist oppression and win freedom for their homeland during India's struggle for independence.[1] The Pashtuns, who live predominantly in Afghanistan and on the North-West Frontier area of the Indo-Pakistani subcontinent, are Muslim and have been often characterized as a brutal, backward, and tribal people. In 1848, when this area was taken over by Britain, the British divided it into two parts: the settled districts, which were under strict government control, and the tribal area, where the people lived their traditional lives with less outside interference, under the tribal *jirga* (council).[2] Later, the danger of Russia's approach to India and internal unrest in the NWFP concerned the British, and in 1893 they established the Durand Line to separate their empire from Russian influence.[3] The settled districts were under the administrative authority of the governor of Punjab, while the tribal areas were semi-independent.

British Administration and Ghaffar Khan's Early Work

In 1902, the British viceroy, Lord Curzon, brought the settled districts and tribal areas under one administrative unit and called it the North-West Frontier Province in an attempt to counter the internal and external challenges there. A series of measures were taken to suppress and counter antigovernment actions taking place there. In the settled districts, the Frontier Crimes Regulation, a set of laws widely seen as repressive and unfair, was adopted to fight antigovernment activities. The police were given the authority to destroy buildings that were used by anti-British elements. Authority to inflict collective punishment was also given to police to punish families, villages, or even whole communities for the acts of one person. In addition, the Tranquility Act was enacted in order to strictly control the people's right to assemble. The British undertook major expenses to build roads and railways to increase and assure the mobility of its strong military forces in order to control the NWFP.

Oppressive measures were taken by the government to counter the introduction of unwelcome political ideas and to bestow favors on particular religious leaders and others who were helping to improve the British image among the people. The expense of a large-scale police force and army in the NWFP was an unbearable burden on the settled districts, because the tribal areas did not pay taxes. As most of the province's budget was centered on financing the huge military, police, and other projects, social assistance, education, and sanitation did not receive enough attention. Only 25 out of 1,000 men, and a far lower percentage of women, were literate in 1911. This served the interests of the colonial authorities, who intentionally paralyzed political growth in the province. Political, social, and economic reforms that the British applied in other provinces of India were denied to the NWFP.

Khan Abdul Ghaffar Khan, the son of a well-respected landowner in a village near Peshawar, started his mission as a reformer in 1912. He opened schools throughout the districts of Mardan and Peshawar, seeking to educate the villagers and prepare them to understand the reforms that he intended to introduce. Soon this education movement spread to all parts of the NWFP. The British authorities resented these activities and warned Ghaffar Khan to cease his work, even pressuring his family to stop him. In 1919, when he ignored the warning, the government arrested him, his 95-year-old father—who was released after three months—and other members of his family. After serving a six-month sentence, Ghaffar Khan was released later that same year and received a warm welcome from his people. He joined the Khalifat movement, which began as a Muslim protest against British conduct in Turkey after World War I but later became a popular anti-British resistance struggle with Hindu participation.[4]

Ghaffar Khan soon returned to the NWFP to carry on with his work. He founded the organization Anjuman-Islah-e-Afaghina (Afghan Reform Society) to increase education and reform. The organization developed rapidly, and soon established branches throughout the province. Ghaffar Khan himself frequently traveled on foot to villages, educating the rural population. His reforms touched on various social problems. He appealed to his people to become involved in other kinds of work besides farming. To set an example, Ghaffar Khan opened a commission shop in his home village. He took these actions to convince the Pashtuns to live peaceful, productive lives, free from dependence on the British occupiers.

A New Strategy of Struggle

The government did not approve of Ghaffar Khan's work, and the chief commissioner of the North-West Frontier Province, Sir John Maffy, warned him to cease his activities or suffer the consequences. Ghaffar Khan ignored the warning and continued with his mission even more rigorously. By 1921, before being arrested once again and sentenced to a three-year term in one of the most notorious prisons in India, he had toured every village in the province and completed his goal of spreading his ideas to the villages surrounding Peshawar. In 1924, when Ghaffar Khan was released from jail, a huge gathering was summoned in his home village. Prominent workers and thousands of people from all districts of the province participated in the assembly and resolved to start a popular movement. During this meeting, in appreciation for his sacrifices, the people gave him the title of Fakhr-i-Afghan (Pride of the Afghans).

After attending the Grand Conference in Mecca in 1926,[5] Ghaffar Khan changed the strategy of his activities. With the support of his contemporaries, he founded the Pashtun Jirga (Pashtun Council). This body had a program centered on education, social, and political matters. Most of the members of the new organization were educated in schools run by Ghaffar Khan and others who were his long-time associates. The Pashtun Jirga also began publishing a journal called *Pashtun*. The new organization quickly gained momentum and, in 1929, a new contingent of volunteer members was added. This body was called the Khudai Khidmatgar (Servants of God). This group was designed to be the most efficient and orderly force among the Pashtuns. It later developed into a disciplined nonviolent army to fight for the independence of India from the British. Before being accepted into the Khudai Khidmatgars, the new recruits had to take the following pledge:

In the presence of God I solemnly affirm that:

1. I hereby honestly and sincerely offer myself for enrollment as a Khudai Khidmatgar.
2. I shall be ever ready to sacrifice personal comfort, property and even life itself to serve the nation and for the attainment of my country's freedom.
3. I shall not participate in factions, nor pick up a quarrel with or bear enmity towards anybody. I shall always protect the oppressed against the tyranny of the oppressor.
4. I shall not become a member of any other organization and shall not furnish security or tender apology in the course of the nonviolent struggle.
5. I shall always obey every legitimate order of my superior officer.
6. I shall always live up to the principle of nonviolence.
7. I shall serve all humanity equally. The chief object of my life shall be attainment of complete independence for my country and my religion.
8. I shall always observe truth and purity in all actions.
9. I shall expect no remuneration for my services.
10. All my services shall be dedicated to God; they shall not be for attaining rank or for show.[6]

A genuine popular movement, the Khudai Khidmatgar's main objectives were to win complete independence for India and drastically reform the social, political, and economic life of the Pashtuns while preserving Hindu-Muslim unity, all strictly within the framework of nonviolent means. Although it was a local resistance movement centered in the NWFP, the Khudai Khidmatgar was part of India's civil disobedience struggle and the Indian National Congress, the main nationalist party. The Khudai Khidmatgar pledged an informal cooperation with the broader struggle.

In December 1929, during the famous meeting of the Indian National Congress at Lahore, Jawaharlal Nehru—earlier an advocate of a violent war of liberation and later Prime Minister of India—declared the commitment of the Congress to obtain full independence for India. To achieve this objective, a major civil disobedience campaign was proclaimed. Ghaffar Khan as well as the vice president of the Provincial Congress Committee and other notable political leaders from the NWFP were also present at the conference. Ghaffar Khan approved the Congress plan, and in early 1930 the Peshawar Congress Committee announced that Ghaffar Khan and the Khudai Khidmatgar were its partners for the coming disobedience struggle. Ghaffar Khan traveled to key places in the province and urged the people of the NWFP, together with the Khudai Khidmatgar, to take part in the Congress civil disobedience campaign. In August 1931, the relationship became a formal alliance that continued until the day of India's independence, August 15, 1947.

Training, Volunteering, and Schooling

After being accepted in the Khudai Khidmatgar organization and taking the oath, individuals were required to participate in training camps, where they received instructions about the goals and programs of the movement. The reform programs demanded a considerable change in the cultural model of Pashtun society, so an elaborate program of training and instruction was prepared to be carried out in the training camps.[7] At the beginning, during the early 1930s, these camps were not well organized, but gradually they developed into an efficient system of training for potential resisters. Participants included Khudai Khidmatgar members, as well as others from the surrounding areas who wished to take advantage of the general educational courses offered by the camps.

The basic ideas of the reform operation were explained to new volunteers in the first meeting by Ghaffar Khan himself. Benefits of cleaning and sweeping houses and spinning one's own cloth were explained. Cleaning houses of nonmembers of the movement, in which high-ranking officials, as well as Ghaffar Khan himself, personally participated, was intended to render services and win the loyalty of the people. Working for and with one another improved unity and cooperation and set the groundwork for future nonviolent action. It was reasoned that such activities as digging, spinning, and cleaning, and other physically demanding work that was performed in the camps raised social and political awareness and taught discipline and hard work. Also, these activities psychologically prepared the volunteers for nonviolent struggle with the British. This idea of volunteer work was an integral part of the movement throughout the struggle, and would remain so even at the height of its civil disobedience campaign.

Opening schools where writing, reading, political awareness, cleaning, and sanitation could be taught was one primary task of the Khudai Khidmatgar. The schools also communicated to the public that one goal of the movement was to make the country self-sufficient, and therefore economically independent of the colonial power. In order to strengthen the nation's handloom weavers against imported British cloth, the Khudai Khidmatgar distributed *charkha* (spinning wheels) and taught people to spin thread. In a similar vein, pressing oil seeds for cooking oil and grinding wheat for flour to feed camp volunteers were considered important tasks for camp residents.

Participants were required to attend late afternoon meetings, where they were often joined by residents from nearby villages. In these meetings, anticolonial ideas and issues were addressed. Discussions centered on planning for action, the importance of unity among the people, information about prisons—such as how to survive and endure them—and, most important, the necessity of adhering to the organization's principle of nonviolent discipline. After one instance of violence, Ghaffar Khan fasted for three days to admonish the perpetrators.[8] Mukulika Banerjee reports that the persons who committed violence, including Ghaffar Khan's son Ghani, were dismissed from the movement. Such persons usually asked for a pardon but were readmitted only after at least three years of good behavior.[9] Also important at the meetings were poetry and skits to explain various concepts and ideas to the people. There was time for music and amusement.[10] The unity of all Pashtuns was emphasized, and as a precondition, members were asked to completely resolve all internal differences and feuds before joining the movement. "We are at war against the British for independence, but we have no weapons; our only weapon is patience. If you can fight this war, then wear a red uniform and come and join us," Ghaffar Khan said.[11]

A large tent was used for conducting general educational courses (as distinct from Khudai Khidmatgar training programs), holding meetings, and spinning thread. The Khudai Khidmatgar lived separately from other people under a policy of strict regulation. Here they performed their routine, military-style drills. Another large tent was used as a medical clinic, a mosque, and a supply depot. The usual routine for the Khudai Khidmatgar in the camp included drills, physical exercise, and running to prepare for long marches and daylong protests. Also included was practical instruction for proper cleaning and good sanitation in the camp. In addition, they took classes focused on political subjects, such as nationalist movements (with special attention to the history and duties of the Khudai Khidmatgar movement), and spinning raw cotton into threads and grinding wheat into flour to make bread for the camp.

Nonviolent Discipline: Red Shirts against the British Empire

Introducing and stressing to the Pashtuns the importance of maintaining non-violent discipline in the movement was a complicated task. The leadership of the Khudai Khidmatgar succeeded by serving others and practicing teamwork, preaching religious and moral principles, and strongly advocating the elimination of internal rivalries. One particular measure to promote adherence to nonviolent discipline in the movement was to administer the nonviolent Khudai Khidmatgar in the form of a military organization. Ranks and titles (captain, lieutenant, colonel, general, etc.) were used for officers, and the organization had units and subunits (company, brigade, etc.).[12] Members of the Khudai Khidmatgar were obligated to live under strict discipline and daily routines.

The strategy of organizing the Khudai Khidmatgar in a military style was not only desirable for the conduct of successful operations, but also proved that contrary to the characterization portrayed by the British, the Pashtuns, like all people, had the ability to organize themselves and establish self-government. The drills and long marches that resembled military activities were performed only to instill in the participants the importance of discipline, not as preparations for future violence, as some have suggested.

Ghaffar Khan stressed that the Pashtuns were "unable to defeat the British on the battlefield...[and instead] we were doing politics and that we had to defeat them politically."[13] Ghaffar Khan understood that a violent uprising by the Pashtuns could not be sustained because of the superior military capabilities of the British and the lack of resources and ammunition of the Pashtuns in the NWFP. Violence would only succeed in provoking further British atrocities and repression against them. On this he concluded, "Earlier, violence had seemed to me the best way to revolution...but experience taught me that it was futile to dig a well after the house was on fire."[14] That is, he was aware that the British had succeeded in firmly entrenching themselves in the NWFP militarily and otherwise, and that violent, military resistance would not be useful.[15] Before marching to demonstrations and picketing, the importance of maintaining nonviolent discipline was stressed and it was openly stated that those who intended to use violence should leave right away.

The Khudai Khidmatgar wore red uniforms, earning the nickname the Red Shirts. The name was intentionally introduced and spread by the British to be used as a substitute for the name "Khudai Khidmatgar," which had the connotation of religious piety and godliness. After popularizing the name Red Shirts, the government labeled the Khudai Khidmatgar as a communist or "quasi-fascist" group because not only did they wear red uniforms, but they were the only organization that advocated a policy of service without payment.[16] The communist charge was denied by the Khudai Khidmatgar, which stated that this was a very obvious attempt by the British to discredit the movement and raise alarm among anticommunist forces in both India and London. Furthermore, they asked how they could have "the slogans *Allah-O-Akbar* (God is great) in our demonstration and call ourselves Khudai Khidmatgar (the Servants of God)" and at the same time be followers of communism, an atheistic ideology. The Khudai Khidmatgar explained their reasoning for using the dark red color for uniforms: fabric of this color was very cheap and readily available in the area.[17] The authorities were not convinced, and the police often seized their uniforms and burned them. During 1931, the police confiscated and burned more than 1,200 Khudai Khidmatgar uniforms.[18]

"The technique of nonviolent confrontation was the very opposite of guerrilla campaigns," Mukulika Banerjee notes, "and in place of the Pathans' traditional use of stealth and camouflage, the Khudai Khidmatgar was a determinedly extroverted and highly visible presence."[19] The cooperation between the Muslim Khudai Khidmatgar and the predominantly Hindu Indian National Congress concerned the British, who persistently tried to sever this relationship. The British continually accused the Khudai Khidmatgar of being a "paramilitary group" and charged that they were fundamentally opposed to the Congress policy of nonviolent struggle. The British also took advantage of Hindu-Muslim difference by telling the pro-government *mullahs* (Muslim religious leaders) in the NWFP to call Ghaffar Khan and the Khudai Khidmatgar friends of Hindus. This misinformation campaign was used by the British to turn Pashtun opinion against the Khudai Khidmatgar and to label them as *kafir* (unbelievers). The interfaith unity made the colonial power so nervous that in the mid-1930s, they directed a great deal of time and effort toward creating the Muslim League and undermining the Red Shirt–Congress alliance.[20]

Methods of Nonviolent Struggle and Opposition

During the 1930–1934 civil disobedience campaigns, the Khudai Khidmatgar used the following methods:

- refusing to pay taxes or rent to the government
- picketing of government offices
- boycotting of foreign goods (cloth, etc.), and a full-scale boycott of liquor stores in Peshawar
- noncooperation with the government administration and contracted services, such as delivering mail
- refusing to settle criminal and civil cases in government courts, opting instead for village councils
- commemorating anniversaries of important events; for example, the massacre in the Kissa Khani Bazaar in Peshawar in April 1930, when 200 demonstrators were killed by troops under British command
- encouraging officials in the villages who worked as tax collectors or other state workers to resign or be socially ostracized[21]

In 1930, the Khudai Khidmatgar volunteers numbered around 1,000. By the end of 1931, this number had reached 25,000, and by 1938 membership had grown to more than 100,000.[22] During the 1930 civil disobedience campaign, thousands of Pashtuns of the NWFP participated in nonviolent picketing campaigns. The Khudai Khidmatgar included among their members Hindus, Sikhs, and women and preached a policy of inclusion of all people. In Bannu, 400 miles from Peshawar, women were involved in picketing and boycotting the institutions of the British rulers, including courts, police, army, tax offices, and schools.[23]

It was a common understanding among the Khudai Khidmatgar that there was no difference between the rich and poor in the struggle to oust the British from their land. The country belonged to both rich and poor, and people joined the movement for different reasons. Some were attracted to the organization for good business opportunities, others for economic improvement, and still others for non-economic reasons, like the call for unity and an eventual end to the British rule that was the root cause of the unjust situation. Despite the diversity of the members' backgrounds, after entering the Khudai Khidmatgar, they all strictly followed the movement's policy. The Khudai Khidmatgar were enormously popular among the population and with a great number of people who, although outside the organization, actively participated and supported the struggle.[24]

Some of the wealthy, landowning *khans* (tribal leaders) and others who benefited financially from the British opposed the Khudai Khidmatgar inside Pashtun society. The religious groups in the NWFP were divided in their support. One group of prestigious mullahs supported the Khudai Khidmatgar and had become members. Other groups opposed British rule, but favored traditional jihad and the use of violence; they criticized the nonviolent technique adopted by the Khudai Khidmatgar.[25] Although Ghaffar Khan had developed the idea of nonviolent struggle independently from Mohandas Gandhi, "nonviolence" was considered to be a Hindu concept. Another group of mullahs, mainly in rural areas, who received monetary compensation from the government preached obedience to the British government and discouraged people from antagonizing the government. Using fear of the military strength of the British, they told people that there was no use hitting their heads against the mountains.[26]

On April 23, 1930, one month after Gandhi's well-known Salt March, which defied the British Salt Law, a delegation of Indian National Congress officials was scheduled to arrive in Peshawar from Delhi to investigate complaints from the NWFP against government policies that were widely regarded as cruel and unjust. The grievances included, especially, complaints about the Frontier Crimes Regulation, the set of laws that targeted the Pashtuns.

A large gathering with several hundred Khudai Khidmatgar was waiting in Peshawar Station to receive the delegation, but they were told that the Indian National Congress committee had been detained in Punjab and denied entrance to the province. Outraged by the news, the Provincial Congress leaders staged a general demonstration and threatened the British authorities, asserting that they would start picketing liquor stores and foreign goods stores the following day.

During the demonstration, two police cars crashed into each other, causing a fire. Soldiers then began shooting at the resisters and continued without interruption for three hours. An estimated 200 people were killed.[27] According to other sources, the number of dead was in the "hundreds," with many wounded.[28] The government was determined to arrest Ghaffar Khan and some of his followers and charge them with "sedition and wrongful assembly." Ghaffar Khan was arrested that day and his journal, *Pashtun,* was banned.

The horror of the Kissa Khani Bazaar massacre (as the incident came to be called) shocked all of India. The British government appointed a committee to investigate, while at the same time making it very difficult for information about the matter to reach other provinces in India. The refusal of two platoons of the Royal Garhwal Rifles to fire on the peaceful and unarmed civilians further concerned the authorities and put in doubt the loyalty of the military forces. As a consequence, the disobedient soldiers were treated harshly, and each received a jail sentence of 10 to 14 years.[29]

Eventually, the news of the massacre managed to reach other provinces and regions of India. A new, higher-level commission of the Indian National Congress was established to investigate the massacre, but it too was prevented from entering the province. The commission therefore started its work in Rawalpindi in Punjab, far from the scene. The Congress report revealed that during the Kissa Khani Bazaar incident, the "Peshawaris demonstrated a high standard of heroism, love for their country, and were consistent with the spirit of nonviolence."[30]

The incident forced the British to withdraw from Peshawar because of the inability of its limited number of forces in the NWFP to control the angry city after the massacre of peaceful, unarmed people.[31] The Provincial Congress essentially took over the city for nine days. At the same time, the activities of the Khudai Khidmatgar and the difficulties of travel and communication crippled the government's rule in much of the adjacent rural areas for more than two months.[32]Soon false news spread throughout the NWFP and the surrounding region that the British were abandoning the entire province and even leaving India.

Repression and Violent Resistance

On May 3, the British declared the Provincial Congress and the Khudai Khidmatgar to be illegal. The following morning the city of Peshawar was surrounded by reinforcement troops, and government control over the city was restored. Congress activists were arrested, and a curfew was imposed on all movement for 24 hours.

Although nonviolent discipline was strongly stressed by the Khudai Khidmatgar leadership and was strictly observed by its members, violence was not completely eliminated from the struggle. The earlier killings of the nonviolent Khudai Khidmatgar in Peshawar provoked the population and tribes against the British, and occasionally they reacted by using violence. Sometimes, violence occurred in the tribal regions, carried out by individuals unaffiliated with the Khudai Khidmatgar organization, and also in some rural areas. This violence produced a brutal response from the government. Although the British justified their use of violence in the NWFP by a propaganda campaign that sought to portray the Pashtuns as a rebellious group that favored the use of violence, the people of the province proved themselves otherwise during the Kissa Khani Bazaar massacre, when for the most part they remained nonviolent in face of the most brutal actions against them.[33]

On May 30, in the village of Takar, in Mardan district, the villagers attempted to prevent the arrest of the Khudai Khidmatgar leaders in their area and marched with them as they were led toward the district center.[34] A small group of police intervened to stop their procession. During the confrontation, an English police officer was killed. Three days later, in retaliation, the police attacked the village and killed several individuals. The original objective of the British authorities in arresting the Khudai Khidmatgar officials was to provoke a violent response from the villagers and find justification for the government's continued suppression and atrocities.

Bannu was the second largest area of resistance, after Peshawar. A combination of clergy, tribal chiefs, and politicians from the cities kept the antigovernment uprising alive. On August 24, 1930, a large gathering convened in Spin Tangi, in Bannu district, although many people were prevented from assembling by the government. At the meeting, a British soldier fired on Qazi Fazil Qadr, a prominent local leader. Even though there was a strong commitment to nonviolent discipline among the participants, a very small number of people had weapons, and a fight broke out. When the fighting stopped, the government had arrested 300 people, killed 80, and wounded many more. During the fighting, a British captain was killed with swords and axes. Qazi Fazil Qadr was taken to the police station, where the deputy commissioner taunted him to give an anti-British statement. He was too weak, however, and passed away. The British sentenced him posthumously to 14 years imprisonment, buried him in Bannu prison, and refused to release his body to his family for the required religious funeral.[35]

During 1931, the tribes in Peshawar Valley and Waziristan further complicated the government's problem. For example, the Afridis—the largest single Pashtun tribe and skilled in warfare—twice violently invaded Peshawar. Starting on 7 August, they paralyzed the government for 12 days. The violent uprising forced the viceroy to declare martial law in Peshawar district on 16 August. The tribal revolt was an unsolicited response to the government's atrocities against the nonviolent protestors in Peshawar. The Afridis continued scattered raids until October 1931.

In December 1931, while Gandhi was negotiating with the British government in London at the Roundtable Conference, the authorities increased their pressure in the NWFP. The Provincial Congress and the Khudai Khidmatgar were banned. Ghaffar Khan and other leaders were jailed, and strict control was placed on the Khudai Khidmatgar and its antigovernment activities. The police and the army were given unlimited power to crush the Khudai Khidmatgar, and they often fired on protesters, killing and injuring many of them.[36] Gandhi returned from London on 28 December, docking in Bombay. The day of his arrival, Gandhi declared in a public speech, "Last year we faced *lathis* [steel-shod bamboo rods], but this time we must be prepared to face bullets. I do not wish that the Pathans in the Frontier alone should court bullets. If bullets are to be faced, then Bombay and Gujarat also must take their share."[37] Gandhi attempted to talk to the viceroy about the imprisonment of Ghaffar Khan and the crackdown on the Khudai Khidmatgar, but was ignored.

The massacre of Kissa Khani Bazaar and its aftermath shocked the British. The deputy commissioner was blamed for failing to accurately perceive the situation in the NWFP before the event. The local government was accused of inaction against the growing danger of the Khudai Khidmatgar. In an attempt to repair the damage caused by the massacre and to appease the people, the colonial government increased financing for education, health and agriculture, and veterinary medicine. Later, in 1932, the government also replaced the chief commissioner with the power of governor, bringing the NWFP to the same level of administration as other provinces of India. Urban and rural elections slowly followed.

Although the Khudai Khidmatgar movement had won some short-term successes, the government had more brutal designs for the NWFP in the form of propaganda, torture, and suppression. Following the Kissa Khani Bazaar tragedy, the government launched its intensified propaganda war against the Khudai Khidmatgar and accused it of being a paramilitary group for wearing uniforms, drilling, and organizing like a military establishment. The Khudai Khidmatgar rejected the charges.

To prevent incidents like that of the Kissa Khani Bazaar, the British were determined to use extreme force in order to terrify the population from rising against
their authority. Various means of harsh repression were inflicted. Houses were
burned, and stocks of grain were destroyed. According to an American tourist,
"gunning the red shirts was a popular sport and pastime of the British forces in the
province."[38] Members of the Khudai Khidmatgar were unclothed and forced to run
down the middle of rows of British soldiers while being kicked and jabbed with rifle
muzzles and bayonets. They were thrown from rooftops into filthy ponds, often in
extremely cold temperatures. Torture, often to the point of causing serious physical and psychological damage to the individuals, was prevalent.[39] Banerjee also
reports that women's *purdah* was sometimes verbally and physically violated.[40]
Male prisoners were sometimes exposed to overnight extreme cold and stripped in
front of women; some were castrated and sexually abused.[41]

From April 1930 to December 1932, the British jailed 12,000 Khudai Khidmatgar members who allegedly took part in demonstrations and picketing. In
Haripur jail alone, 7,000 Khudai Khidmatgar were imprisoned under extremely
harsh conditions, sleeping on the floor with two worn blankets in severely cold
temperatures. Members were forced to march in Peshawar city in their bare feet in
pajamas.[42] Forced labor was another method of punishment, particularly when the
prisons were full. The prisoners were taken to various work sites to perform hard
labor. They were ill fed, they slept on site, and they were eventually sent home without payment. There were also reports, cited by Banerjee, that the authorities paid
agents to poison food in the Khudai Khidmatgar training camps.[43] The villagers of
the settled districts who helped the Khudai Khidmatgar were also targeted, and in
1932 some 92 villages were fined a total of 20,000 rupees.

Civil Disobedience Suspended

In April 1934, Gandhi suspended the civil disobedience struggle all over India, and
the government freed all Congress activists from jails in most of India. By this time,
the civil disobedience movement had lost its effectiveness. The Khudai Khidmatgar
and the Provincial Congress leaders were not included in the amnesty. The activities of these organizations remained prohibited.

When Ghaffar Khan and his brother were released in 1935, they were not permitted to enter the NWFP. The authorities almost instantly subjected Ghaffar Khan
to another laborious two-year sentence for giving "antigovernment and seditious
speeches" in the Punjab. After some six years of imprisonment, the leader of Khudai
Khidmatgar returned to his home in November 1937. At the time, the political
environment was relaxed, and the government had allowed some political reforms.
The civil disobedience struggle of the previous years was eventually replaced by
electoral party politics as the relationship between India and the British Empire
entered a new phase during the years preceding partition and independence.[44]

Notes

This chapter is based on the chapter of the same title from *Waging Nonviolent Struggle:
20th Century Practice and 21st Century Potential* (Boston: Porter Sargent, 2005). Research
assistance for this chapter was provided by Jamila Raqib. This chapter has only been modified slightly.

1.   They are also called Pushtuns or Pathans.
2.   The Pashtuns themselves refer to the region as Pashtunistan, or the Land of the Pashtuns.

3. The Durand Line formed the border between Afghanistan and British India.
4. Mukulika Banerjee, *The Pathan Unarmed* (Oxford and Karachi: Oxford University Press, 2000), 49. In 1920, Ghaffar Khan participated in the Khalifat flight to Afghanistan, where he met Afghan king Amanullah Khan.
5. The conference was organized by the king of Saudi Arabia, Sultan Ibn Saud, during the Hajj to discuss problems facing Muslim nations. On this occasion, Ghaffar spoke to the delegations of many nations, whose views greatly increased his understanding of the dilemma of colonized nations.

    After performing Hajj, Ghaffar Khan visited other parts of the Middle East, including Egypt, Iraq, Lebanon, Palestine, and Syria. During meetings with the subjects of these nations, he found that it was the vast resources of India that enabled the British to keep these nations under control. He concluded that independence of India from the British would also free other nations from the grip of this colonial power. Indian soldiers had not only fought for the British in World War I (and would go on to fight for them in World War II in the coming decades), but they also fought many wars in Africa, China, the Far East, as well as the Middle East. He stated, "Therefore, at the same time we are slaves ourselves, we are the means of enslaving others as well, from this point we should develop our strategy of non-cooperation with our alien ruler, to free ourselves from its oppression and also help other oppressed nations to liberate themselves." Mohammad Yunus, *Frontier Speaks* (Bombay: Hind Kitabs, 1947), 11.
6. Pyarelal [Nair], *A Pilgrimage for Peace: Gandhi and Frontier Gandhi among N.W.F.P. Pathans* (Ahmedabad, India: Navajivan, 1950), 50.
7. The idea of the "unruly" Pashtun masses as an organized and unified movement not only surprised outsiders, but also required a change in the way Pashtuns viewed themselves. The issue of violence was closely attached to honor, which in turn was deeply embedded within Paskhtunwali. Rejecting the use of violence was closely linked to notions of financial self-sufficiency, family pride, and individual autonomy. The Pashtuns' acute sensitivity to insults and the egalitarianism of Pashtun society did not lend themselves to the emergence of a disciplined hierarchically organized army of activists. Also, an extremely heightened sense of individualism made it difficult for people to cooperate with one another or to offer or accept assistance. The prevalence of fatalism and discouragement led many to believe (with reinforcement by religious leaders) that they should simply bear their difficulties in the hopes of a better afterlife. The movement required that ordinary people begin to think that they themselves could improve their conditions.
8. Banerjee, *The Pathan Unarmed*, 121.
9. Ibid., 121–22.
10. Ibid., 75–76.
11. Ibid., 80.
12. It is important here to note that leadership in the organization was democratic. Candidates were nominated to their various positions and elections were held.
13. Banerjee, *The Pathan Unarmed*, 81, as reported by Mukarram Khan.
14. Ibid, 49.
15. Ibid.
16. Ibid., 105.
17. Ibid., 103–7.
18. Ibid., 88.
19. Ibid., 87.
20. Ibid., 111.
21. Ibid., 73–102.
22. Ibid., 60.
23. Ibid., 93.
24. Pyarelal, *A Pilgrimage for Peace*, 37.
25. Jihad, Muslim struggle, is usually interpreted as "holy war."

26. Banerjee, *The Pathan Unarmed*, 109.

27. Ibid., 57.

28. Yunus, *Frontier Speaks*, 117.

29. These soldiers' release was not included in the negotiated Gandhi-Irwin Pact in March 1931, so they served their full prison terms. See Yunus, *Frontier Speaks*, 118; and Gene Sharp, *Gandhi Wields the Weapon of Moral Power* (Ahmedabad, India: Navajivan, 1960), 196.

30. Jawaharlal Nehru compared the British atrocities in the NWFP with the first Indian war of independence in 1857, when the British slaughtered thousands, and also with the massacre of Jallianwalla Bagh, in Amritsar, Punjab, in 1919, when General Reginald Dyer's troops, by official count, killed 379 unarmed people and wounded another 1,137 during a peaceful gathering.

31. Stephen Alan Rittenberg, *Ethnicity, Nationalism, and the Pashtuns* (Durham, NC: Carolina Academic Press, 1988), 84.

32. Ibid., 66.

33. Banerjee, *The Pathan Unarmed*, 58. There were some acts of violence against individual British soldiers in the streets in addition to raids of administrative buildings and attacks on military posts.

34. The Pashtun have a tradition of giving sanctuary to someone in trouble in their territory.

35. Banerjee, *The Pathan Unarmed*, 195.

36. In Kohat Valley, 50 demonstrators were killed during protests.

37. S. W. A. Shah, *Ethnicity, Islam and Nationalism: Muslim Politics in the North West Frontier Province, 1937–47* (Oxford and Karachi: Oxford University Press, 1999), 36 and 49 n. 79.

38. Yunus, *Frontier Speaks*, 118.

39. Pyarelal, *A Pilgrimage for Peace*, 50.

40. Purdah is the traditional Muslim and Hindu practice of seclusion and veiling of women.

41. Banerjee, *The Pathan Unarmed*, 118–19.

42. Ibid., 111.

43. Ibid., 114.

44. Ibid., 71.

9

Noncooperation in the Golan Heights: A Case of Nonviolent Resistance

R. Scott Kennedy

Here is a modern day example of a nonviolent campaign, of a people very small in number, facing incredibly powerful odds militarily, saying, "We don't have a military option. It doesn't pay for us to throw rocks or stones. We can never 'out violence' the Israeli army. But we can— through unity, cooperation and taking a principled stand, and accepting suffering—just refuse to cooperate and withhold our consent, and reasonably come to a solution that reserves and preserves our own rights and interests, at least in some measure."

—Jonathan Kuttab, Palestinian human rights lawyer,
interview, January 1983, Jerusalem

The Syrian Druze of the Golan Heights are a distinct Arab population in the Middle East whose tenets "developed in the eleventh century as an offshoot of the *Isma'illiya*, itself a radical fringe of Shiite Islam."[1] In the face of centuries of persecution at the hands of orthodox Sunni Muslims and the more mystical Shiites, "the Druze developed the concept of *taqiya*—camouflage—keeping their religious communal identity secret."[2] This communal secrecy is reinforced by a prohibition on marriage outside of the sect, insistence that one must be born a Druze and cannot through conversion become Druze, and restraint from proselytizing.

The Arab Druze eventually settled more easily defensible mountainous areas in the southern parts of the Mt. Lebanon range in what is now Lebanon and Syria and the Carmel range in Israel. In the mid-1980s, there were 580,000 Druze throughout the world: 300,000, mostly in the Chouf mountains of Lebanon; 13,000 in the Golan Heights of Syria; 50,000 to 60,000 on Israel's Mount Carmel; 27,000 in the United States; and small groups in Jordan and India.[3]

The Druze proved themselves a tight-knit, fiercely independent, politically flexible, pragmatic, and sometimes militant force in Middle Eastern politics— all important attributes for a minority religious sect in sometimes hostile host countries. According to Hebrew University's Moshe Sharon, the Druzes' "history as a small, persecuted sect within the world of Islam can be summed up in two enduring principles: the survival of the community and the exclusivity of territory. Over the centuries, the Druze have developed the military prowess to ensure both."[4]

Arab Druze from the Golan were among the leaders in the struggle in Syria against French colonial rule. Arab Druze began to be conscripted into the Israel Defense Forces (IDF) shortly after the creation of the Jewish state in 1948 through an accommodation reached between Israeli authorities and the Druze community's traditional leadership. The Druze are known to be among the toughest soldiers in the IDF and often serve in the elite Border Patrol units.

In the wake of Israel's invasion of Lebanon in June 1982, the Druze living in Lebanon became a key element in the Lebanese National Movement, a leftist coalition. Walid Jumblatt, the leader of the Druze in Lebanon and head of the Progressive Socialist Party, generally represented, and continues to represent, the Druze in negotiations in Lebanese politics. Receiving much less publicity than the Druze in the IDF and in Lebanon are the Syrian Druze villagers in the Golan Heights who waged a courageous and effective nonviolent campaign against the Israeli occupation in spring 1982. In a region and a conflict often characterized by violence, the Arab Druze of the Golan demonstrated the power and efficacy of nonviolent resistance as a method of social struggle that can be utilized by unarmed civilians confronted with overwhelming police and military force.

Occupation and Identification

The Golan Heights sit on Israel's northeastern corner as a plateau rising dramatically above the Galilee bounded by Lebanon to the northwest, Syria to the north and east, and Jordan to the south. The Druze have farmed the region for generations and are famous for the olives and apples they produce within sight of Mt. Hermon's snowy slopes. Israel considers the Golan strategically vital. From 1948 to 1967, Syrian soldiers from the Hula Valley fired down on Israeli kibbutzim and towns that encroached on areas declared a no-man's land in the 1948 ceasefire.[5] The slopes of Mt. Hermon came to be called Fatahland, because Palestinian guerrillas took advantage of its terrain to infiltrate into Israel.

During and soon after the 1967 Arab-Israeli war, in which Israel captured the Golan, some 110,000 Syrians living there either fled or were forced from their homes. Nearly 13,000 Arab Druze citizens of Syria refused to leave their handful of villages at the foot of Mt. Hermon near the headwaters of the Jordan River. Like the other Israeli-occupied territories—the West Bank, Gaza Strip, and East Jerusalem—since 1967 the Golan has undergone a continual and systematic process of annexation, not least in economic terms, to the state of Israel.[6] Many Druze work as day laborers in the factories and agricultural settlements of northern Israel. Israelis have settled on land confiscated from the Druze and absentee Syrian landowners and claimed major sources of water for their exclusive use. Other sources of water have been diverted for use in Israel.

For a decade, the Golan was frozen in its status as militarily occupied land. Following the U.S.-brokered Camp David Accords between Israel and Egypt in 1979, Israel pressured Syria to join the peace process or risk losing the Golan permanently. The United States tacitly supported this maneuvering by de-emphasizing and eventually dropping the Golan from its list of topics for discussion in negotiations about the return of territories occupied by Israel in 1967. In 1979, the Israeli Knesset passed a law making Jerusalem its capital. This action provoked widespread opposition in most countries, including in the United States. The international community rejected Israel's unilateral annexation of Arab land beyond its pre-1967 borders. On the Golan, Israel began de facto assimilation to avoid the harsh and nearly unanimous criticism along the lines of that elicited by its actions concerning Jerusalem. Israel seemed to be following David Ben Gurion's dictum: "What matters is not what the Gentiles will say, but what the Jews will do."[7] Israeli leaders thought that providing citizenship to the Druze would blunt criticism of the gradual annexation of the occupied Golan. Beginning in 1979, they made it known that Golani Druze could ask for Israeli citizenship, promising favored treatment to those choosing it. Most Druze rejected the offer, viewing citizenship as a portent of the eventual annexation of the Golan to the Jewish state.

According to Jonathan Kuttab, "The Israeli policy was to attempt to drive a wedge between them as Druze and between other Muslims or Arabs. 'You are Druze but not Arabs.' "[8] This policy had worked in Israel, where a "divide and rule" approach sharply distinguished Druze from other Arabs. In the 1950s, the Israelis had offered to help Lebanese Druze leader Kamal Jumblatt set up an independent Druze buffer state between Israel and Lebanon and Syria.[9] Many of the residents who remained in the Golan after Israel's occupation in 1967, partly in reaction to this attempt at "divide and rule," insisted on their identification as Arabs. According to one resident of Majd al-Shams, "We in the Golan do not like to be called Druze in the political frame. We are Arabs by nationality, Syrians by citizenship, and Moslems that belong to the Druze offshoot."[10]

Israel tried to entice Golani Druze into accepting Israeli identification from 1979 until the end of 1981. Some Druze workers in Israel lost their jobs or faced harassment for resisting the measure. Opposition solidified among the Druze, and those who accepted identity cards were often shunned by the entire community. According to Palestinian journalist Daoud Kuttab, "[The Druze] decided that anyone who accepts Israeli identity cards is really cutting themselves off from the community: 'They are no longer one of us, no longer a Druze.' "[11] Few would speak to or enter the homes of Druze with Israeli identification. They were not welcomed at religious gatherings or invited to such events as weddings or funerals. Their dead were denied the community's prayers. Such tremendous social pressure guaranteed that all but a few diehards returned their cards. Those who recanted were required to do so publicly, going door-to-door to apologize to their neighbors or contributing money to support the families of Druze imprisoned by Israel.

Other incentives reinforced Druze resistance. Their political sympathies generally favored the Palestinian and Arab cause—most had relatives living in Syria, some of whom were prominent officers in the army—and they did not want to serve in the IDF, like Israeli Druze, and end up fighting their kin and coreligionists. In addition, Jordan had recently declared as traitors any Palestinians cooperating with the Israeli-backed collaborationist Village Leagues in the West Bank. Many Druze remained confident that the Golan would eventually be returned to Syria and expected similar harsh treatment by Syrian authorities should they cooperate with the Israelis.

Annexation Feeds Resistance

On December 14, 1981, in a sharp departure from normal parliamentary procedure, Prime Minister Menachem Begin's ruling Likud coalition forced through the

Knesset the requisite three readings and final passage of legislation to formally annex the Golan. The unprecedented speed with which the legislation passed prevented debate and organized opposition. Annexation abrogated Syrian sovereignty, denied national self-identification to the people still living in or who had fled from the Golan, and defied the declared U.S. position on the status of the occupied territories as well as the international community's stance toward them.

With formal annexation, the Druze would be forced to accept Israeli identification. The Druze petitioned, but to no avail, for a reversal of the Knesset's action. They then pronounced their intent not to cooperate with any attempt to be convinced or coerced into adopting Israeli citizenship. "We're not fighting Israel; we cannot.... We're not against Israel's security interests. Israel can do whatever it wants to us: they can confiscate our land. They can kill us. But they cannot tell us who we are. They cannot change our identity."[12]

Druze laborers refused to work, crippling industry in northern Israel for several weeks. Many lost their jobs. As previously, those who accepted Israeli IDs were ostracized. Israeli authorities placed nine "ringleaders" of resistance under administrative detention (imprisonment without trial). They also fabricated press reports that the Druze had abandoned their resistance efforts, but as more became known of their struggle, an astonishing story of nonviolent resistance was revealed.

When one village ran short on food, residents of a neighboring village walked *en masse* to deliver food to it. The villagers overwhelmed, in sheer number, the IDF soldiers who had been deployed to isolate the village. The elderly and young violated strict curfews to harvest crops. The arrest of elders created intensified resolve among the villagers. When soldiers arrested some of the children and carried them away in helicopters, even more ran out into the fields, hoping to get a ride.

In another incident, groups of women surrounded Israeli soldiers, wrested at least sixteen weapons from them, and handed the guns over to army officers while suggesting that the forces be removed. Guns sometimes were exchanged for the release of jailed Druze. Villagers once locked several soldiers inside a stable and took the keys to the commanding officer; they told the officer where the soldiers were and suggested that he free them and send them home. In another episode, Israeli soldiers reportedly refused direct orders to fire from helicopters on Druze villagers protesting in a town square.

One village took advantage of Druze laborers on strike from jobs in Israel to complete a major sewer project for which Israel had refused funds and permits for years. A "strike-in-reverse" resulted in trenches being dug and pipelines installed. Villagers also began developing cooperative economic structures, such as sending the entire community out to spray trees with the understanding that the crops would be shared by all. They even began to set up their own schools as alternative institutions.

At one point, rumors circulated that Israel planned to erect a fence around Majd al-Shams and return the Druze village to Syrian control. The villagers joked, "If they do that, we will have succeeded in liberating Arab territory for the first time since 1948. Where all the Arab armies have failed, at least we might liberate this one little section of land. Why not?"[13] After four months of negotiations between village leaders and the Israeli government, a victory for civilian noncooperation seemed within grasp. The Druze were led to believe that on April 1, 1982, the government effort to force citizenship upon them would end. Instead, the Israelis escalated the situation with outright repression.

Approximately 15,000 Israeli soldiers swarmed the Golan. They seized schools for military camps and sealed the territory. They also cut electricity and water to villages and destroyed several homes. Nine people were wounded when soldiers broke up a demonstration, and at least two people died because blockades disrupted ambulance service to nearby hospitals. Another 150 people were arrested on each of several days; 14 Druze received four-to-five-month prison sentences. Most received fines for failing to produce Israeli identification upon demand. The Israeli press, members of the Knesset, lawyers representing the Druze, and international observers were denied access to the Golan as Israel imposed a state of siege that would last 43 days.

Israeli troops went door-to-door, forcing entry, and confiscated villagers' identification papers from the period of Syrian rule or military occupation and left Israeli identification papers behind. On following mornings, the town squares of the various villages would be littered with Israeli identity cards. The Druze had refused, under direct and immediate threat of personal harm and communal suppression, to accept Israeli identification. As a result, the Israeli government eventually relented and lifted the siege, withdrawing its troops, dismantling checkpoints, and leaving the Druze alone. Druze resistance to the imposition of Israeli citizenship continued, nonetheless, at a reduced level of intensity, until the June 1982 Israeli invasion of Lebanon. The Druze adopted a "wait-and-see" attitude on July 19, 1982, when they agreed to suspend the strike "after Galilee Druze leaders [in Israel] said that the government would negotiate with the Druze community regarding their demands."[14]

According to the Palestinian English-language weekly *al-Fajr*, which covered the Golan situation at length, "The popular consensus in July 1982 was to accept the Israeli compromise...which stated that the Israeli government [would] not interfere with the residents' basic civil, water and land rights, and [would] not impose army service on youths."[15] Israel promised Golan residents identity cards specially designed with the term "Arab" (rather than "Druze") printed next to "nationality." This addressed the primary concern of Druze, such as activist Suleman Fahr Adin of Majd al-Shams: "The Druze is one sect of the Islamic movement, not a nation. We are a religious sect, not more."[16] The agreement was short-lived. According to Daoud Kuttab,

> [T]he formula regarding the acceptance of Israeli ID cards failed because the Israeli government did not honor its promises to find an alternative solution for the [residents without identity cards]....Forced by the lack of action on the [part of the] Israeli government, most Golan residents have unwillingly taken ID cards, primarily in order to travel to their work. Most residents compare their situation to East Jerusalem, which, like the Golan, was annexed by Israel against the will of its residents. The Golanis point out that Palestinians of East Jerusalem [who] have not become Israeli citizens are not allowed to vote in the Israeli Knesset elections unless the residents make a separate application requesting citizenship. Only 300 of Jerusalem's 120,000 residents have applied for and accepted it to date.[17]

Other conditions of the agreement were also not fulfilled, including commitment to the acknowledgment that the ownership of land is indisputable, that there would be no Israeli interference with the Golan water sources, that there would be open bridges to Syria and freedom to sell local produce there, and assurances that there would be no transfer of land ownership in times of war or peace. Although the Golani residents were spared the income tax and "value added tax" that Israelis are obliged to pay, they were forced to pay an "Operation Peace for Galilee" tax to offset the costs of the 1982 invasion of Lebanon. The Druze continued to struggle with Israeli authorities over confiscation of land and denial of water rights. They attempted to strengthened their autonomy by establishing their own, alternative institutions, including medical clinics and a college.

It is difficult to know how the strike would have played out had the war in Lebanon not intervened. Although one Druze villager suggested that the Druze had followed Gandhi's example and suspended the strike, rather than take unfair advantage of the Israelis' fighting elsewhere, most scoffed at this assertion, arguing that no further concessions could have been won with the war in progress. According to the *Jerusalem Post*, "Operation Peace for Galilee put an end to the strike without further fuss. The government and the press no longer had time for Druze demands."[18]

Twelve Golani Druze arrested during the spring 1982 strike filed a formal appeal before the Israeli High Court of Justice contesting the law requiring Israeli identification for Golanis. The court rejected the appeal on May 22, 1983, ruling that issuing identity cards to Golani Druze was "a technical issue which is necessary to running the affairs of the local residents in the administered territories." The decision finessed the legal status of the residents of the Golan Heights without ruling whether the territory had been legally annexed or made part of Israel and avoided the key issue of Druze nationality.

Meanwhile, the Druze of the Golan continued their noncooperation, simply carrying on their affairs without any kind of legal identification, a particularly courageous posture given Israel's practice of harassing, imprisoning, or deporting Arabs who do not possess proper identification. In one instance, five Druze villagers were arrested for not carrying identity cards and put on trial. In response, all the villagers turned themselves in and demanded that they too be tried because they were equally guilty.

Roots of Success

In August 1983, the *Jerusalem Post* reported, "The prolonged and bitter dispute within the Golan Druze community over the issue of Israeli identity cards ended unexpectedly at a modest ceremony earlier this month when Druze clergymen pledged to lift the religious and social ban imposed on those who had accepted Israeli identity cards.... It remains to be seen whether this step will be accompanied by a change in the government's attitudes [toward] the local Druze population in the Golan."[19] Other sources reported that the Druze community had not lifted its social and religious ban on Druze with Israeli citizenship. According to Druze leader Shaykh Ahmad Qadamani, "Nothing has changed in the attitudes of Golan Heights residents against the Israeli occupation and the law annexing the Golan Heights. They still maintain their loyalty to their homeland, Syria."[20]

On September 23, 1983, a special gathering was held in the Golan one week after the death of Kamal Kanj Abu Saleh, the spiritual head of the Golani Druze and a leader of the strike who had been jailed in 1982. A funeral procession from Majd al-Shams drew an estimated 15,000 people on the Syrian side of the cease-fire line and 20,000 Golani Druze and supporters on the Israeli-occupied side. Lebanese Druze leader Walid Jumblatt and Khaled Fahoum, chair of the Palestine National Council, addressed the large crowd, praising the Golani Druze for their 1982 strike. The Druze had convincingly demonstrated the power of concerted nonviolent action in the face of tremendous odds and harsh and repressive military action.

Several unique factors had contributed to the relative success of the Golani Druze's nonviolent action campaign. Few populations have so distinctive a community identity as the Druze, enabling them to act largely as a unit, as though by virtue of group instinct. One Israeli scholar likens "the Druze 'communal identity' [or] their communal link to that which binds Jews throughout the world.... When it comes down to Druze survival, the communal bond cuts through national boundaries."[21] The strike was also conducted on a relatively small scale: four villages of less than 13,000 people. Application of the same methods with a larger and less tightly knit population would be an entirely different proposition.

The Golani Druze benefitted from the unique position of the Israeli Druze being able to serve in the Israeli army and expressing solidarity with their Golani coreligionists. At one point, a military parade held annually in the Israeli Druze villages on Mt. Carmel was canceled because of boycotts planned in solidarity with the Druze of the Golan. Israeli officials, anticipating the invasion of Lebanon, felt pressure to defuse the crisis in the Golan because they knew Israeli Druze soldiers and Lebanese Druze were certain to be involved. Israel clearly feared further alienating the Israeli Druze.

Although some Israeli Druze think their community's support for the Golani Druze was sentimental and sectarian, rather than political, there was concern in Israel nonetheless about a growing tendency among Israeli Druze to identify with the Palestinian cause, even to the point of refusing military service.[22] A small but vocal sector of Israeli Jewish society also spoke out in defense of the Golani Druze's civil and human rights and opposed the annexation. The Israeli government, ultimately, could compromise with the Druze without paying too great a price. The Golanis were not demanding liberation from Israeli occupation. They simply sought a return to the status quo ante.

The unique aspects of the Druze's struggle may temper enthusiasm about their apparent success or qualify the applicability of their struggle to other situations. Nevertheless, a great deal can still be learned from their use of nonviolent resistance. The Golan Druze demonstrated the advantage and the power of organizing nonviolent struggle around realistic objectives. The strike was not an open-ended general strike demanding self-determination or an end to Israeli rule. The Druze candidly assessed the political context in which it took place and avoided ill-defined or hopelessly unrealistic objectives. So practical an approach may not satisfy the maximalist goals of revolutionary rhetoric or ideological dogmatism. Yet the strike gave the Golani Druze a concrete experience of their power in united action and a tangible experience of success against a military occupier.

The Druze struggle suggests that effective nonviolent struggle can manifest a broad cultural cohesion, rather than serve as the means by which a new culture is created. The Druze have a cultural cohesion that is rare, especially in more developed countries. The Druze also had a realistic assessment of the resources available to them. According to one Majd al-Shams activist, "We fight with hands and sticks against the Israelis. What can we do? We cannot wait for them to hit us and to fight us. They came to fight us in our villages and our homes. They attacked us for 16 years. And now also they are attacking us. We reject it with our own rights. We have the specific conditions. We have to choose the place to put pressure and against what. We have to choose correctly and to test correctly our methods and our facts. Force must be met with counter-force, not passivity."[23]

George Lakey, a leading advocate of nonviolent social struggle from the United States, has observed, "Nonviolent struggle doesn't just happen. It comes out of a social context, and people who actually do the action are responding to a variety of things. They may be responding to a change in conditions or changes in attitudes. They may see a glimmer of hope where they didn't see it before. They may see a particularly brutal event. Whatever the initial cause, what people are actually doing is casting off submission and getting rid of their passivity."[24] Once people decide to reject submission and engage in social struggle, the objective of nonviolent action becomes, according to the scholar Gene Sharp, "to make a society ungovernable by would-be oppressors."[25] Despite the difficulties encountered by the Golani Druze and shortcomings in terms of what they achieved, their 1982 general strike is a remarkable example of the action of which both Lakey and Sharp speak. A chief source for the strike's effectiveness was the Druze's deep sense of identity. The Israelis provided the symbol of their campaign: the identity card. The objective of their resistance was simple and attainable: "If you are a Syrian Druze, you cannot be an Israeli, so don't accept the identity card!" It was as simple as that.

Younger, secular, and more politically radical Druze and older, religious, and more traditional leaderships were able to come together and compromise on questions of style, authority, political analysis, and personal status. They arrived at decisions through a consensus process that as one Palestinian remarked rivaled the participatory democracy of American's best town meetings. On five different occasions, as many as 2,500 people gathered to make decisions. The decision-making process for villages was centered within their religious practices and hence was largely immune to overt Israeli interference. During the initial stages of the strike, Druze villagers refused to work in their own fields or across the 1967 border in Israel. During the last two months of the strike, farmers returned to the fields, but according to a Majd al-Shams villager, "Everyone was deciding for the other one. It means farmers cannot decide for themselves and workers cannot decide for themselves."[26]

Leaders among the Druze may have helped to ascertain the advisability of various actions, but they were primarily responding to what the community as a whole had arrived at through consensus. This allowed for continuity in the campaign and built momentum from one success to the next, even when leaders were placed under house arrest or jailed. The Druze demonstrated that a deeply rooted collective morale and social solidarity are decisive factors in social struggle. Druze villagers were prepared to undergo considerable personal sacrifice, including loss of jobs and crops, imprisonment, and physical harm. Their willing acceptance of suffering inspired and encouraged others and rallied support.

One unexpected source of support came from within those soldiers sent to enforce edicts against the villagers' will. Villagers defied a strict curfew confining them to their homes to place tea and cookies outside their doors for the Israeli soldiers. They engaged soldiers in conversation and chose not to curse them. The early decision to talk with the Israeli soldiers resulted in villagers actively seeking soldiers out and speaking with them in Hebrew, which they had been forced to learn in school. According to Jonathan Kuttab, "The soldiers were really being torn apart, because they couldn't handle that type of nonviolence." The Druze exposed the vulnerability of military force to nonviolent means of struggle. Kuttab continued, "Israeli soldiers generally function so effectively, at least in part, because of the widespread conviction that they are acting out of genuine security needs of their fellow Israelis and because so many of the situations in which they are stationed give them cause to fear for their own lives. In the face of a disciplined unarmed civilian population, which threatened neither Israeli security, nor the lives of the individual soldiers, the morale and discipline of Israeli soldiers began to break down. According to several reports, the division commander complained that the Golan situation was ruining some of his best soldiers."[27]

The nonviolent resistance of the Golani Druze is a provocative example of the power of a well-disciplined campaign against tremendous military might. It proved to be difficult to manage by the Israelis, who depended ultimately on residents' cooperation in all of the occupied territories in order to maintain control. Perhaps of most significance, the Golani Druze's militant nonviolent struggle embodied an alternative for the Palestinians under occupation. International law expert Richard Falk observed that Palestinians could make a decisive contribution toward the peace process "by moving away from armed struggle as [their] central image of the politics of self-determination."[28] It is significant that Israeli Jews, active in movements in opposition to annexation of any of the occupied territories, began to speak in similar terms. Daniel Amit, cofounder of the Israeli Committee against the War in Lebanon, commented, "My personal vision is that the [Israeli] peace movement has to develop nonviolent civil resistance tactics on a large scale. The human and numerical potential is there. If the Palestinians will come along, it will be like a forest fire."[29]

The potential impact of the Druze campaign on the Palestinians was not lost on the Israelis. Several Palestinian activists and Americans working in the occupied territories noted that Israeli military officials devoted much more time to examining possible uses of nonviolence by the Palestinians than did the Palestinians themselves. The Israelis began actively developing means to reduce the potential impact of nonviolent struggle for the Palestinians through legal strictures drastically curtailing the ability to organize and through harsh repression of any militant nonviolent action. Political demonstrations by Palestinians were outlawed at the beginning of the occupation in 1967. Soon after the Golani strike, the Israeli military governor of the West Bank forbade demonstrations by *Israelis* in the occupied territories as well. This order was meant to nip in the bud a series of demonstrations by various Israeli peace and human right groups against Jewish settlement in the West Bank. It is telling that the military governor also forced an American organization to change the job description of one of its workers in the West Bank to eliminate "nonviolence education." Clearly the Israelis perceived nonviolent action as a threat to its ability to maintain control over the Palestinians.

Although the Arab Druze campaign in the Golan may not serve as a textbook for nonviolent struggle, or a clear direction for Druze in other geographical locales, perhaps those struggling against oppression in other areas will be able to hear the words of an Israeli antiwar activist who commented to a group of Majd al-Shams villagers, "When you are able, competent and generous, you don't need arms."[30]

Notes

A version of this chapter was originally published as "The Golani Druze: A Case of Nonviolent Resistance," *Journal of Palestine Studies* 13, no. 2 (Winter 1984): 48–64. © 1984 by the Institute for Palestine Studies. It has been edited for length, style, and content.

1. Joseph Berger, "Members of Druze Sect Guard Privacy, Keep Tenets of Faith Secret," *United Methodist Reporter* (October 21, 1983): 5.
2. Professor Moshe Sharon, "Why the Druze Are Formidable," *Jerusalem Post* (international edition), September 18–24, 1983, 14. Sharon is chairman of the Department

of the History of Islamic People at Hebrew University and a former advisor on Arab affairs to Prime Minister Menachem Begin.

3. According to Jamal Muadi, chairman of the Druze Initiative Committee, interview, Dalayat al-Karmel, Israel, 1983. The Druze Initiative Committee is an anticonscription association and supporter of Palestinian rights in Israel founded in the mid-1950s.

4. Sharon, "Why the Druze Are Formidable," 1.

5. In a 1976 interview with *Yediot Aharonot*, Israel's largest daily newspaper, former Israeli defense minister Moshe Dayan described how Israel provoked military incidents on the Golan Heights: "I know how at least 80 percent of the clashes there started. In my opinion, more than 80 percent, but let's talk about 80 percent. It went this way: We would send a tractor to plough someplace where it wasn't possible to do anything, in the demilitarized area, and knew in advance that the Syrians would start to shoot. If they didn't shoot, we would tell the tractor to advance farther, until in the end the Syrians would get annoyed and shoot. And then we would use artillery and later the air force also, and that's how it was." Dayan gave the interview on the condition that it not be published until after his death. Cited in Avi Shlaim, *The Iron Wall: Israel and the Arab World* (New York: W.W. Norton, 2001), 236–37.

6. The economic assimilation of the occupied territories is graphically detailed in the statistical studies of Meron Benvenisti, a former vice mayor of Jerusalem. See, for example, Meron Benvenisti, *The West Bank and Gaza Data Base Project: Pilot Study*, no. 1 (Jerusalem, 1982).

7. From "David Ben Gurion," *Looklex Encyclopaedia*, http://i-cias.com/e.o/ben-gurion.htm.

8. Jonathan Kuttab, interview, May 1, 1983, Resource Center for Nonviolence, Santa Cruz, CA. Kuttab had heard Golani villagers speak in these terms to an American journalist accompanying him on a visit to the Golan.

9. Mention of the alleged Israeli offer to Jumblatt was heard in several conversations involving Golani Druze villagers during this author's visit to Majd al-Shams on February 5, 1983. Israel's apparent aim was to establish the Druze as a geographically independent national entity, closely allied to Israel and serving as a buffer between Israel and surrounding Arab states.

10. Taiser Merei, from the community organization Golan for Development, e-mail communication, December 12, 2008.

11. Daoud Kuttab, "Nationalism Flares," *al-Fajr* (Jerusalem) (international English edition), October 7, 1983, 7.

12. "Golan Residents Must Carry IDs," *al-Fajr* (international English edition), May 27, 1983, 13.

13. Suleman Fahr Adin, interview, Majd al-Shams, February 5, 1983.

14. Kuttab, "Nationalism Flares," 7.

15. Ibid.

16. Fahr Adin, interview, February 5, 1983.

17. Kuttab, "Nationalism Flares."

18. *Jerusalem Post* (international edition), August 21–27, 1983.

19. Ibid.

20. *Al-Fajr*, August 19, 1983; also *Israeleft*, August 15, 1983.

21. Sharon, "Why the Druze Are Formidable," 1.

22. The Druze Initiative Committee for Conscientious Objection was founded in 1972, according to Andreas Speck, "Druze Conscientious Objectors: Discrimination, Silence and Ignorance," an article based on discussions at a meeting in Haifa, January 2003, and originally published in *The Broken Rifle*, no. 58 (May 2003): www.wri-irg.org/pubs/br58-en.htm. The Druze Initiative Committee claimed to have collected 600 signatures by Druze opposing military service. During a February 7, 1983 visit and sev-

eral previous visits, this author met a dozen Druze in Israel who had either refused or avoided military conscription in the Israeli army.

23. Fahr Adin, interview, February 5, 1983.
24. Canadian Broadcast Corporation, "Alternatives to Violence Video, 1999, Forum," section 2, produced by WTL/TV.
25. Ibid.
26. Adin, interview, February 5, 1983.
27. Reports of dissension within the Israeli military have not been independently confirmed by Israeli sources, but were mentioned by several sources, including Jonathan Kuttab, Druze villagers in the Golan and in Israel, and American nationals serving in various capacities in service organizations on the West Bank.
28. Richard Falk, "*Toward Arab-Israeli Peace*," CALC [Clergy and Laity Concerned] Report, November–December 1982, 34. Falk is professor emeritus of international law at Princeton University and has traveled in the Middle East and written extensively about the Arab-Israeli and broader Middle Eastern conflicts. Falk is currently the United Nations special rapporteur on the human rights situation in the Palestinian territories occupied since 1967.
29. Nat Hentoff, "Can Israel Create Its Own Gandhi, Muste or King?" *Village Voice,* June 28, 1983.
30. Israeli Jewish anarchist and pacifist Yeshya'ahu Toma Sik, World Service Authority and War Resisters International (Israel section), Tel Aviv, during a February 5, 1983 visit to Majd al-Shams.

10

Palestinian Civil Resistance against Israeli Military Occupation

Mary Elizabeth King

In 1987 Palestinians in the West Bank, Gaza Strip, and East Jerusalem launched a massive social mobilization against the Israeli military occupation that had resulted from the June 1967 war. Four Palestinian deaths at an Israeli checkpoint on December 9 touched off a month of chaos. By January 1988, however, synchronized nonviolent actions were discernible—marches, civil disobedience, demonstrations, public prayers, strikes, and vigils. It was the start of a movement to lift a belligerent occupation using classic nonviolent methods. A spread of knowledge about nonviolent strategies throughout Palestinian society for almost two decades shaped an uprising that would remain relatively coherent until March 1990, despite harsh reprisals.

For more then two years, Palestinians inside the territories militarily occupied by Israel refused to use firearms, setting aside a tradition of armed struggle—including some of the twentieth century's most notorious attacks on civilian targets—in favor of nonviolent struggle. Israeli retaliations failed to alter the fundamental Palestinian decision not to use weaponry against thousands of armed Israeli soldiers and settlers in their midst. It was a pivotal opportunity in contemporary world history. The movement would by its third year disintegrate into violence after Israel's incarceration, deportation, or discrediting of the very activist intellectuals who had sustained the uprising's nonviolent character and had throughout the 1970s and 1980s worked to bring about the new political thinking that produced the intifada.

Background

In 1917–1918, the British occupied Palestine and imposed the Balfour declaration, promising a "national home" for world Jewry in Palestine. Jewish, Christian, and Muslim communities had been living peaceably together in Palestine for centuries, until the time of the British Mandate and massive immigration of European Jewry. During the 1920s and 1930s, the Palestinian Arabs sought to maintain their way of life and land. They responded primarily with nonviolent methods in challenging the British mandate, immigration of Jews, and exclusive enterprises being developed under Zionism.[1] Their protest actions included presenting petitions, organizing delegations, and displaying black (mourning) borders on Palestinian newspapers when British officials visited Jerusalem. They also used noncooperation methods, including social, economic, and political boycotts and resignation from jobs in the British colonial administration. Palestinians mounted frequent strikes, including possibly the longest in history, which lasted for 174 days in 1936.[2] Palestinians generally pleaded for abrogation of the Balfour Declaration, an end to the British Mandate, and national independence. They asked for limits on Jewish immigration, restrictions on land sales to Jews, and establishment of a national government.

Without obscuring three major, yet aberrant, turns to violence that occurred in 1921, 1929, and 1937–1939, historical review discloses a pattern in which the British and Zionists responded to violent outbreaks, but chose to dismiss the more indicative overtures made through nonviolent sanctions. A British and Zionist prototype of responding to violent struggle but not to collective nonviolent action by the Palestinians over changes to their land and society became entrenched.

In 1933, the National Socialists were elected in Germany and the migration of Jews to Palestine increased.[3] Cities, ports, and agricultural land underwent conspicuous changes, as the Zionist newcomers built restricted institutions and economies. On November 29, 1947, the infant United Nations adopted General Assembly Resolution 181, calling for the partition of Palestine into two states: a Jewish state and an Arab state, plus an internationally managed section for the Old City of Jerusalem. Coinciding with the departure of the British and rejection of the partition plan by Arab states, full-scale war broke out between the Arab states and Jewish forces after the May 14, 1948 proclamation of the state of Israel.

By the end of 1948, Israeli forces not only held the areas designated by the UN for the Jewish state, but they had also captured large parts of the proposed Arab state. When armistice agreements were signed in 1949, Zionist forces controlled three-quarters of the country. The new state was overwhelmed with the arrival of immigrants, many of them survivors of the European Holocaust. For the Palestinian Arabs, the war meant disaster on an inconceivable scale. The Arab state never materialized. The remaining one-quarter of the country came under Jordanian and Egyptian control and would become the West Bank of the Jordan River and the Gaza Strip.

During the 1948 war, approximately 750,000 Palestinian Arabs fled in fear, often assuming that they could return in a few weeks, or they were expelled from their homes. Besides those killed, more than half of the Arab population took flight or were driven out, devastating Palestinian society. Mostly peasants who had tilled the land, they became refugees and resettled in the West Bank and Gaza, or in Syria, Jordan, and Lebanon. Throughout the 1950s in refugee camps outside what had been Palestine, the ideologies of armed struggle fermented. Palestinian guerrilla movements formed calling for armed struggle. The Palestine Liberation Organization (PLO), comprised of refugees, grew out of a 1964 summit meeting in Cairo. In 1968 the PLO revised its charter, stipulating armed struggle as the *only* way to liberate Palestine. Most of its attacks would be directed against Israeli civilians.[4]

In 1967, Egypt's president Gamal Abdul Nasser raised tensions in the Islamic world against the Jewish state, and Egypt's ships blockaded Israel's Red Sea port, closing Israeli shipping lanes. Israel interpreted the blockade as an act of war. The United States condoned an Israeli preemptive strike, resulting in six days of war and more than 40 years of military occupation. The Israelis took control of the remaining one-quarter of historic Palestine, and occupied the West Bank, including East Jerusalem, and Gaza.

Inside the Israeli-occupied territories, some Palestinians began to question armed methods. Others ventured a conciliatory view of Israel. Abandoning the dream of recovering the land by military means, still others recognized that they had no one to turn to but themselves. Even those pledged to the dogma of armed struggle began to participate in nonmilitary organizations that for more than twenty years, without any definite plan, would build the corporate capacity for the intifada.

Among the armed factions growing in the refugee camps outside the Palestinian areas, many rejected the UN partition plan since it allocated 55 percent of the land in mandate Palestine to the Jewish minority. The communists accepted the 1947 UN partition plan and did not hold to the requirement of "armed struggle" to liberate Palestine, a position otherwise thought to be consensus.

Palestinians inside the occupied territories started organizing themselves in civilian, nonmilitary mobilizations. Some underground military cells persisted, but armed struggle generally held little allure for the disarmed residents inside what remained of mandate Palestine. This situation arose not so much from moral revulsion as the fact that Israeli reprisals for cross-border raids and sorties fell upon them, not the guerrillas carrying out the attacks.

The saga of the uprising includes misperceptions by the target group, the Israelis, toward the mass nonviolent mobilization that emerged in 1987. Many Israelis viewed the uprising through the lens of the PLO's refusal over the years to distinguish between civilians and military targets; the front had taken responsibility for thousands of attacks, the majority of them against Israeli civilians. This denial of a differentiation is important, as is the Israelis' perception that the conflict over land was not and is not exclusively between themselves and the Palestinians, but between themselves and all the Arab states. Overreactions and existential fear, especially among the older generation of Israeli leaders, and brutal reprisals also derived from a view of Israel as vulnerable to destruction. Despite Israel's military advantage, stranglehold of Gaza, control of land and roads in the West Bank, and unwavering support from the United States, Israeli fearfulness still constitutes part of the strategic dilemma facing the Palestinians.

The Emergence of Nonviolent Civil Resistance

The adoption of nonmilitary strategies in the 1987 Palestinian uprising against Israeli occupation resulted from three developments that occurred under military occupation: (1) movements of committees constructed a Palestinian civil society, which became the wellspring for the intifada; (2) activist intellectuals redefined the canon of armed struggle, advanced alternative ideas on how to oppose the occupation, and proffered compromise and negotiations, thereby affecting viewpoints on negotiating with Israel; and (3) knowledge of nonviolent sanctions spread to the occupied territories from nonviolent civil resistance movements in other parts of the world.

Networks of Committees

Nearly two decades of social mobilization provided the infrastructure for the 1987 uprising, as Palestinians developed networks of civilian organizations within view of omnipresent Israeli military forces. A resulting fragmentation and decentralization of authority in Palestinian society would contribute to changes in power configurations and allow the nonmilitary contours of the intifada to form, also helping Palestinians later to survive retaliations from Israel.

In 1969 the Palestine Communist Party broke the Israeli ban on Palestinian political activity in the occupied territories and openly advocated political rather than military methods and popular organizing of small, locally-governed institutions. The communists' stance caught the political imagination of others and soon prodded Fateh, the largest and most dominant faction of the groups in the PLO, to move toward civilian nonmilitary mobilization. The numerically small communist party, which was not part of the PLO, considered self-sufficient institutions the best way to pursue national independence, because building localized institutions could help attain long-range political goals that were achievable only through comparably far-reaching changes in the social structure. Local, clandestine PLO-affiliated military factions soon appreciated that they would lose numbers if they failed to adopt similar approaches. Civilian organizing accelerated among youth, women, labor, students and academicians, and professionals in the 1970s.

Voluntary work committees started in 1972, as schoolteachers and college instructors in the Ramallah and al-Bireh area joined under the sponsorship of al-Bireh's mayor, Abd al-Jawad Saleh. Tens of thousands of young lecturers and civic-minded Palestinians volunteered for these committees during the 1970s; the majority of them were not members of PLO factions. Community renewal initiatives flourished. Local sports and youth clubs multiplied. Student and faculty associations became the largest power centers under occupation. Trade unions expanded. The four major PLO factions each established women's committees, which organized tens of thousands of peasant women. Teachers formed federations. In 1979 Palestinian clinicians began formal associations of health professionals, many of which still deliver health care. Gradually recognizing that the occupation would not soon be lifted, as initially thought, the Palestinians in the territories built an infrastructure for addressing their social needs.

A "movement of movements" formed, as networks of civilian, nonmilitary committees allowed the Palestinians to oppose and counteract occupation. By the dawn of the intifada, possibly 45,000 such committees were at work. A prisoners' movement developed, and coordinated large hunger strikes inside Israeli prisons, without any visible means of communications between the Palestinians incarcerated in various penal complexes; the first one occurred in 1970. One of the small civilian committees was the Arab Studies Society, established in 1980 in East Jerusalem by Feisel Husseini, son of Abd al-Qadir al-Husseini, a renowned Palestinian killed in 1948. The society's initial purpose was to translate into Arabic articles concerning the Palestinians from Israeli newspapers, because such accounts often divulged Israeli plans pertaining to the Palestinians.

Organizers of thousands of such civil society groups prepared for incarcerations with diversified leaderships so the organizations could carry on after anticipated arrests by the Israelis. Diffusion of power assured survival of the committees no matter the members jailed, as new leaders assumed the duties of imprisoned predecessors. Persons who proposed ending the occupation by means other than armed struggle—or who would not in any instance have joined the *fedayeen*, literally "self-sacrificers," or guerrilla commando units—thus had the opportunity to rise to positions of leadership, further encouraging pluralistic outlooks. Palestinians advocating armed insurrection through covert PLO-related military cadres comprised various poles of power, yet these were no longer monopolistic.

The voluntary committees and civic organizations were based upon strategies that relied for their success on broad civilian participation and nonviolent means.

A new politics was developing, its internal processes egalitarian, cooperative, and democratic. Leaders were elected; groups governed themselves in a broad social mobilization that would provide the infrastructure for the intifada.

Activist Intellectuals

In a development second only to the building of civil society, Palestinian activist intellectuals championed compromise, negotiations, and nonviolent means. Complementing the very committees in which some played catalytic roles during the 1970s and 1980s, especially in student and faculty unions, a small number of academicians, professionals, lawyers, editors, and journalists questioned the efficacy of armed struggle as a strategy for ending the occupation.

The first visible harbinger of a political metamorphosis underway and deliberate selection of nonviolent methods after 1967 was a series of Palestinian-Israeli committees, whose spokespersons were Feisel Husseini and Gideon Spiro. Scion of an aristocratic Jerusalem family, Husseini was also related to Haj Amin al-Husseini, a controversial 1930s Palestinian leader who ambiguously advocated violent resistance and nonviolent methods and for three decades opposed Zionist political goals. At the start of the 1980s, Husseini sought out Spiro, an Israeli journalist and former conscript paratrooper. In 1982 he became a founding member of Yesh Gvul (There Is a Limit), a movement of Israeli military reservists who refused to serve in Lebanon after Israel's invasion that year and which contested that war's legality.[5]

FIRST PERSON: AN INTERVIEW WITH GIDEON SPIRO

The Committee of Solidarity with Bir Zeit University (CSBZ) was the first serious Israeli expression of solidarity. It was essentially an Israeli committee, including Israeli Arabs, and it worked with Palestinian partners and organizations, including Feisel Husseini and Orient House, in East Jerusalem, which he ran. We became active when the government of Israel closed Bir Zeit University at the end of the 1970s. CSBZ called for total Israeli withdrawal from the occupied territories and negotiations leading to a Palestinian state. Our scope of issues later widened to engagement with lecturers at BZU, and organizing joint exhibitions in Jerusalem, Tel Aviv, Haifa, and East Jerusalem of Israeli and Palestinian painters who advocated peace without occupation. At its core were perhaps sixty Israelis, but when there was a planned action, hundreds would participate. At the start of the 1980s, at the Daheisha Palestinian refugee camp near Bethlehem, we organized a one-day work camp to facilitate the building of a road, because the roads around and in the camp were not paved properly and became gutted from the winter weather. We could not finish the road, because the Israeli army declared it illegal and evicted us.

By 1985, another group, the Committee Confronting the Iron Fist (CCIF),[6] was in full swing. Against the background of CSBZ, it represented major change, because it was a *joint* Palestinian and Israeli group—the first of its kind, comprehensively addressing the military occupation. During the years that I worked with Feisel Husseini in CCIF, he was often under house arrest after 8:00 p.m., so I would frequently stay with him at his home at night. Feisel had a very sensitive understanding of the importance of working with Israelis. We...worked against the harassment of Palestinians and confiscation of their land and property.

I was among the Israeli soldiers who captured Arab East Jerusalem in 1967. When I finished my military reserve duty, I made the personal decision that I would never again put myself in a situation of controlling another people.

My peace activities deepened as the military occupation intensified. Later, I was among the founding members of Yesh Gvul (There Is a Limit), a movement of Israeli reserve soldiers who refused to serve in the 1982 war in Lebanon, formed when 2,500–3,000 reservists signed a petition refusing to serve. Of the petitioning reservists, 170 were court-martialed and imprisoned. Yesh Gvul's members believed that Israel's 1982 war with Lebanon was unlawful and that they were morally and politically required to refuse to participate in it. This was the first time that Israelis had refused to participate in a war. Yesh Gvul's members were not pacifists—they were committed to defense, ready to serve in the army, but were not ready to oppress another people. Such selective refusal made the Israeli authorities very nervous.

During the 1982 Lebanon war and the first intifada, we could not be ignored. Yesh Gvul's civil disobedience recalled Israel's own denial of the validity of Nazi war criminals who claimed they were merely obeying orders. Ours was a "diamond" of civil disobedience—an exquisite example of persons refusing to obey government orders without using violence, acting with civility, and ready to pay the penalty. We received our orders, and we said No. Civil disobedience is not well understood in Israeli society—the Israeli public is completely obedient, especially on security issues. We don't need military coups d'état in Israel! Israeli former military generals are everywhere: in government, leading economic institutions, mayors of municipalities, totally integrated in the overall system. Israeli society is highly militarized.

> Gideon Spiro, two one-hour telephone interviews with the author,
> November 12, 2006 and May 27, 2008.

In contrast to the PLO's military doctrine of "all means of struggle," the joint committees of Israelis and Palestinians used strategies based on public disclosure and methods such as boycotts, demonstrations, marches, petitions, picketing, speeches, and vigils to argue for lifting the occupation. Setting aside metaphors of revenge, the joint committees imagined shared solidarity between Israelis and Palestinians, who would together seek to end the mutual degradation of military occupation that humiliated the occupied as well as the occupier. Husseini explained:

[W]e decided that the main enemy is the occupation, the main enemy for the two communities—for the Palestinian community and the Israeli community—and that the occupation can hurt the morals of those controlling the occupation, no less than the people who are under it, maybe more. So we reached this argument that we must, Palestinians and Israelis working together, end this occupation....It was in the interest of the Israelis to end this occupation as well as the Palestinians.[7]

Aziz Shehadeh, a Ramallah lawyer, often met with Husseini and influenced his thinking. Shehadeh may have been the first Palestinian quoted publicly in news media advocating two states side by side; as early as 1948, he prepared the way for a two-state solution as an alternative to the liberation of all of Palestine. Shehadeh's advocacy of a negotiated two-state solution envisioned statehood as a matter of citizenship, a symbolic entitlement rather than literal retrieval of lost ancestral properties (as implied by "liberation"). Shehadeh was also persuasive with the lawyer Jonathan Kuttab, and supervised Kuttab's legal work. Shehadeh's son, Raja, also a jurist, and Kuttab in 1979 founded the first Palestinian human rights monitoring organization, al-Haq (Law in the Service to Man). Embarking on a prolonged challenge to the thousands of legal restrictions imposed by the Israeli military administration, their approach utilized Israeli standards and military orders to document and contest Israel's legal claims on its own terms.

Husseini had begun making speeches in Hebrew in 1968 in which he advocated a strictly nonviolent course in resolving the conflict with Israel. The Palestinian lawyer Ziad Abu Zayyad, also speaking in Hebrew, joined Husseini in promoting peaceful coexistence. With metaphors of lifting an occupation that degrades both peoples, symbols of coexistence, and imagery of two states side by side, Israelis and Palestinians marched together with placards written in Arabic, Hebrew, and English.[8]

Throughout the 1980s, Sari Nusseibeh, a philosopher, wrote to redefine Palestinian nationalist concepts. Returning to Jerusalem after studying politics, philosophy, and economics at Oxford and doctoral studies at Harvard, he became involved in the 1980s student and faculty movements to resist Israeli Military Orders 854 and 947, which encroached on academic freedom. In 1985, he advocated a one-state solution based on the principle of one-person-one-vote.[9] In Arabic and English outlets, Nusseibeh deconstructed revolutionary military dogma and ideology. He proffered a right of return in which the *person* returns and is granted citizenship in a state, rather than recovering precise parcels of familial land. Citizenship in a Palestinian state, he penned, can substitute for lost land. The entitlements in his writings pertained to universal human rights, fast on their way to becoming international norms after the 1975 Helsinki Accords.

The activist intellectuals expressed their political thought in action. Three documents drafted by Nusseibeh substantiate interplay between new ideas and organized action. One of these, the "Jerusalem Paper," would later guide an unseen leadership cooperative for more than two years during the intifada. The organizer intellectuals believed that Palestinian behavior should demonstrate the viability of statehood. Seeking to change the goal from the liberation of all of Palestine to an independent state alongside Israel, to be arrived at through direct negotiations, they advocated nonviolent methods because they would improve the odds of entering into talks with Israel.

The diffusion of the centers of power and fragmentation of authority that accompanied the organizing of thousands of civilian committees also permitted the voices of the activist intellectuals to be heard. Once the intifada began, the organizer intellectuals would gain the upper hand vis-à-vis the advocates of militarized strategies for more than two years as members of "unofficial" Fateh, along with others from differing factions. They worked together through a think tank that included all of the Palestinian factions as well as unaffiliated, independent persons. The PLO's second in command, Khalil al-Wazir, nom de guerre Abu Jihad, advocated for the leadership in the territories with the PLO's chief, Yasir Arafat, who approved the initiatives of the intifada's activist intellectuals and their concentric circles, which also included members of military cadres who had suspended their violent action. Nonetheless, the PLO leadership's ambivalent posturing—most of them never fully appreciated, understood, or espoused the nonviolent strategies— oftentimes combined with their guerrilla cadres' vituperative rhetoric to undermine the social mobilization underway in the territories.

The only perplexity more astounding than the ability of the activist intellectuals to guide a mass nonviolent uprising after decades of PLO ideological insistence on armed struggle has been the failure of outside observers to recognize the enormity of the struggle within a struggle that these local leaders were waging in reconstructing political thought. Their accomplishment, evident in the construction of the intifada, was fundamental: they had unraveled bellicose guerrilla ideologies, advocated sharing the land with Israelis, and opened Palestinian society to a post-Helsinki discourse of human rights.[10]

Transmission of Knowledge

FIRST PERSON: AN INTERVIEW WITH MUBARAK AWAD

Mubarak Awad, a Palestinian-American clinical psychologist born in Jerusalem, teaches in the international peace and conflict resolution division, School of International Service, the American University, Washington, D.C.

The idea for a Palestinian Center for the Study of Nonviolence did not begin with me or with the concept of nonviolent action.... For me, the idea that people could empower themselves originally came from psychology....

The Pakistani political scientist Eqbal Ahmad was the first after the 1967 war to argue with the Palestinians, in Beirut, against armed struggle. He told them that the best weapon they had was the weapon of nonviolence: they should burn their tents, they should not accept themselves as refugees, and they should march to the borders and have every leader and Palestinian, including children and women, saying, "We must go back to our homes," like Gandhi's 1930 Salt March. Eqbal asserted that nonviolent action for the Palestinians means using very big events....Professor Hisham Sharabi of Georgetown University,pushed hard in 1984 to get a center for the study of nonviolence set up in East Jerusalem....We concluded that we would have the Palestinian Center for the Study of Nonviolence, and I would go back to East Jerusalem and work for a year and see how it went. Sharabi was the first who was able to give us some funding...I went back for a year. There was no salary. I volunteered.

Not all of the Palestinians were able to grab the concept of nonviolence. The Palestinians outside the occupied territories were not able to feel (I am talking about the PLO) they were not able to *feel* the strength of the Palestinians inside the territories, when they resisted without the gun, when they resisted without bombs. They couldn't grasp it. They weren't seeing Israelis with a look in their eyes that showed *they* were afraid of us, even with their guns, because we were confronting them and were not willing to move, even if they started shooting at us.

I don't think the PLO understood. Within the PLO there was a competition between themselves of who could do [the biggest] act of violence—there was no competition on an act of nonviolent struggle. But Abu Jihad got it. He begged all the factions, "Let's give those people a chance to do it on their own; they are doing a much better job than with any kind of bombs." We were so unhappy and angry when we would learn that Palestinians from outside [beyond the occupied territories] had sneaked across the borders to attack the Israelis. That was the worst sabotage of the whole concept of the intifada.

Mubarak E. Awad, one-hour interview with the author,
February 14, 1995, Washington, D.C.

Mubarak Awad and Jonathan Kuttab in 1983 started workshops on the technique of collective nonviolent action in East Jerusalem and Ramallah. Advertised in local newspapers and open to any Palestinian or Israeli, in the workshops Awad and Kuttab distributed a booklet they had written in Arabic about wielding nonviolent power to accomplish political goals without clandestinity. Published in Awad's name to protect Kuttab's ability to continue to practice law as a member of the Israeli bar, the booklet, *Nonviolence in the Occupied Territories*, illustrates the Palestinians' search for methods that might resonate with the target group, Israelis, potentially splitting their ranks. In 1984 Awad and Kuttab established the Palestinian Center for the Study of Nonviolence in East Jerusalem. Volunteers disseminated the 1983 booklet, mimeographed translations, and distributed pamphlets on nonviolent civil resistance.

Arguing that the Palestinians should cease using violence to resist the occupation—because it confronted the Israeli military and government where the Palestinians were at their weakest—these activist intellectuals organized pilot marches, parades, and demonstrations. In trial runs of direct action jointly sponsored with the Israeli branch of the International Fellowship of Reconciliation, Israeli participants were enlisted as allies in actions designed to confront and entreat Israeli sensibilities. Carrying experiments into forty or fifty villages and refugee camps on the West Bank, the center organized nonviolent direct action in Qatanna, Hebron, Tqu (Tekoa), and elsewhere. Tendering no political blueprints, its representatives maintained that taking action was better than inaction, that civil resistance was less costly than armed struggle, and that nonviolent struggle fit the limited abilities of the disarmed Palestinians and would be more successful than armed struggle in redressing fundamental injustices.

For four years prior to the intifada, the center distributed thousands of copies, reprints, translations, and booklets on nonviolent resistance. The center's materials and translations of the Boston scholar Gene Sharp reinforced assertions also being advanced in the essays of the university-based activist intellectuals that the Palestinians could without violence prevent Israeli authorities from accomplishing their goals and create a more level bargaining situation. The materials were analogous to *samizdat* (Russian for "self-published"), the manifestos, charters, and clandestine writings of the Eastern European nonviolent revolutions of the same period, which replaced Soviet-backed communist regimes with fledgling democracies.

In November 1986, Gene Sharp traveled to the region for the first of three such trips. In Israel, he spoke with strategic studies specialists in Tel Aviv and visited the Knesset. Sharp's three-volume 1973 cross-cultural analysis, *The Politics of Nonviolent Action*, had been circulating for more than a year among Palestinians. Sharp spoke with Palestinians, Israelis, and mixed groups, analyzing historical cases of nonviolent struggle. He described how civil resistance can cause dissent within the ranks of the target group, while violent struggle consolidates opposition against any challenge. Acts of terrorism produce international isolation, he explained, while nonviolent struggle can stimulate support. With Palestinians, he stressed how military occupation is dependent upon the obedience of the occupied. Disputing the "blind faith" in violence that he had found despite its devastating results, he maintained that unquestioning Palestinian belief in violence prevented the deliberation of alternatives and criticism of failure. Only a few might participate in violent struggle, he explained, in contrast to the mass involvement possible with nonviolent struggle. Sharp recommended building small, local, self-reliant institutions for survival under probable reprisals, advice that dovetailed with the thousands of committees created in the civilian movements of the 1970s and 1980s.[11]

Recognition that the submission of a populace to a belligerent occupation is required for its subjugation, and that in this respect, the Palestinians themselves had the power to refuse to cooperate with Israel was vocalized by Husseini, penned by Nusseibeh, articulated in Awad's *samizdat*, and deciphered in Sharp transla tions. It was the single most significant change in political thinking that galvanized the uprising. It would be expressed in the street leaflets of the intifada as "disengagement."

The First Intifada

On December 9, 1987, four laborers from Gaza were crushed as an Israeli truck collided with their two vehicles as they waited to pass through an army roadblock after a day's work in Israel. The funeral for three of those killed was attended by four thousand people. Israeli officials called the crash an accident, but rumors spread among Palestinians that the deaths were in retaliation for the murder of an Israeli in Gaza City the preceding day. By 10 December, smoke from barricades of burning tires covered much of Gaza. Despite Israeli forces' use of tear gas and bullets coated with a thin veneer of rubber, demonstrators of all ages and walks of life remained in the line of fire, throwing stones and advancing toward the soldiers, in December 1987 and into January 1988. A Gaza funeral for a Palestinian drew 35 thousand Palestinians. In the coming weeks, protests by Palestinians erupted across the occupied territories, blocking roads and impeding Israeli army movements.

Within the first month of the uprising, Israel placed 200,000 Palestinians under curfew in the West Bank and Gaza. By December 1989, one million Palestinians were confined to their homes. The intifada's ability to continue despite crackdowns relied on hundreds of "popular committees," often started and run by women, which burgeoned as if instantaneously from the extended process of civilian mobilization. The West Bank village of Beit Sahour (pop. 12,000) organized itself into 36 committees. In providing necessary infrastructure, the committees complemented and helped sustain a local leadership that was unknown beyond the immediate neighborhood, with broad participation across class, gender, and educational lines.

The widening awareness and new political thinking that generated the uprising were disclosed early, at a news conference in East Jerusalem on 14 January, 1988, five weeks after the initial outpouring of the *intifada* (figure 10.1). A list of demands was released, grouped in fourteen clauses, and presented by "Palestinian nationalist institutions and personalities from the West Bank and Gaza," in a document known as the "Fourteen Points."[12] Among those standing up to issue it were the newspaper editor Hanna Siniora, Hebron mayor Mustafa Natsheh, acting president of Bir Zeit University Gabi Baramki, clinical psychologist Mubarak Awad, lawyer Jonathan Kuttab, and philosopher Sari Nusseibeh, who drafted this and other key documents.

After the first frenzied month of demonstrations and protests, geographic harmonization and diversity of nonviolent methods became visible. A leadership collective, the Unified National Leadership Command of the Uprising, called simply the Command, acted as an unseen, acephalous coordinating mechanism. It was clandestine to avoid the arrest of its members by Israeli authorities. Consisting of representatives from the four main secular-nationalist factions in the occupied territories, it *coordinated* actions, rather than directing the population. Tens of thousands of local voluntary committees and professional associations by then rooted

Figure 10.1   In late 1987 in East Jerusalam, Haj 'Abd Abu-Diab (hands clasped), manager of the East Jerusalem Electric Company and among the first to volunteer with the Palestinian Center for the Study of Nonviolence in East Jerusalem, led a demonstration marking what was then 20 years of Israeli military occupation. Posters at the time were typically written in Arabic, Hebrew, and English. They read "Down with the Occupation."

Credit: Hashomer Hatzair Archive, Givat Haviva, al-Hamishmar Collection, Eliyaho Harati.

in villages, towns, and refugee camps also made independent decisions on actions or yielded freely to the Command when they deemed.

The Command communicated by periodic leaflets, which appeared clandestinely with appeals for action steps. None of the Command's dated and numbered leaflets bade the destruction of Israel or death to the Jewish people. Rather, they presented the Palestinian strategy as one aimed at peace through negotiations and disclosed an uprising built on three political aims: acceptance of Israel in its pre-1967 borders; removal of Israeli authority from the occupied territories; and establishment of a Palestinian state. Behind the Command stood some two dozen Palestinian activist intellectuals, who, acting as a political think tank, advised and guided the Command. These included many of the same academicians, editors, and journalists whose writings during the 1980s had promoted symbols of coexistence, championed negotiations, and helped change thinking on Palestinian resistance. Sari Nusseibeh and colleagues in Ramallah acted as the lodestar.

Intifada is a linguistically nonviolent term, meaning "shaking off." The massive mobilization of Palestinians was possible because of their developing civil society with a consensus for self-reliance, popular participation, nonmilitary strategies, and willingness to compromise. The new thinking and external sources explain how Palestinians employed more than 100 methods from an international repertoire of nonviolent sanctions in withdrawing cooperation from the occupation or evincing opposition to it. This also accounts for how diverse methods filled the Command's leaflets: closing shops (or opening stores ordered shut); symbolic funerals, defying school closures, unfurling forbidden flags, local or general strikes, organizing boycotts, public prayers, refusing to fill out forms, rejecting identity cards, and renaming streets and schools.

Demonstrations of protest and persuasion occurred almost daily in the first three months. From December 1987 to March 1988, women alone conducted more than 100 demonstrations. Noncooperation was enacted not only in strikes, but in job resignations (600 police officers resigned on a single day, representing virtually the entire cohort of Palestinians working in the Israeli police force) and tax resistance. Civil disobedience, hunger strikes, pray-ins, and defiance of blockades were widespread. Alternative institutions, or parallel institutions—among the most sophisticated nonviolent methods—helped to make the territories "non-governable" by Israeli authorities, while Palestinians governed themselves. In the "siege of Beit Sahour," from 22 September to October 31, 1989, Palestinians enacted the ancient method of tax resistance with textbook exactitude. A protracted strategic debate on civil disobedience reveals itself in the clandestine leaflets. This policy deliberation on whether the Palestinians should adopt "total" civil disobedience lasted for 18 months and disclosed the extent to which Antonio Gramsci's "hegemonic consent" over ideologies of military liberation had been achieved.[13]

Some Israeli reprisals became, ironically, an accessory to the uprising. In January 1988, Israel closed 16 Palestinian community colleges and a month later shut 900 schools and 6 universities. Alternative education programs began as 300,000 pupils found themselves at home. Contravening normal gender separation, boys and girls attended class together in church halls, clubhouses, gardens, and mosques. The school closures helped to spread ideas about nonviolent struggle. A Palestinian educational publication reported, "the Israeli authorities...[are] no longer in control of the process and contents of Palestinian education."[14] Most accounts of the intifada have missed the happenstance of 14,500 university students and professors being sent home to their villages and refugee camps. There, the baker sat with the physics professor or student to plan distribution of bread or debated the next nonviolent sanction against the occupation. Israeli retaliations broadened the intifada's consolidation, as intellectuals and academicians meshed directly with youthful street organizers and popular committees, and the population took power into its own hands. The notion asserted by some experts that the Palestinians in the occupied territories were robotic automatons taking orders from the PLO in Tunis is contradicted by the evidence, as is the misbegotten view of the leadership in the territories, including in the Command, as "subordinate" to the PLO abroad. The young in Gaza who sparked the uprising were not allied with PLO factions.

The throwing of stones in the uprising aroused Israeli fears, however, instead of reassuring Israelis of the absence of arms. These acts would ultimately lessen the achievements of the uprising. Children learned quickly that if they threw stones, television crews would appear. No matter who hurled them, the stones hindered the use of nonviolent sanctions in a way that might have caused division in soldiers' ranks or splits among Israeli sectors. Regardless, this issue also requires examining the deaths of Israeli soldiers, thousands of whom were on active duty in the territories. The Palestinians' restraint of arms was such that the Israel Defense Forces (IDF) officially reported the following: four Israeli soldiers killed in the West Bank and none in Gaza in 1988; two soldiers killed in the West Bank and two in Gaza in 1989; two soldiers killed in the West Bank and one in Gaza in 1990; and one soldier killed in the West Bank and none in Gaza in 1991. Against the 12 Israeli soldiers slain during this four-year period, the IDF spokesperson noted, Israelis killed 706 Palestinian civilians (figure 10.2).[15]

Figure 10.2   In 1988, a joint Israeli-Arab peace march, "Jews and Arabs against the Occupation," started in kibbutz Rosh Hanikra in northern Israel and after a week's marching climaxed in Jerusalem, near the Knesset. It was organized by Red Line (Kav Adom in Hebrew), an Israeli peace organization set up by Dov Yirmiya, a former colonel in the Israeli Army; Yoram Verete, a poet; and Alon Porat, an artist. More than 100 Israeli peace organizations or groups supportive of the uprising came into being or reactivated during the first intifada.

Credit: Hashomer Hatzair Archive, Givat Haviva, al-Hamishmar collection, Boaz Lanir.

Israel ordered severe crackdowns. Defense Minister Yitzhak Rabin outlawed the alternative popular education that had replaced the closed schools and universities, establishing 10-year jail terms and fines equivalent to $5,000 for any teacher involved. Ten-year prison terms were imposed for membership in the popular committees, disproportionately affecting women, who ran so many of the committees. Food scarcity, restricted movements, and controls on the passage of travelers through roadblocks and checkpoints were circumvented by the committees, but incidents of trauma rose sharply, along with deportations, massive arrests, and preemptive detentions. Economic constraints were harsh, as Palestinian laborers were prohibited from traveling to Israel for day jobs. Within the Command, long incarcerations had a debilitating effect. The ability to resist collapse or withhold names of contemporaries under torture became a rite of passage. Prohibitions against media access to the occupied territories prevented a full airing of Israel's reprisals.[16]

The civilian movements of the 1980s, with their thousands of micro-organizations, had also given a hearing to voices espousing violence, including that of Hamas. *Hamas* is a non-Quranic word meaning "zeal" and an acronym for Harakat al-Muqawama al-Islamiyya (Islamic Resistance Movement). Hamas evolved from a decision by the Muslim Brotherhood, founded in Egypt in 1928 and in Jerusalem in 1945, to partake in the intifada, though not in accordance with the protocols of nonviolent civil resistance prescribed by the Command. It published its covenant in

August 1988 to distinguish itself from the Command, which produced the leaflets guiding the intifada and in them appealed for recognition from Israel while simultaneously confronting its policies. A more accurate date for Hamas's origin would be late 1987, after the outbreak of the uprising, when, led by Sheikh Ahmad Yasin, the group's kindergartens, clinics, and youth centers became visible.[17] Within the circumference of the uprising, although Hamas endorsed armed struggle and refused to recognize Israel, otherwise improbable bargains could still be struck. Hamas found common ground with Fateh in 1990. They agreed to a 13-point pact of honor in September, with Feisel Husseini signing for Fateh, and Sheikh Jamil Hamami for Hamas. In the pact, and not for the last time, Hamas softened its position by endorsing the lifting of Israel's military occupation. By accepting the end of occupation as a goal, Hamas implied the possibility for sharing the land, reversing its position against accepting the partition of Palestine.

Figure 10.3 In late 1989, a human chain encircled the Old City of Jerusalem. A demonstration in favor of a Palestinian state and a Jewish state side by side, it was organized by the Israeli organization Peace Now, Israeli women's organizations, several members of the Knesset, Feisel Husseini, and numerous Palestinians. More than 25,000 Arabs and Jews held hands around the approximately two-and-a-half-mile perimeter.

Credit: Hashomer Hatzair Archive, Givat Haviva, al-Hamishmar Collection, Rachamim Israeli.

Two months after the outbreak of the intifada, on February 9, 1988 Gene Sharp traveled again to Israel and the occupied territories. At the invitation of former IDF chief psychologist Reuven Gal, he spoke to Israeli strategic specialists. Stressing that the Palestinians' grasp of the technique of nonviolent resistance was superficial, Sharp emphasized that the Israeli government should be cautious in reacting, because ruthless reprisals could affect its ability to bring an end to terrorism. Soon after, Gal imparted Sharp's insights to Gen. Matan Vilnai and his senior officers. According to Gal, his outline of Sharp's thinking would hasten eventual Israeli recognition that military solutions would fail to defeat the intifada (figure 10.3).[18]

A Newfound Cognizance of Power

In the intifada, a newfound cognizance of power, a byproduct of actions in which all persons could participate and be empowered, underscored the advantageous properties of nonviolent civil resistance as an alternative to doing nothing or joining a commando unit. The thinking of the Palestinian organizer intellectuals had in some cases been cross-fertilized by education abroad and also was influenced by contact with Israeli sympathizers, some of them dissenters from within the ranks of Israel's military forces who were prepared to challenge its occupation tangibly. The alterations in political thought that resulted—along with concepts borrowed from struggles elsewhere—located the Palestinian uprising within the larger nonviolent quest for human rights that in the late 1980s swept the world from Chile and Argentina, across Eastern Europe, into the Soviet Union, to Burma—which is not to say that it was recognized as such in Israel by authorities, news media, academia, or for that matter in the diplomatic corps.

To view this homegrown movement as controlled by exiles, as many observers did, is to misunderstand its consequentiality. Power had shifted to the territories, where organizer intellectuals were making the decisions. The PLO preoccupied itself unnecessarily with the possibility of the new local leadership posing a serious challenge to it.[19] Palestinians in the territories were more pragmatic and ready to compromise with Israel than was the exiled leadership in Tunis, which did not share or comprehend the perspective in the territories on the need to undermine Israeli justifications for extremist policies that played on fear. Nusseibeh would fax the draft leaflets to Tunis, via a prearranged intermediary in Paris, hoping to influence the thinking of the PLO in Tunis and seeking to bind them to the strategy hatched locally. Palestinians in the "think tank" and Command in the territories visualized themselves as originating actions, organizing demonstrations, and maintaining communications, while the PLO would articulate their grievances in the international halls of power.

Vexation began eventually to spread from the meager fruits of maintaining nonviolent discipline. It took years for Israel to recognize that the uprising had political rather than military goals. Meanwhile, the Command survived four waves of arrests. The template of nonviolent struggle could not hold, as Israel either locked up or deported the main nonviolent protagonists. The consensus had been preserved for two and a half years, despite Israeli counter-brutality, lack of PLO support, and the weak posture of the international community. As a result of the disregard for the deliberate forswearing of firearms in the uprising, the consensus on nonviolent strategies in the territories collapsed in the third year. Voices propounding desiccated theories of military retaliation rebounded. By March 1990, the PLO, which had not in reality comprehended the nonviolent strategies and logic for noncooperation, took over the intifada. Muhammad Jadallah, among the original organizers of the 1970s professional associations, elaborated:

> 1988 and 1989 were two pure years organized by local leadership, but when the interference of the [PLO] leadership started taking place, things started to suffer....[Prior to 1990] the interrelations among the [factions] were great, with high responsibility, good cooperation, coordination, and there was space and place for everyone to operate separately. There was room for joint work, and there was room for individual work, so everybody was involved. This was the case until the [PLO] leadership took over....By [March] 1990, it was their intifada. This is when the uprising was aborted. The intifada was strangulated by the PLO, before it was strangulated by the Israelis.[20]

Three and a half years after its start, Husseini called for a reassessment and retooling of the intifada, but the balance of power had reverted to the governing elite in exile, whose foremost concern was to preserve its supremacy.

Where disputing parties possess severely asymmetrical power, the smaller or weaker side may be unable to obtain any hearing apart from staging a nonviolent struggle, which can bring parity between the sides of an otherwise unbalanced adversarial relationship. Nonviolent resistance may be the *only* way to reach negotiations. The uprising neither lifted the military occupation nor stopped the implanting of Israeli settlements in lands set aside for the Palestinians by the United Nations. Nonetheless, the uprising's nonviolent sanctions achieved more than had decades of armed attacks on largely civilian targets.

The intifada produced the most considerable effort of the United States to date to encourage a comprehensive settlement of the Arab-Israeli conflict—an international peace conference held in October 1991 in Madrid. The Palestinians had hitherto been absent from Middle East peace talks, but made their debut in this forum, upending Israel's longstanding refusal to countenance the Palestinians as a negotiating partner. Israel's explicit veto of PLO members and residents of East Jerusalem resulted in a joint Jordanian-Palestinian delegation. A separate guidance committee was established with Feisel Husseini as coordinator, and professor Hanan Mikhail Ashrawi as spokesperson. They and the other Palestinians, primarily physicians or academicians with doctorates in various disciplines, were segregated from the conference delegates, who represented 40 countries as "advisers," but 5,000 reporters covered the discussions, giving the Palestinian issue a human face, that of Husseini, Ashrawi, and Haidar Abd al-Shafi, a Gaza physician in whose home early planning meetings for the intifada had been held. The activist intellectuals chronicled here, and their political thinking, gained exposure on the world stage.

U.S. Secretary of State James Baker's extensive preparations for the conference included more than a half dozen meetings with Husseini, Ashrawi, and other East Jerusalem organizer intellectuals, who were instrumental in the intifada. When he visited Jerusalem in March 1991 for the first encounter with them, Husseini and others maintained that they were emissaries from PLO chairman Arafat, who had approved the session; however, as *Washington Post* reporter, Glenn Frankel, notes, "in fact, they were, for the first time, calling some of the shots themselves."[21] The Madrid conference broke the psychological barrier against direct talks between the Israelis and Palestinians, a tangible breakthrough that was among the results from changes in political thought nurtured during the period in which the Palestinians in the occupied territories were the most disciplined in their use of nonviolent action.

Gains and Reversals: The Oslo Accords and a Second Intifada

While the Madrid 1991 international conference had been produced by the first intifada, the Oslo process derived from Israelis on the political Left. Designated Israelis and Palestinians met in Oslo without public acknowledgment. The residents of the occupied Palestinian territories expected that a Palestinian state would soon exist alongside Israel—the formulation agreed in the intifada—yet this outcome was not provided in Oslo.

The Declaration of Principles of the Oslo accords was signed at the U.S. White House on September 13, 1993, denoting the first Israeli recognition of the PLO. In an exchange of letters between Yasir Arafat and the Israeli prime minister, Yitzhak Rabin, without which the signing would not have transpired, the PLO letter recognizes the state of Israel, but Israel's does not identify the right of the Palestinians to establish their own nation-state. In recognizing Israel, the Palestinians accepted that nearly four-fifths of historic Israel (lands within the boundaries of Israel before the 1967 war) was no longer under consideration. Any upcoming negotiations over land would involve adjustments from the West Bank and Gaza Strip; in sum, the Palestinians' land would get smaller, while the Israelis' territory would enlarge.

The declaration was an agenda for talks, with a schedule, rather than an agreement. Held for future parleys, pursuant to implementation of an interim agreement, were the issues of Jerusalem, the question of the Palestinian refugees, and the status of Israeli settlements in the occupied territories. The declaration of principles emphasized process over content, specifically an Israeli withdrawal from Gaza and Jericho, subsequent incremental transfer of civil functions from Israel to the PLO, and ultimately Israeli withdrawal from Palestinian population centers. Israeli involvement in final negotiations was made contingent on a favorable outcome in peaceful implementation of the interim agreement.

The first Israeli military forces to leave the Palestinian territories militarily occupied in 1967 departed from Jenin, on November 13, 1995, the day after Prime Minister Rabin was assassinated and one week ahead of schedule for the planned withdrawals. Earlier, in May 1994, an infant self-government, the Palestinian Authority (PA), had been established in Gaza and nominally in Jericho, also as provided in the accords. Israel had rejected as insufficient the 1996 verbal nullification of offending articles of the PLO's charter. On December 14, 1998, U.S. president William J. Clinton went to Gaza to witness voting with a show of hands to amend the Palestinian National Charter, which Israel accepted, implying further impetus for statehood.

Despite bloody attacks by the Islamic revivalist organizations Hamas and Islamic Jihad, intended to halt the process, Israel and the PLO signed the Interim Palestinian-Israel Agreement regarding the West Bank and Gaza Strip, or Oslo II, on September 28, 1995, at the White House. In 300 pages, it provided for elections of a Palestinian council, transfer of legislative authority to it, withdrawal of Israeli forces from Palestinian population centers, and division of the West Bank into three areas.

Recurring boundary closures led to deteriorating standards of living in the West Bank and Gaza and increasing poverty. Israel and the PA both condoned human rights abuses in the name of security. Unabashed building of settlements continued. Shimon Peres formed a government after Rabin's assassination, but lost to Benjamin Netanyahu in 1996 elections, largely in response to Hamas suicide bombs in major Israeli cities. Still more setbacks transpired.

The arrival of 100 thousand [ditto] Palestinian exiles from Tunis brought strains and pressures. The second intifada started on September 28, 2000, when the Israeli opposition leader Ariel Sharon took more than 1 thousand security and border police into the Old City of Jerusalem, onto the site known by Jews as the Temple Mount and by Muslims Haram al-Sharif (august sanctuary). The following day, Palestinians conducted a nonviolent demonstration. Israeli police fired live ammunition and killed four protesting youths. The territories were torn by upheaval. The initial weeks of the second intifada (also called al-Aqsa intifada) were fundamentally another upsurge of civil resistance. "We cannot emphasize the fact enough," according to Israeli peace activist Michel Warschawski, "Palestinian soldiers joined in the confrontations with the Israeli army only after Israeli soldiers armed to the teeth, often with rifles with telescopic sights, had killed several dozen young demonstrators."[22] The police and security of the returning exiles took almost no part in the early weeks of the second intifada, neither contributing to it nor trying to end it, as enraged youths hurled rocks at Israeli soldiers. The young had become dismayed as Israeli settlements condemned by the international community annually grew in number and size despite the Oslo accords.

Some youths joined the Fateh *tanzim* (organization), a militia that embarked on armed actions. With the *tanzim,* for the first time, Israeli settlements with armed Israeli settlers were attacked, having increased in size and number, often next to Palestinian urban settings. The first intifada had meticulously avoided contact with the settlements. According to Palestinian journalist Daoud Kuttab, "The Palestinians' use of firearms, especially against settlers and settlements near populated Palestinian communities" was a critical difference between the two uprisings; furthermore, "not since the 1967 war has Israel used such heavy weapons against Palestinians."[23]

Small, Local Movements against the "Separation Barrier"

The Palestinians' withdrawal from the cycle of violence as in the first intifada continues in pockets of nonviolent civil resistance across the West Bank, where small, nonviolent movements are attempting to minimize the destructiveness of the "separation barrier" being built by Israel among their communities. Thus another example of the repudiation of armed struggle as the means to a limited end is perceptible nearly two decades after the salient years of 1987–1990.

According to UN sources, Israeli settlements and related infrastructure occupy approximately 40 percent of the West Bank, including an "Israeli-only" road network and a system of barriers separating land settled by Israelis from Palestinian-held lands and dividing established Palestinian communities, towns, and villages. In April 2002, the Israeli government announced its plans for the construction of "separation barriers" with the ostensible purpose of preventing the infiltration into Israel of suicide bombers, who had launched a number of attacks during the second, or so-called al-Aqsa, intifada that erupted in September 2000.

Parts of the barrier, on which construction continues, consist of 25-foot-high segments of concrete—two to three times the height of the Berlin Wall. Armed sniper towers rise every 300 meters in some sections, and trenches also help deter efforts to breach the structure. In the *New York Times* on June 4, 2008, Thomas L. Friedman, described the landscape: "The West Bank today is an ugly quilt of high walls, Israeli checkpoints, 'legal' and 'illegal' Jewish settlements, Arab villages, Jewish roads that only Israeli settlers use...."

Despite the officially pronounced purpose of preventing attacks by physically separating the West Bank and Israel, only some 20 percent of the barrier's 450-mile route was slated to run along the Green Line, as the border between them is called.[24] As a consequence, more than 530,000 dunums of land (approximately 132,500 acres), representing 9.5 percent of the West Bank (including East Jerusalem), were to be situated between the barrier and the Green Line, that is, on the "Israeli side." This area contains 21 Palestinian villages, home to more than 30,000 residents, and some 200,000 Palestinians who hold Israeli identity cards and live in East Jerusalem. With the completion of the barrier, all of these people will be separated from the West Bank. In addition, as a result of its winding route, the barrier will surround on at least three sides 50 more Palestinian villages, in which 244,000 persons live, that lie on the "Palestinian side" of the barrier.[25] Official pronouncements aside, the actual effect of the separation wall is to confiscate Palestinian land, isolate Palestinian communities one from another, and compromise their viability individually and collectively, as, according to analysts Catherine Cook and Adam Hanieh, "in places, the barrier dips several miles into the West Bank, leaving settlements, fertile Palestinian land, and valuable water resources on the Israeli side."[26] The Israeli human rights organization B'Tselem insists that the route of the barrier "defies all security logic and appears politically motivated."[27]

The large Israeli settlement of Modi'in Illit (Upper Modi'in) is built on land belonging to the Palestinian villages of Bil'in, Dir Qadis, Kharbata, Ni'lin, and Saffa. The fastest-growing settlement in the West Bank, its population is projected to grow to 150,000 by 2020. Modi'in Illit is representative of the major settlements that successive Israeli governments have regarded as non-negotiable settlement blocs intended for annexation to Israel in any agreement with the Palestinians. The unchallenged growth of Modi'in Illit has already damaged life for the Palestinian farmers of Bil'in, a village of 1,700 inhabitants, and the settlement itself reveals the association between the construction of the separation barrier and the expansion of settlements. The wall being constructed between Modi'in Illit and Bil'in consumes half the village's remaining lands, or about 450 acres. It threatens to rob many others of their lands and condemn them to living in tiny, isolated enclaves.

Since February 2005, the residents of Bil'in have led a local nonviolent struggle against the wall consuming their lands. Accompanied by Israeli peace activists and international volunteers, they have demonstrated each Friday before bulldozers and Israeli soldiers. They have made common cause with other Palestinian villages directly affected by the wall, including Biddu, Budrus, Deir Ballut, Jayyus, and Nil'in, which for more than four years have also used nonviolent methods to campaign against the encroachment of the barrier. Local popular committees have organized these collective nonviolent actions. Some call the campaign "the intifada of the wall." Their gains have been significant, but ultimately producing only modest results: they have managed to impede or slow the progression of the system of barriers but they have not halted them outright. In the case of Budrus and Deir Ballut, persistent civil resistance combined with legal appeals and solidarity campaigns has actually changed the course of the wall, enabling some communities to regain lost pastures, water sources, and vineyards.[28]

More than 200 persons have been injured in Bil'in during rallies, and many have been arrested. Deployed against the unarmed challengers are the army, police, border guards, and private security enterprises, armed with live ammunition, clubs, teargas, and "rubber bullets" (ballistic metal coated with a thin veneer of rubber). Israeli forces routinely try to deter members of the Bil'in popular committee with arrests and late night sweeps. Evidence has come to light of Israeli special forces having been positioned in Bil'in, along with Israeli agents provocateurs in Arab disguise, who joined demonstrations and sought to incite demonstrators to use violence. The local committee has prevented such provocations from instigating lethal escalations.

On some Fridays, 100 Palestinian villagers in Anin are joined by 80 or more members of the International Solidarity Movement (ISM), an organization that has facilitated involvement and witness by activists from around the world.[29] Its volunteers have more than once faced Israeli gunfire.[30] In December 2006 in Bethlehem, the Archbishop of Canterbury, Rowan Williams, spoke out against the separation barrier, proclaiming them a "sign of all that is wrong in the human heart," but the role of international third parties has yet to be fully utilized in the struggle against the wall.

On June 30, 2004, Israel's High Court of Justice ordered changes in the route of the barriers, because the course was causing harm to the local Palestinian population. Scantily reported outside Israel, the court ruled that "the route disrupts the delicate balance between the obligation of the military commander to preserve security and his obligation to provide for the needs of the local inhabitants." Such impairment must be minimized, the court held, even if it results in less security for Israel. The Israeli security establishment insists consistently before the court that the barrier is being constructed to prevent suicide bombers from entering Israel, so its route is determined by security needs.

In September 2007, the High Court ordered the government to revise a mile-long segment of the barrier that had separated the population of Bil'in from much of their farmland. This and other rulings by the court were ignored by the Israeli military, which regards them as lacking implementation authority. Furthermore, the rulings of Israel's highest court do not follow the doctrine of stare decisis; that is, they do not set or hold precedent. On December 15, 2008, the High Court requested additional revision of the wall's section in Bil'in, holding that an alternative route offered by the government ran primarily through private Palestinian land and was not based purely on security needs.[31]

Shortly after the Israel High Court's June 2004 ruling on the barriers' routing, in The Hague the International Court of Justice (ICJ), the principal judicial organ of the United Nations, had urged the United Nations to enforce the court's ruling that Israel tear down the separation barrier and compensate the Palestinians for the hardship it had caused them. On July 9, 2004, the ICJ found that the wall "gives expression" to Israeli settlements and annexation of East Jerusalem, because the region through which the wall proceeds is territory under military occupation according to international law; thus international legal instruments governing armed conflicts apply. In addition, Israel, it noted, is under an absolute obligation to respect international humanitarian law, as defined by the Regulations of 1907 and by the Fourth Geneva Convention of 1949. The court held that any part of the wall built on land occupied by Israel in 1967 violates the Fourth Geneva Convention and other treaties.

The 15 ICJ justices were almost unanimous in supporting the opinion, and although the court's ruling is not binding, the body's legal position was clarified and guidelines laid out for future action by the General Assembly and international community. In the same month, the General Assembly overwhelmingly reaffirmed the ICJ's judgment that the separation barrier violates international law and called on Israel to demolish it or re-route it to follow the Green Line. The Israeli government has ignored the violations of territory—80 percent of the projected route of the wall is inside the West Bank—and the Israeli military considers the ICJ's judgments as but "opinions." Nonetheless, the modest achievements of local nonviolent campaigns against the wall suggest some potential for future challenges and applicable approaches not based on violence. They reflect the residual effects of Palestinian civil resistance and civil society developments of the 1970s and 1980s

Conclusion

In any future Palestinian state, popular comprehension of the power of noncooperation could be crucial for restraint of Palestinian despotism. It is thus important, apart from the Israeli-Palestinian conflict, not to overlook, ignore, or mischaracterize the discipline represented by the first intifada and current small Palestinian movements against the Israeli separation barriers. Residual knowledge of nonviolent civil resistance is an asset for a future state, enhancing the capacity for self-criticism and reform. Moreover, historical analysis verifies that nonviolent struggle often acts as a predictor for outcomes of democratic governance. This is not a result of ideology. Authoritarian and militaristic structures of armed guerrilla movements often lead to coercive systems, whereas nonviolent movements *tend* to select democratic results and leaders who are democratic in ethos.

The first intifada opened and democratized Palestinian society. It produced the strongest civil society to date in the Arab world and minted the first authentic Arab model of democracy. From this popular resistance would emerge the most cogent pressure to date to create a Palestinian state alongside Israel, with inherent acceptance of the latter's permanence. The moment was not unique in the sense that the Palestinians had employed nonviolent struggle as a dominant technique in the 1920s and 1930s when pleading their case before the British, asking them to honor their promises to the Arabs as they had to world Jewry. Yet the first intifada was epochal because alterations in political thinking about sharing the land and ending armed struggle were forged by Palestinians inside the territories, despite continual advocacy or ambiguity on a policy of armed struggle by many in the PLO, whose pronounced orthodoxies of guerrilla warfare were inconsistent with their goals. The implications of the first intifada are seismic, yet these alterations cannot stand without reciprocity. Changes in political thought are evanescent, contingent, and always in need of reclamation.

Notes

1.   The Zionists migrating into Palestine did not seek to become part of the local institutions and economies, but developed their own, exclusive enterprises. Sociologist Gershon Shafir explains that Jewish colonization rested upon two doctrines: Hebrew labor, or conquest of labor, which sought to replace Arab workers with Jewish workers, and Hebrew land, or conquest of land, which meant that Arab land, once purchased by the land-acquisition arm of the World Zionism Organization, could not be resold to Arabs. Gershon Shafir, *Land, Labour and the Origins of the Israeli-Palestinian Conflict, 1882–1914* (Cambridge: Cambridge University Press, 1989).

2. The 1920s and 1930s saw extensive employment of nonviolent methods by Palestinians in seeking to preserve their way of life. From the first large peaceful demonstration against the British on February 27, 1920, to the 174-day general strike of 1936, the Palestinians employed archetypal methods of nonviolent struggle. For example, in Gaza several hundred veiled Muslim women marched on April 25, 1936. Far from playing auxiliary roles, women's groups stood in the vanguard by April and May 1936 in calling for a boycott of Zionist- and British-made products and withdrawal from the British Boy Scout movement.

    Local strike committees across Palestine ran the 1936 countrywide general strike. These committees, like those in the first intifada, possessed independence and individuality within the broader context of nationalist appeals for limiting immigration and establishing self-government in Palestine. The local committees were largely autonomous, possibly explaining the strike's durability. As officials locked up one local leader, another stepped forward. The first intifada reasserted this quest for recognition of civil and political rights of the 1920s and 1930s.

    This record of utilization of nonviolent methods in the 1920s–1930s, reintroduced in the first intifada, has been ignored and misrepresented. (This narrative has also been eclipsed by shock and horror from acts of terrorism.) In ignoring the Palestinians' nonviolent methods, the British and Zionists reinforced those sectors that were advocating violent resistance, including the forerunners of today's Islamic revivalist organizations. By 1938, the historian J. C. Hurewitz states, "these events [had] taught the lesson that the use of violence as a political weapon produced results which otherwise appeared unobtainable." J. C. Hurewitz, *The Struggle for Palestine* (New York: Schocken Books, 1976), 93. For details on the Palestinians' use of nonviolent sanctions in the 1920s and 1930s, see Mary Elizabeth King, *A Quiet Revolution: The First Palestinian Intifada and Nonviolent Resistance* (New York and London: Nation Books, 2007; Perseus Books, 2008), 25–93.

3. Martin Kolinsky, "The Collapse and Restoration of Public Security," in *Britain and the Middle East in the 1930s*, ed. Michael J. Cohen and Martin Kolinsky, 147 (New York: St. Martin's Press, 1992); Royal Commission of Enquiry, July 1937, *Palestine Royal Commission Report*, Cmd. 5479 (London: H. M. Stationery Office, 1937), 279 (hereafter Peel Commission Report). Extralegal immigration especially distressed the Arabs. Zvi Elpeleg, *The Grand Mufti: Haj Amin al-Husaini, Founder of the Palestinian National Movement*, trans. David Harvey, ed. Shmuel Himelstein (London: Frank Cass, 1993), 36, as cited in King, *Quiet Revolution*, 43, 369 n 127. Between 1932 and 1936, the Jewish population virtually doubled.

4. Banned by the Israelis, the PLO's main base was in Jordan until 1970, when its fighters were forced to relocate to Lebanon after challenging the government of King Hussein. The front was routed by Israel's invasion of Beirut in 1982, ending up in Tunisia, in remote North Africa.

5. Yesh Gvul began when 2,500 reservists asked not to be assigned to military service in Lebanon.

6. CCIF also called itself the Committee to Confront the Iron Fist. "Confronting the iron fist" meant challenging the policies of the State of Israel. Israeli Prime Minister Yitzhak Shamir had not coined the term *iron fist* but frequently linked himself with it. David Ben-Gurion, Israel's first prime minister (simultaneously defense minister) used the expressions *yad hazaqah* (strong hand), and *barzel Yisrael* (iron of Israel). Israeli officials employed these terms in the 1980s. Scott Atran, "Stones against the Iron Fist, Terror within the Nation: Alternating Structures of Violence and Cultural Identity in the Israeli-Palestinian Conflict," *Politics and Society* 18, no. 4 (1990): 484.

7. Feisel Husseini, one-hour interview with the author (East Jerusalem, January 30, 1996). Such meetings were illegal, hence a form of civil disobedience.

8. The appeal of writings by the Italian Marxist, Antonio Gramsci, were enhanced by 11 years spent in Mussolini's prisons and his disagreement with the Bolsheviks' seizure of power through violence. Gramsci views "organizer intellectuals" as the primary historical agents of change in opposing despotism and nonviolently promoting lasting political change. In his view, resistance movements must possess popular support and permeate the structures of civil society *before* attempting to take control of state power. This means alliances among movements on behalf of civil liberties, peace, students, or women. Gramsci's concept of *egemonia* (hegemony), also *direzione* (direction, or leadership), suggests that major change through nonviolent action becomes possible when groups opposing a state apparatus gain widespread consent within civil society.

9. Nusseibeh, interviewed for the first time for an Israeli periodical, proffered a one-state solution. On November 13, 1985, in *Koteret Rashit*, the Israeli interviewer Michal Sela inquired what the Palestinians would do if they did not get a state. Nusseibeh replied that Israel should annex the Palestinians and give them rights, which would result in their obtaining between 12 and 16 seats in the Knesset. If they were not a majority at that time, he suggested, within 10 years the Palestinians would have a demographic plurality. Michal Sela, "Nusseibeh: Yes, to Annex; Interview of Sari Nusseibeh," trans. comm. Zoughbi E. Zoughbi, *Koteret Rashit*, November 13, 1985, as cited in King, *Quiet Revolution*, 184, 404 *n* 92.

10. The nascent Palestinian civil society produced new leader-spokespersons, among them Radwan Abu Ayyash, Haj Abd Abu-Diab, Ziad Abu Zayyad, Mamdouh Aker, Hanan Mikhail Ashrawi, Mubarak Awad, Mahdi Abd al-Hadi, Feisel Husseini, Muhammad Jadallah, Zahira Kamal, Ghassan Khatib, Jonathan Kuttab, Raja Shehadeh, Riad al-Malki, Khalil Mahshi, Sari Nusseibeh, Haidar Abd al-Shafi, and Hanna Siniora. Directly addressing the Palestinian, Israeli, and international news media for attribution, they spoke without noms de guerre. The descent of a few from notable families that opposed the British amplified their message. With deliberate openness—in contrast to the stealth of covert military cadres—they stated limited, achievable political goals. They scorned the threatening, grandiose language of the guerrillas. Clear communication is an adjunct to the technique of nonviolent struggle, linked to the need to explain grievances clearly when seeking change from an adversary.

11. A work by Sharp, written with no specific conflict in mind and translated by the center, contends that civilian defense (a subfield of nonviolent resistance) should dispense with the notion that defense is synonymous with military strength. Central to the theory of civilian defense is the proposition that an entity occupying through military force has no true power without the consent and obedience of those who are occupied (even if cooperation is exacted by brute force, punishment, or threat). Through planned noncooperation, the citizenry can make a society ungovernable for the oppressor or attacker, deterring aggression. Originally entitled *Power, Struggle and Defense*, Sharp's work was translated into Arabic as *al-Muqawama bi la-Unf* (Resistance with No Violence, meaning Nonviolent Resistance). In 1983–1984, between 4,000 and 7,000 copies of this translation circulated on the West Bank. In the mid-1980s, Mifras Publishing House brought out a Hebrew edition in Israel titled *Hitnaggedut Lo Alima* (Opposition with No Violence, or Nonviolent Opposition). The first chapter of Sharp's *National Security through Civilian-Based Defense* (Omaha, NE: Association for Transarmament Studies, 1970) bears close resemblance to the Arabic translation. Gene Sharp, two-hour interview, Cambridge, Massachusetts, October 19, 1995, and Jonathan Kuttab, two-hour interview, East Jerusalem, December 12, 1997.

12. The Fourteen Points propose the convening of an international peace conference with the PLO acting as the sole legitimate representative of the Palestinian people. It requests Israeli compliance prior to the start of the conference in order to create an atmosphere

of equality and imply recognition of the national rights of the Palestinian people, including self-determination and the "establishment of an independent Palestinian state on Palestinian national soil." Among its demands are Israeli compliance with international conventions on human rights, including those concerning deportations, prisoners, imprisonment, actions by settlers and soldiers, and the right of political freedom; Israeli military withdrawal from Palestinian population centers and an end to the "siege" of refugee camps; a halt to the implantation of Israeli settlements and confiscation of Palestinian land; respect for Muslim and Christian holy sites; cessation of direct taxes levied on Palestinian residents; the lifting of restrictions on building permits, agriculture, and industrial programs; the free movement of products from the occupied territories; and legal political contact between the residents of the occupied territories and the PLO. See Hanna Siniora and Fayez Abu Rahme, "The Fourteen Talking Points of West Bank–Gaza Palestinians, January 14, 1988," in *The Middle East: Ten Years after Camp David*, ed. William B. Quandt (Washington, DC: Brookings Institution, 1988), Appendix J, 484–87.

13. See note 8. *Total* civil disobedience was the term used in debates and leaflets in envisioning a program of across-the-board noncooperation with Israeli occupying authorities, such as mass hunger strikes, boycotts, withholding of fines and bail, withdrawal of funds from Israeli banks, resignation from jobs, refusal to patronize Israeli businesses, and labor unions' contracting with local enterprises.

14. "Education during the Intifada," *Educational Network* (Ramallah) 1 (June 1990): 1, as cited in King, *Quiet Revolution*, 223, 419 n 151. Published quarterly by Khalil Mahshi and teachers at the Friends School in Ramallah, the *Educational Network* detailed punitive measures against educational institutions in the West Bank and reported on the alternative, or parallel, structures created to compensate for school closures.

15. Lt. Col. Yehuda Weinraub, IDF spokesperson and head of information, Tel Aviv, records pursuant to a telephone request of 18 March 1997, trans. Reuven Gal.

16. On Israeli censorship of television coverage of the uprising, see James V. D'Amato, "How Regimes Profit by Curbing U.S. Television News," *Orbis* 35 (Summer 1991): 351–56. Former U.S. secretary of state Henry Kissinger recommended at an off-the-record breakfast with American Jewish leaders, "Israel should bar the media from entry into the territories involved..., accept the short-term criticism of the world press for such conduct, and put down the insurrection as quickly as possible—overwhelmingly, brutally.... Under no circumstances should Israel make any concessions during the present insurrection." Julius Berman, "Behind Closed Doors," *Harper's*, June 1988. On 4 March, Israel attempted for the first time to close the entire West Bank to journalists. Alan Cowell, "Israel Curbs Coverage of the West Bank," *New York Times*, March 5, 1988, 5.

    Despite such prohibitions, more than 100 Israeli peace groups or organizations supportive of the intifada came into being or reactivated. Sociologist Naomi Chazan, member of the Knesset, estimated that 86 new groups formed as a result of the intifada, while a large number of moribund Israeli protest movements revived themselves. Naomi Chazan, one-hour interview, East Jerusalem, 6 June 1988. On particular aspects of Israeli responses to the uprising, see King, *Quiet Revolution.*, 242–55, 275–77, 292.

17. Hamas had come into existence with official Israeli assistance (but would become a Pandora's Box for Israel and in the 1990s and 2000s sponsor waves of suicide bombings, fight Fateh with military weaponry, and militarily seize control of Gaza). The Israeli Foreign Ministry admitted in an interview that the welfare programs of Hamas and a desire to weaken the PLO, by supporting a challenger to the front, were among the justifications for Israel's support of Hamas in its early days. Yigal Caspi, Israeli Foreign Ministry spokesperson in 1994 when Shimon Peres was foreign minister, one-hour interview, Jerusalem, November 10, 1994. The Israeli brigadier general in charge of Gaza told David Shipler of the *New York Times* that he had funded Islamic factions to strengthen

them against the PLO. David Shipler, *Arab and Jew: Wounded Spirits in a Promised Land* (New York: Times Publishers, 1986), 176–77. Retired Brig. Gen. Binyamin Ben-Eliezer, coordinator of operations in the occupied territories (1983–1984), implied in interviews that Israel had a policy of encouraging Muslim forces to weaken the PLO. Susan Hattis Rolef, "Israel's Policy toward the PLO: From Rejection to Recognition," in *The PLO and Israel: From Armed Conflict to Political Solution, 1964–1994*, ed. Avraham Sela and Moshe Maoz (New York: St. Martin's Press, 1997), 259.

18. Reuven Gal, two-hour interview, Zichron Yaakov, Israel, March 16, 1997.

19. The activists and organizers in the territories had no desires or plans to substitute themselves for the sitting PLO leadership. They wanted a division of responsibility and for the PLO to take on the job of conducting negotiations for the independent state that they hoped would eventuate from the intifada. The relationship between the PLO in Tunis and the activist intellectuals who stood behind the Command inside the occupied territories was fraught with disagreement. On the disjuncture between the PLO's concerns for its own survival versus the potential for progress toward the full negotiated settlement sought by the West Bank and Gazan organizer intellectuals, see Raja Shehadeh, *From Occupation to Interim Accords: Israel and the Palestinian Territories*, Cimel Book Series no. 4 (London and The Hague: Kluwer Law International, 1997), esp. 103–21, 128–29, and 157–61.

20. Muhammad Jadallah, two-hour interview, December 15, 1997.

21. Glenn Frankel, "Divided They Stand," *Washington Post Magazine*, October 30, 1994. Also see Sarah Helm, "Pragmatist Will Speak for Palestinians," *Independent*, April 26, 1993, 12; Michael Sheridan, "Middle East Conference: New Breed Who Will Plead Palestinian Case; The Collapse of Armed Struggle against Israel Has Shifted Influence towards a More Bourgeois Western-Educated Selection of Representatives," *Independent*, October 30, 1991, 10.

22. Michel Warschawski, *Toward an Open Tomb: The Crisis of Israeli Society*, trans. Peter Drucker (New York: Monthly Review Press, 2004), 12.

23. Daoud Kuttab, "The Two Intifadas: Differing Shades of Resistance," February 8, 2001, Information Brief no. 66, Washington, D.C., Center for Policy Analysis on Palestine.

24. This is the boundary between Israel and the West Bank of the Jordan River based on the 1948 border of Israel as agreed to in the 1949 armistice. It is named for its green color on official armistice maps, to distinguish it from the customary black or occasionally purple lines on UN maps to denote anticipated final borders.

25. *Under the Guise of Security: Routing the Separation Barrier to Enable the Expansion of Israeli Settlements* in the West Bank (Jerusalem: B'Tselem, 2005), 5.

26. Catherine Cook and Adam Hanieh, "The Separation Barrier: Walling out Sovereignty," in *Struggle for Sovereignty*, eds. Beinin and Stein, 338–47.

27. *A Wall in Jerusalem: Obstacles to Human Rights in the Holy City* (Jerusalem: B'Tselem, 2006), 13. The Israeli Information Center for Human Rights in the Occupied Territories, or B'Tselem, was established in 1989 by Israeli academicians, attorneys, journalists, and members of the Knesset, to document human rights violations in the occupied territories and to inform the Israeli public and policymakers about them.

28. See Gadi Algazi, "Settlers on Israel's Eastern Frontier," *Le Monde Diplomatique*, August 2006, 4. Concerning one of the Israeli participants who regularly take part, Nimrod Ronen, see Meron Rapaport, "Symbol of Struggle," *Haaretz*, September 10, 2005, www.haaretz.com/hasen/objects/pages/PrintArticleEn.jhtml?itemNo=622829.

29. The ISM was founded in 2001 by Huwaida Arraf, a Palestinian American, and her Jewish husband, Adam Shapiro.

30. Johann Hari, "Walking towards Gunfire: The Peace Protesters Who Stand Up against Violence," *Independent* (London), August 1, 2008.

31. Isabel Kershner, "Israeli Court Orders Revision of West Bank Barrier Route," *New York Times*, December 16, 2008, A16.

11

The Nonviolent Struggle for Self-determination in Western Sahara

Salka Barca and Stephen Zunes

In 1975 the kingdom of Morocco conquered Western Sahara on the eve of that territory's anticipated independence from Spain. In doing so, it acted in defiance of a series of UN Security Council resolutions and a landmark 1975 decision by the International Court of Justice asserting the right of Western Sahara's inhabitants to self-determination. With threats of a French and U.S. veto at the United Nations preventing decisive action by the international community to stop the Moroccan invasion, the nationalist Polisario Front—which had been previously fighting the Spanish colonialists—launched an armed struggle against the new occupiers. In February 1976, the Polisario declared the establishment of the Sahrawi Arab Democratic Republic (SADR), now a full member state of the African Union and recognized by almost eighty countries. Mauritania, which had administered the southern third of Western Sahara with Morocco, renounced its claim to the territory in 1979 and withdrew its forces.

Meanwhile, the majority of the indigenous population, known as Sahrawis, was forced into exile, primarily to Polisario-run refugee camps in the southwestern desert region of Algeria adjacent to Western Sahara. Morocco eventually was able to take control of most of the territory, including all the major towns, building a series of fortified sand berms in the desert that effectively prevented penetration by Polisario forces into Moroccan-controlled territory. Regardless, the Polisario continued to mount attacks against Moroccan forces along the wall, resulting in ongoing human and financial costs to the Moroccans. After a series of diplomatic victories resulting in widespread international support for self-determination and ongoing nonrecognition of the Moroccan takeover by the international community, Morocco and the Polisario agreed to a cease-fire in 1991. Their cease-fire agreement was based on an understanding that there would be an internationally supervised referendum on the fate of the territory. Morocco, however, refused to allow the referendum to move forward. With French and U.S. support for the Moroccan government preventing the UN Security Council from providing the necessary diplomatic pressure to advance the referendum process and the lack of a realistic military option by Polisario forces, the struggle for self-determination has shifted to within the Moroccan-occupied territory and even parts of Morocco, where the remaining Sahrawi population has launched a nonviolent resistance campaign against the occupation.

The human rights situation in the occupied Western Sahara has been quite poor since the start of the occupation, and open expressions of nationalist sentiments have been severely suppressed. The repressive apparatus under King Hassan II, who launched the invasion in 1975 and attempted to consolidate the occupation until his death in 1999, was relatively quiet, with kidnappings of suspected nationalists taking place in the middle of the night. His son and successor, Mohamed VI, engaged in a series of important liberalizing measures within Morocco itself, allowing more political debate, allowing the elected parliament a greater role in policy making, and enacting a relatively progressive new family law protecting the rights of women. However, despite some initial hopes otherwise, repression has actually increased in severity in the occupied Western Sahara, with some of the worst repression taking place in broad daylight and involving large numbers of police and military. Meanwhile, Morocco moved more than 200,000 settlers into Western Sahara, where they now number twice the population of the indigenous Sahrawis.

Despite the ongoing repression, nonviolent resistance by Sahrawis has continued to grow in Western Sahara. From its beginnings in the form of hunger strikes by prisoners to its expansion over the last two decades, nonviolent action has become the primary means of resistance by Sahrawis and their allies against Moroccan occupation. Sahrawis from different sectors of society have engaged in protests, strikes, cultural celebrations, and other forms of nonviolent resistance. These acts, which have focused on such issues as educational policy, human rights, the release of political prisoners, and the right to self-determination, have helped to organize Sahrawis, raised the cost of occupation for the Moroccan government, and increased visibility to the Sahrawi cause. They have also helped to build support for the Sahrawi movement among international nongovernmental organizations and solidarity groups as well as among some sympathetic Moroccans.

Sahrawi Nonviolent Resistance

Between 1976 and 1979, Moroccan authorities imposed a totalitarian level of control in Western Sahara. In urban areas, they established checkpoints on every major street. Extrajudicial killings, torture, and sex crimes became widespread. The majority of the population at that time was rural, and after having their livestock killed and wells poisoned, most fled to refugee camps in Algeria, where they and their descendents remain to this day.[1]

Starting around 1979, however, the Moroccan government realized that it could not suppress the Sahrawis' desire for self-determination, so it sought to win their support through development schemes that turned the sleepy colonial capital of al-Aaiun into a modern city. Repression became quieter, but persisted, with up to 1,500 Sahrawis—a full 1 percent of the population—reported as disappeared.[2] The territory remained a closed military zone, allowing the population little contact with the outside world. Foreign journalists, including Moroccans, were rarely allowed entry. The Moroccan secret police controlled the population with an iron fist. Some Saharawis, out of fear or opportunism, worked closely with the Moroccan intelligence agency, the Direction de la Surveillance du Territoire (DST, Directorate of Territorial Surveillance), but collaboration remained at a fairly low level.

With the cease-fire agreement in 1991, the Moroccans released a few hundred of the disappeared Sahrawis who had been secretly detained at the Magouna prison. The public welcomed them as heroes, inspiring greater resistance within the occupied territory, especially among the younger generation. Among those encouraged to resist were those Sahrawis more recently arrested, who had grown up largely under Moroccan occupation; they were inspired particularly by prisoners' stories of defiance while in detention, including hunger strikes during the holy month of Ramadan and on other occasions. Beginning around 1998, some leading Sahrawi activists, among them Algaliya Djimi and Aminatou Haidar, began traveling to Rabat to meet with representatives of Moroccan and international NGOs and personnel from foreign embassies to discuss human rights issues. In addition, these representatives took advantage of relaxed restrictions on visitors to Western Sahara to visit the territory.

There had been scattered, impromptu public acts of nonviolent resistance over the years, most notably in 1987, when a UN committee's preparations for a proposed plebiscite on the fate of the territory occasioned a major human rights protest in al-Aaiun. The success of this demonstration was all the more remarkable given that most of the key organizers had been arrested the night before, and residents placed under a strict curfew. Most resistance activity remained clandestine, however, until early September 1999, when Sahrawi students organized sit-ins and vigils for more scholarships and transportation subsidies from the Moroccan government. Because an explicit call for independence would have been brutally suppressed, the students tested the boundaries of dissent by taking advantage of their relative intellectual freedom.

Sahrawi workers from nearby phosphate mines and a union of unemployed college graduates soon joined the nonviolent vigils, as did former political prisoners seeking compensation and accountability for their state-sponsored disappearances. The Moroccans suppressed the movement within a few months. Although the demands of what became known as the first "Sahrawi intifada" appeared to be nonpolitical, the movement served as a test of the Sahrawi public and the Moroccan government and paved the way for Sahrawis to later make bolder demands and engage in larger protests to directly challenge the Moroccan occupation.[3]

The Polisario had had active cells in the occupied areas since the Spanish colonial period, and shortly after this first major protest, other groups began to emerge. These new organizations focused on international humanitarian law, demanding the release of all political prisoners and justice for those who had never received due process. Though committed to national self-determination, they avoided explicit calls for independence, as this would have invited more repression than the dissident community could handle. By focusing exclusively on human rights issues—taking advantage of promises of liberalization in Morocco by King Mohamed—they hoped to create enough of a political opening to ultimately allow discussion of self-determination and eventually make it possible to advocate more openly for independence. Such efforts increased Sahrawis' awareness of their rights. In addition, Moroccan human rights groups began to interact with their Sahrawi counterparts within the occupied territory and with Sahrawi students attending Moroccan universities. As these meetings became more public, even modest shows of solidarity subjected Moroccans to the wrath of the authorities with such gatherings being forcibly broken up and those in attendance beaten, detained, and subjected to harsh questioning.

In 2004, upon the release of the prominent Sahrawi activist Mohammed Daddach, who had spent nearly 30 years in prison, massive public celebrations took place throughout Western Sahara. Of significance, these protests included the most explicit calls for independence at a public gathering since the Moroccan occupation began. In another unprecedented act of resistance, flags of the Sahrawi Arab Democratic Republic were put up overnight along major streets.

A second Sahrawi intifada, which became known as the "intifada al-istiqlal"— the intifada of independence—began in May 2005, as thousands of Sahrawi demonstrators, led by women and youths, took to the streets of the Hay Maatala quarter of al-Aaiun to protest the ongoing occupation and demand independence.[4] Moroccan troops and settlers met the largely nonviolent protests and sit-ins with severe repression. Within hours, leading Sahrawi activists had been kidnapped and disappeared. Sahrawi students at Moroccan universities organized solidarity demonstrations, hunger strikes, and other forms of nonviolent protest. Though mischaracterizing the almost exclusively nonviolent protests as being riots, the Moroccan media, including Channel 2 and the al-Aaiun local channel, were allowed for the first time to cover the demonstrations.

The intifada continued throughout 2005 with spontaneous and planned protests, all of which were met with harsh Moroccan responses. Many of the protests took place during visits by international figures to highlight the poor human rights situation, which had been largely ignored by the international community (figure 11.1). The excessive force unleashed against women and the elderly by Moroccan authorities, a particular affront in Islamic societies, resulted in the deaths of at least two nonviolent protestors, and served to broaden support for the movement, even among some Moroccan settlers and ethnic Sahrawis in southern Morocco.[5] The Internet and cell phones had become widely available in Western

Figure 11.1 Sahrawi protest in the liberated territory on a day of solidarity with those protesting in the occupied territory; Western Sahara; May 2005. Courtesy saharatik.com.

Sahara by 2001, which greatly assisted in organizing the resistance and building international solidarity.[6] Internet communication became a key element in the Saharawi struggle, with public chat rooms evolving as vital centers for sending messages and breaking news, leading activists to refer to them as the Sahrawi CNN. Internet access, though available, continued to be monitored by the DST through electronic and human surveillance. Conditions in the remote refugee camps in neighboring Algeria severely limited Internet access there, but the new technologies have nonetheless provided at least some contact with the refugee population as well.

News of the growth of the nonviolent resistance campaign reached external actors, especially those in the Saharawi diaspora outside the camps, most of whom live in Spain. These exiles have become the largest and most significant voice in the diaspora, remaining in touch with the Sahrawis in Western Sahara as well as those in the refugee camps. Despite attempts by the DST to disrupt these contacts, the diaspora continues to be able to provide financial and other forms of support to the resistance movement, an effort also supported by Polisario leaders. The Sahrawi diaspora, together with Polisario representatives in Washington and solidarity supporters, played a seminal role in Aminatou Haidar, a leading figure in the Sahrawi nonviolent resistance movement, being awarded the 2008 Robert F. Kennedy Human Rights Award (figure 11.2).[7]

Technological advances allowed the diaspora and international solidarity groups for the first time to closely monitor the situation in the occupied territory on a daily basis. Moroccan authorities had succeeded in 2007 in closing Paltalk

Figure 11.2 Aminatou Haidar, the "Sahrawi Gandhi" and winner of the 2008 Robert F. Kennedy Human Rights Award, celebrating her release from prison with Sahrawi women activists, Western Sahara, January 2006. Courtesy saharatik.com.

chat rooms by convincing the U.S.-based company offering them that the main chat room was used to promote violence linked to international terrorism in the territory. Following an e-mail campaign by Sahrawi exiles and human rights activists, however, Paltalk reinstated the service in Western Sahara, and a chat room now called Western Sahara: Voice of Intifada opened, supported by donations from the diaspora. Efforts by Moroccan secret police to monitor the cybercafes in Western Sahara has proved to be difficult, in particular because the preferred language is the Sahrawi dialect of Hassaniya. Although some Moroccan authorities have a basic understanding of the language, they are unable to decipher the meaning of certain slang, code words, and proverbs common in the chat rooms.

The Current Struggle

After Moroccan authorities' use of force to break up the large and prolonged demonstrations that began in 2005, the resistance subsequently opted primarily for smaller protests, some of which were planned and some of which were largely spontaneous. Today, at least one minor public act of protest, symbolic or otherwise, takes place each day somewhere in the occupied territory. The resistance movement is active in every inhabited area of Western Sahara, with the exception of some neighborhoods populated exclusively by Moroccan settlers. The cities of Smara and al-Aaiun tend to be more active than Dhakla or Boujadour, because they are larger towns and are home to the most prominent activists.

Most nonviolent actions occur in al-Aaiun or in one of the territory's other urban centers. A typical protest begins on a street corner or a plaza when someone unfurls a Sahrawi flag, women start ululating, and people begin chanting pro-independence slogans. Within a few minutes, soldiers and police arrive, and the crowd quickly scatters. Other tactics include leafleting, graffiti (including tagging the homes of collaborators), and cultural celebrations with political overtones. Though Sahrawi protests begin nonviolently, some demonstrators have fought back with violence when attacked by the police. Some resistance leaders have argued the importance of not retaliating against violence with violence, but there appears to be little systematic emphasis on maintaining nonviolent discipline. Demonstrators typically have had minimal or no formal training in strategic nonviolent resistance. Little evidence points to resistance leaders having a coordinated, strategic plan of nonviolent action, although key writings about civil resistance and strategic nonviolent action training guides have been translated into the local languages and disseminated via PalTalk and other sources. The protests that take place appear to be more the result of individual initiative, largely because of the relative newness of the organized internal struggle as well as the level or repression and the lack of resources. Still, the Moroccan government's regular use of violent repression to subdue the Sahrawi-led nonviolent protests suggests that this form of resistance is seen as a threat to Morocco's control over the territory.

El Carcel Negra, Inzigan, Magouna, and other notorious prisons in which hundreds of Sahrawis have spent years in incarceration became educational centers for new activists. Judicial hearings in Moroccan courts have been used as a rare public forum to denounce the occupation. On several occasions, prisoners engaged in noncooperation at their hearings, to protest beatings and other abuses while in custody. Hmad Hamad, a former political prisoner, spoke in only Spanish and Hassaniya, demanding an interpreter, telling the court that he is not a Moroccan and would not converse in Darja, a Moroccan dialect. Public demonstrations are theoretically legal under Moroccan law if a permit is granted after organizers submit information regarding the day, time, location, and duration of the action. Such permits, while usually granted in Morocco (though never to Saharawis), are denied in Western Sahara.[8]

Moroccan authorities have used a variety of means to repress the human rights and pro-independence movements. Those in custody are routinely beaten and tortured.[9] The Moroccans at one point pursued all participants in the nonviolent struggle, but more recently have focused on leaders, as well as on raiding offices and confiscating materials. Uniformed soldiers are increasingly being replaced by undercover police. Activism can get one fired from his or her job, which cannot be taken lightly in an area with such high unemployment. Sons and daughters of activists are punished in school. In addition, Moroccan authorities pressure young activists to emigrate and have even allegedly helped facilitate and force their illegal immigration to the nearby Spanish-controlled Canary Islands.[10]

The Resistance

Prior to 1991, Sahrawi resistance inside Western Sahara was largely armed and directed by the Polisario, but this is no longer the case. Like most of the international community, today's activists recognize the Polisario as the international face and diplomatic representative of their cause, but the internal struggle is autonomous and democratic. While acknowledging that the leadership of the Polisario has made some mistakes, most in the resistance believe that as long as the national question is paramount, they will not dwell on political differences, such as possible changes in leadership.

The Polisario appears to recognize that by having signed a cease-fire and then having had Morocco reject the diplomatic solution expected in return, it has essentially played all its cards. As a result, there is a growing recognition that the only real hope for independence has to come from within the occupied territory. As Mohamed Yislim Baysat, the former Sahrawi representative to South Africa, describes it, "We have given the chance to the peace plan. Our plan at this time is to support the intifada with our diplomatic means and solidarity with our people inside the occupied territory, southern Morocco and in the Moroccan universities."

At the same time, some Sahrawi activists suspect that the Polisario leadership— primarily of an older generation rooted in the tradition of national liberation through an armed vanguard—is worried about leadership being assumed by the intifada activists inside Western Sahara. For example, after the murder of Hamdi Limbarki, a nonviolent activist, by Moroccan authorities, conditions seemed ripe for an upsurge in the nonviolent resistance campaign. Instead, in a radio broadcast, Polisario leader and SADR president Mohamed Abedalaziz called on Sahrawis to wait, to be patient. In response to the anger and disappointment expressed by many in the internal resistance and in the diaspora, some of the Polisario reiterated support for the intifada as a complementary approach to their diplomatic effort.

There are two primary wings of the internal movement: the semi-legal wing recognized or tolerated by Moroccan authorities advocating for human rights (comparable to similar groups within Morocco) and the clandestine wing openly agitating for independence; the latter includes a few underground Polisario cells. Both wings coordinate their activities and maintain regular communication. The clandestine wing remains open to a return to armed struggle if deemed necessary, though the current consensus clearly advocates a strategy of expanding the nonviolent resistance movement inside the territory while the exiled Polisario leadership continues to pursue efforts for an internationally supervised referendum or other means to gain independence. Although the Polisario periodically threatens to relaunch the armed struggle in response to Morocco's refusal to live up to its obligations under the cease-fire agreement,[11] lack of support from Algeria—historically the Polisario's principal diplomatic supporter and military supplier—and the effectiveness of the Moroccan-built separation wall make this unlikely.

The younger generation of Saharawis who grew up under Moroccan occupation appear to be at least as strongly in favor of independence as their parents, perhaps a reflection of family heritage but also of personal experience living under oppressive, foreign military rule. Most families have had a member killed, jailed, or disappeared. Youth comprise the majority of those active in demonstrations; some are as young as 10 years old. As a result, authorities target young people and generally treat them with suspicion. Though most activists were educated under the Moroccan school system, in Western Sahara through high school and in Morocco for higher education, they use many of the same pro-independence slogans that their parents and grandparents had adopted against the Spaniards in the early 1970s.

Only a small percentage of Saharawis supports the integration of Western Sahara into Morocco. Such advocates are generally those benefiting economically from the status quo, such as being provided shares in Moroccan companies invested in the territories and pocketing subsidies provided by the central government to the territory. Some prominent Sahrawis have received well-endowed posts in the Royal Advisory Council for Saharan Affairs (CORCAS). Overall, however, although the Moroccan government has gone to great lengths to try to "Moroccanize" the indigenous Sahrawi population, this policy has met with little success. The Sahrawis maintain their distinct dialect and cultural identity. As a result, cultural celebrations and wearing traditional clothing have become acts of resistance that some activists refer to as "the silent protest." Sahrawis have also established an underground educational system, the most significant being private language institutions in which classes in Hassaniya and Spanish are offered by recent university graduates who, like most Sahrawis, find themselves with little chance of finding employment in Morocco despite having degrees.

The Moroccans

Moroccan occupation authorities and Moroccan settlers quietly acknowledge that the overwhelming majority of Sahrawis want independence and that their control of the territory remains based primarily on force. Although a Moroccan autonomy plan for the territory put forward in 2006 has been criticized by the Polisario and much of the international community for not meaningfully addressing the Sahrawi right of self-determination, it nevertheless constitutes a reversal of Morocco's historical insistence that Western Sahara is as much a part of Morocco as other provinces by acknowledging that Western Sahara is indeed a distinct entity.[12] Protests in Western Sahara in recent years have begun to raise some awareness within Morocco, especially among intellectuals, human rights activists, pro-democracy groups, and some moderate Islamists—long suspicious of the government line in a number of areas—that not all Sahrawis see themselves as Moroccans and that there exists a genuine indigenous opposition to Moroccan control.

One of the obstacles to the internal resistance movement is that Moroccan settlers outnumber the indigenous population by a ratio of more than 2:1 and by even more in al-Aaiun and Boujadour. This makes certain tactics used instrumentally in similar struggles more problematic in Western Sahara. For example, although a general strike could be effective, the large number of Moroccan settlers, combined with the minority of indigenous Sahrawis who oppose independence, could likely fill the void resulting from the absence of large segments of the Sahrawi workforce. Although such a situation might be alleviated by growing pro-independence sentiments among ethnic Sahrawi settlers from the southern part of Morocco, it still presents some challenges with which largely nonviolent struggles in other occupied lands—among them the Baltic republics, East Timor, Kosovo, and the Palestinian territories, where the overwhelming majority of the resident population favored independence—did not have to contend. It is also important to note that most Moroccan settlers are in Western Sahara because of the generous subsidies and tax breaks offered by the government, and unlike many Israeli settlers, for example, they do not have a strong ideological commitment to being on the land. Few actually own their homes, which tend to be on property owned by Sahrawis or the Moroccan government. Most keep in close contact with and regularly visit their extended families in the Moroccan communities from which they come. Few consider Western Sahara home.

The failure of the vast majority of Sahrawis to assimilate and increasing acts of open resistance have led most settlers to become more aware that rather than simply having moved into a part of Morocco liberated from Spanish colonialism as they had been told, they are in fact colonists on somebody else's land. A minority of settlers, either on their own or with the active encouragement of authorities, have been violently hostile toward Sahrawis openly supporting independence. During the 1999 protests, DST agents helped organize Moroccan mobs to attack protesting Sahrawis; such incidents have been rare in the resistance campaign renewed in 2005. The decline is in part due to the resistance encouraging Sahrawis to avoid such confrontations as well as less willingness among the settlers to confront them.

Some Moroccans who fully understand their quasi-colonial status have chauvinistic and paternalistic attitudes toward the Sahrawis. Similar to other North Africans raised in urban coastal areas, they look upon the traditionally nomadic peoples of the desert as backward Bedouins, making it easy for them to accept the government's line that the Sahrawis need to be educated and uplifted as part of a Moroccan *mission civilisatrice*. Regardless, the Polisario has indicated that settlers would be welcome to stay in a Sahrawi state as long as they abide by Sahrawi law.[13] Despite Morocco's successful efforts at colonizing Western Sahara, the current opposition by Moroccan settlers to independence may not be insurmountable given that they have no strong attachment to the land and that they have little to fear if they decide to remain.

In the workplace and other public spaces inside the occupied territory, a fair amount of integration and mutual respect exists between Sahrawis and Moroccans. Family celebrations and other cultural activities tend to be segregated, however, and there is virtually no intermarriage. The Moroccan-Sahrawi issue is clearly not an ethnic conflict, but one of occupation. Of significance, approximately one-third of the Moroccans settled in 1991 are ethnic Sahrawis, from the southern part of Morocco, and have increasingly begun to exhibit nationalistic sentiments in recent years. As a result, one must count them as potential allies in the nonviolent resistance struggle. One must also remain mindful of other new settlers from the Atlas region in Boujador, Dakhla, and Smara.

Conclusion

A Sahrawi strategy to neutralize the primary sources of support for the occupation must include components that appropriately effect Moroccan settlers, the

Moroccan intelligence and military apparatus, the government's economic and ideological motivation, and the government's foreign supporters.

As noted, one problem confronting the Sahrawis is that they are now the minority within Western Sahara. Another is that Morocco has been able to persist in its defiance of its international legal obligations toward Western Sahara largely because France and the United States have blocked the enforcement of resolutions in the UN Security Council.[14] As a result, at least as important as nonviolent resistance by the Sahrawis against Morocco's occupation policies is the potential of nonviolent action by the citizens of France, the United States, and other countries that enable Morocco to maintain its occupation. Such campaigns played a major role in forcing Australia, Great Britain, and the United States to end their support for Indonesia's occupation of East Timor.[15] Networks in solidarity with the Sahrawis have emerged in dozens of countries around the world, most notably in Spain and Norway, but they have yet to have a major impact on the countries that matter the most.

Taking fuller advantage of new communications technologies, a better-organized, sustained, and media-savvy nonviolent resistance movement within the Western Sahara would not only make the territory more difficult for the Moroccans to rule on a day-to-day basis, but would also help toward building international support capable of eventually forcing governments to push Morocco to cease repressive actions and accept a Sahrawi right of self-determination. A major factor in whether nonviolent resistance succeeds in bringing freedom to Western Sahara depends upon the ability of the Sahrawi resistance to raise international awareness that Moroccan control of the territory is not legitimate or a true fait accompli and to make it an issue in foreign capitals, primarily through building international solidarity with NGOs and civil society organizations in Europe and the United States (figure 11.3).

A successful nonviolent independence struggle by an Arab Muslim people would establish an important precedent in demonstrating how, against great odds, an

Figure 11.3   March led by Sahrawi solidarity supporters in Bilbao, Spain, May 2008. Courtesy saharatik.com.

outnumbered and outgunned population can win through the power of nonviolent resistance in a part of the world where resistance to autocratic rule and foreign military occupation has tended to spawn acts of terrorism and other violence. Furthermore, the participatory democratic structure within the Sahrawi resistance movement and the prominence of women in key positions of leadership could help serve as an important model in a region in which authoritarian and patriarchal forms of governance have traditionally dominated. The outcome rests not just on the Sahrawis, but also on whether the international community determines that such a struggle is worthy of its support.

Notes

1. See Anne Lippert, "The Saharawi Refugees: Origins and Organization, 1975–85," in *War and Refugees: The Western Sahara Conflict,* ed. R. Lawless and L. Monahan (London: Printer, 1987), 151.
2. Of these, more than 500 never returned and are presumed to have been executed.
3. On the historical and strategic evolution of the Sahrawi "intifadas," see Maria J. Stephan and Jacob Mundy, "Battlefield Transformed: From Guerilla Resistance to Mass Nonviolent Struggle in the Western Sahara," *Journal of Military and Strategic Studies* 8, no. 3 (Spring 2006).
4. Ibid.
5. See, for example, Amnesty International USA, "Morocco/Western Sahara: Sahrawi Human Rights Defenders under Attack," November 24, 2005, www.amnesty.org/en/library/info/MDE29/008/2005.
6. During 16 years of armed struggle in Western Sahara, Moroccan authorities had limited the use of telephones or faxes to government-run centers, which strictly monitored all communications. With the 1991 cease-fire agreement, it became possible to reach Morocco from a private phone, and by 2001, one could call internationally.
7. Haidar's selection is a testament to the growing strength and prominence of the nonviolent struggle taking place in Western Sahara. Suzanne Scholte, chairman of the U.S.-Western Sahara Foundation, nominated Haidar for the award. She worked closely with Mouloud Said, the Polisario representative in Washington, along with Sahrawi diaspora and U.S.-based human rights activists and policymakers, to promote Haidar's candidacy.
8. For example, in 2008 the mothers of 15 Sahrawi youths who disappeared in December 2005 approached the local authorities in al-Aaiun to seek a permit to protest. After they were turned away, the mothers protested in the center of al-Aaiun; they were severely beaten by the police shortly after the protest began.
9. See Human Rights Watch, "Morocco: Investigate Police Beating of Rights Activists in Western Sahara," December 27, 2007; Amnesty International, *Amnesty International Report, 2008—Morocco and Western Sahara*, May 28, 2008.
10. In November 2006, the Spanish League for Human Rights reported that 14 Saharawis died on the coast of the occupied city of Bojador while 26 others were reported missing after trying to escape "the brutal repression" exercised in the territories of the Western Sahara. The League denounced the fact that the illegal migration of the Saharawi youth is "encouraged" by Morocco with an aim to "destroy the (Saharawi) internal resistance". ("The Spanish League for Human Rights asks for the protection of the lives of the Saharawi youngsters," Sahara Press Service, 11/29/06. Accessed 29 June 2009 at: http://www.spsrasd.info/sps-e291106.html#3.)
11. In one example of Moroccan obfuscation, it insisted on expanding the voter rolls, to include large numbers of Moroccan settlers, for the UN-supervised referendum to decide the fate of the territory.

12. Important matters, such as control of Western Sahara's natural resources and law enforcement (beyond local jurisdictions), remain ambiguous. In addition, the proposal appears to indicate that all powers not specifically vested in the autonomous region would remain with Morocco. Indeed, since the king is ultimately invested with absolute authority under Article 19 of the Moroccan constitution, the autonomy proposal's insistence that the Moroccan state "will keep its powers in the royal domains, especially with respect to defense, external relations and the constitutional and religious prerogatives of His Majesty the King" appears to afford the monarch considerable latitude of interpretation. On a fundamental level, because the autonomy proposal rules out the option of independence, it denies the Sahrawis their right to self-determination as called for by the International Court of Justice and a series of UN resolutions. Indeed, to accept Morocco's autonomy plan would mean that for the first time since the founding of the United Nations and the ratification of the UN Charter more than 60 years ago, the international community would be endorsing the expansion of a country's territory by military force, thereby establishing a dangerous and destabilizing precedent.
13. Bachir Abi, Saharawi representative to Nigeria.
14. France and the United States have also served as principal suppliers of the armaments and other security assistance to Moroccan occupation forces.
15. See Stephen Zunes and Ben Terrall, "East Timor: Reluctant Support for Self-Determination," in *Contemporary Cases in U.S. Foreign Policy: From Terrorism to Trade*, ed. Ralph Carter (Washington, DC: CQ Press, 2001).

12

Lebanon's Independence Intifada: How an Unarmed Insurrection Expelled Syrian Forces

Rudy Jaafar and Maria J. Stephan

On March 14, 2005, some 1 million Christians, Muslims, and Druze from all parts of Lebanon gathered in Beirut, carrying signs and waving flags, to demonstrate for a free and independent Lebanon.[1] The scope, intensity, and distinctly nonviolent character of the civilian uprising, referred to variously as the Cedar Revolution or the "independence intifada," was unprecedented in Lebanese history.[2] Over the course of approximately two months, what had begun as relatively small, spontaneous protests after former prime minister Rafiq al-Hariri's assassination on February 14, 2005 quickly developed into an organized, broad-based opposition movement that would lead to the resignation of the prime minister and the withdrawal of Syrian forces, which had occupied Lebanon for almost 30 years. Understanding the dynamics of this "people power" movement is necessary for deciphering the country's subsequent turbulence. What brought more than a million Lebanese onto the streets of Beirut on 14 March? To what extent was this popular uprising strategically planned? What were its achievements and shortcomings?

Incipient Resistance and Growth

Syrian troops were deployed to Lebanon in 1976 following the country's descent into civil war. The 1989 Saudi-sponsored Ta'if agreement brought closure to the Lebanese conflict, but it also marked the beginning of Pax Syriana, as the government in Damascus extended its influence in Lebanon by reinforcing its vast security and intelligence apparatus in the country and continuing to manipulate sectarian politics by strengthening its patronage of the various religious and political groups.

Resistance to Syrian hegemony had existed even before the official end of the civil war. During the Ta'if negotiations in the late 1980s, a government led by Lebanese Army commander Michel Aoun carried on a "liberation war" against Syrian influence in Lebanon.[3] The popularity of Aoun's stance transcended religious affiliation. In a notable feat of civil resistance, hundreds of thousands of demonstrators surrounded the presidential palace in Baabda in December 1989, forming a "human shield" to protect Aoun's government. In October 1990, Syrian forces and Lebanese factions opposed to Aoun moved against him.[4]

Aoun sought political asylum in France, from where he established himself as the vanguard of the opposition to the Syrian occupation. He then founded the Free Patriotic Movement (FPM), and his followers in Lebanon persistently, although far from decisively, continued to challenge Syria's grip on the country for some time. The FPM was active in a number of professional and academic circles. The movement also organized boycotts, demonstrations, and sit-ins, which were especially popular with youths and led to several thousands of them being detained and jailed.[5] There were also acts of resistance by other political parties and their affiliates, and by religious leaders and ordinary Lebanese citizens, but their resistance lacked an overall strategy, was limited in nature, and was mostly confined to the Christian community.[6] There was little hope or expectation that such weak opposition could, by itself, end Syrian hegemony in Lebanon.

The situation began to change when the system of control established over a decade by long-time Syrian leader Hafiz al-Asad was increasingly challenged following his death and the succession of his son Bashar al-Asad in July 2000. Although surrounded by many of his father's closest aides and having been given the "Lebanon file" by his father before his death, the new president lacked the authority that Hafiz had commanded. As agitation grew in Lebanon, the level of repression increased; opposition activists were arrested and beaten, and the culture of fear, intimidation, and self-censorship intensified. Opposition to the Syrian presence would steadily grow during the coming months and years.

In early August 2001, plainclothes security agents arrested some 250 activists from the FPM and other Christian opposition parties agitating against Syria's role in Lebanon in advance of a francophone summit to be held in Beirut. The crackdown drew strong condemnation from Lebanese politicians, religious leaders, journalists, and civil society groups, as well as members of the international community. A year later, in September 2002, the government banned MTV broadcasts after the network aired interviews with the exiled Aoun in which he criticized the Lebanese-Syrian relationship. This action infuriated many Lebanese youth.[7]

The opposition understood that it needed to expand its base of support while chipping away at its opponent's base in order to pose an effective challenge to the Syrian-backed Lebanese government. This meant building coalitions, a fundamental process in a normal democracy and a crucial component of effective nonviolent struggle.[8] On April 30, 2001, a group of Christian intellectuals, businessmen, and politicians, had met in the town of Qornet Shehwan and called for a new relationship with Syria based on equality and respect. Although the group's leading members were all Christians, its mission and mandate transcended religious and sectarian divisions.[9] A few months later, Cardinal Mar Nasrallah Boutros Sfeir visited the predominantly Druze Shuf region—the first such visit in 200 years by a Maronite patriarch—where he met Druze leader Walid Jumblat.[10] The Maronites and the Druze shared a bloody history dating at least to the nineteenth century. This attempt at reconciliation indicated the willingness of Lebanese sects to try to transcend the past in pursuit of a larger national goal.

Meanwhile, the policies emanating from Damascus brought to the fore critical fissures in the Lebanese political landscape where two camps, crystallizing around Prime Minister Rafiq al-Hariri and President Emile Lahoud, clashed repeatedly under Syrian tutelage. Hariri, a self-made billionaire with close ties to the Saudi royal family and Western leaders, had overseen Lebanon's reconstruction following the civil war. Although at one time a close ally of Damascus, Hariri's allegiance appeared to slowly shift with the death of the elder Asad to the point that he became a thorn in the side of Lahoud and other staunch Syrian allies in the Lebanese government.

Tensions between the Hariri and Lahoud factions reached a tipping point on September 3, 2004, as Lahoud's term came to a close. Under Syrian pressure, the Lebanese parliament voted to pass a constitutional amendment to extend Lahoud's term for an additional three years.[11] The unpopular extension of Lahoud's mandate galvanized opposition forces and led to the formation of the Committee for the Defense of the Constitution and the Defense of the Republic, which included the Qornet Shehwan coalition, the Jumblat-led Progressive Socialist Party (PSP), the Democratic Left Party, and others. The committee, later called the Bristol Gathering, after the hotel where its leaders met, formed the backbone of an opposition that became the driving force behind the independence intifada.

Hariri stepped down on October 20, 2004 to protest the extension of Lahoud's presidential mandate. According to opposition sources, Hariri was quietly gravitating toward the opposition to explore the prospect of forming a tripartite (Sunni-Maronite-Druze) electoral alliance capable of defeating Lahoud supporters in upcoming elections. The likelihood of such an arrangement increased in January 2005, when Hariri's political party, the Future Movement, dispatched representatives to attend ongoing opposition meetings at the Bristol Hotel.[12] The alliance hoped to sweep the parliamentary elections scheduled for May 2005. On February 14, 2005, a massive car bomb pulverized Hariri's convoy in downtown Beirut, killing him and 20 others.[13]

Funeral Protests and Freedom Camp

Few Lebanese believed that Hariri, a larger-than-life Sunni Muslim figure who had bankrolled Beirut's revival from the destruction of the civil war, would be the target of deadly violence. Hariri's assassination united large segments of the Lebanese population in grief and anger against their government and the Syrian regime. Lebanese officials declared a three-day mourning period, but the Hariri family, supported by the parliamentary opposition, announced its decision to hold a public funeral for the slain leader on February 16. It also made it clear that Lebanese state officials should not bother to attend.

The start of what became a movement of more than a million people included spontaneous protests and candlelight vigils involving smaller groups primarily consisting of students and women.[14] Youth leaders from the nine opposition political parties joined forces to organize a peaceful march from the site of the assassination to Martyrs' Square, the heart of Beirut's downtown district. Well-known Lebanese personalities, including Nora Jumblat, wife of Druze leader Walid Jumblat, joined them, inviting the media to cover the nonviolent protest. According to Nader Nakib, a youth leader, "The media was on our side. People were watching TV all the time, and we were covered."[15]

Almost a quarter of a million Lebanese, along with a number of prominent international figures, turned out for Hariri's funeral, which was also an occasion for anti-Syrian demonstrations. Subsequent rallies in Beirut grew larger, with the times and locations of daily protests communicated via cell phones and SMS, technologies that have played crucial roles in a number of recent "people power" movements,[16] enabling thousands of Lebanese to mobilize quickly. Growing demands from parliament and in the streets for "the truth" pressured Lebanese officials into getting to the bottom of the crime. "The government's weak resolve and inability to provide a serious and satisfactory explanation," wrote one analyst, "increased its vulnerability."[17] To exploit this weakness, the political opposition presented a united front and developed a strategy to channel popular discontent into concrete action.

As the anti-Syrian and anti-government protests grew larger, political leaders from the opposition met at the Bristol Hotel on 18 February to announce a set of demands: the immediate and total withdrawal of Syrian troops, the resignation of the government led by Prime Minister Omar Karami, and the holding of free parliamentary elections. Their demands were clear, specific, and the same ones being made by the Lebanese rallying in the streets. At the press conference following the meeting, opposition spokesperson Samir Frangieh, wearing a red and white scarf around his neck, announced the start of a "peaceful and democratic intifada for independence." With these few words," wrote one Lebanese analyst, Frangieh "psychologically liberated the Lebanese people from thirty years of servitude. The process of self-liberation began and there was no turning back."[18]

On the same evening, a group of Lebanese students belonging to opposition parties raised a tent in Martyrs' Square.[19] Taking a cue from the 2004 Orange Revolution in Ukraine, these Lebanese protestors decided to build a permanent camp on the site.[20] After the overnight sit-in on 18 February, other political factions and civil society groups quickly followed suit, erecting more tents. The area, dubbed Freedom Camp, became the opposition's hub during the popular uprising.

"La Chambre Noire"

In the days and weeks that followed, a dynamic, iterative relationship developed involving Bristol Gathering leaders and Lebanese civil society groups at the level of strategists and "foot soldiers" in nonviolent struggle. Although most of the early street protests, demonstrations, and sit-ins had occurred spontaneously, a few key individuals eventually took charge of strategic planning for the movement. Around 19 February, a small group of friends and political activists began discussing the situation on the ground and planning for the sustainability and growth of the movement. Saleh Farroukh, director-general of the Beirut Association for Social Development, a group established in 1998 by Hariri, said that the small working group, sometimes called *la chambre noire* (the black room) "began initiating the general plan of the movement," exploring "how to ensure the continuity of this intifada to reach the objective of getting Syria out."[21]

The core members of this planning circle, each representing a political wing of the opposition, included, in addition to Farroukh, Samir Kassir, a leader of the Democratic Left Party, a journalist for *al-Nahar*, and a vehement critic of the Syrian presence in Lebanon; Ziad Majed, another leader in the Democratic Left Party; Nawaf Salam, a professor at the American University of Beirut; Nora Jumblat; Samir Abdelmalak, a spokesperson for the Qornet Shehwan group; and Gibran Tueni, a member of parliament and owner of *al-Nahar*. Others joined the group on an ad-hoc basis, including representatives of the FPM (until Michel Aoun's return from exile). This operational corps would play a crucial role in the nonviolent struggle.[22]

The political opposition passed on to the working group general directives, which they discussed and the group helped translate into coordinated action in the "operations room," an office made available by Tueni in the strategically located *al-Nahar* building, overlooking the southwest corner of Martyrs' Square. Although there was nothing secretive about this group, few Lebanese knew that it existed. "The strength of the working group," said Abdelmalak, "was that it was not exposed." He added, "Our numbers were changing as people came and went."[23] Decisions made by members of the working group were supported by their political superiors in the Bristol Gathering.

One of the working group's first decisions was to support the youth in the tent city. Nearly two weeks after the first tent went up, Asma Andraos, an events organizer, was tasked to enter the site and assume responsibility for camp logistics. Andraos and her team led the effort to ensure sufficient food, water, blankets, beds, sheets, gas, toilets, and other amenities for the hundreds of young people spending nights in the camp. Like the tent city erected by Ukrainian youths on Maidan Square in Kiev, the Freedom Camp on Martyrs' Square became the symbol of the popular resistance in Lebanon. In addition to the financial and logistical support from the working group, the tent city was sustained thanks to the generous contributions of thousands of ordinary Lebanese who deposited money into an account set up in the Lebanese Saradar Bank.[24] Because security forces had cordoned off the area, many of the supplies had to be smuggled into the camp, sometimes in cars owned by opposition politicians who had legal immunity and clout.[25]

Samir Abdelmalak helped create and oversee a "dialogue tent" in the camp where youth from different parties, clans, and religious backgrounds could come together. He considered the intracommunal dialogue among young people, possible future leaders of the country, to be one of the most important developments of the popular uprising.[26] The camp as well as the rest of the movement featured great diversity. Both, however, lacked a large Shiite presence.

Marketing an Intifada

To promote unity and a common sense of purpose, an opposition movement must craft messages that encapsulate the shared aspirations of diverse audiences. Movement leaders must develop and propagate a "galvanizing proposition" that inspires ordinary people to take action for a common purpose.[27] It is important that targeted communication "attract people to your mission and, eventually, inspire them to act for social change."[28] The Lebanese independence intifada benefited from the savvy marketing and messaging efforts of Quantum Communications, a political communications firm headed by Eli Khoury. According to Khoury, also the CEO of Saatchi & Saatchi Lebanon, he and Samir Kassir, a part-time senior writer at Quantum, saw what was happening in the streets and decided, "[T]his is it. We need to brand it!"[29]

Khoury said that the choice of "Independence '05" as the central slogan of the opposition movement was meant to create a sense of urgency and momentum. "How many times have we said that we wanted to liberate the country and nothing happened? So I said we need...a deadline....[T]his time, we're going to get rid of the Syrians." In the lead-up to the 2000 presidential elections in Serbia, the youth-led Otpor! (Resistance) movement rallied an aggrieved population around the slogan "Gotov Je!" ("He's Finished"), in reference to President Slobodan Milosevic. In a similar manner in Lebanon, the opposition set a timeframe for action. A former Otpor! activist, in fact, met with Lebanese youths to share experiences and information about strategic nonviolent action in the lead-up to the 14 March demonstration.[30]

A second key marketing decision involved the choice of the Lebanese flag and national anthem to represent and unify the opposition. Despite the reservations of some people, Khoury said that he believed that the Lebanese flag would resonate with all of the country's communities. He called a few influential Lebanese and "everybody agreed to take the gamble—it was successful."[31] Bristol Gathering leaders, notably Walid Jumblat, asked opposition supporters to leave their party flags at home and to rally around the national flag. For a country whose politics are defined along sectarian lines, noted Nora Jumblat, the one-flag policy was "a very powerful and important decision."[32]

The first large rally organized by the working group took place on 21 February, when some 70,000 Lebanese demonstrated in Beirut, which was awash in the national flag and signs that read "Independence '05" and "The Truth." Meanwhile in parliament, the opposition called for a debate on the circumstances surrounding Hariri's assassination and a vote of confidence in the government. Also at this point, a growing coalition of groups, including the Beirut Merchants' Association and the Lebanese Bar Association, along with other labor unions, syndicates, and professional organizations, called for a general nationwide strike and mass rally in Martyrs' Square on 28 February.[33] As the number of Lebanese organizations and institutions prepared to engage in nonviolent civil disruption grew, so too did the power of the opposition movement.

A Decisive Standoff

The Lebanese government, with its economic and political pillars of support endangered, decided to crack down.[34] On 27 February, it banned all public demonstrations. The head of the army declared that protestors had until 5:00 a.m. the following morning to comply with the ban. Thousands of soldiers and police set up cordons and checkpoints around Martyrs' Square and at entrances to the city. The opposition had good reason to fear that government forces would use violence to dismantle the tent city before the parliamentary debate and vote of confidence the next day. Lebanese officials could not ignore what had happened in Serbia (2000), Georgia (2003), and Ukraine (2004), where the opposition movements occupied the parliament prior to taking control at the pinnacle of these popular uprisings.[35] At this crucial juncture in Lebanon, politicians and masses of civilians joined forces against a well-armed opponent and collectively defied the government.

Televised images of the mass mobilization in Freedom Square had created a snowball effect, encouraging citizens, some traveling great distances, to come join the protest. The security forces, in the thousands, were quickly outnumbered and outflanked by the unarmed protestors.[36] At this point, it became clear that many of the members of the security forces sympathized with the protestors. This was likely at least in part a result of actions by the opposition designed to shift their loyalties. Notably, the protestors fraternized with the members of the security forces, placed flowers in the barrels of their guns, and avoided any action that could be construed as threatening.

The sheer number of civilian protestors and the high level of nonviolent discipline they maintained would have made it politically costly for the security forces to use violence against them. Of equal importance, the larger the number of Lebanese participating in the demonstrations, the more likely the chance that members of the security forces might encounter someone they knew or possibly even a family member. The fear of injuring or killing loved ones during mass demonstrations has been cited often by members of security forces as the rationale behind their refusal to obey orders to crack down on protestors.[37]

Protestors at Martyrs' Square were instructed that in the event of an attempted assault, they should immediately sit in tight rows, join arms, and form a human chain to make it more difficult for the security forces to carry them away.[38] Although sirens were heard at around 4:30 a.m., the 5:00 a.m. deadline came and went without incident. By mid-morning, the police barricades had been removed, allowing thousands more people to enter the square. By successfully defying the ban, the opposition undermined the government's authority and neutralized its security forces—two major sources of power required by a regime or power-holder to effectively control its population.[39] Later that afternoon, at the conclusion of parliamentary debate and with a few hundred thousand Lebanese protesting in the streets, Prime Minister Karami announced the resignation of his government. With the media attributing "people power" to the toppling of the government, the opposition proclaimed the first victory of the intifada for independence.[40] U.S. undersecretary of state Paula Dobriansky used the term "Cedar Revolution" for the first time to describe the events unfolding in Beirut.[41]

In early March 2005, international pressure on Syria intensified. At a meeting in Riyadh, Saudi crown prince Abdullah advised President Asad to "rapidly" withdraw Syrian troops from Lebanon.[42] France and the United States continued to push for the implementation of UN Security Council Resolution 1559, which called for the withdrawal of all foreign troops from Lebanon and the disarming of all Lebanese militias (read, Hizbullah. Walid Jumblat, meanwhile, proclaimed the beginning of a "Beirut Spring" to force Syrian troops from the country. On 5 March, Asad announced his intention to withdraw all Syrian forces from Lebanon, a retreat completed less than two months later and the most impressive victory of the intifada.

The March 8 and March 14 Movements

Asad's announcement set the stage for another showdown in the streets of Beirut, this time between two popular Lebanese movements. For the first time since the start of the independence intifada, the two main Shiite factions, Hizbullah and Amal, decided to assert themselves. Hizbullah—feeling isolated by the anti-Syrian protests and perhaps fearing that more opposition victories would lead to greater international pressures on the group to forego one of its fundamental tenets, armed resistance against Israel—called for a massive rally.

On 8 March, hundreds of thousands of Lebanese rallied in Riad al-Solh Square, not far from Martyrs' Square, to show appreciation for Syria, denounce UN Resolution 1559, and show that Hizbullah could not be ignored. During this mass nonviolent demonstration, which was to date the largest in Lebanese history, Hizbullah supporters took a page from the opposition and carried only Lebanese national flags. The fact that no yellow party flags could be seen was "a hint that Hizbullah, while it found itself hesitant about turning against its Syrian supporters, also did not find itself in total disagreement with the mainstream opposition."[43]

The size and magnitude of the mostly Shiite rally, and its pro-Syrian message, surprised opposition leaders. Indeed, 8 March proved to be a galvanizing event for the opposition, whose leaders met the next day in the operations room at *al-Nahar* to plan a mass demonstration on 14 March to commemorate the one-month anniversary of Hariri's murder. The working group engaged in meticulous planning and preparation for its biggest event hitherto. They secured enough drinking water for an expected half million people, prepared an outdoor stage and set up a sound system in Martyrs' Square, mass produced flags, signs, and banners, put crowd control devices in place, and took care of countless other tasks, down to the creation of a lost child location service.[44]

Eli Khoury reiterated that *how* the mass gathering would be perceived by the rest of the world was as important—if not more important—than the actual number of participants: "If you win the heart of the media and the heart of the international community, you will win the war. We suffered in the past when we had large numbers of people demonstrating but failed to win international hearts and minds." The rally, covered live by CNN and other major Western and Arab networks, was a global spectacle that attracted more than a million participants (figures 12.1 and 12.2). Lebanese of all ages, religions, socioeconomic backgrounds, and political affiliations poured into Beirut. (Again, however, a Shi'a presence was lacking.) No flags were burned, rocks thrown, or clashes with security forces.

The independence intifada remained nonviolent, helped along by extensive media coverage, good communication among different parts of the movement, and a cadre of leaders who advocated nonviolent resistance from the start. There was not a single injury or piece of broken glass on a day when a quarter of Lebanon's population participated in an antigovernment demonstration. When asked to explain the high degree of nonviolent discipline exhibited by the protestors, Saleh Farroukh said that there seemed to be a common understanding among the politicians and the people that violence would be futile and counterproductive: "Nowadays, the nonviolent struggle is a very important struggle, and a civilized one. [Lebanese] learned from everywhere that violence breeds violence. . . . [V]iolence would make the army turn against you. . . . The Palestinians lost when they moved from a nonviolent to a violent struggle."[45]

Although the 14 March Movement received significant political and diplomatic backing from powerful external actors, including the United States, the popular uprising was homegrown and, it appears, mostly self-financed. "The foreign help would not be useful if there were no domestic, homegrown movement. They complemented each other," Farroukh pointed out.[46] Opposition movements must be able to secure access to material resources in order to sustain their resistance activities.[47] The Lebanese opposition movement also benefited greatly from the Hariri family's tremendous fortune. A significant amount of the money used to buy flags, signs, banners, pins, and other materials came from the Hariri family's Beirut Association for Social Development. Other wealthy Lebanese businesspeople and countless Lebanese citizens also contributed amounts, small and large and often anonymously, to keep the movement going.[48]

After the 14 March demonstration, the zenith of the struggle against Syrian hegemony, the opposition movement began to secure its central demands. On 7 April, the UN Security Council passed Resolution 1595 calling for the establishment of an international commission to investigate Hariri's murder. Lebanese security chiefs, who had come under heavy criticism for their handling of the investigation into Hariri's assassination, either resigned or were replaced.[49] The greatest achievement of the independence intifada occurred on 26 April, when the last uniformed Syrian soldier left Lebanon. For the first time in nearly three decades, Lebanon was free of Syrian domination.[50] On 5 May, the United Nations verified the complete withdrawal of Syrian forces, paving the way for the freest Lebanese elections since the end of the civil war in 1990, a major development in Lebanon's history.

Figures 12.1 Mass nonviolent demonstration in support of Lebanese independence in downtown Beirut, March 14, 2005. Courtesy Rami Khouri.

Figures 12.2 Mass nonviolent demonstration in support of Lebanese independence in downtown Beirut, March 14, 2005. Courtesy Rami Khouri.

The Independence Intifada and Post-Syrian Politics

The independence intifada successfully shattered long-standing taboos, notably concerning Lebanon's relationship with Syria, opening the door to substantive dialogue between traditionally competing, and at times openly hostile, political factions. Syrian control over Lebanon vitiated genuine reform and planning, as Damascus played divide and rule. Continued Syrian control would likely have led to ongoing stagnation in Lebanese political, economic, and cultural life. Therefore, the removal of Syrian influence was a necessary, although not wholly sufficient, condition for a veritable "revolution" in Lebanese domestic politics.

Indeed, the aftermath of the Syrian troop withdrawal proved to be disappointing for many Lebanese, particularly those pining for a "revolution" that would open the political process to new blood and greater democratic participation and end control by entrenched elites (who have dominated the political process for most of Lebanese history). Freshly empowered by the successful democratic effort to oust the Syrians, many Lebanese were distressed to see the traditional elites from various clans maintain their grip on power.[51] Worse still, as Michel Aoun and the FPM split from opposition ranks because of internal squabbling, parliamentary elections in summer 2005 consolidated emerging divisions between the March 8 and March 14 camps, producing a dangerous chasm in Lebanese society.

The disappointment shared by many Lebanese following the elections highlights a fundamental weakness of the independence intifada, namely, that it did not articulate a long-term vision and plan of action that extended beyond a Syrian troop withdrawal. Missing was a "vision of tomorrow" to address the need to reform Lebanon's antiquated confessional system of government.[52] In the lead-up to parliamentary elections, opposition politicians who had played a dominant role in guiding the popular movement from the beginning reverted to the pursuit of personal interest over the common good. Meanwhile, the country lacked a nonpartisan organization or movement that could have united all Lebanese around specific, reformist goals. Samir Abdelmalak reflected on this general shortcoming: "We knew that the excitement would diminish as new objectives were met. The apex was on 26 April when the Syrian army left the country; this achieved most of our objectives. Also, by then the security chiefs were in jail and the international investigation had begun. This was the beginning of the countdown of the movement. The question became 'What's next'? The elections came and separated the people again, putting everyone back in their camps. This is something normal during elections, and we tried to reduce the negative consequences of this. Nonetheless, there is still no basis from which new leadership can emerge."[53] In hindsight, hope was misplaced that those who had led the independence intifada would work to reform the sectarian system from which they derive benefits.

Since the intifada, Lebanese leaders have not lost an opportunity to threaten their rivals with *vox populi,* and the "street" has become ordinary usage in Lebanese political discourse. Although there had been demonstrations in the early 1970s that threatened established Lebanese governments, these protests were undirected and sometimes involved random violence against the security forces and private property. Today, the Lebanese have awakened to the fundamentally different nature of strategically planned movements, wherein a group of mobilized individuals can, without recourse to violence, exact tremendous costs on a government and bring the country to a standstill. On December 1, 2006, Hizbullah and its allies brought Beirut to a halt with a rally attracting slightly less than a million people.[54] They also established a permanent tent city, where thousands of protestors camped on a daily basis, the hub of their campaign against the March 14 coalition and for a greater share of power in the Lebanese government.[55]

Although it could be argued that nonviolent action is more moral and more effective than recourse to violence—the method used in the Lebanese civil war—the populist abuse of nonviolent means to settle deep-seated conflict can be dangerous. Strategic nonviolent action is frequently used when existing structural channels are blocked, as was arguably the case when Syria controlled Lebanon. As a form of extra-institutional (and sometimes extra-legal) activity, nonviolent direct action is often used to challenge institutional deficiencies and create those structural changes necessary for reform and continued political evolution. In post-intifada Lebanon, however, elites on both sides of internal political conflicts have called on their followers to protest for reasons that have little to do with changing the country's outdated and deficient system of government. It is in fact a symptom of the weakness of the Lebanese governing structure that politicians revert to such noninstitutional methods to further their own interests. The use of nonviolent action for the purpose of flexing one's factional muscles can bring about a precarious stasis where each camp's nearly identical numerical weight cancels out the other. Stagnation and failure to reach a political resolution to the underlying governance dilemma serve only to further polarize Lebanese society and entrench stalemate, which could facilitate the intervention of foreign powers or precipitate, once again, an outbreak of violence. The latter is what happened in early May 2008, when opposition forces stormed the capital and neutralized pro-government armed groups.

Because of Lebanon's size and open society, it is difficult for it to shield itself from the geopolitical storms of the Middle East. It is urgent, however, that the Lebanese at least agree on a better formula for governing themselves, one not prone to the repeated crises of consociational balance-of-power structures, for which the 2008 Doha accords were the latest solution.[56] Indeed, that is the very meaning of self-determination. If capitalized upon, the independence intifada, which set the stage for uninhibited dialogue regarding the future of Lebanon, could be the opening of a more promising chapter in Lebanese history.

Notes

1. Although individuals of Shiite background participated in the demonstration, Lebanese Shiites, numerically the country's largest confessional group, were notably absent as a community from this event.
2. Dozens of Syrian immigrant laborers—of which there are several hundreds of thousands in Lebanon—were attacked or murdered during the independence intifada. These acts of violence, however, were committed by individuals, not as part of any strategy by those leading or actively involved in the uprising. In fact, leaders throughout the country explicitly condemned such actions. The violent nature of these acts, limited in scope, did not affect the strategic decision of the Syrian or Lebanese governments during this period. Notwithstanding this tragic loss of life, Lebanon's independence intifada is a nonviolent chapter in Lebanese history.
3. In 1988 a failure to elect a new president led to Aoun being appointed as caretaker prime minister by outgoing president Amin Gemayel and the refusal of the sitting prime minister, the Syrian-backed Selim al-Hoss, to relinquish power. Thus Lebanon found itself with two rival governments.
4. The United States gave a green light to Syrian actions after Damascus agreed to cooperate with the U.S.-led multinational coalition aligned against Iraq following the August 1990 Iraqi invasion of Kuwait.

5. Gary Gambill, "Michel Aoun," *Middle East Intelligence Bulletin* 3, no. 1 (2001).
6. This does not mean that Lebanese citizens from other communities did not resist Syrian dominance. It is known, for example, that Syrians hesitated to venture inside Beirut's southern suburbs because inhabitants there, mostly Shiites and poor, resented the influx of hundreds of thousands of cheap Syrian laborers who competed with them for jobs. The Shiites as a community, however, represented by leaders from Hizbullah and Amal, were strategically allied with Syria in the greater struggle against Israel. Christian leaders, on the other hand, were split; although many were allied with Damascus and benefited from the status quo, there were others who resisted Syrian dominance of Lebanon.
7. Gabriel Murr, "Des voix libres pour réanimer la foi en la liberté," *L'Orient Le Jour*, special supplement, February 13, 2006, 42.
8. Peter Ackerman and Christopher Kruegler, *Strategic Nonviolent Conflict: The Dynamics of People Power in the Twentieth Century* (Westport, CT: Praeger, 1994), 26–30.
9. Samir Abdelmalak, interview with Rudy Jaafar, March 9 and 15, 2006, Beirut, Lebanon.
10. Gary Gambill, "Lebanon's Shadow Government Takes Charge," *Middle East Intelligence Bulletin* 3, no. 8 (2001).
11. Neil MacFarquhar, "Behind Lebanon Upheaval, Two Men's Fateful Clash," *New York Times*, 20 March 2005; Majdoline Hatoum, "14 MPs Claim They Were Coerced To Back Lahoud," *Daily Star*, 23 February 2006. For a comprehensive account of the Hariri-Lahoud feud, see Nicholas Blanford, *Killing Mr Lebanon: The Assassination of Rafik Hariri and Its Impact on the Middle East* (London: I. B. Tauris, 2006).
12. Samir Abdelmalak, interview; Blanford, *Killing Mr Lebanon*, 6, 8, 117, 120.
13. Hariri's drift toward the opposition remains a nebulous affair, as does the theory of the Syrian regime's culpability in his assassination that has gained popularity among supporters of the March 14 Movement, the name later given to the various groups and parties that challenged Syria's occupation of Lebanon. The United Nations International Independent Investigation Commission (UNIIIC) investigating Hariri's murder has yet to issue its verdict. Nevertheless, the conviction among opposition supporters and a large portion of the Lebanese public that Damascus bears responsibility was sufficient to galvanize them into launching and joining the independence intifada.
14. Rallies on 8 and 14 March drew a staggering percentage of the Lebanese population, which was estimated at a little less than four million in 2005. The Population Reference Bureau, "2005 World Population Data Sheet," www.prb.org/pdf05/05WorldDataSheet_Eng.pdf.
15. Nader Nakib, interview with Rudy Jaafar, December 12, 2005 and February 15, 2006, Beirut, Lebanon.
16. "Mobiles, Protests, and Pundits," *Economist*, October 26, 2006.
17. Oussama Safa, "Lebanon Springs Forward," *Journal of Democracy* 17, no. 1 (2006): 30.
18. Michel Hajji Georgiou, "Comme un volcan qui se réveille," *L'Orient Le Jour*, special supplement, February 13, 2006, 29.
19. Nour Merheb, activist, interview with Rudy Jaafar, March 14, 2006, Beirut, Lebanon.
20. The Orange Revolution succeeded in enforcing lawful election results and ousting the incumbent political party from power.
21. Saleh Farroukh, interview with Rudy Jaafar, March 3, 2006, Beirut, Lebanon.
22. Kassir was assassinated in June 2005. Tueni was assassinated in December 2005. Salam later became Lebanon's ambassador to the United Nations. On the strategic importance of the "operational corps" in nonviolent struggles, see Ackerman and Kruegler, *Strategic Nonviolent Conflict*, 21–53.
23. Abdelmalak, interview.
24. The working group and Asma Andraos administered the Martyrs' Square Fund, which collected some $200,000.

25. Saleh Farroukh mentioned in his March interview with Jaafar that opposition MPs frequently crossed security checkpoints with goods and supplies for the camp.
26. Abdelmalak, interview.
27. Jack DuVall, "The Right of Resistance: The Legitimacy and Support of Nonviolent Civic Force," paper presented at the Social Activism Speaker Series, California Institute of Technology, Pasadena, May 11, 2006.
28. Srdja Popovic, Andrej Milivojevic, and Slobodan Djinovic, *Nonviolent Struggle: 50 Crucial Points* (Belgrade: Center for Applied Nonviolent Action and Strategies, 2006), 60.
29. Eli Khoury, interview with Rudy Jaafar, March 1, 2006, Beirut, Lebanon.
30. See Hélène Michaud, "Roses, Cedars, and Orange Ribbons: A Wave of Nonviolent Revolution," Radio Netherlands Worldwide, June 30, 2005.
31. Ibid.
32. Nora Jumblat, interview with Rudy Jaafar, 30 January 2006 and 21 February 2006, Beirut, Lebanon.
33. Michel Touma, "Le 27 février, la nuit ou tout a basculé," *L'Orient Le Jour*, special supplement, February 13, 2006, 34.
34. See Hardy Merriman chapter's in this volume (chapter 1) for a discussion of the pillars of support.
35. Nora Jumblat, interview with Rudy Jaafar.
36. The nonviolent conflict literature refers to this as "muting the impact of the opponent's violent weapons." See Ackerman and Kruegler, *Strategic Nonviolent Conflict*, 21–55. The use of violent repression by powerful (security) forces against unarmed protestors often ends up weakening the former, a process that Gene Sharp calls political ju-jitsu. See Gene Sharp, *There Are Realistic Alternatives* (Cambridge, MA: Albert Einstein Institution, 2003), 42. Brian Martin developed a more nuanced and refined description of political ju-jitsu, which he refers to as "backfire." See Brian Marin, *Justice Ignited: The Dynamics of Backfire* (Lanham, MD: Rowman and Littlefield, 2007).
37. See Anika Binnendijk and Ivan Marovic, "Power and Persuasion: Nonviolent Strategies to Influence State Security Forces in Serbia (2000) and Ukraine (2004)," *Communist and Post-Communist Studies* 39, no. 3 (2006): 411–29. On the refusal by Soviet troops to use violence against protestors during the anti-coup resistance in 1991, see Brian Martin and Wendy Varney, "Nonviolence and Communication," *Journal of Peace Research* 40, no. 2 (2003): 213–32.
38. Touma, "Le 27 février," 35.
39. See Hardy Merriman's chapter in this volume (chapter 1) for discussion of the sources of power.
40. Karima Rhanem, "Lebanon Heading toward Democracy: Public Protest Brings Down Pro-Syrian Government," *Morocco Times,* March 1, 2005.
41. Washington preferred to avoid the expression "independence intifada." Jefferson Morley hypothesized, "It's easy to see why the Bush administration prefers not to adopt the 'intifada' label. *Intifada* is an Arabic word meaning 'shaking off.' It was coined by Palestinians during their spontaneous uprising against Israeli military occupation in 1987. To speak of Lebanon's 'intifada' places this month's events in the tradition of the Palestinians' struggle against Israeli occupation. And it implies that Syria, a decaying Arab autocracy, and Israel, a favorite U.S. ally, have something in common as occupying powers." Jefferson Morley, "The Branding of Lebanon's Revolution," *Washington Post,* March 3, 2005, www.washingtonpost.com/wp-dyn/articles/A1911–2005Mar2.html.
42. Richard Beeston, "Saudis Tell Syria To Get Troops Out of Lebanon Quickly," *Times* (London), March 4, 2005, www.timesonline.co.uk/tol/news/world/middle_east/article 418896.ece.
43. Safa, "Lebanon Springs Forward," 33. See also Blanford, *Killing Mr Lebanon*, 117.
44. Nora Jumblat, interview.

45. Saleh Farroukh, interview.
46. Ibid.
47. Peter Ackerman and Christopher Kruegler, *Strategic Nonviolent Conflict*, 30–33.
48. Reports of foreign, specifically U.S., funding for the intifada could not be substantiated by the authors. Reports that the 14 March Movement was driven by external actors were vehemently denied by officials; indeed, such reports could have been used in an attempt to delegitimize the movement as a U.S.-manufactured coup. The fact remains, however, that there was little need for external financial assistance when opposition leaders, especially the Hariri family, had sufficient capital to finance the endeavor.
49. As of late 2008, the four security chiefs had yet to be tried.
50. Syrian president Asad said before the withdrawal, "Our problem concerning our presence or no presence in Lebanon wasn't with the international resolutions but with whether or not it was supported by the people of Lebanon. What happened following the assassination of President Hariri was a fundamental reversal by large numbers of Lebanese who, distracted by the media and other Lebanese leaders, responded in an emotional manner." See Daoud Sayegh, "Le prix d'un retour à soi," *L'Orient Le Jour*, special supplement, February 13, 2006, 22.
51. Stephen Zunes, "The United States and Lebanon: A Meddlesome History," *Foreign Policy in Focus*, April 26, 2006, www.fpif.org/fpiftxt/3237.
52. Robert L. Helvey writes that if a movement is created to struggle against an oppressive government, its leaders must think not only about how to remove the oppressor from power, but also what form of government will replace it. A movement's "vision of tomorrow" should include "the form of government to be selected by public consensus based on the characteristics of the society that the citizens want in place at the end of the struggle. Unless citizens give some thought to what should replace a repressive regime, they may remove one tyrannical government only to bring another, more despotic government into power. Thus it is necessary that 'visions of tomorrow' be translated into objectives that will result in pragmatic changes.... Attention should be directed to defining those core issues representing government policy, actions, or style of rule that adversely affect the actual or potential prospect for 'a better life' of its citizens. With clearer definitions of the problems to be attacked, resources can be more wisely apportioned." See Robert L. Helvey, *On Strategic Nonviolent Conflict: Thinking about the Fundamentals* (Boston: Albert Einstein Institution, 2004), 48–50.
53. Abdelmalak, interview.
54. The White House weighed in, excoriating Hizbullah for threatening "illegal" street protests to topple the pro-Western government of Fouad Siniora. One should note, however, the similarity between Hizbullah's demonstrations and those that led to the withdrawal of Syrian troops and the election of the Siniora government.
55. "Protestors Set Up Camp in Beirut," *BBC News*, December 2, 2006, http://news.bbc.co.uk/2/hi/middle_east/6201084.stm. The camp was dismantled following the Doha accords of May 21, 2008.
56. The Doha accords established a new distribution of executive power among the various Lebanese political factions following the May 2008 crisis. For the deficiencies of consociationalism in Lebanon, see Joseph G. Jabbra and Nancy W. Jabbra, "Consociational Democracy in Lebanon: A Flawed System of Governance," *Perspectives on Global Development and Technology* 17, no. 2 (2001); Rudy Jaafar, "Democratic System Reform in Lebanon: An Electoral Approach," in *Breaking the Cycle: Civil Wars in Lebanon*, ed. Youssef Choueiri (London: Stacey International, 2007), 285–305.

Part II

Case Studies

(b)

Challenging Domestic Tyranny and
Promoting Democratic Reform

13

Iran's Islamic Revolution and Nonviolent Struggle

Mohsen Sazegara and Maria J. Stephan

The 1979 Iranian Revolution ousted an unpopular monarchy and led to the establishment of an Islamic republic following an intense period of mass mobilization and collective civil disobedience. Earlier attempts to depose Mohammed Reza Shah Pahlavi's regime through assassinations and guerrilla warfare had failed to achieve what mass protests, strikes, stay-aways, and noncooperation achieved in less than 100 days. Whereas the main guerrilla groups in Iran were infiltrated and decimated by the shah's security apparatus in the 1970s, the civil resistance that began in earnest in late 1977 exerted significant pressure on the monarchy and became impossible to contain or suppress. The withdrawal of consent and cooperation by Iranian workers, students, professionals, clerics, and others separated the regime from its most important social, economic, political, and military pillars of support. The final page turned on the monarchy when on February 11, 1979 the joint staff of the Iranian armed forces declared that the military would "remain neutral" in disputes between the shah's regime and the Iranian people.

Origins of the Monarchy and the Islamic Republic

In Iran, the idea that Islam contains the answers to all of humanity's needs, including government, was first discussed during the 1906 Constitutional Revolution, which ushered in parliamentary government. Devout members of Iran's majority Shiite community strove for several decades afterward to extract from Islam and the precepts of Islamic law (*sharia*) everything that seemed fitting to them in the modern world, ranging from issues relating to sanitation and medical treatment to physics and thermodynamics and from social systems to economics and management. On the basis of this maximalist reading of religion, theologians tried to relate every aspect of life in the modern world to Islam and the precepts of sharia or to "Islamize" them. When this approach faced off against the shah's dictatorship, it gave birth to revolutionary Islam.

Mohammed Reza Shah Pahlavi came to power in 1941, after his father, Reza Shah, was deposed following an invasion of allied British and Soviet forces. The shah ruled until 1953, when he was temporarily forced to flee the country following a power struggle with Prime Minister Mohammed Mossadegh, a democratically elected leader who had nationalized the country's oil fields and had attempted to gain control over the armed forces. Following the 1953 military coup supported covertly by the Central Intelligence Agency and MI6, Mossadegh was arrested, and the shah returned to power. (The shah's opponents consistently challenged his legitimacy because of the way in which he retook power.) Like his father, who looked to Kemal Ataturk's Turkey as a model, the shah sought to modernize and "westernize" Iran while marginalizing the role of the *ulama* (clergy). Reforms enacted through his so-called White Revolution in 1963 included land redistribution to the peasantry, a campaign against rural illiteracy, and civil and political rights for women.

These reforms could not, however, mask the repressive authoritarianism, rampant corruption, and extravagance that characterized the shah's rule.[1] The shah imprisoned political activists, intellectuals, and members of the ulema who opposed him, shut down independent newspapers, and used an extensive security apparatus and secret police, SAVAK, to suppress dissent. By the late 1960s, his regime had officially banned all opposition parties, unions, and formal and informal associations. In 1975 the shah established a single party, Rastakhiz (Resurrection), to which the entire adult population was required to belong and pay dues.

The shah's domestic legitimacy was further weakened by the widely held belief that he was a puppet of the West—primarily the United States, which had supported his rise to power and his anticommunist position—whose values were regarded as corruptive of Iranian culture and traditions. Certain of the shah's policies were considered deeply offensive to Muslims and provoked the ire of the clerical establishment. For example, in 1976 he changed the start of the country's calendar from the Prophet's migration (*hijra*) to the advent of King Cyrus's rule in Persia and hosted an annual arts festival in Shiraz that included international programs with content that many Muslims considered offensive. The shah's economic policies were similarly unpopular. He promised economic rewards from the oil boom of 1974, but instead Iranians suffered under high inflation; the economic disparity grew between the rich and poor and between urban and rural areas.[2] The shah's economic austerity policy, including an anti-profiteering campaign that resulted in the arrests of hundreds of businesspeople, alienated major sectors of society, including middle-class government workers, bazaar merchants, and oil workers, "who would not normally have been rebellious."[3]

Islamist and Other Challenges of the 1960s and 1970s

Following a typical revolutionary pattern, the Iranian middle-class and liberal intellectuals—long-standing targets of the shah's repression—initiated organized dissent, demanding political reforms and liberal freedoms.[4] The Second National Front, a group founded in July 1960 by former colleagues of Mossadegh, headed early opposition to the shah. University students, professional unions (such as the teachers' union), and Islamist and Marxist activists joined forces with the Front, which sought free elections and other political reforms. The shah's regime effectively suppressed the National Front in 1963, as it had the communist Tudeh Party before it. The other main opposition groups during this time were the Liberation Movement of Iran, consisting of religious figures associated with the Front (including Mehdi Bazargan and Ayatollah Mahmud Taleqani), along with the Third Force, an opposition political group formed around Khalil Maleki. They supported constitutional efforts to bring about political reforms inside Iran, and many advocated return to a constitutional monarchy.

The other major challenge to the shah came from Ayatollah Seyyed Ruhollah Khomeini and his clerical supporters. Khomeini had received the honorific *seyyed* because his family allegedly descends from Musa al-Kazim, the seventh of the Twelve Imams. His father and his two grandfathers had also been clerics. Khomeini lectured at seminaries in Najaf and Qom for decades before he became a political figure. Although he did not have a large religious following inside Iran before he was forced into exile in 1964, his long-standing opposition to the shah's regime lent him considerable moral authority. His embrace of mysticism, a philosophy with deep roots inside Iran, contributed to his charismatic appeal. Khomeini and his followers rejected the reforms proposed by the shah under the 1963 White Revolution and the regime's anti-clerical positions. Khomeini declared that the shah had "embarked on the destruction of Islam in Iran."[5] He condemned the shah's close cooperation with Israel and his decision to grant diplomatic immunity to U.S. military personnel.

Khomeini's arrest in June 1963 led to the first outbreak of nationwide riots since the 1953 coup. The regime's brutal suppression of the 1963 demonstrations, resulting in the deaths of hundreds of protestors,[6] represented a major turning point in the anti-shah movement. The regime's reaction to the protests prompted many Iranians inside and outside the country to conclude that armed struggle was the only viable option for challenging the shah's government.[7] Shortly after the protest, in 1964, Khomeini was exiled, first to Turkey and then to the holy city of Najaf in Iraq, where he would spend fifteen years before moving to Paris in 1978.

Iran experienced a veritable Islamic revival during Khomeini's exile, as leading Muslim intellectuals, among them Ali Shariati, popularized revolutionary Shiite messages and texts, in the process attracting new listeners and followers; Jalal Al-e-Ahmad denounced the *gharbzadegi* (Western cultural plague). In a series of lectures in 1970, Khomeini, building on a maximalist interpretation of Islam, developed the concept of an Islamic state with a government headed by the leading Islamic jurist (*vilayat al-faqih*). His lectures were transcribed and published as *Islamic Government.*[8]

Khomeini's concept of a government ruled by clerics was revolutionary, but it was not readily discussed by non-clerical anti-shah forces before and during the revolution. Although Shiite scholars had been debating for centuries the relationship between religious scholars and political power, Khomeini broke from their traditional scholarship by insisting on the deposition of the Iranian monarchy and the concentration of ultimate Islamic authority and political power in a single individual.[9] To avoid creating divisions within the ranks of the opposition during the revolution, however, Khomeini never spoke of the practicalities of the Islamist government during discussions or interviews. Indeed, as Gene Burns has argued, the "ambiguous ideology" that characterized the Iranian Revolution helped unite a disparate Iranian population around an anti-shah and anti-imperial platform. This ideological ambiguity would also set the stage for a struggle over the meaning of the revolution after the fall of the monarchy.[10]

Firsthand: Early Opposition to the Shah

Iran's political groups during the last century were dominated by monarchists, Islamists, Marxists, nationalists, and ethnic minorities. Most of political organizations were either Marxist or nationalist. On the whole, the Islamists and the Marxists were more determined and radical in their activities against the shah. The Islamists and their supporters consisted primarily of clerics, bazaaris, and academics.

In May 1961, Mehdi Bazargan, Yadollah Sahabi, and Ayatollah Mahmud Taleghani announced the formation of the Liberation Movement of Iran, which was comprised of academic Muslims. The group established good relations with other segments of the Islamic movement like bazaaris and clerics, and at the time of its founding, advocated a democratic reading of political Islam. (Later, this was replaced by a revolutionary political Islam based on Shariati's ideas.)

During the 1960s and 1970s, the shah jailed political activists, clerics, and intellectuals who opposed him, censored the media; banned political parties, and established Rastakhiz (Resurrection) as the only legal party. The shah's opponents, especially the Marxists and Islamists, were of the view that only through armed struggle and guerrilla warfare could they successfully fight against his regime.

Inspired by Marxist-Leninist writings and influenced by the anticolonial struggles in Algeria, Angola, Cuba, and other parts of the world, Iranian Muslims developed an ideological and revolutionary Islam that justified armed combat. After the 1963 uprising, even those who had advocated reform from within the system became outspoken advocates of armed struggle. Dozens of small armed groups formed, but the most significant factions were the Organization of People's Feda'i Guerrillas (Feda'iyan), the People's Strugglers of Iran (Mojahedin-e Khalq-e Iran), and the Marxist-Leninist Mojahedin-e, an offshoot of the latter established in 1975.[11]

The Feda'iyan, a Marxist-Leninist group formed in 1971, conducted mostly urban attacks from 1971 to 1979.[12] The Mojahedin-e Khalq, established in 1965, was a revolutionary guerrilla group that "represented a genuine attempt by young Moslem revolutionaries to reinterpret traditional Shi'a Islam and infuse it with modern political thinking in order to turn it into a viable revolutionary ideology."[13]

Firsthand: The Mojahedin-e-Khalq

The Mojahedin-e-Khalq Organization (MKO) was established in 1965 by Mohammad Hanif Nejhad, Saeed Mohsen, and Ali Asghar Badie Zadegan, young members of the Liberation Movement of Iran. They believed in a revolutionary Islam and armed struggle. A faction of the leadership and the members of this organization converted to Marxism in 1976 and tried to control the organization through bloody, internal conflicts. For this reason, two MKOs existed for a while, one Marxist and one Islamic. In 1978 the Marxists left MKO and established their own organization, Peykar dar Rahe Azadie Tabagheh Karegar (Struggle for the Liberation of the Proletariat).

The Feda'iyan's first guerrilla action took place on February 8, 1971, when its members attacked a gendarmerie post in the small village of Siyahkal, in the northern province of Gilan. The attack proved disastrous: the guerrillas' contact in the village had already been captured by SAVAK, and the local farmers turned against them. The shah's government sent in thousands of troops and deployed helicopters to clear the countryside of the guerrillas.

One of the goals of the violent struggle was to refute the myth of the absolute power of the shah and SAVAK. The guerrillas also wanted to show the people that they were not absolutely powerless. This "two absolutes" thesis was based on the assumption that the people would be heartened if they saw that average people could inflict blows to the shah and SAVAK and that this would pave the way for revolution. The failure of this strategy was made clear when the regime crushed the larger guerrilla organizations in 1976 and 1977. The remaining guerrilla forces continued to launch sporadic armed attacks into the late 1970s, but their activities were overshadowed by mass nonviolent resistance.

What effectively shattered the notion of two absolutes was the election of Jimmy Carter as president of the United States. In 1976 Carter campaigned for the presidency on a platform that emphasized the promotion of human rights through U.S. foreign policy and as a tool against the communist bloc. His focus on human rights worried the shah, a cold war ally who publicly insisted that Iranians were not ready for rights, but instead needed strong tutelage for the foreseeable future as the country developed socially, economically, and politically.[14] The shah received strong U.S. support to hold on to power, and assumed that given Carter's foreign policy approach, he would have to reconsider his governing style. When the shah started to moderate his policies, his opponents seized on the opportunity to broaden and strengthen their struggle.

Intellectuals and other members of the opposition, who were few in number in the early 1970s, began to publish open letters critical of the shah and calling for constitutionalism and respect for human rights. In summer 1977, they began to organize semi-public protest activities treated with relative leniency by the shah's security forces. The death later that year of Ali Shariati, a leading Islamist intellectual with a significant following among religious students, led to large demonstrations in memory of Shariati and in support of Khomeini. Ten consecutive nights of poetry readings with political overtones attracted thousands of Iranians to the Iran-Germany Association in Tehran in October. The regime forcefully broke up the gatherings. In October 1977, a group of moderate oppositionists formed the Iranian Committee for the Defense of Human Rights.

Firsthand: "The Shah Must Go"

When President Carter's policies were announced in winter 1977, the Liberation Movement of Iran, a clandestine organization of which I was a member, came to the conclusion that there was now the possibility for change in Iran's political atmosphere. Those of us who were abroad demonstrated this clearly in an article entitled "US Caught in the Impasse of Militarizing Iran," which was published in the movement's journal, *Payam-e Mojaehd* (Struggler's Message). We suggested that a pivotal slogan—we settled on "The Shah Must Go"—could now be raised and pursued. On the basis of this analysis, we sent a message to Mehdi Bazargan, the leader of the Liberation Movement who was in Iran, and told him that it would be a good idea for him to disseminate and distribute this proposal openly in the form of a statement in an open letter signed by opposition figures.

When Ebrahim Yazdi, one of the leaders of the Liberation Movement abroad, traveled to Najaf and raised this idea with Ayatollah Ruhollah Khomeini, who was living there in political exile, he found Khomeini to be enthusiastic about it; his only advice was that once Bazargan had written the statement, he should try to persuade all the individuals and groups who were in some way opposed to the shah to sign it. Muslim or non-Muslim, it makes no difference; invite everyone who is opposed to the shah to sign the statement. This, in short, was Khomeini's instruction. In Iran, Bazargan wrote a comprehensive, 60-page statement, which ended with the following words: "The country is at a crossroads. Either a single individual has to be sacrificed for a nation or a whole nation has to be sacrificed for an individual. So, there is no alternative: The Shah must go." Discussions over the statement between the country's political forces began in Iran. Numerous meetings led to unity around the specific aim of deposing the shah. Ayatollah Khomeini, for his part, strove, via his students, to create the same unity against the shah among the clergy. Ultimately, it is possible to say that, thanks to this method, nearly all of Iran's political forces, from a gamut of persuasions, ranging from left-wing to nationalist, from ethnic minorities to Muslims, were united and mobilized against the shah and the monarchy in the last few months before he was forced to leave the country.

"The Shah Must Go," or in the words of the people, "Death to the Shah," became the pivotal slogan of the revolution. In the people's minds, this simple and universally comprehensible slogan had turned into the cure for all ills and the key to all locks to the point where revolutionary crowds sometimes would chant, "This homeland won't be a homeland until the shah is in a shroud."

Expectations that the Carter administration would apply significant pressure on its cold war ally and major oil and arms trading partner to improve its human rights record were soon dashed. When the shah visited Washington in November 1977, human rights issues were discussed only in private and mostly in positive terms. When Carter in turn visited Tehran the next month, he famously offered the shah this toast: "Iran, because of the great leadership of the shah, is an island of stability in one of the more troubled areas of the world. This is a great tribute to you, Your Majesty, and to your leadership and to the respect and the admiration and love which your people give you."[15]

The level of repression inside Iran increased after the shah's meeting with Carter in November. The security apparatus began to break up poetry readings and student protests with force. As opposition leader Mehdi Bazargan told U.S. diplomats several months later, "Following the Shah's visit to Washington, repression again seemed the order of the day."[16] An internal State Department memo noted in December 1977 that the shah's government was "substantially increasing its use of force in dealing with political opposition."[17]

On December 20–21, Islamists turned the annual processions of Tasu'a and 'Ashura into occasions for mass political demonstrations. Thousands of protestors carrying signs with anti-shah slogans marched through the bazaars in Tehran. Riot police attacked and arrested them. By the end of 1977, Islamists began to believe that their consciousness-raising activities and parallel institution building of the 1960s and early 1970s, when they founded independent schools, publishing houses, and disseminated journals and pamphlets, had finally borne fruit. As Khomeini acknowledged in a speech on 12 November that was recorded, smuggled into Iran, and distributed to his followers, demonstrations indicated "hate towards the tyrannical regime [of the shah] and an actual referendum on the vote of no confidence towards the treacherous regime....The nation—from the clergy and academics to the labourers and farmers, men and women—all are awakened."[18]

Khomeini's supporters began to mobilize at the end of 1977, reactivating the Society of Qom Seminary Instructors and the Society of Struggling Religious Scholars, which began to issue pronouncements. The exiled leader spoke of an "awakening" inside Iran after his eldest son, Mostafa, had died suddenly on 23 October and thousands of devout Muslims attended mourning ceremonies in Qom that took the form of mass street demonstrations. Mass mobilization at this point became a distinct possibility. Mourners in Shiraz and Tabriz marched out of mosques and began shouting "Death to the Shah"—the first time the slogan was publicly chanted.[19] A week later, merchants at the Tehran bazaar commemorated the death of Khomeini's son by organizing a general strike.

The shah's security forces launched a massive crackdown on the protestors a couple of weeks after the mourning ceremonies began. This failed, however, to deter religious Muslims, who began to mobilize seminary students in Qom for even larger mourning ceremonies scheduled for the fortieth day after Mostafa Khomeini's death (as per Shiite tradition). The fortieth day was marked with merchant strikes and overtly political speeches by religious leaders, who presented a "fourteen-point resolution" calling for, among other things, the return of Khomeini from exile, the release of political prisoners, the reopening of religious and university institutions, free speech, a ban on pornography, protection of the right of women to wear the *hijab* (headscarf), an end to relations with Israel, and support for the poor.[20]

During this period of intensified repression, the opposition began to increase its protest activities, aided by the powerful mosque network in Iran. More than 9,000 mosques in Iran in the early 1970s were linked by religious leaders in every town and village. The activation of the mosque network did not occur automatically. Rather, Islamic radicals and students applied pressure on moderate clerical leaders to support the revolutionary cause. On January 7, 1978, after an article ran in the state-run *Ettela'at* newspaper mocking Khomeini and insinuating that his opposition to the shah's modernization policies had been bought with British oil interests, a group of seminary students and scholars from Qom won the backing of leading ayatollahs to organize a day-long strike. The strike on 9 January closed down the bazaar. Thousands of protestors joined students as they marched door to door to pressure religious leaders to offer them public support. Specific instructions had been given to the protestors to avoid antagonizing the security forces.[21] Rather than shouting angry slogans, the protestors marched in silence.

As long as the protests remained fairly small, they were vulnerable to repression by the security forces. A bloody crackdown on protestors in Qom on 9 January proved to be another turning point in the revolution. When a group of demonstrators approached a police barricade, someone—either a protestor or an *agent provocateur*—threw a brick through a bank window. The security forces, in response, began to fire live rounds into the crowd. Less than a dozen people were killed, but rumors spread that hundreds had died, and their bodies taken away by government trucks. The Qom shootings triggered a wave of demonstrations that touched all parts of the country.

"Doing the Forty-Forty"

The people killed in Qom were commemorated on the fortieth day of mourning, generating protests in other cities. Protestors killed by the shah's security forces in Tabriz, Yazd, and other cities were similarly commemorated 40 days after their deaths, triggering a cycle of mobilization that some called "doing the forty-forty."[22] A ceremony mourning the deceased on the fortieth day after his or her death is traditionally a small event in Shiite Islam, usually attended by close family and friends. Iranian Islamist leaders transformed this religious custom into a political event to promote mass mobilization.[23]

The shah began retreating, ordering some of his senior administrators arrested. Leading the ranks of the detained was Amir Abbas Hoveida, who had served as prime minister for 13 years. The shah blamed these officials for the country's shortcomings, causing a great deal of uneasiness among all who had remained loyal to the monarchy. Far from calming the masses, however, these arrests emboldened them. They now recognized the shah's vulnerability. The two absolutes had been breached; the engine of the revolution was started. The mosque network provided crucial infrastructure and sanctuary for the revolutionaries, and was the main distributor of audiocassettes smuggled into Iran containing speeches and instructions from Khomeini and his close advisors. Abolhassan Sadegh, an official with the Ministry of National Guidance, noted at the time that cassettes were stronger than fighter planes.[24]

Firsthand: The 1978 Mass Mobilization

In summer 1978, I returned to Iran from the United States. Apart from the messages and documents that I secretly took to fellow members of the foreign-based liberation movement, my most important undertaking was to join the various links of the chain of fellow religious activists. For some years, an extensive network of Muslim students in universities and high schools had been establishing libraries in mosques and organizing plays and other artistic activities in order to strengthen revolutionary ideas.

Our strategy was to establish links between Islamic activists, in effect stringing together all the dispersed beads of active cells; unite all the shah's opponents, regardless of political persuasion, around the slogan "The Shah Must Go" and isolate those advocating compromise in light of the shah's retreat; create unity between Muslim intellectuals and clerics, who also had the bazaaris on their side; and promote the idea that Ayatollah Khomeini should be the leader of all opposition activists in view of the fact that he was the first Islamic jurist to issue a *fatwa* holding that the monarchy had contravened Islam. We tried to attribute any accomplishment that we made to Khomeini so that his authority would grow with every passing day. With this strategy, we sought to encourage various groups of people to go on strike and to paralyze the country so that we could put pressure on the shah to step down.

The Shah's Concessions and Escalating Protests

The shah's conciliatory overture of arresting some of his top officials in summer 1978 threatened to split the opposition; in addition to fighting against corruption, the shah had also made a promise to gradually free political prisoners. Whereas the exiled Khomeini declared the shah's announcement "a trick," leaders of the moderate opposition were more enthusiastic about the possibilities afforded by the shah's concession. Mehdi Bazargan—a leading moderate Islamist and close advisor to Khomeini who would become prime minister of the interim Islamic government after the revolution—expressed cautious support for the shah's proposals and called for a "step-by-step" approach in dealing with the monarchy.

The Islamists, however, quickly rejected the gradualist approach favored by Bazargan and others and began to revive street protests and demonstrations in cities across the country. "The response [to the shah's liberalizing overtures] was larger crowds of demonstrators chanting for an Islamic State."[25] During the long, hot summer, two occasions demonstrated the effective unity of forces' thinking: a series of poetry nights at the Goethe Institute in Tehran organized by the Association of Writers, mainly comprised of left-wing intellectuals, and speeches delivered every night during Ramadan after prayers at Quba Mosque in north Tehran. After Id al-Fitr prayers marking the end of Ramadan, the worshippers embarked on a march during which they chanted "Death to the Shah."

Expanding beyond a core group of supporters and building a truly mass movement remained a central challenge for the Islamist leadership. A few demonstrations had attracted 50,000 protestors, an impressive number but a relatively small proportion given a population of more than 35 million. After dozens of protestors were killed in Isfahan on 10 August, the government declared martial law in the city, sending in tanks and implementing a nightly curfew. Solidarity protests took place in cities throughout Iran, and Khomeini accused the shah of seeking to destroy the country as he was being forced to relinquish power.

The protest movement expanded considerably after a fire at a movie theater in Abadan on 19 August killed 400 people. When it was discovered that the doors to the theater had been locked from the outside and that the fire department had been slow in responding, many Iranians blamed the government for the deadly arson. Shouts of "Burn the Shah!" were heard at protests held in mourning; such demonstrations multiplied in number and intensity after the theater massacre. By the end of August, eleven cities had been placed under martial law. At this point, the shah took a series of steps designed to appease the Islamists, among them appointing a new reform-minded prime minister, Ja'far Sharif-Emami, on 27 August and returning to the Muslim calendar. He closed casinos and instituted new press freedoms.

Firsthand: Gaining Momentum

The shah tasked his new prime minister, Ja'far Sharif-Emami, with forming a new cabinet. (Sharif-Emami replaced Jamshid Amouzegar, who had been appointed a year prior to replace Amir Abbas Hoveida.) Sharif-Emami was a long-standing freemason and a proponent of national reconciliation, especially with the clergy. He imagined that by making concessions to the clergy and granting the people a few freedoms, he would be able to quell the revolution. These new freedoms created the climate that we needed. Although martial law had been declared in a few cities, pressure from SAVAK had eased a bit, and we could extend strikes to government departments and factories. Our tactic everywhere was to establish strike committees and to bring departments to a standstill. We were trying to paralyze the country, and we were careful to ensure that no one deviated from the theme that "The Shah Must Go."

At this point, two events greatly helped take the revolution forward. One was the reopening of schools and universities at the start of the new academic year. This meant that as students joined the strikes, almost the entire country and every family would be involved in the revolution. The other event was the travel of Ayatollah Khomeini from Najaf to France. The Iraqi government, led by Saddam Hussein, had pressured Khomeini, telling him that he could not work against the shah from Iraq. At the time, relations between the two countries had been improving, after the signing of the 1975 Algiers accord, and the two regimes were trying to normalize ties. Khomeini decided to leave Iraq. Ebrahim Yazdi had gone to visit Khomeini in Najaf as the ayatollah was preparing to depart with a few of his cohorts, so Yazdi joined them. When the Kuwaiti government refused to allow them entry, Khomeini decided on a Western, democratic destination. Thus, Paris became his next place of residence.

I joined the group in France a week after their arrival. The openness of France was exactly what we required. As the struggle in Iran intensified, media interest in Ayatollah Khomeini grew. During his stay there, he was interviewed more than 430 times, so the entire world heard the voice of the revolution. Neauphle-le-Château, in the Paris suburbs, turned into the revolution's headquarters. Three telephone lines and a dubbing machine that allowed us to make three copies of audiocassettes at a time were the equipment at our disposal for communicating with Iran. Whenever Khomeini delivered a speech, we would make a master copy, which would open with me announcing the time and place of the speech. Masoud Manian would then make copies and arrange for passengers to take them to Iran. The content of the tapes were also transmitted to Iran via telephone and then copied and distributed there. This was why the Islamic revolution became known as the "audiocassette revolution," as Iran's constitutional revolution became known as the "telegraph revolution."

In Neauphle-le-Château, apart from helping translate during interviews, every night I prepared for Ayatollah Khomeini summaries of reports and articles from more than 20 high-circulation newspapers and journals. Every few days, we held discussions to analyse the situation. I drafted summaries of these discussions for Khomeini as well. Since we thought the struggle against the shah would continue for quite some time, we were also thinking about forming a popular army. This idea later materialized in the form of the Revolutionary Guards after the revolution's success. The model that we had in mind was the Algerian revolution. We never thought that the shah could be so easily toppled using the tactics of nonviolent struggle, which were unfamiliar to us at the time.

Most protest activity continued to be spontaneous, but a large-scale demonstration on Eid al-Fitr expanded the base well beyond core Islamists. Bazaaris, liberal oppositionists, and leftists joined the Islamists for a massive demonstration, prompting Khomeini to refer to that year's celebration as an "Eid of epic movement."[26] On 8 September, one day after a mass demonstration, the shah declared martial law in Tehran and other cities. Several thousand protestors gathered on Zhaleh Square in Tehran in an act of defiance. After security forces fired tear gas into the growing crowd, they began to shoot live rounds. Casualty counts on that day, which came to be known as Black Friday, ranged from fewer than a hundred to several thousands.[27]

After Black Friday, the opposition halted outdoor protests and demonstrations and shifted to other tactics. In the weeks following, wildcat strikes spread throughout the country, starting with workers from the oil refineries on 9 September.[28] By the first week of November, members from almost every sector of Iranian society had held work stoppages, including journalists, national airline and railroad workers, customs officials, and power plant and bank employees. "The stranglehold on international trade was so complete that for awhile the central bank was forced to stop issuing Treasury bills to raise money for the Government because the ink for certification was held up on the quayside."[29]

The oil workers' strike had the most profound effect on the Iranian economy, as the oil fields were the regime's most important source of revenue. When oil workers went on strike in October 1978, Iranian oil exports dropped from more than five million barrels a day to less than two million barrels in two weeks' time. As Asef Bayat notes, whereas workers had called strikes numerous other times in Iranian history, their demands had tended to focus on purely economic issues, such as increased pay and subsidized housing. This time, however, their demands included an end to martial law, support for striking teachers, release of political prisoners, and the Iranianization of the oil industry.[30]

Khomeini did not intend for the national strike to go on for an extended period of time. He stated, "Nobody will die of hunger from several days of striking shops and businesses, in submission to God."[31] It was not until a month later, in November, that Khomeini expressed support for an indefinite national strike until the regime collapsed. In early November 1978, with strikes being launched throughout the country, high school students organized a demonstration in front of Tehran University that turned violent when students clashed with security forces. Several people were killed, triggering a student-led riot the next day. Buildings throughout Tehran were torched, including the British embassy compound.

At this point, the shah launched a major crackdown. He fired his civilian prime minister and appointed a military government. With martial law declared, tanks and armored vehicles entered cities and towns across the country to prevent further demonstrations. The army took control of the National Iranian Radio and Television and clamped down on the print media; only the ruling party newspaper was allowed to go to press. The government arrested leading opposition figures. The army forced oil workers to go back to work, and strike committee leaders were instructed to increase oil production or risk death.

The shah, in his announcement of the new military government, insisted that he was sympathetic to some aspects of the revolution and promised to crack down on lawlessness and corruption and to restore a national unity government to oversee free elections. He condemned the wave of strikes that had paralyzed the country, notably in the oil sector, and demanded that the strikes end and that order be restored. Some scholars contend that the shah's health at the time—he was, unbeknownst to the population, dying of cancer—helps to explain his vacillating, inconsistent response to the revolutionary movement. Because the state had been constructed to rely on the shah, his diminished capacity paralyzed it.

Firsthand: Martial Law versus Jihad

When in November 1978 the shah instituted military rule under General Gholam-Reza Azhari, martial law was declared in most cities. Newspapers, which had only had a taste of freedom for a few months, were banned. In effect, an iron fist policy went into effect. A number of clerics and politicians were sending messages to Ayatollah Khomeini, suggesting that he issue a fatwa for jihad so that the people could fight back against the military government, which had deployed troops and tanks on the streets. Ayatollah Morteza Motahhari, who had been close to Khomeini, traveled to Paris from Iran to propose this path to Khomeini. He stated that the people might be too intimidated by martial law to demonstrate in the streets and that their excitement and enthusiasm would peter out unless they did. We were opposed to this idea and Ebrahim Yazdi, Khomeini's closest adviser in Paris, persuaded him at a lengthy meeting that there was still plenty of time for issuing a fatwa for jihad and that the threat of such a fatwa could be held over the shah's head like Damocles' sword.

If the people are to take up arms in obedience to a fatwa by Khomeini and to go to war against the army, to kill and be killed, why not start by asking them to do simpler things? In this way, it could be determined whether they were prepared to follow the instructions of the revolutionary leader. For example, he could ask them not to pay their water and electricity bills or to disobey the regime's regulations. Moreover, if there were to be clashes with the army, it would be best to first try to create divisions in its ranks. Ask soldiers to leave their garrisons or ask young officers not to obey their generals and commanders. Call on officers' wives to encourage their husbands to disobey their superiors. Ask the people to hug their brothers in the army and invite them to join the nation's struggles. A few years later, when the memoirs of the shah's generals began to appear, one revealed the minutes of a Joint Staff meeting in which a military commander had said that with so many soldiers and officers deserting, "We'll melt away like snow."

When Khomeini issued statements based on these ideas, the atmosphere of the struggle changed, and Iranians became more united. People would place flowers in soldiers' gun barrels and ask, "Brother Soldier, why kill your brothers?" or assert, "Soldier, we give you flowers, you give us bullets." At night, when the curfew would go into effect at 10 o'clock, people would go onto their rooftops and shout repeatedly, "God is Great." In this way, people could express their opposition to the shah and military rule without clashing with soldiers. When Gen. Azhari declared in a speech that only a small number of people were opposed to the shah and that it was these people who were playing cassette recordings of "God is Great" from rooftops at night—not the people en mass—street demonstrators began shouting, "Azhari is a four-star ass, says it's cassettes, even though cassettes have no legs."

The census taken after the revolution recorded that in the final year of struggle against the shah's government, some 700 people had been killed in street clashes nationwide. This figure is, first, amazingly low given the country's population—at the time about 35 million—and, second, some of the casualties can be blamed on troops' inexperience and lack of preparedness in dealing with street demonstrations.

Not only were there too many protestors for the shah's police to arrest in fall 1978, but the security forces simply did not have the resources or manpower to enforce martial law or sufficient space in jails and prisons to accommodate detainees. Transcripts of a security meeting held in January 1979 reveal that Iran's military chiefs discussed plans to arrest 100,000 opposition activists, but an assessment of the facilities available showed that only 5,000 additional detainees could be held.[32] Some people already serving time were released to make room for new prisoners.

Even more problematic from the regime's perspective, the shah's soldiers and police were incapable of running the organizations and institutions over which they had assumed control. When the military attempted to force state-run television to run pro-shah programming, the officials in charge warned that their workers would see the programs and refuse to report to work. Employees at electrical facilities began cutting power for two hours each night to disrupt the state-run evening news and to offer the cover of darkness to protestors violating the 10 o'clock curfew. The shah's security forces lacked the personnel to take over the facilities in order to stop the blackouts.

Taking control of the oil refineries proved similarly impossible. The shah sent in hundreds of navy technicians to operate the pumping stations, but they did not know how the system functioned. The government tried to force oil workers to return to the oil fields, sometimes invading their homes and dragging them to work. The workers decided to return to the fields, work for a short time, and then launch another walk-out. A recognizable pattern developed in all of Iran's major industries, including the national airline, telecommunications, banking, and customs office: "Industries would strike, return to work when forced to, and then go back on strike as soon as possible."[33] Seemingly acknowledging the inability of his regime to rely on force to keep the population in line, the shah said in an October 1978 interview, "You can't crack down on one place and make the people on the next block behave."[34]

Neutralizing the Security Forces

The weakening of the shah's most important pillar of support—the security forces—was the death knell for his regime. Opposition leaders met with security officials and asked them to join their cause or at least to disobey orders to crack down on protestors. Khomeini pleaded with the security forces, "Proud soldiers who are ready to sacrifice yourself for your country and homeland, arise! Suffer slavery and humiliation no longer! Renew your bonds with the beloved people and refuse to go on slaughtering your children and brothers for the sake of the whims of this family of bandits!"[35]

Fraternization was an important part of the opposition strategy. During demonstrations, protestors handed flowers to the soldiers and chanted the slogans, "Brother soldier, why kill your brothers?" and "The army is part of the nation." A Tehran-based religious scholar ran an operation to assist deserters, whereby foot soldiers were given civilian clothes to change into, and higher-ranking officers were sent back to the barracks to collect intelligence.[36] While the effectiveness of these forms of pressure is unclear, and the number of actual desertions remained relatively low until the shah left Iran, what is clear is that the opposition efforts lowered morale in the army and police. Authorized leaves increased dramatically, the number of small-scale mutinies began to rise, and evidence existed of decreasing loyalty among junior personnel.[37] In early January 1979, Chief of Staff Abbas Gharabaghi estimated during a meeting with fellow officers that the military was running at about 55 percent capacity.[38]

By late 1978, protestors simply outnumbered and outmaneuvered the shah's security forces. As Charles Kurzman points out, "The Shah's military-security complex was not so much weakened as overwhelmed. No system of repression is intended to deal with wholesale popular disobedience like that which emerged in Iran in late 1978."[39] The opposition began to produce fake cassettes with a voice sounding like the shah's giving generals orders to shoot demonstrators. While most Iranians never directly confronted the shah's security forces, preferring to stay at home, where they would shout anti-shah slogans from their rooftops, casualties only seemed to intensify the mass mobilization.

The Shah Flees, Khomeini Returns

At the end of 1978, the shah offered the prime ministerial post to key members of the moderate opposition. While these reform-minded individuals almost assuredly would have accepted the offer at an earlier time, to do so in late 1978 would have been political suicide. In December on the shah's orders, Shapour Bakhtiar, a nationalist leader opposed to the shah, took over as prime minister from Gen. Azhari. With the country engaged in mass rebellion, the shah fled to Aswan, Egypt, on January 16, 1979 under the pretext of seeking medical attention in the United States.

Firsthand: Revolutionary Government

Although the shah had cancer and had announced that he was going abroad for medical treatment and to rest, his departure caused a wave of joy among the people. They chanted in the streets, "We say we don't want the shah, [but only] the prime minister changes / We say we don't want a donkey, [but only] the donkey blanket changes." Iranians were beginning to sense victory, which boosted their morale. Nothing could stop them now. They were only a few steps from toppling the monarchy.

The shah's newly appointed prime minister tried to take control of the situation, but time was not on the side of the caretaker government. Meanwhile, in Paris, Ebrahim Yazdi prepared a four-step plan for the creation of an Islamic government, which Ayatollah Khomeini approved: announce the formation of a Revolutionary Council; paralyze the country and deprive the shah's government of all control over Iran's affairs; form a provisional government (proposed by the Revolutionary Council and approved by Khomeini) and work to win international recognition for itself; have Khomeini return to Iran.

Prime Minister Shahpour Bakhtiar tried to take up the reins of government and play for time with the hope that people would tire and the government would be able to survive the pervasive strikes that had paralyzed the country. Khomeini called on civil servants to prevent Bakhtiar's cabinet members from entering ministries and to withdraw cooperation from them. Bakhtiar's government lasted only 37 days. In practice, the third and fourth stages of the four-stage plan occurred in reverse. That is, Khomeini returned to Iran and then announced the formation of a provisional government. He had worried that people's enthusiasm might wane as Bakhtiar tried to stall for time. It was obvious that Khomeini's return to Iran would create a wave of popular excitement big enough to sweep away the Bakhtiar government and what remained of the monarchy.

On February 1, 1979, Ayatollah Khomeini returned from exile. His arrival on an Air France flight had been negotiated between opposition members and the Bakhtiar government. Enthusiastic supporters mobbed him. Bakhtiar remained in office, but regardless, Khomeini took matters into his own hands and appointed Mehdi Bazargan provisional prime minister on 4 February. For two weeks, Iran had two governments.

On the evening of 9 February, fighting broke out at a Tehran air force base between pro-revolution military technicians (homafaran) and the shah's Imperial Guards. The guards fired on pro-Khomeini officers and members of a crowd outside, killing at least two people. When word of the incident spread, civilians rushed to the base to defend mutineers. The high council of the army announced a curfew to start at 4:00 p.m. Khomeini called on the people to disobey martial law. At the same time, however, he refrained from calling for a violent jihad. As one scholar has noted, "Khomeini never needed to declare a holy war. Iranians were already fighting one."[40]

In Tehran, the masses of citizens, who were already in the streets in large numbers, headed for and seized garrisons in solidarity with the revolutionary military personnel. Around the country, crowds of people surrounded different military installations and prevented military reinforcements from reaching the capital. Imperial Guard tanks made their way through hostile (and now highly armed) crowds, fighting with insurgents and killing tens of protestors in two days. On

February 11, after tanks failed to reinforce the besieged guards of a Tehran munitions factory, the armed forces chiefs of staff met and declared that the military would remain "neutral" in the political dispute between the nation and the state and that soldiers would be returning to their garrisons. At this point, Iran's Islamic revolution had effectively triumphed.

Aftermath of the Revolution

After assuming power and appointing Bazargan prime minister, Khomeini filled his cabinet with a number of other moderate oppositionists. Hopes that an acceptable power-sharing arrangement would pave the way for a peaceful transition in postrevolution Iran were, however, short-lived. Within the Revolutionary Council, a split emerged, with Bazargan and his allies on one side and the clerics on the other. The revolutionary groups were also unsatisfied with the cabinet. Bazargan tried to step down on several occasions, but Khomeini refused to accept his resignation. On 3 November, when Iranian students stormed the U.S. embassy and took American diplomats hostage—an action supported by Khomeini—Bazargan again submitted his resignation. This time Khomeini accepted.[41] At this point, the liberals were frozen out of the cabinet and ultimately forced out of postrevolutionary electoral politics. Violent clashes between Islamists and Marxists that had begun before the shah's overthrow intensified after the revolution. Khomeini had warned during the revolutionary period against "those who deviate and oppose Islam" and had condemned leftist groups for a long time. Competition over control of the oil industry in southern Iran furthered the hostility between these groups. Soon, the Marxists resorted to bombings, and the Islamists resorted to arrest, torture, and executions.

Firsthand: Revolutionary Violence

The Iranian Revolution triumphed with minimal casualties, but because the political groups involved all subscribed to violent and revolutionary theories, violence against the shah's officials began on the morrow of the revolution and then extended to clashes with left-wingers, nationalists, and religious and ethnic minorities.

Among the five political "families" that were active in Iran during the course of the revolution, four united against one—the monarchists. Of the four, one—the religious activists—took power. Because none of these groups espoused a democratic philosophy, there was, in effect, no means of resolving the struggle for power in a democratic manner. In other words, these groups' theories of revolution licensed the violence and fighting that began to rage among them.

With the start of the eight-year Iran-Iraq War on September 21, 1980, the atmosphere of violence intensified. At this time, I was deputy for political affairs in Prime Minister Mohammad Ali Raja'i's government. In spring 1981, after six months of discussion and coordination with the judiciary, we issued a 10-point declaration that called on all groups to hand in their weapons in exchange for which the government would recognize their right to participate freely in political activity. We thought that this would calm the atmosphere and represent the first step toward democracy; it was a naive notion.

The Mojahedin-e Khalq Organization, which professed a radical, left-wing Islamic ideology and had reorganized after the revolution, was the strongest armed group in the country and opposed the plan of disarming in order to participate in politics. The central revolutionary prosecutor's office, headed by Assadollah Lajevardi, also opposed the plan, on the grounds that it would give counterrevolutionary groups time to organize for the overthrow of the new regime. These two bodies traded insults over our heads and eventually engaged in armed clashes. Lajevardi banned 60 journals and newspapers in a single night, and the Mojahedin-e Khalq, for their part, opted for combat. The state's response, approved by Khomeini (after persuasive arguments by his son Ahmad), resulted in thousands of killings and executions. The repression then was extended to all dissident groups. In effect, the Islamic activists who had come to power crushed all the other political groups. The jails filled with prisoners, and thousands of people were executed by firing squad.

We had misunderstood violent revolution. We did not know that the theories of violent revolution, which had been widely advocated but never really practiced during the revolution, had supporters who would not be satisfied until a great deal of blood had been shed. After a few years, the Islamic activists were able to gain the upper hand over all the other groups and establish a monopoly on power.

By 1982, the organized left in Iran had been virtually eliminated.[42] Liberals, leftists, nationalists, and ethnic minorities were all targets of the radical clerics who controlled the new theocracy. Nearly 20,000 people were killed in the postrevolutionary period; the Islamic Republic cites a figure of 12,000. Thousands of citizens were jailed, and a decade later, in summer 1988, on the orders of Ayatollah Khomeini 4,448 of these political prisoners were executed. These events led to an accumulation of hatred and vengefulness in Iranian society. At present, the quest for vengeance is one of the biggest problems that any nonviolent movement faces in Iran.

Conclusion

Whereas only a tiny percentage of the Iranian population fought as guerrillas— mostly young men (but also some women) from urban areas—the masses became the vanguard in the nonviolent resistance of the Iranian Revolution. Resistance to the shah, which began in late 1977 and rapidly accelerated after summer 1978, was characterized by mass participation from nearly every segment of Iranian society. With young clerics in the forefront, and with the assistance of a decentralized ulema-bazaari network that facilitated the mass mobilization, mourning ceremonies that took the form of street demonstrations spread throughout Iran and later included a national strike that paralyzed the country.

Rather than attacking the regime's security forces—the main target of violent revolutionaries—the civilian-led opposition fraternized with the shah's soldiers and police and undermined their reliability. Although the regime responded to street protests with violence, and later attempted to force the striking population to return to work to restore normalcy, no amount of violent coercion could suppress an entire population refusing to cooperate. Guerrilla attacks caused the occasional disruption of the shah's control over society, but they did not fundamentally threaten the shah's sources of power; they also gave justification to the shah's violent crackdowns. In the end, mass nonviolent resistance was responsible for systematically neutralizing or eliminating the monarchy's sources of political, economic, and military power.

Ayatollah Khomeini and his close students succeeded in bringing a large segment of the clergy into the arena of political activity against the shah. In this way, the country's large network of mosques was put at the revolution's disposal. Hence, various religious rituals, especially annual mourning ceremonies, also served revolutionary purposes. The activation of the mosque network, backed by a young generation of revolutionaries and the powerful bazaari community, was the most significant component of revolutionary recruitment. At the same time, many moderate and conservative religious leaders were suspicious of the aims and objectives of Khomeini and the radical clerics and were loathe to become actively involved in revolutionary activities. It took pressure by local leaders, including radical clerics and their allies among bazaaris, students, and moderate politicians, to transform the mosque network into a tool of mass mobilization. Many Iranians were linked to the mosques and through neighborhood religious associations (hay'at- I madhabi), many of which were run by bazaaris.[43] The perception that the revolutionary movement had a chance at success, coupled with the ease with which ordinary people could participate in nonviolent acts of resistance and defiance through informal networks, made recruitment to nonviolent resistance relatively easy.

The revolutionary movement proved to be resilient in the face of the shah's repression for a variety of reasons, one of which was the fact that the movement drew support and recruits from broad segments of society. This made it impossible for the shah's government to concentrate on repressing one group of people in the hopes of controlling the actions of others. Some of the most active supporters of the movement were student networks at the universities, which enhanced the movement's sustainability by providing a steady reservoir of young recruits with relatively few inhibitions about engaging in protest activity against the shah's regime and more moderate oppositionists.[44] Many women also supported the movement and were encouraged by Khomeini to join in demonstrations, in modest garb deemed appropriate by Islamists.[45] Some secular women wore the hijab as a symbol of opposition to the monarchy.

The movement's resilience was further enhanced through the active participation of workers and members of professional groups. They provided skills and resources that the shah depended on for power. The shah's coercive efforts to force workers back to their jobs in late- 1978 proved to be ineffective in the face of mass noncooperation. The shah's regime did not have the capacity or the resources to arrest and detain hundreds of thousands of opposition activists, nor could it effectively manage the takeover of industries and institutions after imposing martial law.

The opposition employed a diverse repertoire of nonviolent sanctions, which also kept the movement going. The 40-day period of mourning followed by a memorial observance, which took the form of street demonstrations, expanded the geographic scope of protests. This transformation of recognizable cultural referents served revolutionary purposes and created a dilemma for the shah, because repression of the memorial observances would have been taken as an affront to Islam. Stay-aways, boycotts, and symbolic activities (like shouting from rooftops) permitted mass participation while shielding the population from the regime's use of force. After the declaration of martial law in November 1978, the power of dispersed acts of noncooperation was revealed when the entire country went on strike. At that point, it did not matter that the shah continued to receive the backing of the

U.S. government or that security forces had deployed to coerce the population back to normalcy. The power of mass disobedience had neutralized the state's repressive capacity.

When the most important pillar of support for the monarchy—its military and other armed defenders—experienced a significant deterioration in morale and eventually broke into loyalist and pro-revolutionary factions, there was no way for the monarchy to wield effective control over Iranian society or the opposition. These divisions did not occur automatically; mass mobilization by the opposition, combined with conscious appeals to the army and police and acts of fraternization, significantly weakened this pillar of support, thereby enhancing the opposition's leverage. When this pillar fell, the Pahlavi dynasty ended.

Notes

1. Sandra Mackey and Scott Harrop, *The Iranians: Persia, Islam, and the Soul of a Nation* (New York: Plume Publishers, 1998), 236, 260; Desmond Harney, *The Priest and the King: An Eyewitness Account of the Iranian Revolution* (London: I. B. Tauris, 1999), 37, 47, 67, 128, 155, 167.
2. Robert Graham, *Iran: The Illusion of Power*, rev. ed. (New York: St Martin's Press, 1980), 94.
3. Gene Burns, "Ideology, Culture, and Ambiguity: The Revolutionary Process in Iran," *Theory and Society* 25, no. 3 (June 1996): 359; Marvin Zonis, "Iran: A Theory of Revolution from Accounts of the Revolution," *World Politics* 35 (1983): 586–606.
4. Burns, "Ideology, Culture, and Ambiguity," 359; Shaul Bakhash, *Reign of the Ayatollahs: Iran and the Islamic Revolution* (New York: Basic Books, 1986), 14; Ervand Abrahamian, *The Iranian Mojahedin* (New Haven, CT: Yale University Press, 1989), 29–30.
5. Baqer Moin, *Khomeini: The Life of the Ayatollah* (London: I. B. Tauris, 2000), 75.
6. Accounts vary about the exact number of protestors killed during the 1963 demonstrations and other anti-shah protests. Emaduddin Baqi, a well-known Iranian journalist and head of the Association for the Defense of Prisoners' Rights, has documented higher numbers of protestor deaths than those cited by the government. See "Amar-e Qorbaniyan-e Enqelab" (Statistics of the lives sacrificed in the revolution). On the number of deaths during the 1963 protests, Shaul Bakhash writes that "the number left dead was certainly higher than the figure of 200 cited by the government." Shaul Bakhash, *The Reign of the Ayatollahs: Iran and the Islamic Revolution*, rev. ed. (New York: Basic Books , 1990), 30.
7. See Maziar Behrooz, *Rebels with a Cause: The Failure of the Left in Iran* (London: I. B. Tauris, 1999).
8. According to Mohsen Sazegara, around 5,000 copies of *Islamic Government* were published outside Iran and fairly negligible numbers were published inside the country.
9. Charles Kurzman, *The Unthinkable Revolution in Iran* (Cambridge, MA: Harvard University Press, 2004), 65–66.
10. Burns, "Ideology, Culture, and Ambiguity," 375.
11. One of these groups, the clandestine Coalition of Islamic Associations (Hey'atha-ye Mo'talefeh-ye Islami), was a 1963 merger between three smaller groups with close links to the bazaar and Ayatollah Khomeini-led ulema. In January 1965, Muhammad Bukhara'I, a bazaari and a member of the coalition, assassinated Prime Minister Hasan Ali Mansour, after which he and some of the group's key members were executed. Its activities had come to a halt by 1971. The Revolutionary Organization of the Tudeh Party of Iran (ROTPI) was established in February 1964 as a Maoist offshoot of the communist Tudeh Party that had been largely decimated by the shah in the late 1950s.

ROTPI members participated in a small rebellion in south-central Iran that was easily crushed in 1965. That same year, one of its members attempted to assassinate the shah and was killed in the process. Some of its members had attempted to join a rebellion in Iranian Kurdistan in 1967, but the rebellion was crushed, and its leaders killed before ROTPI guerrillas arrived. "As with the Tudeh and the Islamic Coalition, all attempts by the ROTPI to establish a network inside the country were frustrated by the end of the 1960s." Maziar Behrooz, "Iranian Revolution and the Legacy of the Guerrilla Movement," in *Reformers and Revolutionaries in Modern Iran: New Perspectives on the Iranian Left,* ed. Stephanie Cronin (London: Routledge Curzon, 2004).

12. Behrooz, *Rebels with a Cause;* Abrahamian, *The Iranian Mojahedin.*
13. Behrooz. "Iranian Revolution and the Legacy of the Guerrilla Movement." Some of its prominent members were Muhammad Hanifnezhad, Sa'id Mohsen, and Ali Asghar Badi'zadegan.
14. Kurzman, *Unthinkable Revolution,* 12–13.
15. Ibid., 14.
16. Ibid., 20.
17. Ibid.
18. Ibid., 31; Ruhollah Khomeini, "Ayatollah Khomeini's Letter to the Iranian People, November 12, 1977," *Review of Iranian Political Economy and History* 2 (1978).
19. Kurzman, *Unthinkable Revolution,* 27.
20. Ibid., 28.
21. Ibid., 36.
22. Ibid., 50.
23. Ibid., 55.
24. Stephen Zunes, "Nonviolent Resistance in the Islamic World," *Nonviolent Activist: The Magazine of the War Resisters League* (January–February 2002).
25. Karen Rasler, "Concessions, Repression, and Political Protest in the Iranian Revolution," *American Sociological Review* 61 (February 1996): 144.
26. Kurzman, *Unthinkable Revolution,* 64.
27. Ibid., 75. After the revolution, a coroner claimed that his office buried 555 persons killed on Black Friday. Sar Malek, quote from *Ruz-Shomar-e Enqelab-e Eslami,* vol. 5, 287. Another report based on Martyr Foundation documentation concluded that 88 were killed on Black Friday. See Baqi, "Amar-e Qorbaniyan-e Enqelab."
28. A wildcat strike is a spontaneous work stoppage or one that begins without union approval.
29. Kurzman, *Unthinkable Revolution,* 78, citing Asef Bayat, *Workers and Revolution in Iran* (London: Zed. 1997), 98; Roy Assersohn, *The Biggest Deal* (London: Methuen. 1982), 25.
30. Asef Bayat, *Workers and Revolution in Iran.*
31. Kurzman, *Unthinkable Revolution,* 78–79.
32. Ibid., 112.
33. Ibid., 113.
34. Ibid., 114.
35. Pronouncement of September 6, 1978. Ruhollah Khomeini, *Islam and Revolution: Writings and Declarations,* trans. and anno. Hamid Algar (New York: Kegan Paul, 2002), 236.
36. Ibid., 115.
37. Ibid., 115.
38. Ibid., 115
39. Kurzman, *Unthinkable Revolution,* 165.
40. Ibid., 160.
41. One of the criticisms against Bazargan was a meeting he had with Zbigniew Brzezinski, the national security advisor to President Carter, in Algeria. Foreign Minister Ebrahim Yazdi also attended the meeting.

42. Kurzman, *Unthinkable Revolution*, 147.
43. Rasler, "Concessions, Repression, and Political Protest," 141.
44. The idea of the revolution and a revolutionary Islam came from the universities and university-educated intellectuals. The university was the most important resistance base against the shah's regime for several decades; the revolutionary ideas were popular among students. Clerics joined the university communities during the revolution against the shah.
45. Secular women eventually came to feel threatened when they refused to wear the hijab. They were harassed, and rumors circulated that women who did not wear proper hijab would have acid thrown on them. Kurzman, *Unthinkable Revolution*, 152.

14

Enough Is Not Enough: Achievements and Shortcomings of Kefaya, the Egyptian Movement for Change

Sherif Mansour

President Hosni Mubarak has governed Egypt under emergency rule since assuming power in 1981 after the assassination of his predecessor, Anwar al-Sadat.[1] In recent years, Mubarak has used the fight against terrorism as a pretext for dismissing calls for political reform and lifting emergency rule. The government has cracked down on dissenters across the political spectrum, including liberal and secular voices that had initially backed the government's efforts on the terror front. Mubarak refused to suspend the Emergency Law even after destroying the network of radical Islamists responsible for high-profile attacks in the late 1990s.

At the start of the twenty-first century, Egypt's political system remains stagnant. Opposition parties, including the Muslim Brotherhood, face severe restrictions on their political activities, and the media operates under tight government control. Antigovernment protests typically have been met with violent, heavy-handed repression. According to the Egyptian Organization for Human Rights, approximately 16,000 persons were detained without charges in the 1980s and 1990s on suspicion of engaging in illegal political activity or involvement in terrorism.[2] Several thousand individuals were already serving sentences for convictions on similar charges.

In summer 2003, the political scene began to change in Egypt as the country experienced an unprecedented increase in public activism. American and European interest in democratization in the Middle East, along with the U.S.-led invasion of Iraq and overthrow of one of the region's most hated dictators, intensified the debate on political change in the country and how it should be achieved. A coalition of groups of varying ideological, religious, and political persuasions established the Egyptian Movement for Change, popularly known as Kefaya, to challenge Mubarak and the possible succession of his son Gamal to the presidency. Kefaya's ability to bring together diverse groups and organizations around a common cause was unprecedented in Egyptian politics. The movement raised its profile significantly during the 2005 constitutional referendum and presidential campaigns by introducing a new style of protest to the Egyptian political arena.

Leadership, Organization, and Ideology

The word *kefaya* means "enough" in Arabic. According to Kefaya spokesperson Abdel-Halim Qandil, the decision to call the burgeoning Egyptian movement Kefaya came about spontaneously during preliminary meetings of what would become the movement. He added, "The word has a very local [origin] and was always used to characterize popular discontent in Egyptian history; even crowds in Egyptian soccer games use it all the time."[3]

Kefaya evolved in 2003 as a loose-knit coalition of diverse political groups and individuals led by a central coordinating cadre. The movement stood in stark contrast to many of Egypt's traditional political parties, which were hierarchical in structure and narrow in ideology, refusing to give space for younger generations or reach out to form broad coalitions. As Benjamin Rey, a French researcher, noted, "Kefaya represents a 'new style' of opposition, with parallels to Ukraine's Orange Revolution and Poland's Solidarity movement."[4]

Kefeya's leadership consisted of a general coordinator, a coordinating committee, and a spokesperson. George Ishaq, a Christian high school principal who got his start as an activist during the 1956 Arab-Israeli War, became the group's first general coordinator. He held this position until 2007, when the coordinating committee elected Abdel Wahhab al-Messiri, another Arab nationalist, to the post. Abdel-Halim Qandil, the editor of the Nasserist newspaper *al-Arabi*, served as the movement's spokesperson until the beginning of 2007. Other key figures in the movement's leadership included Mohamed al-Saied Edris, a liberal academic; Hany Anan, a businessman; Kamal Khalil, a veteran activist who rose to prominence in the February 1968 student protests; Abul Ela Madi, a prominent founder of the moderate Islamist Wasat Party; Ahmed Bhaa Eddin Shaaban, a leftist activist; and Yehia ElKazaz and Magdy Hussein, leading members of the now politically inert Labor Islamic Party.

Most of the movement's leadership was based in Cairo, where it held most of its political demonstrations and where the political parties that associated with it were located. It also, however, opened branches throughout the country that worked independently of the original body. The movement included cross-cutting activist groups, among them professional syndicates, student groups, and political parties with male and female members of varying ages and religious groups, and social classes. Ideologically, the movement drew support from a wide range of groups and individuals, including Nasserists, Islamists, liberals, and leftists, some of whom have deeply rooted ideological differences and had clashed in the past. What brought these various actors together was the shared fear that the Syrian experience of transferring power from father to the son would likely be repeated in Egypt. The movement coalesced in large part around opposition to the Emergency Laws and hereditary succession and support for multiparty elections.

Beginning in 2002, President Mubarak had set in motion a plan to transfer power to his son Gamal. He first appointed Gamal general secretary of the Policy Committee of the National Democratic Party (NDP), the third most powerful position in the country's ruling party; the committee is the starting point for most government action. After a July 2004 cabinet shuffle and the appointment of Ahmed Nazif as prime minister, the cabinet was nicknamed "Gamal's cabinet," as most of the new ministers were chosen from the NDP's Policy Committee. These steps intensified resentment toward Mubarak that was expressed in the form of unprecedented public demonstrations and critiques of the president.

In August 2004, prominent Egyptian activists and intellectuals circulated a petition demanding fundamental constitutional and economic reforms. Most important, the petition called for direct, transparent presidential elections with competing candidates. The 300 signatures of what became Kefaya's founding declaration called for "democracy and reform to take root in Egypt." Two months later, in October 2004, Tariq al-Bishri, one of Egypt's most respected judges, presented what came to be regarded as Kefaya's first manifesto, in which he called on Egyptians to "withdraw their long-abused consent to be governed."[5] Bishri's exhortation was the first public call for civil disobedience in recent Egyptian history.

Kefaya was established, according to its founding manifesto, to "prepare to deter the American and Israeli assaults on the Arab nation and reform the Egyptian despotic system."[6] Although Kefaya represented a diverse group of activists who joined across ideological lines to try to reach the common goal of bringing political reform to Egypt, its overarching ideology was largely secular, steeped in the language of human rights, and imparts an Arab nationalist tone. Regardless, many members of the banned Muslim Brotherhood also became members of Kefaya. The Islamist groups joined with the understanding that they would not use religious slogans or symbols in the movement's activities. Kefaya's organization spawned related groups and movements that maintained their independence, while remaining under the broader umbrella of the Kefaya movement and its activities. Among these are Youth for Change, Workers for Change, Journalists for Change, and Students for Change.

The majority of Kefaya's founders were leaders of student movements in the 1970s and spanned a broad political spectrum, from leftist—Nasserists and Marxists—to Islamist. Since the 1970s, these groups had advocated separately and largely unsuccessfully for political reform. Their efforts were more or less ignored by the international community because countering terrorism inside Egypt was the driving concern of local and international actors. It was not until the al-Qaida attacks on the United States in September 2001 that the issue of reform and democracy in the Middle East became part of a global agenda. Only then did Egyptian activists find diplomatic and public support abroad, particularly in the United States. This momentum led various opposition groups to put aside their ideological differences so that they could work more effectively together in taking advantage of this newfound international support for democracy. They coalesced around the consensus that reform in Egypt should be political in nature. They in particular chose to focus on gaining support for constitutional changes in the way the president is elected.

Regional factors contributed as well to the rise of Kefaya's unifying ideology. In 2003 the second Palestinian intifada was well under way, and the United States and some of its allies were on the verge of invading Iraq. With these circumstances, many Egyptian activists recognized the inability of Egypt to go to the defense of its Arab neighbors, even if it so desired. They therefore came to view their struggle to make Egypt stronger through reform as part of a larger regional effort. Manar Shorbagy, a professor of political science at the American University in Cairo, argues this point: "Clearly, the invasion of Iraq aggravated the sense of Egypt's vulnerability in the minds of Kefaya's founders. The founding statement captures the close connection between the external and domestic forces behind the movement's emergence."[7] It is no coincidence that Kefaya's activism grew largely from nationwide protests against the U.S.-led invasion of Iraq in March 2003. Although Egypt has historically been viewed as the leader of the Arab world—because of its size, history, and established political system—the country has lost much of its clout under Mubarak's rule because the aging president is perceived by many as being a faithful follower of the "imperial" Western powers. The Kefaya movement was therefore able to paint its opposition to the government in Arab nationalist terms and win the support of a broad swath of Egyptians.

As noted, another aspect of the movement's popularity stemmed from widespread dissatisfaction over the issue of presidential succession, which in the mind of ordinary Egyptians implies a continuation of the repression, corruption, and general incompetence of the Mubarak regime. For political and human rights groups, it meant that there would be no legal guarantee of a safe and legitimate transfer of power after Mubarak, who in violation of the Egyptian constitution, has never had a vice president. Mubarak, who turned eighty in 2008, was increasingly sick and frail. In November 2004, he had fainted while delivering a speech to the National Assembly. Egyptians recognized that without a vice president, Mubarak's death would likely lead to Gamal, already being groomed, assuming power. This scenario gave the movement's campaign a sense of urgency and legitimacy in Egypt and abroad. Kefaya expanded its political activities in 2005 as Mubarak, bowing to international pressure, agreed to multicandidate presidential elections for the first time in Egypt's history.

Tactical Innovation and Communication

One aspect that clearly set Kefaya apart from other organizations and movements engaged in political activities in Egypt was its use of innovative tactics and strategies. From 2003 to 2007, Kefaya grew from a few dozen political activists in Cairo to thousands individuals organizing throughout the country. Kefaya's first rally, held on December 12, 2004, was a historic event: It was the first time that a protest had been organized in Egypt solely to demand that the president step aside. Surrounded by riot police, hundreds of activists gathered on the steps of the High Court in Cairo. They "remained mostly silent and [had] taped over their mouths a large yellow sticker emblazoned with the word *Kefaya*" in red.[8] This sticker became the movement's logo. (Egyptians would later be astounded to see South Korean activists demonstrating in solidarity with such stickers and assorted posters in front of the Egyptian embassy in Seoul, the capital of a distant country with which they had never had any interaction.)[9] Successfully asserting their right to demonstrate, despite a ban on large public gatherings under the Emergency Law, was a major victory for Kefaya. The government had not hesitated on previous occasions to use violence against protestors, but it was evident that under outside pressure, the regime thought it wise to allow some space for political dissent, which Kefaya attempted to use to the greatest extent possible.

Another "first" that the movement accomplished was a large-scale petition campaign. Using the Internet, Kefaya collected more than 17,000 signatures affirming the movement's manifesto, which explicitly refers to President Mubarak as a dictator. Although Internet-based, the signature campaign afforded Kefaya's supporters the opportunity to actively engage people in advocating its position. With only 7.5 percent Internet access, few Egyptians had the opportunity to sign the document, but the campaign was effective as a low-risk mobilizer.[10]

The Kefaya movement was also unique in innovatively using cultural symbols and actions against the government. For example, after the government's harassment of demonstrators protesting constitutional amendments on 25 May, the movement organized a protest in June inside the al-Sayeda mosque in downtown Cairo during which hundreds of activists took brooms and swept the floor of the mosque and the area outside. This symbolic action was recognized by ordinary Egyptians as representing the rejection of injustice. Media coverage of the event created a dilemma for the government: If it stopped the demonstration and confiscated the protestors' brooms, it would look silly; if it did nothing, it would still look bad, surrounding helpless demonstrators who only came to sweep and pray.

One of the especially interesting aspects of the Kefaya movement is its association with various artists and cultural icons who became part of the movement. The most famous Egyptian film director, Youssef Shahin, and actors and novelists participated in its events. In August 2007, artists launched an annual Resentment Poetry Festival, to which they invited well-known Egyptian poets to present dissident political works. In another act of defiance, the movement took the national anthem and changed its lyrics to incorporate their slogan, "Enough! Enough! Enough!"

When government repression rose in response to the democracy promotion agenda in 2006 and 2007, Kefaya organized a "stay at home" campaign during the annual celebration of the 1952 revolution, on July 23, 2007. The movement called on Egyptians to refuse to participate in the festival and instead to stay at home and fly the country's flag from their balconies as a low-risk act of protest. No one knows how many people actually participated in the action, but photos of flags on balconies around the country indicated widespread public support for it.

Constitutional Amendment and Presidential Elections

When President Mubarak proposed in February 2005 to amend Article 76 of the constitution to allow multiple candidates to run for president, Kefaya immediately denounced the move as "theatrics" and a "fake reform," a mere "reformulation of the dictatorship"[11] and countered with a call for opening the nomination process to the public, without conditions. Under Mubarak's proposal, each candidate would be required to obtain the support, in writing, of at least 250 elected officials from national or local institutions. Because these bodies were controlled by the NDP, it would be virtually impossible for an opposition candidate to gather the necessary signatures. In addition, political parties that wanted to put their candidates on the ballot would need to have been registered for a minimum of five years and to hold at least 5 percent of the seats in the lower and upper houses of the national legislature. The measure, despite its impression of openness, appeared to be designed to put pressure on established opposition parties and organizations, particularly the Muslim Brotherhood, which had never been allowed to openly put forward a candidate.

Given the government-imposed restrictions on participation, Kefaya accused parties that contested the elections of "aborting people's hopes for freedom and democracy."[12] The movement then decided to launch its own campaign, calling for the "cancellation of the state of Emergency Law and all special laws that restrict freedoms first in order to have meaningful elections."[13] In addition, it attacked the government for its performance in providing social welfare, job creation, and education. In April 2005, simultaneous demonstrations took place in thirteen cities under the banner "No Constitution without Freedom." The judiciary lent support to Kefaya by pressuring the government on the issue of election monitoring. In April at a meeting in Alexandria, 1,200 judges threatened to withdraw their supervision of the presidential and parliamentary contests unless they were guaranteed independence and control of all stages of the elections. The judges acted, however, as nonpartisans, without formally acknowledging or endorsing Kefaya's positions or activities.

On 25 May, the day of the referendum on Article 76, government-backed supporters, thugs, and plainclothes police attacked protestors in demonstrations organized by Kefaya in front of Egyptian Press Syndicate headquarters. Among the victims of this brutality were two women who were beaten and sexually molested. The attacks were captured on digital cameras and cell phones and the images spread worldwide via the Internet. Egyptians were particularly shocked; such actions are extremely shameful in Egyptian culture. This flagrant assault unified the opposition, and Kefaya capitalized on the outpouring of sympathy by holding protests every Wednesday for the rest of the summer.

The Egyptian Independent Committee for Election Monitoring reported that not more than 18 percent of registered Egyptians voted in the referendum.[14] Although the government's estimate put turnout at slightly higher than 23 percent, low voter turnout helped discredit the process and made Kefaya an active player in the presidential elections. The government had traditionally praised high participation in Egyptian elections and utilized the media to mobilize people to vote. That voter turnout was at least 50 percent less than what the government had hoped for meant that the recently established popular movement had "won" against the government, despite its overwhelming resources and capabilities.

Kefaya acted to maintain pressure on the government ahead of presidential elections, scheduled for 7 September. On 8 June, 2,000 people, representing a cross-section of the Egyptian opposition, took part in a candlelight vigil in front of the mausoleum of Saad Zaghul, one of Egypt's national heroes and the leader of the 1919–1921 nonviolent resistance movement against the British, the first and foremost organized nonviolent campaign in modern Egyptian and Middle Eastern history. The writer Amira Howaidi described the demonstration in *al-Ahram Weekly* as "the most organized and impressive demonstration by the reform movement to date."[15]

The government, however, had been emboldened by its success in the May referendum, and increased pressure on Kefaya and the other opposition groups. In Cairo on 30 July, uniformed and plainclothes police wielding truncheons attacked a gathering of 200 activists protesting Mubarak's candidacy in pursuit of a fifth term. According to Human Rights Watch, the actions taken by the authorities were "not just to prevent a demonstration, but also to physically punish those daring to protest President Mubarak's candidacy."[16] The tactics may have played a role in forcing Kefaya to abandon its plan to have several prominent figures run against Mubarak: No prominent figures were forthcoming. Therefore, Kefaya instead adopted a strategy of boycotting the elections.

External Support and Trajectories

As mentioned above, Kefaya was, early on, critical of the United States and Israel. The first chapter of the movement's manifesto was entirely devoted to how Egypt should oppose "American hegemony and Israel's arrogance." When the movement's leader, George Ishaq, participated in a meeting with American and Israeli participants in Istanbul in June 2006, some movement members expressed anger and threatened to leave it.

The overlapping interests of the movement and the U.S. administration following the attacks of 11 September made an attempt at a cooperative relationship between Kefaya and the United States possible. As *Washington Post* journalist Anthony Shadid pointed out, "The [Kefaya] movement leadership admits grudgingly that the pressure the Bush administration exerted in 2004 and 2005 helped curb government repression, providing crucial space for their work."[17] At the same time, as Kefaya leader Abul Ela Madi told Shadid, "Any relationship with any foreign power, but especially the Americans, is the kiss of death.... We don't need this kiss." Shadid went on to explain that U.S. policy in the region had been a story of unintended consequences.

Rather than inspiring reform, the 2003 U.S.-led invasion of Iraq prompted people to pour into the streets in paroxysms of anti-American resentment. Secretary of State Condoleezza Rice's statements in support of democracy in Egypt, while welcomed in some quarters, sounded like a teacher scolding a pupil in others, coming off as another humiliation for a country sensitive to perceptions of its weakness and purported slavish obedience to U.S. policy. "Give Mubarak a visa...and take him with you, Condoleezza!" protestors shouted on the streets of Cairo.[18] Ironically, however, movement members would become angry at the United States when the Bush administration reduced its support for democracy promotion in 2006 and 2007. "The Americans now prefer stability over democracy. I will never trust them again," George Ishaq told the *Washington Post*.[19]

Kefaya's Decline

The Egyptian government had tried to suppress the Kefaya movement since its coalescence in the early 2000s. In addition to repressing protests and harassing activists, the government took actions to intimidate Kefaya's leadership. For example, relatively early on in the movement, Abdel-Halim Qandil was abducted by four masked men and taken in an unmarked van to an area 50 miles outside Cairo, where he was stripped naked, beaten, and abandoned in the desert.[20]

Mubarak also tried to reduce Western support for democracy and human rights in Egypt, primarily by using an electoral victory by Islamists in parliamentary elections in 2005 to pressure the U.S. government into reconsidering its support for democratic reforms. In response, the United States began to shy away from its democracy promotion agenda in 2006 and 2007, giving the regime political cover to crack down on Kefaya. Hundreds of political activists from the movement and the Muslim Brotherhood were thereafter brutally attacked and detained. On May 25, 2006, Muhammed al-Sharqawi, a journalist and member of the Kefaya movement and Youth for Change, was dragged from his car and severely beaten by 15 to 20 plainclothes police and state security personnel. He was then taken to a police station, where he was repeatedly tortured and sodomized.[21]

The government crackdown took place as the movement began to lose momentum, suffering from internal dissent, leadership changes, and general frustration with the apparent inability of the political opposition to pick up the pace of reform. Following the 2005 elections, some observers predicted Kefaya's demise after it fell into political doldrums. Some analysts felt that it suffered from an "identity crisis." There were disputes over tactics between the movement and one of its sister organizations, Youth for Change, particularly over the latter's "vigilante street tactics" (such as small mobile strikes), which tried to relate the discourse of human rights and democracy to the fundamental, daily concerns of the average Egyptian of means.[22] The end of 2006 brought a more serious split within the movement, after an anonymous article posted on Kefaya's Web site apparently supported the anti-veiling stance advocated by Farouk Hosni, the minister of culture. Although the article was removed, seven key figures, all pro-Islamist, announced their intention to leave the movement. One of these individuals, Magdi Ahmed Hussein, later declared that Kefaya had "failed to find the middle ground between the Islamists and liberals."[23]

The movement's first coordinator, George Ishaq, stepped down in January 2007 and was replaced by Abdel Wahhab al-Messiri, a respected scholar and former member of the Egyptian Communist Party as well as the Muslim Brotherhood. Messiri faced the difficult task of reviving the movement following constitutional changes implemented in March 2007 that made it even more difficult for political parties to operate and that extended the state's security powers. Amnesty International described the changes as the "greatest erosion of human rights" since the introduction of the Emergency Powers in 1981.[24]

Kefaya never negotiated with the Egyptian government. At times the movement agreed with some government officials on one topic or another, but there was never a consensus among movement members on how to open a dialogue, explore common interests, or reach understandings with the government. The statement by the minister of culture that women wearing the *hijab* (head covering) was a sign of backwardness thrust Egyptian society into a heated debate. Many government officials and members of parliament expressed disagreement with Hosni, but Ishaq issued a statement supporting the minister's right to freedom of speech. Ishaq's action led to dissension within the movement, prompting the Muslim Brothers and other individuals with Islamist sympathies to announce their withdrawal from it. The movement also never negotiated with opposition political parties. The relations were always tense, with the parties feeling a bit embarrassed by the movement's ability to work around the Emergency Laws, which they had long used as an excuse against effective activism in the streets.

Impact and Legacy

Hani Anan, a prominent member and funder of Kefaya, said in May 2007 that the movement was "dead." "The group appeared and ended and many other movements will emerge from it," Anan pronounced at a workshop organized by the Cairo Center for Human Rights.[25] Despite its importance and innovation, the Kefaya movement fell short of its stated objectives.

When the movement began, it had promised mass civil disobedience and a strong opposition network to pressure the Mubarak regime to reform. Neither of these goals materialized. The movement attracted large numbers of members and supporters, but never enough to influence the government. The movement primarily "preached to the converted," as it largely recruited people already active in opposition groups rather than reaching out to average people in the streets. Also, the movement was never able to target and recruit supporters from within the regime, or at the least, neutralize them; this stemmed from the general attitude inside the movement that everything involving the regime was "evil" and must be fought, regardless of who, what, or why. This lost the movement many potential supporters.

Kefaya remained essentially a protest movement and failed to present an alternative structure capable of reforming or replacing the current regime. After the 2005 elections, the movement did not offer practical solutions to the problems most Egyptians faced on a daily basis, such as poverty, unemployment, corruption, and poor access to education and public services. As Kefaya leader Kamal Khalil told Anthony Shadid, "The simple issue is that we have to make ourselves relevant to the issues, not the other way around." The ever-optimistic Abul Ela Madi was even blunter: "We don't have a vision."[26]

The movement also failed to successfully reach beyond Egypt's borders for support. Its hard-line anti-American and anti-Israeli rhetoric made it difficult for the outside world to approach it. The prospect that in Egypt the democrats would be the most anti-American was a big turn off for many foreign observers, who were always concerned about the prospect of having the Islamist Muslim Brothers in power instead of the pliable Mubarak.[27]

Although Kefaya's vision of a democratic Egypt and free and fair elections (to prevent Mubarak's son from gaining power) attracted widespread support, the movement never produced a charismatic leader or leadership strong enough to sort out internal disagreements and maximize its credibility, impact, and outreach. Some Kefaya members engaged in an ugly exchange of words with figures in well-established political parties, particularly the Tagamu Leftist Party. Rifaat al-Sa'id, Tagamu chairman, ridiculed Kefaya in a series of interviews, describing its leaders as "the kids of George Ishaq."[28] It did not help that Kefaya failed to develop strong alliances with other opposition parties and their leaders, of whom it was always critical. From the start, Kefaya identified all the established political parties as part of the problem, not possible components of the solution. Its aggressive critique of the old guard was in part responsible for raising tensions among potential allies.[29]

Despite its shortcomings, Kefaya was a homegrown nonviolent opposition movement that was successful in some respects. Although it did not achieve its ultimate goal, Kefaya showed people that mobilization in Egypt was possible—that ordinary people could be powerful. It also inspired a new generation of activists and brought diverse groups together in a way that had been unprecedented in the Mubarak era. Kefaya helped create the political space for protest, challenged the taboo against publicly criticizing the government, and paved the way for future movements and opposition activities.

Kefaya's Daughters

Kefaya encouraged other regional movements in the Arab world from 2004 to 2006, including Kabaat (We Are Sick of That) in Jordan, Khalas (Enough) in Libya, and Erhalo (Leave Us) in Yemen. The movement showed signs of rejuvenation in Egypt in 2007 and 2008 on two fronts. The first involved workers' strikes that began in Almahalla City, the biggest industrial compound in the country. In September 2007, 27,000 workers took control of one of Egypt's biggest state-owned textile factories in five weeks of protest over wages and work conditions.[30] It was the longest and strongest worker protest since the end of World War II. In March 2007, the liberal newspaper *al-Masri al-Yawm* estimated that no fewer than 222 sit-in strikes, work stoppages, hunger strikes, and demonstrations had taken place in 2006. In the first five months of 2007, the paper reported a new labor action nearly every day. The citizen group Egyptian Workers and Trade Union Watch documented 56 incidents in April and another 15 during the first week of May alone.[31]

A second wave began building from these strikes, moving beyond workers unions into the broader population. On the one-year anniversary of an April 2007 strike, young Egyptian activists used Facebook, the social networking Web site, to organize two national strikes to support the workers against the government; the action attracted nearly 100,000 members online. "Facebook networking" played a crucial role in broadening support and turnout for the second 6 April textile workers' strike and protest, which again forced the government to concede to their demands of lowering prices and raising wages. Before the first strike, Mubarak had issued a new law to reduce tariffs on many basic commodities, allowing their prices to fall. Before the second strike, Mubarak announced an unprecedented 30 percent increase in all government employees' wages.

The Facebook event fundamentally altered the Egyptian political landscape. For the first time, massive numbers of youth engaged in public life and actively expressed their opinions outside the traditional triangle of power in Egypt—the government's ruling party, weak but legitimate secular opposition parties, and the effective but illegitimate Muslim Brotherhood. Of significance, the Muslim Brothers opposed the April strike, but supported a subsequent unsuccessful strike in May. The Facebook movement raised doubts that "Mubarak's self-fulfilling prophesy as the only alternative to the Muslim Brotherhood will continue to hold Egypt back from the democracy its people deserve."[32] This movement is transitioning from Web-based activism into national organizing involving street activism and moving away from advocating a social agenda and toward a political reform one as well.[33] It is gaining support from political opposition parties[34] and notice by the international media.[35] The movement has certainly rejuvenated the opposition in Egypt, but it is still too early to gauge the odds on how successful it will be in fulfilling what Kefaya set out to do—build a civil disobedience coalition to end the everlasting rule of Mubarak.

Figures 14.1 Protest against the rigging of the parliamentary elections and the death of 11 voters led by the Kefaya and Youth for Change movements, downtown Cairo, December 12, 2005. Courtesy Wael Abbas.

Figures 14.2 Protest against the rigging of the parliamentary elections and the death of 11 voters led by the Kefaya and Youth for Change movements, downtown Cairo, December 12, 2005. Courtesy Wael Abbas.

Figure 14.3   A protester shouts anti-Mubarak slogans in front of the high court building; downtown Cairo, December 12, 2005. Courtesy Wael Abbas.

Notes

1. Egypt's Emergency Law gives the government the authority to detain people without charges and without independent judicial review. The government has been accused of abusing this power, particularly against political opponents.
2. Egyptian Organization for Human Rights, "Egypt: Towards a Society That Respects Human Rights and Fights Terrorism," (in Arabic), www.eohr.org/ar/report/2004/re9.htm.
3. In the early 2000s, students in the country of Georgia formed Kmara (Enough Is Enough), a network of organizations that contributed to the nonviolent ouster of President Eduard Shevardnadze's government in November 2003 in the Rose Revolution, following rigged elections. Kefaya members claim that they were the first to adopt the mantra "Enough." Abdel-Halim Qandil, "Kefaya Is an Egyptian Concept That Appeared before Ukraine" (in Arabic), al-Watan, May 18, 2006.
4. Benjamin Rey, "Will the Kefaya Movement Be Enough to Change Egypt?" *CafeBabel*, March 29, 2005.
5. Tariq al-Bishri, "I Invite You To Revolt," *al-Araby*, www.alarabnews.com/alshaab/ 2004/22–10-2004/aa.htm.

6. The manifesto is available on the Kefaya Web site at http://harakamasria.org/node/803.

7. Manar Shorbagy, "The Egyptian Movement for Change—Kefaya: Redefining Politics in Egypt," *Public Culture* 19 (Winter 2007): 186.

8. Mona El-Ghobashy, "Egypt Looks Ahead to a Portentous Year," *Middle East Report Online*, February 2, 2005, www.merip.org/mero/mero020205.html.

9. See the images of the Korean demonstrators at http://dvd4arab.com/showthread. php?t=256107.

10. Internet World Stats: User and Population Statistics, www.internetworldstats.com/stats1.htm.

11. Rey, "Will the Kifaya Movement Be Enough?"

12. Chris Toensing, "US Stays with Egyptian Dictator," *Middle East Report*, June 30, 2005, www.merip.org/newspaper_opeds/oped060305.html.

13. "Bush Criticizes Oppressing Demonstrators in Egypt Again, *Islam Online* (in Arabic), June 1, 2005, www.islamonline.net/arabic/news/2005–06/01/article05.shtml.

14. Ibn Khaldun Center for Development Studies, *Referendum Monitoring Report*, May 28, 2005, www.eicds.org/arabic/publicationsAR/reports/icme-AR.doc.

15. "A Chronology of Dissent," *al-Ahram Weekly Online*, http://weekly.ahram.org.eg/2005/748/eg10.htm.

16. Sarah Khorshid, "A Cry of Distress: The Egyptian Movement for Change—Kefaya," *IslamOnline.net*, August 25, 2005, www.islamonline.net/English/Views/2005/08/article08.SHTML.

17. Anthony Shadid, "Egypt Shuts Door on Dissent as U.S. Officials Back Away," *Washington Post*, March 19, 2007.

18. Ibid

19. Ibid.

20. Committee to Protect Journalists, "Cases 2004: Middle East and North Africa," November 5, 2004, www.cpj.org/cases04/mideast_cases04/egypt.html.

21. *Amnesty International Annual Report, 2008: The State of the World's Human Rights*, "Egypt," http://thereport.amnesty.org/eng/Regions/Middle-East-and-North-Africa/Egypt.

22. Negar Azimi, "Egypt's Youth Have Had Enough," *Open Democracy*, August 31, 2005, www.opendemocracy.net/democracy-protest/enough_2794.jsp.

23. Frederick Deknatel, "US Skirts the Issue of Egypt's Constitutional Referendum," *Daily Star*, March 22, 2007.

24. Amnesty International, "Egypt: Proposed Constitutional Amendments Greatest Erosion of Human Rights in 26 Years," www.amnesty.org/en/library/info/MDE12/008/2007.

25. Joseph S. Mayton, "Kefaya Opposition Movement Is Dead," *All Headline News: Global News for the Digital World (AHN)*, May 22, 2007.

26. Shadid, "Egypt Shuts Door."

27. Cécile Hennion, "L'Egypte et le paradoxe américain," *Le Monde*, May 28, 2007.

28. Wael Abdel Fattah, "Whither Kefaya: Hal Intahat Harakat Kefaya?" *al-Fajr*, September 3, 2005.

29. Shorbagy, "Kefaya."

30. "Egyptian Workers Occupy Factory," *BBC News*, September 25, 2007, http://news.bbc.co.uk/2/hi/middle_east/7013184.stm.

31. The Egyptian Workers and Trade Union Watch report for the month of April (in Arabic) is available at http://arabist.net/arabawy/wp-content/uploads/2007/05/aprilreport.pdf. The report for the first week of May (in Arabic) is available at http://arabist.net/arabawy/wp-content/uploads/2007/05/1stmay.pdf.

32. Sherif Mansour, "Egypt Facebook Showdown," *Los Angeles Times*, June 2, 2008, www.latimes.com/news/opinion/la-oe-mansour2–2008jun02,0,323158.story.

33. They organized rallies to support Ayman Nour, in prison on charges stemming from his challenge to Mubarak in the 2005 presidential elections, and Ibrahim Eisa, an editor on trial for "spreading rumors" about the president's health.

34. Heads of opposition parties from the right (Muslim Brothers) and the left (Tagamu) and liberals (Ayman Nour from al-Ghad and Osama Ghazali Harb from al-Gabha) were quoted in the media offering their support.

35. David Wolman, "Cairo Activists Use Facebook to Rattle Regime," *Wired Magazine*, October 20, 2008, www.wired.com/print/techbiz/startups/magazine/16–11/ff_facebookegypt; Ellen Knickmeyer, "Fledgling Rebellion on Facebook Is Struck Down by Force in Egypt," *Washington Post*, May 18, 2008, www.washingtonpost.com/wp-dyn/content/article/2008/05/17/AR2008051702672_pf.html; "Crackdown on Facebook Activists," *Los Angeles Times*, July 27, 2008, http://latimesblogs.latimes.com/babylonbeyond/2008/07/egypt-crackdown.html; and Liam Stack, "Egypt Detains Facebook Activists—Again," *Christian Science Monitor*, July 30, 2008, www.csmonitor.com/2008/0730/p04s04-wome.html.

15

The Orange Movement of Kuwait: Civic Pressure Transforms a Political System

Hamad Albloshi and Faisal Alfahad

In Kuwait—a small, rich Gulf state with a history of unstable relations between the ruling royal family and the parliament, or National Assembly—a peaceful, civilian-led movement claimed an important victory in 2006. The Orange Movement began with a simple idea to combat corruption and in the process mobilized a large number of young people, won the support of politicians as well as legislators from different political groupings, and ultimately pushed the Kuwaiti government to accept its demands for electoral reform. Also called Nabiha 5 (We Want It Five), the Orange Movement succeeded in reducing Kuwait's electoral districts from 25 to 5 after receiving support from 29 members of the National Assembly and other politicians who, as one activist noted, "were a parallel line supporting the campaign but...were not the campaign."[1] The reduction represented another step in the reform of a political system in a relatively conservative country where women had gained political rights only in 2005. In May 2009, under the new electoral system, four Kuwaiti women were elected to the parliament—another remarkable change in the relatively young country.

The Orange Movement, named for the color worn by its members, combined sustained bottom-up civic pressure with savvy coalition-building within the Kuwaiti political system. Kuwaitis freely elect members of the unicameral National Assembly (Majlis al-Umma), but the political system is not a purely parliamentary one. As Michael Herb notes, "The parliament can make life difficult for the government, but it does not bear the responsibility of actually running the government or of appointing the people who do."[2] The amir appoints the prime minister, based an Article 56 of the constitution, which does not require that the prime minister to be from the royal family, though by tradition he has been since 1963.[3] It is important for the government and the royal family to have as many supporters as possible in the assembly.[4] The best way to achieve this is to influence elections, which had been done in the past by dividing the country into large numbers of districts, thereby reducing the number of potential voters in each one. This increases the government's ability to interfere in various ways. The five-constituency system advocated by the Orange Movement called for reducing the number of districts—thus increasing the number of voters in each—and thereby weakening potential government influence over electoral results.

Birth of a Movement

Nabiha 5 is not the first nonviolent movement in Kuwait. During 1989–1990, the pro-democratic Constitutional Movement, which tried, but failed, to convince the amir, Jabir al-Ahmad, to restore the constitution, which had been suspended after the dissolution of parliament in 1986. The movement had been started by 32 members of the 1985 parliament under the leadership of Speaker Ahmad al-Saadoun and grew to 45 members when other politicians (from outside parliament) joined in.[5]

The Assembly Law announced by the amir in 1979 had been the main obstacle to organizing public political gatherings in Kuwait, restricting the rights of Kuwaitis to hold meetings and rallies; under this law, they could only organize events with the permission of authorities. To avoid the restrictions of the Assembly Law, the leaders of the Constitutional Movement decided to have meetings every Monday in a *diwaniyya*, an area attached to Kuwaiti homes for private and social meetings.[6] The movement tried to create for authorities the impression that they were not violating the Assembly Law, which allowed social gatherings in diwaniyyas.[7] In reality, movement members wanted to mobilize Kuwaitis to support the restoration of the constitution and parliamentary life. As these meetings increased in number, and to prevent citizens from attending them, authorities employed force. Numerous people were injured and arrested.[8]

The Constitutional Court overturned the Assembly Law on May 1, 2006. Orange Movement demonstrations began four days later.[9] Khalid al-Fadallah, one of the Nabiha 5 leaders, noted that his group's members had organized to launch the movement days before the rejection of the law. Why did the movement take hold at this particular time? According to Fadallah, the movement had developed earlier from discussions among youths about the political and social situation in Kuwait. Most of the participants had graduated from universities in the United States. Many of them were in their first or second year of residence in Kuwait after having lived four to six years in the States. "We were very close and had the same impression about the situation in Kuwait. We used to gather, talk about our nation, and remember our discussions when we were students.... Before coming back to Kuwait we wanted to be good and active citizens," said Fadallah.[10]

Pessimism is one of the primary feelings found among Kuwaitis as a result of the corruption that has come to be seen simply as "part of the culture."[11] This group of young Kuwaitis decided to fight entrenched corruption and reform the political system. At the time, there had been discussion in Kuwait about reforming the electoral system; some of these young people saw this as a gateway for securing more general reforms. The system of having 25 electoral districts played a major role in ongoing corruption. These concerned Kuwaitis decided therefore to launch a campaign to redistrict electoral constituencies in a way that would reduce the likelihood of corruption.[12]

The Kuwaiti Electoral System

Immediately after Kuwaiti independence in June 1961, Amir Abdullah al-Salim called for elections to choose an assembly to write the constitution in December 1961.[13] Abdullah al-Salim hoped to build a modern, constitutional, and democratic Kuwait despite opposition from some members of the royal family.[14] A dispute also arose between the royal family and opposition groups over the electoral system for selecting the constitutional assembly. The royal family wanted to divide the country into 20 districts, but the opposition wanted "one district." Multiple districts would make it easier for the government to intervene in elections in favor of its supporters.[15]

The constitution drafted by the constitutional assembly and approved by the amir on November 11, 1962 established a 50-member parliament, but it did not specify how many electoral districts there should be. According to Article 81, "electoral constituencies are determined by law." The elections held in Kuwait from independence until 1975 were based on 10 electoral districts.[16] In 1980 in the process of restoring the constitution, Amir Jabir al-Ahmad increased the number of districts to 25 without the permission of the parliament, which had been dissolved in August 1976.[17] The government's stated aim was to increase the participation of Kuwaitis in elections by increasing proportional representation in the parliament; each district had two representatives.[18] In reality, however, the amir wanted to "curb the power of the parliament,"[19] by weakening the opposition groups in it and skewing elections in favor of government supporters. He basically wanted a weak parliament with no interest in opposing the government or any real power to do so.

District boundaries were drawn along tribal and sectarian divisions. For example, the majority in the twenty-first district, al-Ahmadi, were Ejmans;[20] the first district, Sharq, mostly consisted of Shiites; and the second district, al-Murqab, was overwhelmingly Sunnis and merchant class.[21] Thus, the nature of the electoral districts decreased the chance of being elected if one did not belong to a certain tribe or sect in his district. The smaller a district and the fewer constituents it has, the better the ability of the government to intervene and manipulate the political process. The 25-district system made it easier for the government to influence the results of the elections by creating more, and therefore, smaller districts. The government supports the campaigns of its preferred candidates by providing them with enough money to purchase votes, especially in the smallest districts, or by ordering cabinet ministers to sign every request (mo`aamala) that pro-government incumbent candidates make. Such candidates are known as "service members" (nowwab al-Khdamat).[22] This practice, common in Kuwait, is one of the main sources of corruption.

Candidates who do not support the government's policies are at a distinct electoral disadvantage because they are denied these rewards. They will not be voted into office if their challengers are seen to have direct access to government-provided services. Hence the significance of the Orange Movement: Having five electoral constituencies increases the number of voters in each district, which consequently decreases the ability of the government to intervene in support of as many candidates by funding them to buy votes or by passing all illegal requests.

Nabiha 5

Since the 1990s, there have been a number of calls to return to the old electoral system of 10 districts. These demands intensified in 2003; the government did not oppose them. In 2003 then-Prime Minister Sabah al-Ahmad said, "We do not have any reservations [about reducing the electoral districts] if it is in the interest of Kuwait."[23] This did not, however, mean that the government lacked an agenda of its own.

The debate over electoral districts continued until the Ministerial Committee presented a proposal to the government on April 16, 2006.[24] The committee had been established by the government in October 2005 to study the problems associated with the electoral system and to find appropriate ways to address them.[25] Its proposal divided the country into five districts with 10 representatives from each of them. Each constituent could vote for four candidates.[26] One day after the Ministerial Committee announced its proposal, Prime Minister Nasir Muhammad al-Sabah asked the National Assembly to give his cabinet a month to study it and to present its view on the issue.[27] The parliament agreed to his request. In the meantime, two major groups formed in the assembly: the 29 Bloc, or the Parliamentary Bloc to Reform the Electoral System (initially consisting of 27 members but later 29)[28] and an "independent" bloc of members opposed to the proposed reforms.[29]

As political elites debated electoral reform, a small group of young Kuwaitis, primarily members of the liberal National Democratic Alliance, decided to express their view by launching a campaign in favor of the five-district plan. They began by designing a Web site, kuwait5.org, "to organize a grassroots campaign" to support the plan.[30] They adopted the slogan "Five for Kuwait." Jassim al-Qamis, who designed the group's Web presence, said, "The Web site was advertised through blogs, which basically started the whole movement to reform the electoral districts."[31] Qamis was a contributor to Sahat al-Safat, a popular blog in Kuwait, and used this association to advertise kuwait5.org and the campaign, which began on April 27, 2006.[32] The group's strategy for their campaign did not initially include public demonstrations.

The organizers aimed to increase the number of supporters of the five-district plan among legislators, politicians, writers, and civil society leaders in Kuwait. This included pressuring those not supporting the plan to change their mind. In order to do this, they asked Kuwaitis to send text messages to the holdouts' personal cell phones or short messages by fax or e-mail. The youths posted most of the legislators' and the ministers' cell phone and fax numbers and e-mail addresses on kuwait5.org. It was not difficult for them to obtain the personal contact information of legislators and ministers because, according to Qamis, "If you know anyone that works as a journalist or in the parliament he'd get it for you." The campaign also posted the e-mail addresses of reporters and commentators for daily newspapers to urge them to support the five-district plan.[33]

The organizers formulated two different messages, one for legislators who supported the five-district plan, and another one for those who opposed it. Fadallah noted, "We wanted to tell members of the 29 Bloc that the Kuwaitis were with them; we wanted them to insist on their demand to reduce the districts to five constituencies."[34] The text massage sent to this group was "Kuwait is with you.... We want five electoral districts."[35] The young activists also worked to convince the members of the independent bloc in the parliament to back the five-district plan. Their message for this group was "Five districts for Kuwait." They also wrote a letter to be sent by fax or e-mail to members of parliament and government ministers.[36] Proponents also could send other messages as long as they contained the primary demand.[37] To reach people without Internet access, the organizers designed an easy-to-print page of their strategy and asked Kuwaitis to distribute it at work, in diwaniyyas, and among their friends and family members.[38]

As part of the effort to build a coalition, the core group of activists approached student organizations and groups, including the National Union of Kuwaiti Students and its branches in different countries, the Democratic Circle (al-Wasat al-Demoqrati), the Independent Column (al-Qai`ma al-Mustaqilla), the Coalition Column (al-Qai`ma al-A`italafiya), and groups at private universities, in addition to Student Unity (al-Wahda al-Talabia) in the United States. As a result of these contacts, 39 student groups and organizations published a signed statement on April 29, 2006 in support of the Ministerial Committee's plan and urged the government to back the proposal.[39]

Support for the campaign grew. At a social gathering, one of the members of the campaign proposed sending a text message calling on Kuwaitis to gather in front of al-Seef Palace, where the cabinet was meeting on May 5 to discuss electoral redistricting. The message was simple: "There will be a gathering in front of al-Seef Palace to demand the reduction of the electoral districts on May fifth, please attend."[40] The organizers then decided to select orange as a theme for the upcoming protest and for the movement. The choice was simple: Kuwait5.org had an orange theme, so orange seemed the obvious color to symbolize the movement.[41] On May 3, the blog Sahat al-Safat urged Kuwaitis to participate in the first demonstration in front of al-Seef Palace and to wear orange. The call was patriotic: "If you believe in the importance of the five-district plan…come, if you want to fight against corruption…come, if you care of your future and your children's future…come, if you love Kuwait…come."[42]

The demonstration, on May 5, the first such protest of the campaign, was relatively small. Between 150 to 200 people gathered for four hours in front of the palace. Although the protest was not large, the ministers discussed it for an hour in the cabinet.[43] The government did not make a decision on the redistricting, but the movement had succeeded in sending a message to the government and legislators that they were serious in their demand to reduce the number of electoral districts. The next day, members of the movement attended a gathering organized by one of the legislators, Muhammad al-Saqer, and included participation by members of the 29 Bloc and other politicians.[44] The movement contingent wore orange shirts and for the first time orange scarves.[45] The conference participants and members of the 29 Bloc expressed their support for the young activists and their demands and even praised them.[46]

The campaign continued. Members next decided to attend a parliamentary session on May 15, the day scheduled for debate on electoral redistricting. The youths designed posters to urge Kuwaitis to support reform of the system and to attend the National Assembly session. They posted these on Sahat al-Safat and other blogs. One of the posters, with the heading "Five Steps for Five Districts," asked Kuwaitis to (1) turn on their car lights during the day, (2) wear an orange patch, (3) express their opinion to five columnists, (4) go the National Assembly on May 15 accompanied by five friends, and (5) send these steps to five other people.[47] The campaign was for the most part successful; the exception involved step one, as not too many people switched on their cars' lights.[48]

As mentioned, Prime Minister Nasir Muhammad al-Sabah had asked the parliament in April 2006 to give his cabinet a month to study the issue and to present its views. The government decided on May 9 in favor of decreasing the number of districts, but only to 10.[49] This was a turning point for Nabiha 5. From inception, the movement's main goal had been to reduce the number of electoral districts to five. It had not supported any other propositions because of concern that the entire discussion about reform would lead to nothing if politicians started talking about different proposals related to electoral reform. At this point, movement members met to discuss the issue and decided to support the Ministerial Committee's original plan for five districts instead of the new proposal by the government.[50]

Although the activists had already decided to go to the National Assembly on May 15, many chose to start demonstrating the preceding day. A number of bloggers announced the protest, and text messages were sent. Approximately 1,000 people protested on May 14. They decided to stay through the night and to go to the parliamentary session the next day. The protest would become known as the Night of Determination (Lailat al-Eradah). Citizens were asked to join in and to stick Kuwaiti flags in the grass in front of the parliament building as a sign of their support for the five-district plan."[51]

"Down with the government!"

On May 15, around 1000 supporters and organizers of the Orange Movement took seats in the gallery of the National Assembly.[52] Before the beginning of the parliamentary session, they gave two of their supporters in the legislature, Muhammad al-Saqer and Ali al-Rashid, copies of a strongly worded statement to distribute to legislators and members of the government.[53] The statement, in part, read, "we are sick of you [the legislators and the ministries] wasting time and postponing our hopes and the next generations'.... [W]e will leave you to your conscience to repair what you have damaged."[54]

The prime minister and his government reiterated their decision to reduce the electoral districts to ten, but then voted in favor of sending its proposal to the Constitutional Court.[55] The parliament began its balloting at 3:40 p.m. on whether to seek the court's opinion. When Minister of Health Ahmad al-Abdullah voted in favor of submitting the 10-district plan to the court, the 29 Bloc withdrew from the chamber. Their walkout was accompanied by shouts from the audience of "Down with the government!" Such exhortation is unprecedented in the Gulf.

According to one of the activists, "We did not want to shout against the government. We did not decide to do that before coming to the parliament, but the government's behavior was shameful....[E]verything was spontaneous. When we saw the members of the 29 Bloc withdrawing, we could not control ourselves. In a way, what happened was an occupation of the assembly."[56] Jassem al-Khorafi, the Speaker of the parliament, lost control of the session, so he ended it and ordered it reconvened the next day. According to Monther al-Habeeb, "The government's behavior was a clear indication that it was not really in favor of reforming the system. How can any government act against itself!"[57]

The support that the Orange Movement received from the 29 Bloc intensified after May 15,[58] but another "occupation" of the National Assembly, could not be tolerated by the authorities, especially by Khorafi. In anticipation of the May 16 session, Khorafi asked the Ministry of the Interior to deploy Special Forces contingents, which are usually called up during domestic rioting, to surround the parliament and prevent citizens from entering the assembly building. Some legislators had informed Orange Movement members of Khorafi's desire to prevent them from attending the next session. To the activists, Khorafi "was provoking violence....It was unprecedented to see such action from him and such bias in his beliefs to the extent that he would use his powers against people he disagrees with."[59] Movement members believed, in the words of Jassim al-Qamis, that the "assembly belongs to the nation, it is our house, and how can anyone prevent us from entering our house?"[60] Thus, they decided to go to the parliament.

Any irresponsible act on May 16 could have resulted in tragedy. The Orange Movement members and supporters, "peaceful by nature," according to Qamis, "did not have any training in peaceful demonstrations"[61] and did not want to clash with the Special Forces or bring harm to anyone.[62] Khalid al-Fadallah went to speak to one of the Special Forces officers outside the parliament to assure him that the activists would not provoke his men. Said Fadallah, "We did not want them to begin to beat us and use force against us. The officer agreed. It was a good deal."[63] This was not the movement's first such meeting with security officers. The activists had informed the Ministry of the Interior about all of their demonstrations; they were not, however, seeking permission by contacting the ministry, but showing their concern for everyone's security by establishing that they were a nonviolent movement.[64]

The National Assembly has two gates. The organizers decided that they should try to enter through the visitors' gate. Fadallah led the protestors, who numbered fewer than a hundred, shouting, "We are the people of Kuwait / We want to enter our house."[65] He repeated the demand three times. After the protestors were denied access at that point of entry, they went to the front entrance, where other Kuwaitis joined them along with some sympathetic legislators who came out to try to help them get into the building. Fadallah describes the situation: "Some of the legislators surrounded us as human shields and tried to help us enter, but they were prevented. A member of the Special Forces put his baton on [Ahmad] al-Saadoun's [the former Speaker of the assembly] chest. We were stunned. We were afraid that Kuwait would face what it had experienced in 1989–1990 when force was used against the advocates of democracy."[66]

Three protestors, including Fadallah, managed to get past the Special Forces. Fadallah then tried to help MP Ali al-Rashid, a member of the 29 Bloc, who was pulling at the front gate in an attempt to open it for the protestors. A Special Forces member beat Fadallah with a baton, angering the protestors.[67] Saadoun, part of the 29 Bloc, urged the youths to restrain themselves. "Please do not clash with the forces. They are your brothers and fathers," he said.[68] The members of the 29 Bloc had not been involved in the Orange activists' decision to go to the parliament that day. Qamis asserted, "No one could have stopped us. They [the legislators] knew that, we, the youths, were leading the movement and all they could have done was to control any damages if they wanted."[69]

As the struggle to enter the assembly took place outside, 15 members of the government and 17 legislators were inside agreeing to send the government's 10-district proposal to the Constitutional Court.[70] After the demonstration in the morning had ended, the Orange Movement called for a protest to take place in front of the parliament building that evening. The demonstration attracted thousands of Kuwaitis. Three members of the 29 Bloc announced their intention to try to impeach the prime minister in light of the government's decision to send its proposal to the Constitutional Court.[71] The following day, Ahmad al-Saadoun, Faisal al-Meslim, and Ahmad al-Mulaifi, all members of the 29 Bloc, submitted an official request for the interpellation of the prime minister on May 17.[72]

To pressure the government, the Orange Movement organized another demonstration to be held in front of the assembly on May 19. Several members of the 29 Bloc attended the event and pledged to support the five-district plan. The event was called Oath Night (Lailat al-Qasam). Eighteen independent legislators opposed to reforming the electoral system chose to hold a separate gathering on May 20 to counter the Orange Movement; they selected blue as the color to represent their movement. They considered the five-district plan to be unjust and unfair. Salah Khorshid, a member of the parliament at that time, said, "I support the redistributing, but it should be based on the constitution, which puts the emphasis on equality."[73] He based his objection on the differences in the number of constituents that would be included in each district under the five-district proposal. For instance, the second district would have some 40,000 voters, while the fifth district would consist of about 95,000 voters.[74] Although the proposal was not a perfect plan given the large differences between the different districts, members of the Orange Movement nonetheless believed that any reform at this point would help in furthering the reformation of the political system.[75]

On May 21 in this politically charged environment—with Kuwait divided between the two movements and dueling demonstrations—Amir Sabah al-Ahmad dissolved parliament and called for new elections.[76] He explained that he had decided on this course of action "because the division in the parliament weakened its ability to perform its responsibilities and encouraged disorder in the society."[77] With parliament dissolved, the Orange Movement activists had to change tactics. They decided to hold off on further protests until after the elections. In the meantime, they would instead engage in traditional campaigning in support of the 29 Bloc candidates and work against legislators and candidates who opposed the five-district plan.[78]

To the astonishment of many, in the elections held on June 29, 2006 candidates supported by the movement were elected to the assembly, and most of those who the Orange activists worked against were defeated.[79] The government, now convinced that the five-district plan had the support of the majority of Kuwaitis, withdrew the ten-district plan from the Constitutional Court on 1 July. The Orange activists organized their last protest in front of the National Assembly for July 7, 2006. Their slogan for the occasion was "The People Delivered Their Message…We Wanted It 5." More than 2,000 people participated in the demonstration. A number of newly elected legislators joined them and gave speeches on the redistricting and urged the government to back the original plan. On 12 July, the new National Assembly voted to implement an electoral system consisting of five districts.

Secrets of Success

The Orange Movement owes its success to two major factors: the organization of its campaign and the broad-based coalition its young members and supporters built.

Organization

The organization of the Orange Movement was simple. It began with a Web site, kuwait5.org designed by Jassim al-Qamis, who earned his bachelor's degree in the United States. "We tried to organize a campaign similar to what we had seen while studying in the U.S. We learned from our experience in the States that in order to mobilize the people, we have to make everything easy and within their reach, and they will implement," revealed Qamis.[80]

The young activists advertised their Web site on blogs, especially Sahat al-Safat, which launched the movement in April 2006 by urging Kuwaitis to do something to reform their electoral system. Sahat al-Safat had a good reputation, earned in part during the dynastic crisis in January 2006 after the death of Amir Jabir al-Ahmad. The blog posted news articles related to the crisis, including from sources inside the royal family.[81] Its performance encouraged Kuwaitis to turn to it as a main source for information and to learn more about the government's policies.

With the exception of al-Qabas, the daily newspapers did not really support the movement. At the time, there were five Arabic- and three English-language daily papers in the country. Although the media in Kuwait is relatively independent of state control compared to in other countries in the region, the government had prohibited new newspapers since 1976.[82] The state of domestic politics often determines the degree of the newspapers' freedom of expression. For example, whenever the National Assembly has been (unconstitutionally) dissolved, freedom of speech has also been negatively affected.

In 2006 some newspapers, including *al-Watan*, were close to the government, so they did not support the Orange Movement; *al-Watan* even published cartoons mocking the movement and calling its leaders "children."[83] For this reason, the blogs were an important alternative media. Bloggers covered the movement's activities and gatherings, writing about events and posting photos and video clips. Moreover, the bloggers urged their readers to participate in the movement. They announced upcoming events and connected protestors to each other online. In addition to promoting the movement, bloggers instructed Kuwaitis about their duties regarding the campaign. According to Khalid al-Fadallah, "We did not have a leader for the movement, we all worked together as a team. Our leader was the net! The youths used to visit the blogs to find out the next step, and they implemented it. This was amazing."[84] Besides Sahat al-Safat, other blogs contributing to the movement included Kila Ma6goog,[85] Zaydoun,[86] Shurouq,[87] al-Tariq,[88] and alommah.org.[89] Some bloggers formed the core of the movement or participated in the demonstrations.

Kuwaiti authorities never attempted to ban blogging or take down sites. Blogs do not fall under the press law passed by the parliament on March 6, 2006.[90] "Blocking blogs is simply stupid," Jassim al-Qamis asserted. He contends that the authorities were not able to ban them, "especially [because] blogs were not doing anything wrong. They were not against the regime, or against the ruling family."[91] Ziad al-Duij, a blogger and a participant in the movement, believes that the authorities did not block the blogs because they did not criticize the amir,[92] whose "person is immune and inviolable."[93] Duij also thinks that the government might not have understood the influence of the bloggers, and for this reason did not move against them.[94]

Some of the movement's actions had a positive effect on Kuwaitis in general. For example, the decision to camp out in front of the parliament on May 14 pointed to the seriousness of the activists. In addition, the symbolism of planting Kuwait's flag in front of the parliament on the same night indicated the movement's patriotism. More important, the activists' attempts to go to the parliamentary session on May 16 despite being barred from it sent a massage to Kuwaitis and the government that the Orange Movement was steadfast in its demand and intended to persist under all circumstances.

A Broad-based Coalition

The movement organizers—among them teachers and professors, reporters and writers, businesspeople and nonprofit professionals—built a broad-based coalition to support reform of the electoral system. "Let's Agree To Make Our Disagreement Amicable in the Future" was one of the slogans that the activists repeated during their campaign. It underscored the decision to work with various groups, parties, and organizations regardless of their political leanings and agendas. This explains in part why the Orange Movement did not have one particular ideology; it was a coalition that spanned the ideological and political spectrum. The movement's central aim was the reform of the electoral system, therefore the core organizers decided to invite other parties and groups to join the movement.[95]

The cooperation between the young Orange activists and the 29 Bloc was another positive result of the campaign. The activists needed parliamentarians who agreed with its position to pass the five-district plan. MPs did not lead the movement, and they did not organize events. Rather, they were invited by the movement to its demonstrations. Jassim al-Qamis insists that the "members of parliament had nothing to do with the Orange Movement."[96] The 29 Bloc was important in providing moral support to the activists and protecting them from possible aggressive actions by authorities in dealing with Nabiha 5.

Despite the relationship that the movement had with some legislators, they were not immune to regime repression. Some Nabiha 5 leaders were subjected to harassment and blackmailed by Amn al-Dawla, the state security service. The movement's core members were informed by friends working with Amn al-Dawla that they were being watched by the service. According to Fadallah, "Some of our friends told us that we should be cautious because they had seen our files in that institute, and that our cell phones were under surveillance." The activists also received threats from people in positions of authority. "Some members of the royal family threatened that they would harm us or harm our families if we did not stop causing problems for some candidates who were close to the government," Fadallah said.[97] Fadallah himself was blackmailed, and an attempt was made to arrest Muhammad al-Oraiman, a Nabiha 5 organizer.[98] To evade phone surveillance, the movement members convinced some foreign workers to obtain new cell phones and give them to organizers to use instead of their own phones. "Obviously, we paid for the new numbers" says al-Fadallah. Kuwaiti authorities dealt, for the most part, quite responsibly and reasonably with the movement.[99] The minister of interior and defense, Jabir al-Mubarak al-Sabah, would tell the activists that his ministry was responsible for the protection of the demonstrators and was not there to harm them.[100]

Conclusion

The Orange Movement succeeded in redrawing electoral districts by orchestrating five protests, bringing about momentous change in Kuwaiti politics. Beyond this immediate transformation, their organization and use of persuasion and some more confrontational forms of nonviolent action had created a model for other activists to use in the pursuit of future goals.[101] After the new National Assembly officially reformed the electoral system in July 2006, the members of the movement began to think about their next step, leading them to raise a number of questions: Do we need to continue the movement? Should we become a political entity in Kuwait?

During a meeting after approval of the five-district plan, the core members of the movement decided to disband it. "We thought that Nabiha 5 was over after achieving our goals," said Khalid al-Fadallah. The organizers wanted to keep their movement "pure" in the minds of Kuwaitis. "We did not want to be like other movements in the world and in history, which began with pure aims, but lost their position in the minds and hearts of their people. We did not want to repeat those mistakes; we wanted to keep our achievements live in the minds of our citizens. We organized the campaign for one particular aim; we achieved it."[102] Fadallah added, "If we decide to address any other problems that the country has, we should organize another campaign."[103] Michael Herb, a political scientist at Georgia State University, believes that the Orange Movement might resurface if the royal family decides to and again succeeds in dissolving the National Assembly.[104]

Although the May 2008 elections under the five-district system led to a reduction in the so-called independent legislators,[105] who tended to be associated with the government, the new National Assembly is overwhelmingly Islamists and tribal. In addition, the elections did not entirely solve the problems associated with the 25-district system, as there were allegations of vote buying in the third and fifth districts. The new system also did not end tribalism, as evidenced in districts one, four, and five, where some of the big tribes conducted illegal "pre-elections." It must be noted as well that sectarianism played a strong role in the balloting, especially in the first district, where Shiites are concentrated. Though thus far largely positive, the full effect of Nabiha 5 cannot yet be measured.

Note: Kuwait held its second parliamentary elections based on the new electoral system in 2009; the results of these elections were totally different because for the first time four women were elected to the parliament and the number of Islamists decreased. In addition, the new assembly has many members who support the government and its policies. Still, tribalism and sectarianism were strong during the campaigns and many sectarian and tribal clashes have occurred in the parliament since May 2009.

Notes

1. Jassim al-Qamis, e-mail interview, March 15, 2008.
2. Michael Herb, "Kuwait," paper prepared for The Transition from Liberalized Autocracy? New Options for Promoting Democracy in the Arab World, a USIP-Muslim World Initiative Working Group and Study Project, October 25, 2005, 6, http://www2.gsu.edu/~polmfh/herb_usip_kuwait.pdf.
3. The constitution is available at http://www2.gsu.edu/~polmfh/kuw_1962_const_arabic.pdf (in Arabic).
4. In Kuwait, some members of the government have seats in parliament although they are not popularly elected. The ruling family and the government need supporters in the National Assembly to back its policies without major opposition and to protect against no-confidence measures.
5. Mary Ann Tétreault, *Stories of Democracy: Politics and Society in Contemporary Kuwait* (New York: Columbia University Press, 2000), 69.
6. Ibid., 70. Diwaniyyas have played important roles throughout the political life of Kuwait.
7. *Kuwait Today*, May 7, 2006, www.mona.gov.kw/Other_Pages/ConstitCourt/Item19.pdf.
8. Tétreault, *Stories of Democracy*, 71.
9. The Constitutional Court, founded in 1972 to resolve disputes between the government and the parliament, overturned the law following a lawsuit brought before the Court of First Instance. Individuals cannot bring cases before the Constitutional Court, but they can try to convince the Court of First Instance to allow a case to proceed to the Constitutional Court. Two Kuwaiti citizens, Mubarak al-Wa`alan and al-Homaidi al-Suba`ie, were able to do this. They had been accused by the Ministry of the Interior of violating the Assembly Law by organizing a convention in 2003 to discuss the interpellation of Minister of Finance Abdullah al-Nuri. The Constitutional Court dismissed the charges against Wa`alan and Suba`ie and revoked the law. See "Parliament Respects Any Measure, Verdict of Constitutional Court—al-Kharafi," Kuwait News Agency, May 1, 2006, www.kuna.net.kw/NewsAgenciesPublicSite/ArticleDetails.aspx?id=1656569&Language=en.
10. Khalid al-Fadallah, interview, Boston, February 2, 2008.
11. Mohammed al-Jasem, "Throwing Stones on the Tankers' Issue," July 27, 2005, www.aljasem.org/default.asp?opt=2&art_id=75.

12. al-Fadallah, interview.
13. Abdo Baaklini, "Legislatures in the Gulf Area: The Experience of Kuwait, 1961–1976," *International Journal of Middle East Studies* 14, no. 3 (August 1982): 359–79.
14. Ahmed al-Khatib, *Kuwait: From Emirate to State,* 2nd ed. (Casablanca and Beirut: Arab Cultural Center, 2007), 1: 223–24.
15. Ghanim al-Najjar, *Introduction to Political Development in Kuwait,* 2nd ed. (Kuwait: Dar Qurtass, 1996), 72.
16. Ibid., 72.
17. Ibid., 99.
18. Ibid., 113.
19. Tétreault, *Stories of Democracy,* 108.
20. Ejmans are one of the major tribes in Kuwait. The tribal system is based on kinship relations. The core of this relationship is the *faza`a*, which means that the members of a tribe are morally required to assist any other member of the tribe if they are asked. This tradition among the Bedouins is obvious during elections. When one candidate, say from tribe "A," is competing with a candidate of tribe "B," the members of each tribe work for and vote for the candidate from their respective tribe regardless of his abilities. The same occurs in districts with predominately Sunni and Shiite populations.
21. For more on this issue, see Michael Herb's "Kuwait Politics Database," http://www2. gsu.edu/~polmfh/database/database.htm.
22. Mary Ann Tétreault, "Kuwait's Annus Mirabilis," *Middle East Report,* September 7, 2006, www.merip.org/mero/mero090706.html.
23. "Sabah al-Ahmed: Kuwait Is Not Free from Ruin, and the Government Does Not Oppose the Reformation of the Electoral System" (in Arabic), *al-Watan,* July 22, 2003, www.alwatan.com.kw/default.aspx?pageid=26&mgdid=186363.
24. Abdul-Mehsen Joma`a, "The Ministerial Committee Approved the Five District Plan and the Voting Will Be by Using the Civil ID," *al-Qabas,* April 17, 2006, 1.
25. "The Prime Minister in a Statement about the Electoral System: We Will Present Our Final Views in the Parliament on May 15," *al-Qabas,* April 18, 2006, 21
26. Nasser al-Otaibi, "11 National-Based Measures Helped the Five District Plan to Succeed," *al-Qabas,* May 5, 2006, 12
27. "We Will Present Our Final Views in the Parliament on May 15," 21.
28. Nasser al-Abdili and Daifallah al-Shemmeri, "27 Legislators Supported the Five-District Plan and Approved the Postponement Request to May 15," *al-Qabas,* April 18, 2006, 1; Nasser al-Abdili, "The Supporters of the Five-District Plan Increased to 29 Legislators," *al-Qabas,* April 19, 2006, 1.
29. *Al-Anba,* April 19, 2006.
30. al-Qamis, interview.
31. Ibid.
32. See Sahat al-Safat, http://kuwaitjunior.blogspot.com/search?updated-max=2006–05-31T10%3A46%3A00%2B03%3A00&max-results=50.
33. Thirty-one columnists issued a statement in favor of the five-district plan on May 19. The statement is available at http://belkuwaitialfasih.blogspot.com/2006_05_01_archive.html.
34. al-Fadallah, interview.
35. "Make the Legislators Hear Your Voice," www.kuwait5.org/mps.htm.
36. "Make the Ministers Hear Your Voice," www.kuwait5.org/ministers.htm.
37. Monther al-Habeeb, a movement participant, phone interview, January 22, 2008.
38. Jassim al-Qamis, interview; "Let Them Hear Your Voice…Five for Kuwait," www.kuwait5.org/ready-print.htm.
39. Amer Zuhair, *When the People Spoke,* DVD part 2, Workshop Media Productions, 2006.
40. al-Fadallah, interview.

41. In an interview, Jassim al-Qamis, who had developed the movement's Web site, said, "When I designed Kuwait5.org...I tried blue, but it was the color for the women's rights campaign. I tried red, but it was too scary. Finally, I decided to choose orange."
42. "We Are Going to the Street: Your Attendance Is Very Very Very Important," May 3, 2006, http://kuwaitjunior.blogspot.com/search?updated-max=2006–05-31T10%3A46%3A00%2B03%3A00&max-results=50.
43. al-Fadallah, interview.
44. Fahad al-Turki and Daifallah al-Shemmeri, "The Five Districts Plan Is the Main Gate to Reformation," *al-Qabas*, May 7, 2006, 6.
45. al-Qamis, interview.
46. Ibid.
47. For this poster, see www.kuwait-unplugged.com/uploaded_images/nabeeha-787850.jpg.
48. al-Habeeb, interview.
49. Nasser al-Abdili, Mubarak al-Abdul-Hadi, and Nasser al-Otaibi, "The Cabinet Approved the Ten District Plan and Decided Not to Amend the Constitution," *al-Qabas*, May 10, 2006, 1.
50. al-Fadallah, interview.
51. Tétreault, "Kuwait's Annus Mirabilis."
52. Ibid.
53. al-Qamis, interview.
54. For a copy of the statement, see http://photos1.blogger.com/blogger/7935/836/1600/DSCN1948.0.jpg.
55. In the Kuwait political system, the parliament and the government both have the right to go the Constitutional Court to seek a ruling on whether an issue or law contradicts the constitution. It is not unusual for one party to threaten to approach the court to make the other party withdraw a proposal that may be found unconstitutional. What is interesting about May 15 is the government's behavior. If it was confident in its plan's constitutionality, it should not have agreed to send it to the court; if it was unsure, it should not have presented it to the assembly.
56. al-Fadallah interview.
57. Ibid.
58. al-Habeeb, interview.
59. al-Qamis, interview.
60. al-Fadallah, interview.
61. al-Qamis, interview.
62. al-Fadallah, interview.
63. Ibid.
64. Ibid.
65. *When the People Spoke*, 2006, a documentary by Amer al-Zuhair.
66. al-Fadallah, interview.
67. Ibid.
68. *When the People Spoke*.
69. al-Qamis, interview.
70. "The Ten District Plan to the Constitutional Court with 33 Votes and the Disagreement of al-Khorafi," *al-Qabas*, May 17, 2007, 16.
71. Walid al-Nusif, Nasser al-Abdili, Abdul-Mehsen Jom'a, and Ibrahim al-Sa'edi, "The 29 Meet at Night and al-Saadoun, al-Mulaifi, and al-Meslim Will Impeach the Prime Minister," *al-Qabas*, May 17, 2006, 1.
72. "The First Impeachment of the Prime Minister," *al-Qabas,* May 18, 2006, 11.
73. Fahad al-Turki and Mahmood al-Mosawi, "The Independence's Protest in Front of the Parliament: We Swear Not to Withdraw the Proposal from the Constitutional Court," *al-Qabas*, May 21, 2006, 8.
74. "A View on the New Districts," *al-Jarida*, March 20, 2008, 7.

75. al-Habeeb, interview.
76. Walid al-Nusif, "The Emir: I Was Forced Psychologically to Dissolve [the Parliament] and I Did Not Sleep Yesterday," *al-Qabas*, May 22, 2006, 1.
77. "The Dissolution Decree," *al-Qabas*, May 22, 2006, 1.
78. al-Fadallah, interview.
79. Salem Ayyob, "Majlis 2006 Was Important Because Women Participated for the First Time in the Elections," *al-Jarida*, March 20, 2008, 5.
80. al-Qamis, interview.
81. Abdul-Latif al-Duij, "The Constitutional Crisis," *al-Qabas*, August 9, 2006, 47.
82. This has changed since 2007, as many other newspapers have appeared in the country.
83. For the cartoon, see *al-Watan*, May 16, 2006.
84. al-Fadallah, interview.
85. See www.ma6goog.com.
86. See www.kuwait-unplugged.com.
87. See http://jabriya.blogspot.com.
88. See www.altariq2009.com.
89. See www.alommah.org/blog.
90. The law forbids any criticism of Allah, prophets, or the Prophet Muhammad's wives, companions, and descendants. It also prohibits criticism of the Amir. For the law, see http://www.irex-mena.org/pdf/kuwait%20Press%20Law%20(Arabic).pdf.
91. al-Qamis, interview.
92. Ziad al-Duij, e-mail interview, March 13, 2008.
93. Article 54 of the constitution states that "the Emir is the head of the State, his person is immune and inviolable," meaning that he is above all criticism.
94. al-Duij, interview.
95. Rakan al-Nusif, movement member, phone interview, March 20, 2008.
96. al-Qamis, interview.
97. al-Fadallah, interview.
98. Ibid.
99. Muhammad al-Jassem, a lawyer and a well-known writer, e-mail interview, January 27, 2008.
100. al-Fadallah, interview.
101. a-Jassem, interview.
102. al-Fadallah, interview.
103. Ibid.
104. Michael Herb, e-mail interview, January 27, 2008.
105. Some such politicians, such as Jamal al-Omar, simply failed to receive enough votes, while others, such as Salah Khorshid and Talal al-Ayyar, chose not to participate under the new system.

Part II

Case Studies

(c)
Movements for Social and Political Rights

16

Hizbullah: Delimiting the Boundaries of Nonviolent Resistance?

Rola el-Husseini

Hizbullah emerged in the mid-1980s as a response to Israeli invasion and occupation and acquired in the 1990s a dual and contradictory reputation. The Lebanese viewed Hizbullah as a legitimate political actor, but the U.S. and Israeli governments considered it a terrorist organization.[1] Two aspects of the party explain this seeming contradiction: on one hand, it operates a large network of charitable organizations and has fielded members and sympathizers in legislative and municipal elections, which has anchored it in the Lebanese polity; on the other hand, its military wing carries out operations against Israel. These same aspects also explain Hizbullah's dual approach to resistance, a concept central to its identity. In Lebanon, Hizbullah's opposition to the government and other political actors has for the most part been nonviolent—despite a recent notable exception—while its resistance toward Israel continued to involve the use of violent force.

Hizbullah's understanding of resistance is easily ascertained. The organization defines itself within the Lebanese polity as a nationalist party, so it is not in its interest to alienate compatriots with the use of violence. Hizbullah has in the past gone the extra mile to try to demonstrate its transcendence of sectarian affiliations, but in recent years, the party has come to feel that it is entitled to more of a say in the government; at the same time, it has sought to retain possession of its weapons. In May 2008, Hizbullah's leaders lost patience with nonviolent efforts to shift the power dynamic in Lebanese politics and turned its guns on fellow Lebanese. It thus fell into the trap of confessional politics and lost its legitimacy for many Lebanese as a *Lebanese* resistance movement.

Emergence and "Lebanonization"

In the 1950s, the economic, political, and social alienation of the Lebanese Shiites had manifested itself in the poverty evident in the community. Notable families had come to monopolize the community's political representation to the point that Shiite religious leaders eventually felt the need to intervene. In the 1960s and 1970s, Imam Musa al-Sadr mobilized the Shiite community socially and politically. Hizbullah traces its origins to the Harakat al-Mahrumin (Movement of the Deprived), established by Sadr in March 1974. Feeling that the community needed to defend itself, he created Afwaj al-Muqawama al-Lubnaniyya (Brigades of the Lebanese Resistance) as a military wing of the movement in 1975. This armed contingent became known by its acronym, AMAL (literally "hope").

In 1982, on the heels of the Israeli invasion of Lebanon, a group of clerics seceded from Amal and established Islamic Amal, the group that would form the nucleus of Hizbullah. Although 1982 is generally considered to be the year of Hizbullah's founding, the party did not actually exist as an organization until the mid-1980s. The group announced its arrival in an open letter released in February 1985. The statement declared that the world is divided between the oppressed and the oppressors, and it designated the United States as the main enemy because of its use of Israel, its ally, to inflict suffering on Lebanese Muslims. As Naim Qassem, Hizbullah's current second in command, notes, "The Party thus declared its ideological, jihad, political and social visions, as well as the launch of its political movement.... With this declaration Hizbullah entered a new phase, shifting the Party from secret resistance activity that ran free from political or media interactions into public political work."[2]

After the signing of the Ta'if agreement that ended the Lebanese civil war in 1989, Hizbullah adopted a conciliatory approach toward Lebanese politics while maintaining its traditional hard line against Israel, which continued to occupy southern Lebanon, a predominately Shiite area. The post–civil war period marked a new era in the organization's history, as several events contributed to a conscious effort by Hizbullah's leaders to transform the movement into a political party. Chief among these events was the death in 1989 of Iran's Ayatollah Ruhollah Khomeini, which brought with it changes in the priorities of the Islamic republic that meant less funding for the party; the end of the cold war in the late 1980s and early 1990s and its effect on Hizbullah patrons Iran and Syria;[3] the actual implementation of the Ta'if agreement, which disarmed all groups in Lebanon—with the important exception of Hizbullah—and opened up the political space for Hizbullah to enter that arena; and Israel's 1992 assassination of Hizbullah secretary-general Abbas Musawi and his replacement that year by Sayyed Hassan Nasrallah, who brought more effective leadership to the helm of Hizbullah.[4]

Emblematic of Hizbullah's shift was the party's participation in 1992 in Lebanon's first postwar legislative elections, an event that has come to be known as the "Lebanonization" of Hizbullah. The term denotes the official shelving of the party's demand for an Islamic state in Lebanon and its acceptance of the rules of the political game, as evidenced in its willingness to run candidates for office in the multisectarian, consociational Lebanese state. Hizbullah has since participated in all the country's legislative (1996, 2000, and 2005) and municipal (1998, 2004) elections. In the 2005 elections, it won 14 seats in the national legislature and allied with other parties to form a voting block of 35 parliamentarians. These elections led to the party participating for the first time in the cabinet.

Hizbullah's Lebanonization was manifest not only in the party's participation in political life but also in the development of the extensive network of charitable works it had begun establishing in the 1980s, primarily geared toward Shiites and other residents of southern Lebanon and the southern suburbs of Beirut. Those charities providing services related to the armed resistance include al-Shahid (established in 1982) and al-Juraha (established in 1990), which help the wounded and the families of those killed while fighting the Israelis. Autonomous outfits that are branches of Iranian institutions include al-Imdad (established in 1987), which distributes social services to the poor; and Jihad al-Bina'a (established in 1988), which focuses on the establishment and management of urban services and on reconstruction, especially in south Lebanon.[5] These charities reflect Hizbullah's perception of itself as the protector of the oppressed and defender of the poor. Its creation of a vast network of parallel structures and institutions constitutes a form of "nonviolent intervention."

Hizbullah crafted for itself the image of an anti-sectarian group challenging traditional politics in Lebanon and the corresponding prevalence of clientelism and corruption. This effort accounts for Hizbullah's hostility in the 1990s toward Prime Minister Rafiq al-Hariri and his economic policies, which it saw as rewarding the rich, privileging the reconstruction of "stone" instead of human capital.[6] Hizbullah further improved its image because of its reputation for efficient and clean local governance in the municipalities in the southern suburbs of Beirut (for example, in Ghubairy). What, however, explains Hizbullah's adoption of resistance to power as a strategy? Is nonviolent resistance, for Hizbullah, justified philosophically or is it simply a pragmatic form of resistance appropriate within the ambit of the Lebanese polity? If the former, what exactly are its philosophical justifications?

Intellectual Underpinnings of Resistance

Hizbullah's adoption of resistance as a strategy was in part inspired by the Iranian Revolution, but also by the discourse of two Lebanese religious leaders—Ayatollahs Muhammad Hussein Fadlallah and Muhammad Mahdi Shams al-Din—through their sermons from the 1980s and 1990s.[7] Shams al-Din, in his book on armed violence, asserts, "Armed political violence, violent political discourse and violent behavior vis-à-vis a foreign invader or occupier is not simple political violence. It's a legitimate *defensive jihad*. . . . It is also a duty for the entire nation. . . . Whether this jihad takes the form of a regular war or that of a public or secret resistance or guerrilla warfare does not impinge on its legitimacy."[8] Resistance then is seen mainly as a violent struggle against an occupying force, in this case Israel. The discourse of these men is a nationalistic one couched in the language of Islam.

According to Fadlallah and Shams al-Din, resistance takes two forms. One form is a fight against an occupier, a "defensive jihad" that uses all possible means, including violent martyrdom operations to defend the land. In such cases, the "bombers give themselves in a spirit of obligation. . . . Their deaths are seen as a sacred duty to sacrifice, to give themselves up totally."[9] Land made holy by martyrdom must not be abandoned to the enemy, which points to the second form of resistance: *sumud* or steadfastness, a passive resistance manifest in a refusal to leave the land. Sumud also has other meanings. It is not only a matter of remaining rooted in the land or enduring a brutal onslaught, but it also involves active nonviolent resistance, manifest in declarations, sit-ins, demonstrations, and civil disobedience. A more passive model of nonviolent action is found in the example of the Prophet Muhammad in the first years of his call to Islam in Mecca. Before migrating to Medina, Muhammad and his followers suffered the persecution of the Meccan elite for 12 years, 610–622 C.E., without retaliating.[10] Note that mere non-retaliation is not the same as nonviolent resistance. Muhammad's actions would be more accurately characterized as avoidance strategy or offering concessions—not nonviolent resistance per se. They, however, are often portrayed in the Arab world, especially in the Palestinian territories as a form of nonviolent resistance and a justification for its use.

In the case of Hizbullah, between November 2006 and May 2008, a period of nonviolent disobedience toward the government, the organization arguably practiced a jihad of the tongue (*jihad al-lisan*) and of the pen (*bi al-qalam*). These types of jihad traditionally have referred to *da'wa* (or proselytizing), but within the recent history of the party one can see a shift in Hizbullah's interpretation of the concept of resistance. Indeed, as "the meaning and application of jihad and martyrdom changed from the battlefield to the elections...Hizbullah's greater jihad was directed towards greater integration into the Lebanese political system and state institutions."[11] This shift increased the importance of speeches, declarations, and television broadcasts (*jihad al-lisan*), in addition to editorials, banners, posters, and leaflets (*jihad bi al-qalam*). For a year and a half, the Hizbullah's use of nonviolent direct action methods consisted mainly of sit-ins and demonstrations.

Resistance as Strategy

Despite entering the forum of official Lebanese politics, Hizbullah continued to maintain its military apparatus after the Ta'if agreement. It is the only group not to have demobilized in postwar Lebanon, ostensibly so it could continue to carry out resistance operations against Israeli occupation.[12] The war of attrition in southern Lebanon between 1992 and 2000 relied on a number of tactics, including suicide bombings used exclusively against military targets in the occupied areas. In 1996 and in retaliation for the deaths of Lebanese civilians, including a fourteen-year old boy, Hizbullah rained missiles on northern Israel. Israel responded with Operation Grapes of Wrath. The so-called Qana massacre during the fighting brought about a nationalist consensus around the idea of "resistance," uniting Christian and Muslim Lebanese against Israel.[13] The election of Emile Lahoud as president in 1998 represented the ascendancy of a strong Hizbullah ally. By the end of the 1990s, Israelis had grown tired of its occupation of southern Lebanon, and in national elections, Ehud Barak campaigned for the premiership on the promise of a unilateral withdrawal by July 2000. After the failure of peace negotiations with Syria and Lebanon, Israel withdrew unilaterally in May 2000, allowing Hizbullah to claim to have driven Israeli forces from the country; its operations had made the cost of occupation too expensive for Israel in human and financial terms.[14] The Israeli-Lebanese border remained relatively calm between 2000 and 2006, with the occasional skirmish between Hizbullah and the Israeli army, especially in the contested Shabaa Farms area.[15]

On February 14, 2005, former prime minister Hariri was killed when a bomb exploded near his convoy en route from parliament to his home. The assassination of Lebanon's most high-profile figure threw the country into a state of shock. Three days of national mourning were declared, and Hariri supporters quickly took to the streets. On 21 February, protestors held a rally at the site of the assassination, calling for an end to Syrian occupation and blaming Damascus and the Lebanon's pro-Syrian president, Lahoud, for the murder. Hariri's death triggered what observers in the West dubbed the Cedar Revolution—known in Lebanon as *intifadat al-istiqlal,* the intifada of independence. As the Jaafar and Stephan chapter in this volume indicates, an estimated 1.2 million to 1.5 million Lebanese protested the Syrian presence at the memorial gathering held on March 14, one-month after Hariri's assassination.[16] Combined Lebanese and international pressure ultimately led Damascus to capitulate. On April 26, 2005, the last of its troops and intelligence agents in Lebanon crossed the border into Syria, and Damascus notified the United Nations of its compliance with

Resolution 1559. Syria's withdrawal left Hizbullah without its main supporter and in danger of being required to disarm by an anti-Syrian Lebanese government. For this reason, Hizbullah decided to participate in the cabinet after the 2005 legislative elections.[17]

The 2006 war and its aftermath suggest that Hizbullah's main agenda initially was a Lebanese agenda. Following on a promise made by Nasrallah to seek the release of all Lebanese prisoners in Israel, Hizbullah crossed the Blue Line[18] and kidnapped two Israeli soldiers on July 12, 2006 with the intent of initiating an exchange.[19] This action triggered the Israeli bombardment of Lebanon during July and August and Hizbullah's firing of thousands of rockets into northern Israel. Hizbullah's action—to fulfill its "truthful promise," also the name of the kidnapping operation—was arguably within the "new rules of the game" governing the low-intensity conflict between the group and Israel after the 2000 withdrawal.[20] Hizbullah's hopes for another exchange were initially dashed when Israel retaliated by launching a full-scale war on the same day of the kidnapping.[21] The military conflict ended on August 14, 2006, three days after the adoption of UN Security Council Resolution 1701, which called for the disarmament of Hizbullah, the withdrawal of Israel from Lebanon, and the deployment of Lebanese soldiers and an enlarged United Nations Interim Force in Lebanon (UNIFIL) in the south. The confrontation had demonstrated Hizbullah's ability to stand against an Israeli onslaught and was perceived by the party as a "divine victory."[22] During the war, the majority of Lebanese rallied around Hizbullah and supported its resistance. Calls for disarmament of the party, rife since the 2000 Israeli withdrawal, ceased—momentarily.

The war provided Hizbullah gains in symbolic capital in some quarters. It had emerged victorious in the eyes of its Shiite constituents and in the eyes of the "Arab street." The party gained respect in Sunni-majority countries, and local Islamist groups expressed solidarity with it.[23] In contrast, the celebration of Hizbullah's victory was far from universal in Lebanon. A large segment of Lebanese, especially Christians and Sunnis, had rejected Hizbullah's claim, made since 2000, that the resistance mission remained unfinished. They saw Hizbullah's position and actions as a cynical means of self-preservation and continuing relevance to the Lebanese polity at the expense of the nation as a whole and its well-being. The tension surrounding this issue became especially acute after the 2006 war, with second-guessing of Hizbullah's actions.[24] Cross-confessional solidarity quickly faded after the cease-fire when some Lebanese began to question Hizbullah's right to provoke Israel and risk massive retaliation against the entire population. Nevertheless, while the war raged, a poll showed that 87 percent of all Lebanese—89 percent of Sunnis and 80 percent of Christians—supported Hizbullah's military response to the Israeli attacks,[25] in contrast to five months earlier, when just 58 percent supported the resistance movement's right to remain armed.[26] The conflict with Israel and the postwar standoff over power between Hizbullah and its allies and the Lebanese government led to a dwindling of support for Hizbullah among Druze, Sunnis, and a segment of Lebanese Christians who do not support former prime minister and military commander Michel Aoun.[27]

Nonviolent Resistance

After the 2006 war, riding on a wave of Arab approval for having held its own against Israel, Hizbullah tried to translate its military "victory" into political power. In September 2006, Aoun, as leader of the Free Patriotic Movement (FPM), called for the resignation of Prime Minister Fouad Siniora and his cabinet and for the creation of a "government of national unity." Siniora refused. Lebanon, trying to recover from its war wounds, had UNIFIL deploying in the south and remained under an air, sea, and land blockade by Israel. In mid-September, Nasrallah slammed the government, accusing it of being an American tool and of failing to protect the country.[28] Nasrallah's criticism came on the heels of a similar attack by a Hizbullah MP who called on Siniora to resign and defiantly vowed that the group would not comply with the UN demand to surrender its weapons.

The postwar attempt by Hizbullah and the Free Patriotic Movement to form a "national unity government" and gain control of more than one-third of the cabinet—to obtain veto power over decision making—points to the Islamic organization's character as a nationalist party concerned with internal Lebanese affairs. During the 2006–2008 stalemate in pursuit of its political goals, Hizbullah used several methods of nonviolent action.[29] Chief among them were staging street demonstrations, organizing a sit-in in downtown Beirut, and blocking the election of a new president by creating gridlock in the political system.

Part of the purpose of demanding greater power was to be able to scuttle attempts to implement Resolution 1701's provision that Hizbullah disarm. In essence, Hizbullah used nonviolent methods to remain armed. This incongruity can be explained by Hizbullah's desire to avoid further antagonizing its compatriots after a war that had destroyed the economy and the country's infrastructure while at the same time catering to the security needs of the Shiite community. The organization also probably sought to reassert its credentials as a "national" defense group.

Hizbullah began its nonviolent campaign to control the government when five Shiite ministers from the party and its Amal ally walked out of the cabinet on November 11, 2006 and a pro-opposition Christian minister resigned. The ministers resigned in November 2006 after the collapse of talks to grant the opposition a stronger role in the government.[30] On December 1, 2006 in Beirut, thousands of Amal and Hizbullah supporters, along with those of Aoun, gathered outside the Grand Serail, the office of Prime Minister Siniora, to stage an open-ended sit-in and campaign to pressure the government to resign:

[H]undreds of thousands of Hizballah and Aoun supporters packed the squares and building sites that make up the southern reaches of downtown. Though the expected speeches and patriotic male-choir music were in evidence, the mood of the demonstration, and the subsequent sit-in, has been less militant than festive. The sounds of drumming and the smells of water pipes and grilled meats have made the sit-in a replica of the carnivalesque rallies of the "Beirut spring," though this sit-in is larger than the 2005 prototype. The participants, too, convey a different air than their 2005 counterparts. Whether the Hizballah supporters clustered around Riyad al-Sulh Square, the Aounist enclave further east or the smattering of others, these people are recognizably less well-to-do than the...revolutionaries of the "independence intifada."[31]

The leadership of Hizbullah coordinated with the protestors on their actions, which included setting up a "tent city." Employees at schools, hospitals, and social organizations run by Hizbullah also participated initially in the demonstrations. Hundreds of women in black chadors and children waving yellow flags were counted among the protestors. When the demonstrations lost steam, after a couple of months, scores of youth remained behind in the tent city. As the ranks of government opponents dwindled, the tent city began showing signs of permanence, with plainclothes Hizbullah security guards manning the makeshift checkpoints surrounding it. One reporter noted in July 2007:

> The full-time inhabitants of the camp are almost exclusively party members. Civilian supporters may pass by in the evenings or on weekends, but they have long since packed up and gone home from the camp themselves.... Despite the dramatic decrease in participation...Al-Manar TV still broadcasts a live show from the camp every evening at 7:00 p.m. The program includes speeches, interviews and shots of protesters gathered in small groups. However, even Manar's attempts to zoom in on protestors to project a better image of the state of the camp fails to convince spectators that people are still eager and committed.[32]

During the early months of the protests, items of daily life had acquired new symbolism. For example, in December 2006 the *Christmas* tree became a symbol of the Hizbullah-led opposition as well as of the government's supporters. On Martyrs' Square, Hizbullah supporters and the Christian followers of Aoun erected a large Christmas tree illuminated with bulbs in the opposition colors of yellow, orange, and green.[33] A few dozen meters away, a coalition of pro-government anti-Syrian parties known as the March 14 movement set up a line of 12 Christmas trees to commemorate prominent critics of Damascus who had been killed in mysterious circumstances in recent years. The names of these "martyrs of the Cedar Revolution" adorned several trees.

The stalemate between the pro- and antigovernment factions led each to adapt new tactics, including spreading their messages via billboards and other types of advertisements. The opposition and the government launched campaigns to boost their cause across radio airwaves, on television networks, and on billboards in and around Beirut. With the sit-ins occupying the two main squares of downtown Beirut, the pro-Syrian opposition also began to pressure the government through visual critiques. For example, protesters hung enormous posters and banners featuring government leaders and their allies, the most important being a poster showing Siniora greeting U.S. Secretary of State Condoleezza Rice with a hug. The poster read, "Thank you for your patience Condi; some of our children are still alive," a reminder of what was described as the "wavering position" of the government in the face of the "American and Zionist" enemy.[34]

The Hizbullah leadership could not control its followers completely, so occasional spasms of violence erupted, but were doused quickly with calls for calm. For example, clashes erupted in January 2007 in the Arab University cafeteria between Sunni and Shiite students. The fighting followed on the heels of Hizbullah-led opposition protests in Beirut on 23 January, right before the Paris III international donor's conference for Lebanon's reconstruction, scheduled to begin on 25 January. The fighting spread from the university to other (Sunni and Shiite) neighborhoods of the capital. Rioters armed with sticks torched cars and tires. Television stations run by both camps blamed the other for the violence. Leaders of both sides appealed for calm. Hassan Nasrallah, who insisted that he did not want Lebanon to tumble into civil war, went on television in the evening to tell followers that it was a "religious duty" to get off the streets and to allow security forces to maintain order. The clashes illustrate how nonviolent resistance can, at times, explode into violence.[35] Once violence occurs, however, the objective often becomes muddied, the level of popular participation diminishes, and the legitimacy of the campaign is called into question as people become fixated on security concerns rather than the underlying (political, social, and economic) issues of the resistance.

According to the International Crisis Group, Hizbullah by and large attempted to moderate sectarian tensions, preferring a step-by-step escalation of its campaign and use of nonviolent protest. It called for "demonstrations in December 2006, a general strike in January 2007 and civil disobedience in March, hoping [that] the government would be compelled to give in. It strived to maintain ties to Sunni Islamists and include Sunnis in its rallies."[36] Despite recurrent talk of the possibility of a new civil war pitting Christians against each other or the expansion of Sunni-Shiite conflict from Iraq into Lebanon, the situation remained calm, if tense, throughout most of 2007.[37] The last civil war was still fresh in the minds of many Lebanese political leaders. Hassan Nasrallah had often stated that Hizbullah's weapons were solely for fighting Israel and would not to be used against fellow Lebanese.

In the meantime, while trying to keep the situation in hand, both sides also took steps to cement their positions. The government continued to assert its legitimacy and refused to back down, much less resign, and the opposition continued to insist on the government's resignation. With the Shiite ministers' resignations and the Shiite community no longer represented in the government, the opposition considered the Siniora government to be illegitimate. The opposition blocked presidential elections at the end of Emile Lahoud's term in November 2007 despite having reached agreement on a compromise candidate; it argued that an agreement on a new government should precede the elections and demanded that new legislative elections be based on a different electoral law (with the hope of winning a majority in those elections). The stalemate was compounded by the fact that each side was supported by regional or international powers. France, Saudi Arabia, and the United States backed the government, seeing in it a burgeoning of Lebanese democracy beyond the reach of Syria. The opposition relied on Iranian and Syrian support. It could therefore be argued that the standoff represented a confrontation, played out on Lebanese soil, between the Bush administration and its allies on the one hand, and Iran and Syria, on the other.[38]

The low-intensity conflict lasted into summer 2007, through the fall, and into early 2008.[39] It remained clear, however, that Hizbullah was still trying to force the hand of the government without resorting to violence. Regardless, long-simmering tensions between Sunnis and Shiites increasingly turned into spurts of violence, raising fears of an Iraqi-style sectarian outburst. The clashes were largely limited to street fights, occurring roughly every few weeks over the last several months of 2007. In January 2008, protestors blocked roads leading to the airport, setting fire to garbage bins and tires, while skirmishes erupted between members of the Sunni and Shiite communities. A strike called by the General Confederation of Workers of Lebanon (known by its French acronym, CGTL), a union close to the opposition, further fanned the flames.[40]

On January 27, 2008, protests over power cuts exploded in violence in Dahiya, Beirut's southern suburbs, a stronghold of Hizbullah.[41] Amal and Hizbullah appealed for calm and urged the demonstrators to go home and allow security forces to restore order. Seven people were killed, the highest death toll to date from the street disturbances. The riots, the worst since January 2007, prompted the army to impose a (brief) curfew for the first time since the end of the 1975–1990 civil war. These events foreshadowed what was to come in May 2008.

Transition to Armed Resistance

As the standoff between the opposition and the government continued into 2008, it appeared to some observers that the two parties might be prepared to wait each other out until legislative elections scheduled for 2009.[42] Such speculation would fall by the wayside in May 2008 because of the decision by the Siniora government to reassign Brig. Gen. Wafiq Shuqair, the airport security chief said to be close to Hizbullah, and to investigate and dismantle the party's telecommunications network.

Hizbullah's communications network had been the subject of discussion in cabinet meetings in August 2007, after which the telecommunications minister slammed the network as a "state violation." He also said, however, that the government was "determined to protect the resistance and the symbols of the resistance from the Israeli enemy but the information that we gathered about the network does not follow this logic."[43] The cabinet considered authorizing a security and technical team to sever the lines of the phone network, but no further actions were taken until May 6, 2008, when the government announced its decision to investigate the network. It accused Hizbullah of violating the country's sovereignty by operating its own communications network and installing surveillance cameras at the Beirut airport. Hizbullah insisted that the network was needed for security purposes and as part of its resistance struggle against Israel; it asserted that the network had played a major role in the success of its war with Israel in 2006. On 5 May, Naim Qassem of Hizbullah stated, "This network is part of our military arsenal and the council of ministers cannot deprive us of it or prevent us from defending the country, whether it pleases some or not."[44]

In a repetition of the events of January, the CGTL had called for a strike on 7 May to protest the cost of living.[45] On this same day, militants loyal to the Hizbullah-led opposition blocked roads to deny access to Beirut's sea and air ports. The violent protests and accompanying strike paralyzed Beirut International Airport (which would remain closed for a week). On 8 May, the violence sparked by Shiite groups spread outside the capital to the eastern Bekaa Valley. In a television interview that day, Hassan Nasrallah said, "The [government's] decisions are tantamount to a declaration of war and the start of a war on behalf of the United States and Israel." He added that the government was planning to hand over control of the airport to the CIA or Mossad, the Israeli secret service. "We are not seeking war with anyone, but the government must go back on its decision and we are being patient." Nasrallah then told the Lebanese people, unconsciously echoing U.S. president George W. Bush: "You are with us or against us."[46] Although Nasrallah did not explicitly call on his supporters to take up arms against the government or against Sunnis in particular, his statement was seen by his supporters as just such an order.

Fighting, with Hizbullah and Amal on one side and Sunni groups on the other, intensified minutes after Nasrallah's statement. On 9 May, Hizbullah gunmen, unchallenged by the army, seized control of West Beirut in a telling demonstration of the organization's military prowess. In short order, they routed groups allied with the al-Mustaqbal movement, led by Saad Hariri, the majority leader in parliament. Hizbullah also forced the closure of all the media outlets belonging to Hariri's family. The Shiite fighters' success in three days of street battles dramatically strengthened the hand of the Hizbullah-led opposition in its political struggle with pro-Western factions over who would guide the country. The Lebanese Army, wary of fragmenting its ranks, remained neutral. Nevertheless, some observers questioned the army's claim of neutrality when it refrained from intervening as Shiite militants surged into West Beirut, trouncing their opponents.[47] The army's performance suggests instead that the better-armed Hizbullah had struck a deal with military leaders.[48] The army had in essence acquiesced to Hizbullah's conquest of territory.

Hizbullah signaled that it was not looking for a bloody showdown by soon pulling back from Sunni areas. It is important to note that Hizbullah did not attempt to occupy Christian areas of Beirut. The order to retreat was given on May 10 after the Lebanese Army revoked the government's decision and reinstated Brig. Gen. Shuqair to his post in the airport and vowed to investigate (but do no harm to) Hizbullah's telecommunications network. After fighting stopped in Beirut, the strife moved to the Druze heartland in the Shuf Mountains and to the north, particularly to the port city of Tripoli, where sectarian tensions were rife between the local Sunnis and Alawites allied with Hizbullah.

By the time the government had reversed its two controversial decisions on 14 May, the conflict had left more than 65 people dead and more than 250 wounded. The consequences for Lebanon appeared to be dire. The fighting had terrified much of the population and created a dangerous precedent: Hizbullah had used its military might against the very civilians that it had claimed to be protecting. The main targets of its attack seemed to be Sunni media outlets and citizens. The *New York Times* reported that Sunni individuals had been kidnapped and tortured for several days "and insulted with sectarian taunts."[49] This use of force is not likely to be forgotten, meaning that it could come back to haunt Hizbullah in the future. There is fear and loathing of Hizbullah in Sunni Beirut and in many other Lebanese communities. The crisis left a large segment of Christians feeling marginalized, without a say in the future of the country,[50] and the Sunnis bitter over the shift in power toward Hizbullah. Lebanon's political process was no longer deadlocked, but Hizbullah's armed disobedience reopened the gate to sectarian conflict.[51]

Hizbullah resorted to violence to dramatically demonstrate the level of its opposition to two government decisions, to mobilize its supporters, and to force the government's hand when it felt that nonviolent resistance was getting it nowhere and inaction might cause it losses. Indeed, violence may have a more immediate "shock value" than nonviolent resistance or civil disobedience, but shock may not always translate into strategic success in the long term. In this case, however, Hizbullah's use of violence against domestic targets was, for the near future, tactically successful as evidenced by the composition of the cabinet announced July 11, 2008 and headed by Siniora, whom President Michel Suleiman (elected in late May) reappointed. Having obtained 11 seats in the cabinet, Hizbullah finally gained control of one-third of the body.

This was, however, a short term gain. The outcome of the 2009 parliamentary elections demonstrated the Sunni and Christian fear of a Hizbullah dominated Lebanon. March 14 won 71 seats of the 128 seat parliament, including two cooperating independents and March 8 was left with only 57 seats. With the Parliament divided between the March 14 and March 8 groups, the 2009 elections saw the emergence of an independent block supported by President Suleiman.[52]

Hizbullah's swift routing of opponents during the deadly street fighting spawned an ominous backlash within Lebanon's Sunni community fed by anger, humiliation, and fear. Indeed, "while the Shiite movements' [Amal and Hizbullah] objectives appeared primarily political, the behavior of their rank and file struck out a clear sectarian chord: armed militants hurled abuse at key Sunni religious symbols."[53] During the week of fighting, the influence of moderate Sunni leaders,

including Saad al-Hariri, dwindled, as their constituents shifted toward more militant groups—such as al-Qaida and its sympathizers—whom they perceived as a
better source of protection against the powerful Hizbullah. As fighting flared in
Beirut, jihadist Web sites buzzed with speculation about civil war in Lebanon and
possibilities of intervention.

Hizbullah's offensive in Beirut may have been intended only as a brief, but potent
shock to discourage the Lebanese government from tampering with the infrastructure of its military wing, but it also delivered a blow to the Shiite party's long-
standing efforts to avoid intra-Muslim discord. According to Timur Goksel, the
former head of UNIFIL, Hizbullah strengthened its position in domestic politics
"but has been considerably weakened in its relations with other major sects," that
is, the Druze, Christians, and Sunnis, "by crossing what has been sacrosanct red
lines of not violating the others' turfs and symbols." In addition, Hizbullah's relations with the military were reported to have "somewhat soured," as some army
officers, particularly those who are not Shiite, felt that the army had lost "considerable prestige" because of the conflict.[54]

Conclusion

In practice, Hizbullah has used techniques of violent and nonviolent resistance
in pursuit of its political goals. Its choices appear to be based on a consideration
of practical outcomes, in other words, their effectiveness as techniques of resistance. Over the years, Hizbullah had come to believe that the best way to deal with
Israel was the biblical "eye for an eye" and the creation of a "balance of terror,"[55]
whereas the domestic political context required a nonviolent form of resistance,
defined as steadfastness by Ayatollahs Fadlallah and Shams al-Din.

The outcomes of resistance for Hizbullah are different types of legitimacy tied
to its success among its constituents, ranging from its own party members to the
Lebanese citizenry at large. The distinction in practice between sumud and violent
resistance established Hizbullah's legitimacy as an anti-imperialist organization
and as opponents of Israeli occupation. By choosing nonviolent methods within
Lebanon, Hizbullah obtained legitimacy as a serious political actor, in addition
to being a national resistance group. By crossing the boundary from sumud into
violence within the context of domestic politics, however, Hizbullah may have not
only diminished its legitimacy as a political actor, but simultaneously weakened its
legitimacy as an organization whose mission is to resist Israel. It became less certain that Hizbullah's weapons were for defending Lebanon against Israel after its
members had been directed them against fellow Lebanese.

In May 2008, Hizbullah went from being a national resistance group, representative of all Lebanese, to being another sectarian party, in this case, one representative of the Shiite community. Its purpose is now to maximize the power of
the Shiite community, similar to other Lebanese sectarian groups that form coalitions with other sectarian groups to advance the objectives of their communities.
Hizbullah thus justified the government's accusations that the organization "far
from representing a national resistance, had become a cover for a Shiite militia."[56]

The agreement reached in Doha, Qatar, on May 21, 2008 between the leaders
of the Lebanese opposition and the government suggests that violence paid off for
Hizbullah. All the demands it presented to the government through nonviolent
resistance since November 2006 were met: it gained legitimacy essentially as a state
within the state[57] as well as veto power in the cabinet and consequently protection

against demilitarization and incorporation into the Lebanese Army (a fate that befell other groups in Lebanon after the Ta'if agreement). Hizbullah's victory was also illustrated in the election of Michel Suleiman to the presidency; he is known to be sympathetic toward Hizbullah and as a former commander of the Lebanese Army had cooperated with it. Although Hizbullah may have won the military battle, it lost the war for the hearts and minds of some segments of the Lebanese population. This has been confirmed by the 2009 elections where fear of a Hizbullah win has led Christians to make a decisive vote against the organization and its allies. Hizbullah's experiment with nonviolent resistance suggests a tactical—but less than strategic—embrace of this form of resistance. Although Hizbullah had in the past appeared to recognize the value of not creating domestic enemies by turning its weapons against fellow Lebanese, its commitment to nonviolent means eventually gave way to violent opportunism.[58] In the meantime, Hizbullah has apparently not considered the potential role that nonviolent civil resistance could play in its territorial dispute with Israel.

Notes

The author wishes to express her gratitude to Dr. Wesley R. Dean for his helpful suggestions during the drafting of this chapter.

1. According to a report by the Congressional Research Service, "In 1995, the President identified...Hezbollah as Specially Designated Terrorists (SDT)....Subsequent legislative and executive initiatives led to the creation of several other lists. Enactment of the Anti-Terrorism and Effective Death Penalty Act of 1996, which also authorizes deportation or exclusion from entry into the United States, generated the Foreign Terrorist Organization (FTO) list. The President issued an executive order to create the Specially Designated Global Terrorists (SDGT) list in the wake of events of September 11, 2001. All these lists were subsequently consolidated into one Specially Designated Nationals and Blocked Persons list (the 'SDN list'), administered by the Department of the Treasury's Office of Foreign Assets Control in 2002....Hezbollah, or individuals associated with [it] are on each of the lists." See "Lebanon: The Israel-Hamas-Hezbollah Conflict," August 2006, http://fpc.state.gov/documents/organization/71845.pdf.

    Canada and Australia added Hizbullah to their lists of terrorist organizations in December 2002 and June 2003, respectively. Despite U.S. pressure and the United Kingdom and the Netherlands's insistence, the European Union has so far refused to include Hizbullah on its list of terrorist organizations. Hizbullah says it opposes terrorism and denounced the September 11 attacks.

2. Naim Qassem, *Hizbullah: The Story from Within* (London: Saqi Books, 2005), 98.

3. Iran and Syria were adversely affected economically and militarily by the demise of the Soviet Union.

4. During the Lebanese civil war, Nasrallah first joined Amal but later decided to join Hizbullah. He had studied Islamic jurisprudence in Iraq in the 1970s and in Iran in the 1980s. The Council on Foreign Relations' biography of Nasrallah argues that he lacked the credentials of his predecessors when he was elected secretary-general and that his appointment had ruffled feathers within the organization. Nevertheless, he was able to win "broad grassroots support by cultivating a social welfare network that provided schools, clinics, and housing in the predominantly Shiite parts of Lebanon." Council on Foreign Relations, "Background—Profile: Hassan Nasrallah," www.cfr.org/publication/11132. Nasrallah's stature in Lebanon and the Arab world grew in 1997, when his eighteen-year-old son, Hadi, died in combat. His popularity further increased after the Israeli withdrawal from southern Lebanon in 2000. Also in 2000,

however, his standing began to decline among certain segments of the Lebanese population who did not approve of Hizbullah's operations in the Shabaa farms area against Israeli forces. His appeal among Sunni and Christian groups took a further hit in 2006 after the large economic losses suffered by Lebanon following Israel's military retaliation for Hizbullah's kidnapping of Israeli soldiers along the border in July 2006.

5. Mona Harb and R. Leenders, "Know Thy Enemy: Hizbullah and the Politics of Perception," *Third World Quarterly* 25, no. 5 (2005): 173–97.

6. Hizbullah and other opponents of Hariri's economic policies use the alliterative *al-hajar* (stone) versus *al-bashar* (people).

7. Naim Qassem refers to Musa al-Sadr as well as Fadlallah and Shams al-Din as the clerics who provided the ideological vision, capabilities, and belief in the need for action that would lead to the coalescing of groups to found Hizbullah. Qassem, *Hizbullah*, 14–17. I have previously argued that resistance lies at the core of Shiite identity and that the discourse on the issues of resistance, jihad, and martyrdom by Fadlallah and Shams al-Din had influenced Hizbullah. The Party of God incorporated this resistance discourse into its ethos and made it its defining attribute if not its raison d'être. Note that Hizbullah is simultaneously a nationalist and an anti-imperialist group. Resistance against occupation is seen as a moral and religious duty. It can take the peaceful form of *sumud* (steadfastness), or it can take shape as military struggle against the occupier. In the latter sense, it becomes a form of jihad. For more on this issue, see Rola el-Husseini, "Resistance, Jihad and Martyrdom in Contemporary Shi'a Thought," *Middle East Journal* 62, no. 3 (Summer 2008).

8. Muhammad Mahdi Shams al-Din, *Fiqh al-ʿUnf al Musallah* (Beirut: al-Mu'asasa al-Dawliah, 2001), 23 (emphasis added).

9. Ivan Strenski, "Sacrifice, Gift and the Social Logic of Muslim Human Bombers," *Terrorism and Political Violence* 15, no. 3 (Autumn 2003): 22.

10. According to Sazai Ozcelik and Ayse Dilek Ogretir, Muhammad "spent the initial 13 years [of his 23 years as a prophet] in Mecca. The Prophet fully adopted the way of active pacifism or nonviolence during this time. There were many...issues in Mecca at that time which could have developed into confrontation and violence. But, the Prophet Muhammad strictly limited his sphere to peaceful propagation of the word of God. This resulted in the call to Islam (*dawa*) that is performed by peaceful means. Even when in Mecca, the Quraysh [tribal] leaders were set to wage war against the Prophet, [but] the Prophet consciously selected the *hijra* (exodus) to Medina instead of reaction and retaliation. *Hijra* (migration) was a clear example of nonviolent activism. After the migration, his antagonists again took the unilateral decision to wage war against him....After the wars, the Prophet still preferred...peace [to] war and he signed a ten-year peace treaty known as Sulh al-Hudaybiya, and accepted all the conditions of his opponents." "Islamic Peace Paradigm and Islamic Peace Education: The Study of Islamic Nonviolence in Post–September 11 World," *Journal of Globalization for the Common Good:* http://lass.calumet.purdue.edu/cca/jgcg/2007/fa07/jgcg-fa07-ozcelik-ogretir.htm.

11. Joseph Alagha, *The Shifts in Hizbullah's Ideology* (Amsterdam: University of Amsterdam Press, 2006), 199.

12. The Ta'if agreement mandates the demobilization of Lebanese militias. In March 1991, as part of the accord's implementation, the main Lebanese militias were declared dissolved and their weapons confiscated. A large number of militia members were incorporated into the security apparatus of the Lebanese state, that is, into the army and internal security forces. Hizbullah refused to disband or disarm, arguing the need for its weapons until the implementation of UN Security Council Resolution 425 (March 1978), which calls for the immediate withdrawal of Israeli forces from Lebanon. For more on demobilization in postwar Lebanon, see Elizabeth Picard, *The Demobilization of the Lebanese Militias: Prospects for Lebanon* (Oxford: Centre for Lebanese Studies, 1999).

13. The "Qana massacre" is the name given to the shelling of a UN compound in April 1996 in which 106 civilians were killed after taking refuge there. The area is marked by a memorial. The same area was shelled again, in summer 2006, during the war between Hizbullah and Israel, resulting in the deaths of 28 civilians, 16 of whom were children, according to Human Rights Watch. See Human Rights Watch, "Israel/Lebanon: Qana Death Toll at 28," www.hrw.org/english/docs/2006/08/02/lebano13899.htm.

14. Hamas has tried to replicate the Hizbullah model to disastrous results, mostly because they have failed to appreciate that the two contexts—historical, cultural, and geostrategic are completely different.

15. Shabaa Farms is a 15-square-mile border region that remains under Israeli occupation. Lebanon and Syria claim that the area is Lebanese territory, but Israel and the United Nations assert that it is part of the Golan Heights and therefore Syrian territory. Israeli scholar Asher Kaufman argues that this situation flows from the clumsy way in which France delineated the Syrian-Lebanese border during the mandate years. After independence, both countries did nothing to rectify anomalies along the border. Syria had not formally accepted Lebanon's independence, and Lebanon was not interested in tending to this issue. Since 1920, maps have located the area within Syria. For all practical matters, however, the area was considered to be part of Lebanon. For more on this issue, see Asher Kaufman, "Who Owns the Shebaa Farms? Chronicle of a Territorial Dispute," *Middle East Journal* 56, no. 4 (2002).

16. For more on the Cedar Revolution, see the chapter by Rudy Jaafar and Maria Stephan in this volume.

17. Nicholas Noe asserts that the "withdrawal of Syrian troops and the ascendancy of a pro-western government in Beirut forced Nasrallah to broaden Hizbullah's participation, and appeal, in the Lebanese body politic. The reason, Nasrallah made clear with ever-greater emphasis, was simple. Hizbullah stands on two legs: resistance and public support for the resistance. Without both legs, Hizbullah and its core constituency of Lebanese Shia would find it next to impossible to function in Lebanon's unique (some say grossly inequitable) system of confessional checks and balances. Thus, in rapid succession it seemed, Hizbullah broke its long-standing self-prohibition against joining the government (to do so it also broke with tradition and sought a Lebanese, and not Iranian, fatwa)." "The Nasrallah Roadmap," 5 October 2007, www.mideastwire.com/downloads/The%20Nasrallah%20Roadmap.pdf.

    Joseph Alagha argues, "As long as the Syrians were in Lebanon, Hizbullah had no ambition to join the cabinet....However, the departure of Syrian troops from Lebanon in 2005 encouraged the Party of God to attempt to fill this political vacuum in order to influence the wording of the policy statements of the cabinet. And, in fact, this has been done rather successfully." "Lebanon: Hizbullah, A Progressive Islamic Party? Interview with Joseph Alagha," Religioscope, 17 May 2007, http://religion.info/english/interviews/article_317.shtml. Other reasons for joining the cabinet might include strengthening its legitimacy by joining a governing coalition for the first time, rather than only having parliamentary representation. This would send a different message to foreign powers and the international community. The party might also have been looking to extend its patronage networks through the use of the state apparatus and the bureaucracy.

18. The Blue Line is the border demarcation between Lebanon and Israel established by the cartography team of the United Nations to confirm Israel's withdrawal of forces in 2000. It is not the official border between the two countries established by the armistice of 1948 following the first Arab-Israeli war. Lebanon, Syria, and Hizbullah have not accepted the legality of the Blue Line because of the Shabaa farms issue.

19. In 2004 Nasrallah had presided over a prisoner swap in which, through German mediation, Israel released more than 400 Arab detainees in exchange for the remains of three Israeli soldiers and for an alleged spy that Hizbullah had lured into Lebanon and captured.

20. Under these unwritten rules of engagement, Shabaa Farms was seen by both sides as a legitimate theater for Hizbullah operations against Israel, and the two sides accepted the principle of "an eye for an eye." Hizbullah could expect such Israeli actions as fly-overs of Lebanese territory. See Daniel Sobelman, "New Rules of the Game: Israel and Hizbollah after the Withdrawal from Lebanon," Jaffee Center for Strategic Studies, Tel Aviv University, January 2004, 67.

21. More than 1,000 people (mostly civilians) died in Lebanon during the conflict, and several thousand were injured. About 1 million people were displaced and economic losses for Lebanon were estimated at $12 billion. In Israel, 43 civilians were killed, and tens of thousands were displaced. Economic losses were estimated at $4.8 billion. See "Israel/Hizbollah/Lebanon: Avoiding Renewed Conflict," ICG Middle East Report no. 59, November 2006, www.crisisgroup.org/home/index.cfm?id=4480&l=1.

22. The term *divine victory* is a pun on Nasrallah's name: in Arabic, Nasr means "victory," and Allah is God.

23. Augustus R. Norton, *Hezbollah: A Short History* (Princeton, NJ: Princeton University Press, 2007), 148.

24. According to a SOFRES poll in February 2008, 59 percent of Christians believe that Hizbullah's agenda is that of Iran. "Road to Ruin: Aoun's Popularity: History or Myth," www.nowlebanon.com/Library/Files/EnglishDocumentation/Other%20Documents/NOW-SR-Eng.pdf.

25. The poll was released by the Beirut Center for Research and Information and based on 800 adult Lebanese citizens surveyed July 24–26, 2006. For the full results, see "Lebanese Public Opinion," *Mideast Monitor*, September–November 2006, www.mideastmonitor.org/issues/0609/0609_6.htm.

26. Nicholas Blanford, "Israeli Strikes May Boost Hizbullah Base," *Christian Science Monitor*, 28 July 2006, www.csmonitor.com/2006/0728/p06s01-wome.html.

27. Aoun, a Maronite and former chief of staff of the Lebanese Army, had been appointed interim prime minister in September 1988 by President Amin Gemayel when the Lebanese legislature failed to elect a president before the expiration of Gemayel's term. As prime minister, Aoun was explicit in his opposition to Syrian control of Lebanon, repeatedly vowing to free Lebanon from foreign domination. Sacked as prime minister in 1989, after the Ta'if agreement, Aoun refused to stand down and instead launched a "war of liberation" against the Syrians that led to the death of thousands of civilians. After being bombed out of the presidential palace in Baabda, Aoun took refuge in the French embassy and then sought exile in France, where he remained until 7 May 2005. Aoun's return to Lebanon 11 days after the Syrian withdrawal marked a new beginning for his political career. For legislative elections held that month, Aoun entered into alliances with a number of former opponents, including some pro-Syrian politicians. Aoun's party, the Free Patriotic Movement (FPM), made a strong showing, winning 21 of the 58 contested seats, including almost all the seats in the Christian heartland. Aoun was one of the FPM candidates elected to the legislature. Along with Hizbullah, Aoun and his Free Patriotic Movement would form the core of the opposition against the government during the period between November 2006 and May 2008. Aoun signed a memorandum of understanding with Hizbullah in February 2006.

28. Nasrallah was voicing a common Lebanese sentiment. According to a poll published by the Beirut Center for Research and Information, more than 70 percent of Lebanese supported the formation of a national unity government and 68 percent liked the idea of early elections. Paul Salem, of the Carnegie Middle East Center in Beirut, observed that the credibility of Siniora's government had been damaged by the widespread perception of the summer conflict as a U.S.-sanctioned war. See Clancy Chassay, "Lebanese Call on Government To Quit over War," *Guardian*, 4 October 2006.

29. Gene Sharp, *The Politics of Nonviolent Action*, Part 2, Methods of Nonviolent Action (Boston: Porter Sargent, 1973).

30. The probe into the Hariri assassination also played a part in the resignations. The ongoing United Nations probe had implicated senior Syrian officials in the bombing, and Hizbullah hoped to protect its ally Syria.
31. Jim Quilty, "Winter of Lebanon's Discontent," *Middle East Report*, 26 January 2007, www.merip.org/mero/mero012607.html.
32. Hanin Ghaddar, "Tent City or Ghost City?" *Now Lebanon*, 19 July 2007, www.nowlebanon.com/NewsArticleDetails.aspx?ID=7204. The Associated Press would report in 2007, "The tents in downtown Beirut stand almost empty, their roofs newly reinforced with plastic covers for winter after the old ones fell apart. As stray cats snatch scraps of food, nearby shops and cafes starve for customers.... Gone are the hundreds of thousands of opposition activists who rallied at the camp in its first weeks, shouting 'down with Saniora' through loudspeakers. The maze of dozens of tents remains home to a skeleton staff of Hezbollah security agents and is surrounded by razor wire and armed troops to separate it from Saniora's office. Together they have turned downtown into a ghost town at night.... Now, people stay away for a range of reasons—the tent city is an eyesore, the traffic flow has been disrupted, and, of course, security concerns." Sam F. Ghattas, "A Year On, 'Tent City' Paralyzes Beirut," *San Francisco Chronicle*, December 1, 2007, www.sfisonline.com/cgi-bin/article.cgi?f=/n/a/2007/12/01/international/i003442S69.DTL&hw=backers&sc=359&sn=007
33. Yellow and green are the colors of the Hizbullah flag; orange is the symbol of the Free Patriotic Movement. It is said that the use of the color orange was inspired by the so-called Orange Revolution of 2004–2005 in Ukraine.
34. The reference to Rice's "patience" is a jab at the reluctance of the United States to call for a cease-fire in the 2006 war between Hizbullah and Israel. It is also a cheeky reference to her infamous comment on July 21, 2006 about "the birth pangs of a New Middle East" as Lebanon was being bombed.
35. Some factors that may contribute to an outbreak of violence in a nonviolent struggle are lack of organization and planning among participants in the nonviolent struggle; inclusion of individuals in the nonviolent struggle who do not understand the strategic reasons for maintaining nonviolent discipline; and a lack of training of participants in the nonviolent struggle. In this case, it is likely that all three factors were present.
36. "Hizbollah and the Lebanese Crisis," *ICG Middle East Report*, no. 69, October 2007, 2.
37. In contrast to the civil war of 1975–1990, the Christians are now divided. Some follow Aoun, and are therefore aligned with the Hizbullah opposition movement, and others follow traditional Christian leaders, such as former president Amin Gemayel, and are allied with the Siniora government.
38. According to Abraham Rabinovitch, Iran provided Hizbullah with $1.5 billion to compensate for losses suffered by fighters and civilians in the 2006 war. "Iran Strips Hezbollah Leader of Power," *Washington Times*, 18 December 2007. In contrast, the United States pledged $770 million in loans and grants to the government, and Saudi Arabia pledged $1.1 billion in aid for the reconstruction effort. Office of the Prime Minister, "Some of the Aid Comes with Strings Attached," January 26, 2007, www.rebuildlebanon.gov.lb/english/f/NewsArticle.asp?CNewsID=784. Note that no one has access to Hizbullah documents detailing the amount of help they receive from Iran. All available figures are based on speculation.
39. Parliamentary sessions to elect a new president would be cancelled or postponed 19 times before former army commander Michel Suleiman would be elected to the presidency on May 25, 2008, after a Qatar-brokered agreement between the Hizbullah-led opposition and government supporters.
40. The strike was aimed at forcing the government to raise the minimum wage—from 300,000 lira ($200) to 900,000 lira ($600)—and to address inflation. The wage demands were not met.

41. Power cuts are ubiquitous in Lebanon and are usually due to problems with the electrical grid or a lack of fuel for generators. Beirut tends to get more electricity than the rest of the country, but it still suffers from power outages.

42. A parliamentarian from the Future Movement group alluded to this. Interview with the author, Beirut, January 7, 2008.

43. Haaretz, "Lebanese Minister Slams Hezbollah Telephone Network," 29 August 2007, www.haaretz.com/hasen/spages/898840.html.

44. AFP, "Lebanon to Probe Hezbollah Telephone Network," 6 May 2008. In a speech on 25 May, Hassan Nasrallah threatened, "If anyone tries to disarm the resistance, we will fight him the way the martyrs fought in Karbala.... We will consider any hand that tries to seize our weapons an Israeli hand, and we will cut it off." Nicholas Noe, ed., *Voice of Hezbollah: The Statements of Sayyed Hassan Nasrallah* (London: Verso, 2007), 349.

45. The government would agree in September 2008 to an increase, though only from 300,000 lira ($200) to 500,000 lira (about $330) rather than to the requested 960,000 lira ($640).

46. Damien McElroy, "Hizbollah 'Ready for War' in Lebanon," *Telegraph*, May 8, 2005, www.telegraph.co.uk/news/worldnews/middleeast/lebanon/1938944/Hizbollah-%27ready-for-war%27-in-Lebanon.html.

47. According to Paul Salem, the director of the Carnegie Middle East Center, "The army has come under intense criticism for doing nothing to stop the onslaught by Hizbollah and its allied militias against civilian areas of the nation's capital and other locations and for simply picking up the pieces of what Hizbollah leaves in its wake. The army defended its inaction by admitting that if it engaged in internal political battles it would be in danger of splitting along sectarian lines, and that it needed to remain neutral among the competing political factions." "Hizbollah Attempts a Coup d'Etat," Carnegie Endowment for International Peace, May 2008, 2, www.carnegieendowment.org/files/salem_coup_final.pdf.

48. Hannah Allam, "Has Lebanon's Army Struck a Deal with Hezbollah?" McClatchy, May 12, 2008, www.mcclatchydc.com/251/story/36767.html.

49. Robert F. Worth and Nada Bakri, "Hezbollah Ignites a Sectarian Fuse in Lebanon," *New York Times*, May 18, 2008, www.nytimes.com/2008/05/18/world/middleeast/18lebanon.html?pagewanted=all. It is important to note that it was not the strategy or objective of Hizbullah to go after civilians; they went after the armed elements of the pro-government parties. However, groups allied with Hizbullah, such as Amal and the Syrian Social National Party, behaved in a more thuggish manner.

50. "The narrow victory scored by Aoun's candidate in the Matn by-election on 5 August 2007 showed the Christian community to be deeply divided, with both sides claiming moral victory. Judging by the numbers, support for the FPM declined (with it receiving one-third less votes than in 2005 election results), while support for the pro-government Christian camp increased (by one-third)." Heiko Wimmen, "Rallying around the Renegade," www.merip.org/mero/mero082707.html.

51. Lebanese columnist Michael Young maintains, "By so foolishly taking over Beirut militarily, the party only scared the other communities into sustained hostility. The two decisions the government went back on were decisions it could never have implemented anyway, so Hizbullah effectively revealed its coup plan at an inopportune time and for little gain.... Its weapons have become a subject of legitimate national discussion." "Something Radically New after Doha," *Daily Star*, May 22, 2008, http://michaelyoungscolumns.blogspot.com/2008/05/something-radically-new-after-doha.html. That Hizbullah's action might lead to civil war has been seconded by local scholars, including Paul Salem, who said "it is also not certain that the security situation can be brought back in hand or whether the devil of sectarian civil war has already been let out of the bottle and cannot be put back again." Hizbollah Attempts a Coup d'Etat," Carnegie Endowment for International Peace, Web Commentary, www.carnegieendowment.org/

files/salem_coup_final.pdf. Another local scholar, Usama Safa, sees the May events as setting a "dangerous precedent": "This means that in the future the opposition could resort to the same violence or threaten to do so." See Al-Arabiya, "Opposition Ends Blockade, Airport Set to Reopen, www.alarabiya.net/articles/2008/05/15/49872.html.

52. In their negotiations to form a government, March 14 and March 8 have effectively brought into being a third party lead by President Michel Suleiman and consisting of five ministers loyal to him. This group will have the opportunity to sway decisions for March 14, or to veto for Hezbollah. Suleiman is effectively the main winner of these elections.

53. "Lebanon: Hizbollah's Weapons Turn Inward," *ICG Middle East Briefing*, no. 23, May 15, 2008, 2

54. Brenda Gazzar, "Lebanese MP: Hezbollah Was Smart To Halt Offensive," *Jerusalem Post*, 19 May 2008. The *New York Times* quotes Paul Salem as saying, "The Sunni-Shiite conflict is in the open now, it's been triggered and operationalized....This is a deep wound, and it's going to have serious repercussions if it's not immediately and seriously addressed." Worth and Bakri, "Sectarian Fuse."

55. Hassan Nasrallah used the expression *balance of terror* to refer to his organization's military buildup along the border with Israel. Should Israel attack Lebanon, Hizbullah would use its weapons against the Jewish state. According to one observer, "that strategic parity...[had] deterred Israel from launching heavy reprisals for Hizballah's Shebaa Farms attacks and other incidents along the border," that is, until summer 2006. See Nicholas Blanford, "Hizballah in the Firing Line," *MERIP Report*, April 2003, www.merip.org/mero/mero042803.html.

56. "Hizbollah and the Lebanese Crisis," 3. Other analysts, including Paul Salem, seem to share this perspective.

57. Hizbullah has its own army and telecommunications system outside the supervision of the state in addition to a network of welfare services. A state traditionally has the monopoly of violence on its territory, but the Lebanese government certainly does not. Hizbullah has taken over that role. That makes Hizbullah a state within the (weak) Lebanese state.

58. Hizbullah's weapons became problematic after the Israeli withdrawal in 2000 and are more so today after their use against other Lebanese. The moment Hizbullah used its weapons internally, it lost the moral high ground.

17

Winning the Mainstream: Arba Imahot, the Four Mothers Movement in Israel

Tamar Hermann

If one accepts the "rational" nature of adopting one form of resistance over another, it is understandable that groups might advocate nonviolent resistance but at the same time—under different conditions—support the right of self-defense through military means. This, indeed, was the case with Arba Imahot, the Israeli Four Mothers movement.[1] Its members used nonviolent means to promote the withdrawal of the Israel Defense Forces (IDF) from south Lebanon and advocated moving from military to diplomatic means to achieve peace and stability in the area. Neither the founders of the movement nor its agenda, however, included anti-militaristic components or called for IDF soldiers to invoke conscientious objection to serving beyond the international border with Lebanon. The Four Mothers based their opposition to the IDF presence in Lebanon on its reading of the deployment as being first and foremost much too costly in terms of soldiers' lives as well as unhelpful, and even counterproductive, in safeguarding Israel's northern border and territory.

The use of nonviolent means was primarily the result of a sober reading of available options. Israel's national ethos and the nature of its security challenges necessitated that the movement's strategy be nonviolent at its core, because otherwise its chances of catching on and gaining political influence would have been nil. In other words, under the circumstances, only a strong adherence to nonviolent means could bring the masses on board, generate positive coverage by the media, and create alliances with mainstream politicians who also supported withdrawal from Lebanon.

Politics and Peace Activism in the Late 1990s

Spring 1997, when the Four Mothers movement emerged, was not a propitious moment for launching a new grassroots peace initiative in Israel. At that time, the prevailing wisdom had it that the Oslo peace process was a dead end. Furthermore, and strongly connected to this view, the right-wing Likud Party under the leadership of Benjamin Netanyahu had won national elections about a year before by promoting the idea that Israel's military forces and capabilities were the country's only "insurance policy." It seemed that the Israeli public had turned its back not only on the Labor Party, but also on the pro-peace agenda that it had tried to promote since the launching of the Oslo process in August 1993.

On another level, the second half of the 1990s found the Israeli peace movement virtually in shambles. It had been "demobilized" to a large extent after the government became involved in the Oslo peace process. As time passed, however, the increasing number of Palestinian attacks in Israel and the halting nature of the peace process led many veteran activists to gradually lose their belief in the possibility of ever attaining a just resolution of the conflict. The peace organizations that remained active and a number of new peace groups that emerged in the late 1990s were much more disapproving of Israeli policies in the occupied territories than previously and thus "lost" the Israeli mainstream.

In addition, the situation on the Lebanese front did not look promising in terms of a dovish position gaining widespread support among Israelis. Having taken over southern Lebanon in 1982, the IDF had by 1985 withdrawn most of its forces with the exception of deployments in a "security zone" along the border with Israel. For more than a decade, leaders of all the mainstream Israeli parties (including Labor) and security experts presented the IDF presence in southern Lebanon as an absolute necessity for safeguarding the villages and towns of northern Israel. These areas were often rocketed from Lebanon by Hizbullah's militia.

Although Hizbullah presented its struggle against the presence of the IDF on Lebanese soil as a struggle of national liberation and resistance, in Israel these attacks were viewed as a clear sign of Hizbullah's hostile intentions. This interpretation was particularly appealing to most Israeli Jews, because Hizbullah's leadership often maintained that their own struggle was meant to assist the struggle of the Palestinians in the occupied territories. This association signaled to many in Israel that a pullout would not put an end to the fire to the north; hostilities would continue along the Lebanese border until the signing of an Israeli-Palestinian agreement, which at that time looked to be an impossibility. Thus in April 1996, following heavy rocketing by Hizbullah of northern Israel, the Labor government launched Operation Grapes of Wrath.[2] Unlike the 1982 invasion of Lebanon, no significant public opposition emerged in Israel to the 1996 campaign.

The growing number of Israeli soldiers wounded or killed in southern Lebanon in the mid-1990s eventually, however, produced a backlash in Israeli public opinion. Slowly but surely, people began to doubt the military necessity and advantage of the IDF presence there. These doubts came to a head in February 1997, when two IDF helicopters carrying 73 soldiers and crewmembers collided en route to Lebanon. The national outpouring of grief was immense. The accident encouraged the emergence of a significant grassroots campaign for complete withdrawal. The Four Mothers movement took the lead in opposing the Israeli presence in Lebanon.

Origin and Agenda

Following the helicopter accident, on July 5, 1997, Yaffa Arbel, Rachel Ben Dor, Ronit Nachmias, and Miri Sela announced the establishment of Arba Imahot, the Four Mothers. All four women, in their forties, were residents of kibbutzim in the north and mothers of soldiers serving in IDF elite units in Lebanon.[3] Their sons had studied together at the same high school; one of their classmates had been killed in the helicopter collision. The "original" mothers' primary motivation was, therefore, highly personal. Through their actions, they basically hoped to protect their own sons, and at the same time, other Israelis' sons posted in Lebanon. Their message pointed the finger at the government elites' responsibility, in their view, for the unnecessary loss of young life, which they severely criticized as a pagan human sacrifice:

> The politicians are shushing the home front by systematically sacrificing our sons to this Moloch [a Canaanite deity to which, by the Bible, children were sacrificed]. They send our sons there in order to sedate and hush Israeli public opinion. I have never understood the difference between killed soldiers and killed civilians. Why is the soldiers' blood so much cheaper than that of the civilians'.[4]

The mothers' personal motivation, along with their living near the Lebanese border, formed a double-edged sword: on one side, it invested the Four Mothers' activities with a strong sense of credibility, but on the other, it cast doubts on their ability to judge the situation from a strategically objective, or rational, perspective. This reservation was fueled by the often-emotional way in which the movement's founders expressed themselves and by their insistence that their criticism of the government's policy was "not political" but came "out of their womb."[5]

Two of the four founders had no previous experience in the political arena or in peace activism. Rachel Ben Dor, later the group's chair, and Miri Sela had participated in Women in Black anti-occupation vigils.[6] The influence of this prior activism on the Four Mothers' agenda and activities was noticeable from the start: on the one hand, the new movement adopted the nonviolent vigil methods that had served Women in Black well; on the other hand, however, the founders of the Four Mothers campaign demonstrated that they had also learned lessons from Women in Black's less-than-optimal strategic and tactical choices.

First, the Four Mothers made the decision to open the movement's door to male activists, thereby avoiding the negative image of being perceived as "radical feminists." Second, they avoided adopting a posture of ideological opposition vis-à-vis the Israeli mainstream, which cherishes the IDF and puts its trust in the military superiority of Israel. The movement therefore never committed itself to ethical nonviolence nor did it express reservations toward the military. In fact, although the Four Mothers were intuitively considered an integral element of the Israeli peace movement by many, in reality they were not, socially or ideologically, part of it. For example, the Four Mothers had no explicit connection to the Palestinian issue, to the occupation of the Palestinian territories, or to any other related matters traditionally at the heart of the various Israeli peace organizations' activities.[7]

During almost three years of activity, the sole item on the Four Mothers movement's agenda was "Israel's unilateral withdrawal from its self-declared security zone in Southern Lebanon."[8] Movement members sought to pressure the government to act on its pledge of 1 April 1, 1998 to abide by UN Security Council Resolution 425, which called for Israel's withdrawal in compliance with international law. It is important to note that at no stage did the Four Mothers campaign propose the means by which unilateral withdrawal should take place, such as without causing many casualties or creating turbulence in the security zone because of the presence of Lebanese militias there that had collaborated with the IDF forces. Furthermore, in order to mobilize maximum public support, its leaders always tried, albeit not so successfully, to avoid being painted with a particular political brush. Thus, on its Web site, the organization declared, "The Four Mothers Movement is unique in the country, a truly grassroots organization, not affiliated with any party, drawing supporters from across the political spectrum. While retaining the name the Four Mothers, the movement now includes a variety of concerned citizens: women and men, married and single, with or without children, students, and ex-soldiers, some of whom have themselves served in Lebanon."[9]

In their well-focused effort to generate pressure on the government to pull out of the "Lebanese mud," the Four Mothers were willing to create political alliances with every potentially influential group or party. For example, they addressed in writing the Kokhav Yair Forum (Hug Kokhav Yair), a highly eclectic group of professional politicians from the left and the right, bringing together members of the Knesset Yossi Beilin (Labor, later Meretz) and Haim Ramon (Labor) as well as Gideon Ezra and Michael Eitan (Likud), who were collaborating on a plan for unilateral withdrawal from Lebanon. In an apparent effort to remove doubts about their patriotism, the founders of the Four Mothers movement stated in their letter to this forum,

> We are residents of the north and mothers of soldiers serving in IDF elite units whom we educated to give everything [to the state] wherever they are asked to do so. We are confident that they will do their best in order to fulfill their orders. Yet we feel that they expect that someone will pull them out of the Lebanese mud in which they are forced to spend their early life.... We know that our sons will be encouraged by the realization that certain people at home are thinking creatively on how to pull the state out of this mess.[10]

In their ongoing effort to remain within the boundaries of the national security consensus, the Four Mothers never, as mentioned above, challenged universal conscription or advocated conscientious objection or refusal to serve in Lebanon.[11] Rachel Ben Dor openly stated the group's allegiance to mainstream thought on the role of the military in Israel: "Naturally we taught our sons that they should serve in combat units and, in general, that when in service one should do one's best, including becoming officers."[12]

Following to a great extent in the footsteps of Mothers against Silence (Imahot Neged Shtika)—which in the early 1980s had also called for the IDF's withdrawal from Lebanon—the founders of the Four Mothers used their maternal status as a political asset.[13] In addition to emphasizing that their protest was maternally motivated, not ideologically driven, the Four Mothers indeed tried to avoid being stigmatized as feminists. This meant that they sometimes butted heads with feminist peace groups that resented the organization's focus on the mother motif rather than a feminist negation of the use of military force. As noted in a *Ha'aretz* article,

> The concern of mothers for their sons is a human, not a feminist issue.... Presenting the mothers' struggle for a solution to this problem [Israel's ongoing military presence in Lebanon] as a feminist one is cynical and short-sighted or a scheme to divert public attention away from the real aim—withdrawal from Lebanon—to a marginal one.... The Lebanon problem should concern the public in general, not only mothers and women. Unfortunately, this is not the case.... The fact that the protestors are mothers of soldiers serving on the front lines who are expressing their personal worries, does not weaken their principal argument against Israel's presence in Lebanon nor rule out their right to protest and demonstrate.[14]

Strategy and Activities

The first action taken by the Four Mothers was a small vigil close to the Israel-Lebanon border to protest the Israeli government's failure to implement a 1985 promise to pull out of Lebanon and the consequences of the "silent war" going on there, exacting the lives of hundreds of Israeli soldiers and unknown numbers of Lebanese.[15] That the Four Mothers were expressing dissatisfaction shared by many other Israelis helps to explain why their protest attracted so much local and international media attention.[16] In a few weeks, more than 25,000 Israeli Jews of different political views had signed the movement's petition calling for the IDF's immediate withdrawal from Lebanon.

The number and scope of the group's vigils, held mostly near major intersections, grew rapidly. Participants were primarily secular, middle-class, middle-aged, center and left-of-center voters; many belonged to a kibbutz. Women tended to be overrepresented in these and other Four Mothers' activities. In other words, despite its rather consensual message, the Four Mothers movement failed—like most other and less-conformist Israeli peace organizations—to reach out to Arabs, the religious community, the lower classes, supporters of the right-wing parties, and young people.

Four Mothers protestors distributed stickers that read, "Leave Lebanon Peacefully." This decision followed the same logic in favor of simplicity that had led Women in Black to adhere to a single slogan: "End the Occupation." Other activities were more creative. One nonviolent action involved stretching a green cloth along the Israeli-Lebanese border to symbolically "re-demarcate" the boundary between the two countries that had been practically erased by the continual post-1982 IDF presence on Lebanese soil.[17] The vigils grew into larger demonstrations across the country and included protests outside of Defense Ministry headquarters in Tel Aviv whenever a soldier was killed in Lebanon. The movement's small, self-elected leaders—its founders—made the decisions on where and when to hold protests as well as the type of activity selected. This mode of decision making later would be attacked by disgruntled members accusing the Four Mothers' leaders of antidemocratic modes of operation. The original leaders disseminated information about upcoming activities via the Internet and social networks as well as through newspapers advertisements, which were financed by the movement's supporters and anonymous donors.[18]

The Four Mothers' vigils and other activities were totally nonviolent, probably purposely because of the group's desire to remain within and palatable to the mainstream. The "other side"—the police as well as the movement's opponents in the political center and on the right who considered unilateral withdrawal a mistaken and dangerous idea—played by the same rules and avoided the use of actual or verbal violent means. Thus, unlike Women in Black protestors, Four Mothers demonstrators never faced police aggression or extremely antagonistic reactions from passersby.

Unlike many Israeli peace organizations, which usually remained small and politically marginal, without access to top decision makers, the Four Mothers movement, with its tens of thousands of supporters and consensual agenda, found the doors of prominent politicians open. In fact, in terms of accessibility to leading figures, it proved more effective than Peace Now, a significantly larger, ideologically more sound and long-lived movement. Four Mothers representatives were granted appointments with President Ezer Weizman, Prime Minister Benjamin Netanyahu, incumbent defense minister Moshe Arens, and former defense minister

Yitzhak Mordechai (who agreed to meet only reluctantly). The delegation also met with most cabinet ministers, various foreign ambassadors and representatives from the U.S. State Department, French and British foreign ministries, and the United Nations. They presented their petition to U.S. President Bill Clinton during his visit to Israel in December 1998. Four Mothers' representatives managed to meet with more than 80 of the 120 members of the Knesset.

One of the movement's strongest supporters and advocates was Labor MK Yossi Beilin, who openly expressed his solidarity with the movement; he later insinuated that the group had taken off because of his encouragement and support, a contested claim best viewed vis-à-vis Beilin's consistently low popularity. The Labor Party won elections in 1999, with Ehud Barak becoming prime minister. Immediately after the election, the Four Mothers presented Barak with their petition, signed by tens of thousands of Israelis. During the campaign, Barak had promised to withdraw Israeli forces from Lebanon. Neither Labor nor Barak had personally embraced the Four Mothers' agenda, so their electoral victory can hardly be attributed to the movement's success in whipping up support. Once in office, Barak kept his campaign promise and withdrew Israeli forces from Lebanon, in June 2000.

Splits in the Movement

The Four Mothers movement, like so many peace groups before and since, quickly became bitterly divided, in this case less than a year after its emergence. On one side stood the four original founding mothers and their supporters from northern Israel; on the other coalesced a group from the political center and the center of the country. The disagreement between the two factions related to the movement's management and strategy. The former considered its management to be totally democratic, while the latter saw it as semi-dictatorial. Members of the dissatisfied faction felt that they were systematically being marginalized and therefore tried, to no avail, to establish their own movement to raise the same banner. The founders and leaders perceived the group's strategy and tone to be careful, while the opposing faction thought them to be too soft, "like kindergarten." The disaffected members never committed to the use of nonviolent means, although they never used violent ones perhaps because their protest never actually took off.

In early 1998, one of the activists said, "It is impossible for an entire movement to operate on the basis of emotions alone.... It should operate rationally, and challenge the decision makers using one argument after another.... We are also outraged by the fact that we have been turned into a group of professional national mourners.... We should move on and take the struggle off the street and into the offices of the decision makers."[19] The splintering tendency of grassroots movements as well as the frustration often involved in adherence to nonviolent methods were manifested in February 1999 in the creation of a new organization, Red Line, or Kav Adom, by former members of the Four Mothers. The Red Line organized its own demonstration for withdrawal from Lebanon in front of Defense Ministry headquarters in Tel Aviv. This protest was more confrontational and obstreperous than those of the Four Mothers movement; participants blocked the crowded street and even burned tires. The new organization's (male) speaker attacked the Four Mothers' softer tactics: "Soldiers are being killed, the army is 'drawing some lessons,' and the mothers only mourn. I left that movement and slammed the door behind me because it is toothless, it doesn't bark and it doesn't bite."[20]

The Red Line spokesperson promised that his new organization would not refrain from using any effective means to achieve their aim: "If we have to, we shall employ force, including harassment of politicians, banging on the doors of those who are responsible for the Lebanon fiasco, blocking traffic, and disrupting life all over the country and the daily routine of the decision makers."[21] Another activist from the same group, which quickly disappeared, also criticized the Four Mothers: "Their line is too soft, they give out flowers, plant trees, but stop nothing in Lebanon. We shall not let anyone shake hands with VIPs and say 'Thank you' anymore."[22]

The Four Mothers founders and their followers feared losing their foothold in the public discourse but insisted that the consensual tone and noncoercive nature of their activism be maintained. To deal with the opposition, the Four Mothers undertook some controversial actions. For example, in May 1999 they sent a message to Syrian president Hafiz al-Asad via a delegation of Israeli Arab MKs visiting Damascus; in it, they asked Asad to undertake confidence-building measures to pave the way for an IDF withdrawal from Lebanon.[23] As a practical measure, it was suggested in the letter that Asad give a green light to prominent Lebanese politicians to promise publicly that hostile activities against Israel would stop if and when it withdrew from Lebanon. There is no public record of a direct or indirect response from Asad.

In addition to strategic and operational disagreements, the Four Mothers also experienced internal tension over gender. At a certain point after the Four Mothers had gained in popularity and members, a number of men joined the movement. Shortly thereafter, the men were moved—or they pushed their way—to the top of the movement's informal hierarchy. As Orit Lavnin-Dgani, one of the angry and frustrated female activists put it, "As I was in the midst of my feminist empowerment process, I suffered a great deal from the fact that a man, and even worse, an ex-general, was put above me, a professional general who of course took control of the group just like that. I was told that this was the only way, because these are the rules of the game in Israel and 'when in Rome, do as the Romans do.'"[24]

Although the Four Mothers movement enjoyed vast public support, it also attracted considerable criticism from various quarters. The most vociferous criticism came from those who believed that the IDF presence in southern Lebanon remained critical from a military and strategic point of view. In this context, the feminine message and composition of the founding group was seen as a major cause for the movement's alleged inability to intelligently and professionally discuss the security implications of withdrawal.[25] Although such criticism was predictable given the source, that from others was less so. More "politicized" female peace activists disagreed with the essentialist, allegedly apolitical, approach of the Four Mothers; they viewed its members as having the right cause but the wrong tactics. The Four Mothers' mainstream-oriented agenda was perceived by them as potentially hampering their own efforts to introduce alternative political thinking and activism challenging the conventional wisdom on security matters. Said a veteran feminist peace activist, "The Four Mothers succeeded because they talked about motherhood. This is always acceptable. This remains within the consensus. However, we refuse to speak in the name of motherhood. We speak out as citizens [not as mothers] and this is why we have remained outside the mainstream. In Israel, not belonging—this way or that—to the blood covenant, not being part of the community of bereaved parents, deprives you of the right to take part in the political-security discourse."[26] Therefore, although on the face of things there would appear to be nothing more natural than cooperation between the well-established women's peace organizations and the Four Mothers, the differences in their respective self-images, agendas, and audiences made such cooperation practically impossible. Said the same veteran activist, "One Friday we tried to join the Four Mothers protest vigil...however, we were greeted with extreme hostility. They were reaching out to the right-wingers and the Orthodox and therefore rejected us."[27]

An opposite criticism came from the political right. Here the critics argued that while allegedly speaking for all Israeli mothers with sons serving in the army, in fact the Four Mothers represented the worldview of the peace camp in disguise. As Chava Pinchas-Cohen, a poet and writer of right-wing views observed, "The Four Mothers used words and took a position that did not represent all mothers....Instead, they used dichotomous, emotional language, declaring only one option as acceptable....The Four Mothers presented one of two halves as the whole. They acted like the proxy of Peace Now, whose name alone is enough to eliminate the option of conducting a meaningful debate on contesting options."[28]

In Retrospect: A Myth of Success?

If a representative sample of Israelis had been asked in an opinion poll in the early 2000s or later which grassroots organization had had the most success in influencing the government's security policy, the most offered answer would probably have been the Four Mothers Movement. Indeed, the movement is considered today by the public and by many political analysts, journalists, and politicians to have been the most successful grassroots organization in Israel's history—the one that brought about the IDF's withdrawal from Lebanon in June 2000. It is often held up as *the* example of the political competence that Israeli civil society organizations can attain: "Sometimes it is soldiers who determine the outcome of a battle; sometimes it is the commanders who shape the course the campaign takes, sometimes certain leaders change the future of their nation, but it seems that there are not many historical examples of a small group of people who are not fighters, commanders, or national leaders, who so clearly and decisively influence the realities of the state and even the region."[29] Reality, however, is often more complicated than myth.

The Four Mothers movement was clearly successful in reading the political mood in Israel and then in leading and adopting a strategy and set of tactics that piqued the emotions of large numbers of Israelis. Thus it garnered strong public support and developed an assertive political voice. Yet, the bottom line on the movement's influence is less clear. For starters, Prime Minister Barak, who it was widely believed had been affected by the Four Mothers movement and therefore had pulled out of Lebanon, strongly asserts that it was his own initiative and his long-standing opposition to the security-zone concept that had informed his thinking on withdrawal.[30] This is not surprising, however, as national leaders usually deny being influenced by the grassroots. Still, the burden of proof lies with those who claim to have influence over national decisions. This challenge has never been met by the Four Mothers or by those who assert credit on their behalf. For example, Yaffa Arbel, one of the original four mothers, openly stated, "It took almost four years since the movement was created until they left Lebanon, can this be a parameter of success? How many soldiers were killed in those four years? Are we so sure that we would not have left Lebanon were there no Four Mothers?"[31]

On the other hand, retired general Ami Ayalon, former commander of the Israeli navy and former head of the General Security Agency (Shabak), had a much different assessment: "I ask you: Why in the end did we leave Lebanon? It was not the government's will to get out; it was the public that forced it to do so."[32] His account is somewhat suspect, however, given that around the time that he presented this perspective in an oral history testimony, Ayalon was himself launching the People's Voice, a grassroots peace campaign for a two-state solution, in league with Palestinian academic Sari Nusseibeh. Ayalon was clearly interested in strengthening the image of the general public as a determinative agent in the national policymaking process. Nonetheless, accepting Ayalon's analysis as the more accurate one, leaves one to grapple with two additional questions: Was the 2000 withdrawal from Lebanon strategically justifiable? Was this alleged success connected in any way to the nonviolent nature of the Four Mothers movement?

The political wisdom of the pressure exerted by the Four Mothers on the government has been called into question after the fact. The movement's critics grew considerably following the outbreak of the second Palestinian intifada in fall 2000. It was often argued that the hasty withdrawal from Lebanon, for which the Four Mothers movement took credit, made the Palestinians believe that if they used violent techniques similar to those that Hizbullah had used in Lebanon, resulting in the loss of many Israeli soldiers' lives, they could also succeed in driving Israel out of the occupied territories. In other words, critics of the Four Mothers actually blamed their nonviolent campaign for bringing about an enormous wave of violence against Israelis. Following the 2006 confrontation between Hizbullah and Israel, this line of criticism intensified: "The culture of hysteria cultivated by the Four Mothers...led the Arabs to think that the state [of Israel] was on the edge of collapse and that the Jewish public would not pass the test by fire."[33] The founders of the Four Mothers strongly rejected such accusations, yet even among them, one can discerns some doubts. Yaffa Arbel is quoted as stating, "One minute I tell myself that at least we had six years of quiet [before the 2006 war], the next minute I tell myself that, yes, but the quiet of these six years was perhaps false, an engine warming up timeout for Hizballah."[34]

The Four Mothers' reliance on nonviolent means was neither based on a pacifist orientation nor did its members preach to domestic audiences about the moral or practical superiority of its strategy. In a way, the opposite is true: The Four Mothers indeed advocated a peaceful pullout from Lebanon and the opening of diplomatic negotiations, but they never dismissed the use of military force as a legitimate means of national self-defense. Their choice to use nonviolent modes of action was a classically rational choice. Nonviolent methods were the only alternative given the national consensus regarding the legitimate operational repertoire of civil initiatives, which strongly opposed physically aggressive grassroots campaigns, on the left or right.[35] Thus, it seems that the greatest success of the Four Mothers movement was in creating the so-called Four Mothers syndrome, the Israeli equivalent of the U.S. "Vietnam syndrome." To this day, Israeli politicians remain hypersensitive about making foreign and security policies that might generate deeply negative public opinion. This, in turn, could prevent Israeli officials from launching military attacks; on the other hand, it could also inhibit them from signing peace agreements that might incite a grassroots backlash.

Lessons Learned

Are there any lessons to be learned from the Four Mothers campaign, particularly concerning the prospects of success for nonviolent peace activism in the context of an ongoing conflict? Against the dismal experience of most other Israeli peace organizations, one lesson from the Four Mothers experience seems to be that the chances of a nonviolent, grassroots campaign gaining widespread public support and the attention of decision makers significantly increases if the image it projects is basically inclusive. In other words, if a campaign's leaders and the majority of its activists look "normal," talk normal, and do not challenge the existing social and political order in lifestyle, behavior, or argumentation, their prospects of staying in the game are better than they might otherwise be. They can be critical of a specific policy—and listened to by the public and national leaders—as long as they do not take it upon themselves to publicly expose the basic defects of the overall sociopolitical order or call for far-reaching political transformation.

A highly discouraging lesson is that in a conflict-ridden society like Israel's, women who emphasize the traditional role of the mother are more highly respected and find that their message is much more tolerated than those of women who put forward their demands for peace based on a gender-neutral citizen status. Indeed, whereas Women in Black were marginalized and ostracized because they made no effort to downplay their feminism, the Four Mothers, who never challenged the traditional societal gender associations and division of labor, were warmly embraced by the general public and in top political circles.

It seems that a campaign that limits itself to specific goals, and even more so, embraces ones that have already been entertained by professional politicians—as opposed to advocating a completely new idea or set of demands—eludes the stigma of being politically naive or politically ignorant. Furthermore, it can much more easily create alliances with the carriers of similar messages in the upper echelons, thereby expanding its access to top decision makers and opinion leaders.

Last but not least, adherence to nonviolent means can reduce the initial level of grassroots and official resistance, thus providing an opening for mobilizing public support. The case of the Four Mothers suggests that a nation involved in an intense external conflict is intolerant of grassroots activities that result in physical aggression. Thus, for example, the right-wing Orange Campaign and the leftist movement Anarchists Against the Wall, which do not reject the use of physical force against the police and the army, were widely denounced. In contrast, the manifestly nonviolent image of the Four Mothers paved the group's way into the hearts and minds of large enough sectors of Israeli society to allow them access to the limited circle of legitimate partners in the national security discourse.

Notes

1. In Jewish tradition, the Four Mothers—Sarah, Rivka, Rachel, and Leah—are the biblical mothers of the nation. See Dafna Lemish and Inbal Barzel, "Four Mothers: The Womb in the Public Sphere," *European Journal of Communication* 15 (2000): 148.
2. The operation lasted from April 11 to April 27, 1996. The Israeli air force, navy, and ground forces targeted Hizbullah units and headquarters in south Lebanon, but nonetheless caused much damage and fear among Lebanese civilians, who fled north in large numbers from their homes. On April 18, an Israeli attack on a concentration of displaced Lebanese and UN peacekeepers killed more than 100 people, including children and women. Israel expressed its regret but refused to apologize, arguing that the residents of the area had been informed by flyers and other means about the pending attack. This, in turn, intensified external pressure to end the operation. Following a UN General Assembly session on April 25, the operation ended with the signing of

an Israeli-Lebanese-Syrian understanding. Hizbullah was not a party to the deal and, indeed, did not consider itself bound by it.

3. The kibbutz movement has always been a "greenhouse" for Israeli peace activists and peace initiatives. It strongly identifies politically with Labor and the political left. This image functioned as a "pull" factor for certain Israeli publics (the Ashkenazi, secular, urban middle classes), but also as an even stronger off-putting factor among others (the Mizrahi, peripheral, low-education and low-income segments of the population).

4. Yaffa Arbel, Four Mothers' Web site, http://4mothers.org.il/peilut/haoref.htm (in Hebrew).

5. Malka Mehulal, "White Days" (Yamim levanim), *al-Hasharon*, January 2, 1998, 44–46 (in Hebrew); Lemish and Barzel, "The Womb in the Public Sphere."

6. For information on the Women in Black movement, see Sara Helman and Tamar Rapoport, "Women in Black: Challenging Israel's Gender and Socio-Political Orders," *British Journal of Sociology* 48 (1997): 681–700.

7. After the IDF withdrew from Lebanon in June 2000 and the Four Mothers movement announced its dissolution, some activists suggested switching the group's focus to the occupation of the Palestinian territories. The majority, however, opposed this reorientation, arguing that the movement had met its one and only goal and should therefore disband, as promised at its inception. Furthermore, many Four Mothers supporters, the majority correctly observed, were not of one mind regarding the territories. Thus, those who wished to deal with the occupation should either join one of the many existing peace groups focusing on the issue or create a new movement. Personal communication with a former Four Mothers activist.

8. Perhaps to avoid evoking anger, the phrasing on the movement's Hebrew homepage concerning the one-sided declaration of the security zone as such reads significantly less critically compared to the English version. See www.4mothers.org.il/peilut/peilut.htm.

9. Ibid.

10. Eran Shachar, "The Home Goes on Attack," *Ha'kibbutz*, April 3, 1997, www.4mothers. org.il/peilut/haoref.htm (in Hebrew). The letter writers used "feel" rather than "know" to make clear that their sons were not involved in their protest in any way. Israeli soldiers are forbidden from taking part directly or indirectly in any political activism, let alone protesting government policies.

11. Despite heated debate over certain security-related matters—such as the rationale of the "territories in return for peace" formula at the heart of the two-states solution to the Israeli-Palestinian conflict—the Israeli Jewish public has always been highly unified around a few key conceptual pillars, often referred to as the "national consensus." Among these is the need for a strong army as well as universal conscription, which was instituted in 1949, shortly after the establishment of Israel. For a discussion of the consensus, see, Asher Arian, *Security Threatened: Surveying Israeli Opinion on Peace and War* (New York: Cambridge University Press, 1995).

12. See http://4mothers.org.il/peilut/haoref.htm (in Hebrew). In the IDF, becoming an officer is optional and requires an extra year of service (at least) on top of the obligatory term, which today is three years for men.

13. For more information about Mothers against Silence, see Haya Zukerman-Bareli and Tova Bensky, "Parents against Silence: Conditions and Processes Leading to the Emergence of a Protest Movement," *Megamot* 32 (1989): 27–42 (in Hebrew).

14. Sari Ben Benyamin, "The Interest of the Entire Public," *Ha'aretz*, September 8, 1997 (in Hebrew).

15. The movement's later declarations and records did not highlight the issue of the Lebanese victims of the so-called silent war, apparently, because emphasis on these victims might have impaired mobilization efforts.

16. For positive coverage, see Hugh Levinson, "South Lebanon: Israel's Vietnam?" *BBC News*, December 23, 1998; for negative coverage, see Daniel Pipes, "Lebanon Turns into Israel's Vietnam," *Wall Street Journal*, March 10, 1999.

17. In their effort to stay within the boundaries of the Israeli Jewish mainstream, the Four Mothers never initiated joint actions with Lebanese groups.

18. The Four Mothers attracted some foreign donors. According to certain media accounts, the European Union allocated 250,000 Euros to the group. This contribution was never used, as the funds arrived after the movement had disbanded following the IDF's June 2000 withdrawal from Lebanon. Yoav Yitzchak, "How the European Union Meddles in Israeli Politics," Ma'ariv, June 22, 2001, available at Israel Resources Review, June 27, 2001, http://israelbehindthenews.com/Archives/Jun-27–01.htm#EU. Although other peace organizations were heavily criticized for taking EU money, the Four Mothers movement—probably because it did not challenge the accepted security narrative—was never denounced for "serving external agendas."

19. Ruth Sinai, "The Movement Has Sunk in the Lebanese Mud," Ha'aretz, January 7, 1998 (in Hebrew).

20. Meital Fried, "A New Organization Is Calling for Withdrawal from Lebanon—Red Line: We Shall Not Refrain from Using Violence," Ha'aretz, March 1, 1999 (in Hebrew).

21. Ibid.

22. Ibid.

23. This action was radical in two respects: First, Syria and Israel were in a state of war. Thus the movement sending messages to Syria's leader outside government channels was illegal. Second, and even more troublesome in terms of losing public support, was the messenger—Arab MKs whose visits to Damascus were always perceived by the Israeli Jewish public as an indication of their disloyalty to Israel and siding with the Arab world.

24. Hedva Isachar, ed., Sisters in Peace: Feminist Voices of the Left (Tel Aviv: Resling, 2003), 143 (in Hebrew).

25. Several years later, when warning against the potential dangers of unprofessional, public intervention in the security policy-making process, a raging high-ranking military officer publicly referred to the Four Mothers as the "Four Floor Rags." http://www.4mothers.org.il/peilut/smartu.htm

26. Isachar, Sisters in Peace, 58.

27. Mehulal, "White Days," 46.

28. Chava Pinchas-Cohen, "Mother Peace: The Fifth Mother," Panim 17 (2001): 44–50 (in Hebrew).

29. Excerpt from a letter sent to the Four Mothers, www.youngknesset.org.il/.sub11/more3.html.

30. Ehud Barak, "The Myths Spread about Camp David Are Baseless," in The Camp David Summit: What Went Wrong, ed. Shimon Shamir and Bruce Maddy-Weitzman (Brighton, UK: Sussex Academic Press, 2005), 129. External observers at the time, however, saw it differently. See Deborah Sontag, "Israel Honors Mothers of Lebanon Withdrawal," New York Times, June 3, 2000.

31. Nava Zuriel, "Because of This Protest," Yediot Aharonot, weekend supplement, February 8, 2008, 16–19.

32. Ami Ayalon, testimony provided June 27, 2002 for "What Went Wrong in the Israeli-Palestinian Peace Process?"—an the oral history research project conducted under the direction of Yaacov Bar-Siman-Tov at the Leonard Davis Institute for International Relations, Hebrew University.

33. Eviatar Ben Tzedef, "A War Middle Account," NRG, July 23, 2006, http://www.nfc. co.il/ArticlePrintVersion.aspx?docId=16962&subjectID=3.

34. Zuriel, "Because of This Protest."

35. The use of forceful means was the primary reason for the failure of the right-wing Orange Campaign to win the support of the Israeli public in 2005 against unilateral withdrawal from the Gaza Strip.

18

Popular Resistance against Corruption in Turkey and Egypt

Shaazka Beyerle and Arwa Hassan

Whoso from you is appointed by us to a position of authority and he conceals from us a needle or something smaller than that, it would be misappropriation (of public funds) and [he] will (have to) produce it on the Day of Judgement.

—Hadith 847 of the Prophet (pbuh)[1]

Corruption remains one of the greatest stumbling blocks to good governance, human rights, and development in the Middle East and throughout the rest of the world. It is a symptom of fundamental economic and political problems that can become systemic when economic opportunities for it prevail and political will to combat it is lacking. When it is systemic—whereby a complex web of graft permeates the political, economic, and social spheres, impeding the basic provision of services to citizens—it can create conditions of social unrest and frustration, which may in turn lead to people seeking an outlet in factional and sectarian groups to provide for their basic needs. Corruption also creates an overall climate of impunity.[2] Civil liberties groups, including Amnesty International, Human Rights Watch, and the Center for Victims of Torture, link corruption to repression and human rights violations, as it impedes government accountability, and can motivate officials and security forces to commit abuses for financial gain.[3]

Throughout the Middle East, people have grown so tired of corrupt politicians that the clean image of Hamas and the Muslim Brotherhood have rendered them appealing. Commentators in Egypt have noted that the Brotherhood changed its slogan from "Islam Is the Solution" to "Fighting Corruption Is the Solution," which contributed to huge gains for it in legislative elections held in 2005.[4]

Over the past 20 years, initiatives to fight corruption and achieve good governance in the Middle East and beyond have experienced exponential growth. At the same time, there is a sense of dismay in the anticorruption community at the scale of the problem and the obstacles in addressing it.[5] Although efforts have been made to amend legislation, introduce reform measures and even launch institutional anticorruption initiatives, the process of change is made difficult by government structures that frequently are centralized and have little accountability or responsiveness to the population at large.

In spite of limited civic and political space, civil society in the broader Middle East is beginning to find a voice. As important, it is harnessing civic power to fight corruption by reaching out to and engaging ordinary citizens, who not surprisingly have begun to question why many of their countries have not reaped more rewards from massive international development efforts and globalization, and in some cases, from natural resources. As a result, the region is experiencing innovative applications of "people power" that are expanding the frontiers of civil resistance beyond "traditional" nonviolent struggles—such as against authoritarian regimes and external occupiers—to systems of injustice with diffuse targets. The 1997 Citizen Initiative for Constant Light in Turkey and shayfeen.com in Egypt and the subsequent Egyptians Against Corruption, cases of civic anticorruption campaigns, offer valuable observations and lessons for scholars and practitioners of nonviolent struggle.

Turkey: Lawyers Mobilize Millions

In 1996 Turkey was plagued by a nationwide crime syndicate involving armed paramilitary entities called *gladios*, drug traffickers, the mafia, businesses, government officials, members of parliament, and even segments of the media. Extrajudicial killings were common, some linked to the mafia and others political in nature. Although scandals in Turkey were not uncommon, on November 3, 1996, one event encapsulated the entire nefarious system. In the early evening, on the road between the coast and Istanbul, a speeding luxury car crashed into a truck near the town of Susurluk. The passengers in the car were a police chief who was also the director of a police academy; a member of parliament who was a large landowner; a mistress; and an escaped convict and paramilitary member wanted by the Turkish courts, Swiss police, and Interpol. This last passenger possessed a fake ID bearing the signature of the Minister ofInterior. Together, these travellers represented some of the key institutions and groups sustaining the system of corruption in Turkey. The car also contained a bag of money, cocaine, weapons, ammunition, and silencers. All but the parliamentarian died in the accident. The wounded truck driver was taken into custody and later to court.

Strategy and Planning

In reaction to the scandal, students held spontaneous protests throughout the country that were harshly suppressed by police. That same day, other students, already on trial for previously breaking the "demonstration law"—for displaying a banner in the parliament about their right to an education—were sentenced to 15 months in prison. Such harsh measures were indicative of the government's use of force and restrictive laws to quell civic dissent.[6]

Despite the repressive political climate, a small group of progressive lawyers decided that this scandal provided an opportunity to tap into public outrage and disgust, mobilize people to action, and push for concrete changes to undermine the system of corruption. The lawyers initiated informal discussions among personal contacts, including public relations experts, political activists, and intellectuals, who together formed the Citizen Initiative for Constant Light.[7]

The group made a series of strategic decisions at the outset. First, they agreed that citizens should feel a sense of ownership in the effort. Ergin Cinmen, one of the attorneys in the group, explained, "Everybody suffered from this [corruption] in Turkey: the working class, the financial sector, and the ordinary people. Because this gladio-mafia combination affected all walks of life."[8] Second, they decided that the campaign would be strictly nonpartisan and non-ideological in order to build a broad alliance, protect against government smear attacks, and attract the broadest possible base of groups and citizenry. Third, they adopted a leaderless organizational structure to defend themselves against reprisals and to reinforce the notion that the initiative belonged to everyone.

Rather than rushing to act, the group carefully planned the campaign. They identified clear, definable goals and publicly disseminated them. One principle objective was ending parliamentary immunity in order to be able to investigate and break connections between crime syndicates, government ministers, and elected officials. For example, although the Minister of Interior whose signature was found to be on the convict's identification papers resigned from his cabinet position, he remained a member of parliament; he, along with the MP who survived the car crash, could not be investigated because of their parliamentary immunity. According to Mebuse Tekey, another of the lawyers, the group sought to "prosecute those who had established the criminal organizations, to protect the judiciary officials [who would be trying the case] from pressure, to reveal the dubious relations hiding within the state. And our last demand was, while doing this, not to undermine democracy."[9]

Understanding the need to forge unity, the group systematically built a broad coalition against corruption by reaching out to non-political groups, including civil rights organizations, the Istanbul Coordination of Chambers of Professions, the Bar Association, unions, nongovernmental organizations (NGOs), and professional associations of pharmacists, dentists, and civil and electrical engineers. According to Tekey, "For the first time, groups that had never joined forces before in Turkey found themselves participating side by side. From the business community to the slum dwellers."[10]

The group developed a sophisticated publicity campaign to spread their message, which constituted something akin to what Jack DuVall, a scholar on nonviolent conflict, has called a "unifying proposition," namely a message encapsulating the cause, the urgency for action, and the call for widespread participation.[11] The campaign proclaimed, "We know everything!...Nothing will be the same after the crash!...Nothing will be the same after Susurluk!" Recognizing the importance of the media as conduits for gaining exposure and, in the case of columnists, as potential allies for the anticorruption cause, the organizers carefully researched, identified, and contacted members of the media who might be interested in the issue of corruption or sympathetic to fighting it. Segments of the media had become deeply concerned about their reputation, because the mafia had recently been exposed as taking control of a major broadcasting corporation by manipulating legislation and business links. The press and National Broadcasters Association were looking for ways to improve the media's image in Turkish citizens' eyes, and prior to the Susurluk crash, had hired a public relations expert, Ersin Salman, to help them. Following the crash, this PR professional became personally involved in the Citizen Initiative for Constant Light.

One Minute of Darkness for Constant Light

The question then became one of how to harness civic power—the voices and demands of ordinary citizens—in collective acts of defiance. The organizers sought to come up with an innovative nonviolent tactic that would overcome real obstacles, including violent crackdowns, imprisonment, and feelings of fear, powerlessness, and hopelessness among the population. They also wanted something that would be highly visible and create a sense of national "togetherness." The teenage daughter of one of the lawyers came up with a simple, low-risk, legal action—a synchronized turning on and off of lights.

In this age before emails and SMS, the lawyers effectively used the technologies and capacities available. They launched a PR campaign and sent a chain of faxes to get word of the action all the way down to neighborhood groups. "We felt the campaign idea should appear to come not from an intellectual or an elite group, but from a street person, a kid, an aunt on pension, etc. The last one had a good ring to it," explained Ersin Salman.[12] In the campaign's printed materials, an anonymous "aunt" gave the call to action: "On February 1, 1997, we will begin to turn off our lights at 9:00 p.m. every night, until the members of the crime syndicate and its connections in the state are brought to the court!"[13] Press releases were sent to the media, signed "The Voice of the Silent Majority."[14]

After three months of strategizing and planning, on 1 February citizens in Istanbul and many other cities turned off their lights at 9:00 p.m. for one minute. Each day the numbers grew, and after two weeks, approximately 30 million people, 60 percent of the population, were participating throughout the country.[15] Feeling empowered, citizens spontaneously began to embellish upon the action. They opened their windows, blew whistles, and banged pots and pans, while those on the road beeped their horns or blinked their lights at the appointed time. By the second week, entire neighborhoods were engaging in street actions, which had a celebratory air. The Citizen Initiative received faxes and phone calls from people in all of Turkey's 36 cities and 81 townships. Organizers learned that in many of the regions, people had organized additional, complementary initiatives.

What was not anticipated was that the military—which viewed itself as the defender of the modern Turkish secular state—would withdraw its support for the government because of what it perceived to be a rapid move toward Islamization. Ezel Akay argues that the mass mobilization of people was so great that it inadvertently opened a window of opportunity for critics of the ruling party and its coalition to bring down the government. The government was forced to resign on 28 February amid the Constant Light campaign, which continued in spite of the political upheaval. Prime Minister Necmettin Erbakan remained in power until the parliament approved a new government six months later.

In all, the campaign lasted six weeks, whereupon organizers called for its halt. In this manner, the initiative ended on a high note, before the mobilization would eventually begin to fizzle, and it produced a sense of victory, which is a key strategic move essential for building a winning record and setting the stage for future actions. The campaign had succeeded in breaking the taboo over confronting corruption, empowered citizens to collectively fight this scourge, and forced the government to launch a series of judicial investigations.

In subsequent months, follow-up civic actions—including more coordinated mass actions, the public presentation of a "citizen's report" on corruption, roundtable meetings to develop a reform proposal, and a letter-writing campaign—kept pressure on the government to prevent Prime Minister Erbakan from using legal loopholes to block the inquiries sparked by the campaign. Reforms continued under the next Prime Minister, Mesut Yilmaz. Court cases progressed, verdicts were handed down, and a new investigative committee prepared a report listing the names of all the people murdered by the crime syndicate. A parliamentary committee was also created to document the syndicate's activities. In 2001, Minister of Interior Sadettin Tantan, in cooperation with the Banking Regulation and Supervision Agency, launched a series of investigations that exposed large-scale embezzlement, resulting in the arrests of well-known business executives.

In spite of these successes, many bureaucrats and elected officials escaped prosecution, including parliamentarian Mehmet Agar, the sole survivor of the car that crashed near Susurluk. By this time, however, most of the old guard had been voted out of office. One line of analysis is that voters punished both the political establishment and the military by electing the AK (White) Party, the re-formulated, moderate Islamic party led by Recep Tayyip Erdogan.[16]

Egypt: A Small Group Empowers People to Speak Out

Egypt enjoys a unique position in the Arab world. Arabs often refer to it as "the mother country." Egyptians are a relatively homogenous people, and in contrast to many of the other countries in the Middle East, their country's borders have hardly changed over the last millennia.[17] Most Egyptians tend to have a pronounced and self-contained sense of national pride and identity. Yet, Egypt's historic stability is not reflected in its civil society landscape, which remains a rocky one. Although literally thousands of registered NGOs exist, there is generally not a tradition of groups working together, including those engaged in anticorruption efforts.

Rivalries among organizations are common, and many groups are not in the habit of sharing and exchanging information. This means that successful efforts expended by one group are not multiplied, perhaps due to resistance by others who may be resentful of that group's profile or success. Adding to this situation, ever-changing laws restricting NGOs' ability to gather and organize—much has been written about Law 84, for example[18]—and a healthy dose of fear of crossing government-drawn lines has produced an atmosphere in which bringing about change is extremely difficult.

Although recent years have seen some positive developments, such as a growth in civic action, particularly opposition movements—including Kefaya (Enough), which, in its choice of name, accurately captures the prevailing spirit of many Egyptians toward government corruption and abuse of power—there remains space for more non-political, people-power style initiatives or civic movements addressing pressing concerns of the day. Although these movements may have political implications, unlike traditional opposition movements, their aim is to bring about positive change, rather than enter government.

Shayfeen.com is a group that has, in spite of all the constraints on Egyptian society, been able to acquire a considerable following and raise awareness using strategic, nonviolent, and other astute means. The name "shayfeen.com" is a clever combination of "we see" (*shayfeen*) and a simple suffix (*com*) that slightly alters "we see" to "we see you," or "we are watching you." It became the driving force behind the creation of a larger movement, Egyptians Against Corruption.

The average Egyptian is confronted with corruption on a daily basis. As in Turkey, corruption has permeated society in Egypt so much so that people feel that it has a life of its own. Most people have little idea of how to begin to counter it. Shayfeen.com began with the basic platform of "report what you see." It was sparked by events following a constitutional referendum in May 2005 that the government presented as paving the way for an "increased choice" in presidential elections, that is, multicandidate campaigns. In theory, this looked like a positive development, but in practice the amendment made it incredibly difficult for any candidate to run against the president.[19]

You Have Eyes. You Can See.

Engi Haddad, one of the founders of shayfeen.com, had worked as a branding consultant for the National Democratic Party, which has held power in Egypt for more than two decades. The May 2005 proposed constitutional amendments on presidential candidates and oversight of the election process, and the demonstrations and unrest they inspired, sparked her change in career. Haddad lost a number of companies in her portfolio when she became active in civic affairs.

Female protestors and other women out protesting against the constitutional amendments were molested and harassed by (unofficial) government forces, provoking considerable outrage. Some of the incidences were filmed and could be viewed on YouTube and similar Web sites; the government denied all responsibility. The reaction among Egyptians was one of disbelief. The prevailing sentiment was along the lines of "we have turned a blind eye for so long that the government must think we are blind." Hence the emergence of "shayfeen" as a slogan and campaign. A pivotal moment was a press conference given by the Minister of Interior and broadcast on Al-Jazeera. A split screen dedicated one side to the Minister's speech, in which he claimed that nothing untoward had happened, and the other side to footage of the women being molested and otherwise attacked. Sheer disbelief and outrage at the attitude of the government motivated people to act.

Haddad, and a group of like-minded friends who happened to all be women, felt that they had to take action. They, including TV personality Bothaina Kamel, were not prepared to let such intolerable actions pass without a response. Moreover, the Zeitgeist was on their side. The results of the referendum—a suspect 80 percent in favor of the proposed amendment—paled in significance alongside the honor of the women who had been violated and the dishonor on everyone who did not act to stop what had happened to them.

In August 2005, the organizers of shayfeen.com announced the organization's official establishment and launched a Web site to monitor government actions. The group began working out of Haddad's office, a successful consulting company and advertising agency, and then from her home. The Web site provided citizens with the opportunity to register complaints and thus a safe space in which to vent their grievances. It was a distinct departure from the standard fare with which people were familiar, such as public protests and demonstrations, the impact of which tended to be, at best, limited.

The small team of women began preparing to monitor the September 2005 presidential elections, a critical endeavor considering that requests to deploy international observers were denied. In the run up to the voting, the group ran a campaign in the independent newspaper al-*Masri al-Yawm* asserting, "This is your election. You have eyes. You can see." It included the shayfeen.com logo of an eye. The shayfeen.com Web site listed more than 20 types of irregularities for people to look for during the election and provided numbers for people to call and report them. Even basic standards, such as minimum privacy when casting one's vote, were not met. Shayfeen.com received 28,000 calls in three days. By the second day, they had set up a tracking system after being overwhelmed initially by the traffic and engagement of everyday citizens.

The group quickly learned that a little innovation and creativity could go a long way. By the time of parliamentary elections in December 2005, shayfeen.com was well known and becoming a force to be reckoned with.[20] They distributed 100,000 tea glasses with the shayfeen.com logo on them, some of which ended up in rural village coffeehouses and tea shops. They printed more than a quarter of a million of the plastic bags used for carrying fresh bread; it carried the slogan "We see you, and at the elections we are observing you," which in Arabic happens to rhyme. The bags were constantly used and re-used; the minister of trade dubbed the people carrying them "the supermarket activists." These were all simple, low-risk methods of raising awareness, visibility, and support for the campaign.

Shayfeen.com also equipped cars with GSM phones, laptops, and digital photography equipment and trained supporters and volunteers in how to use them. Each volunteer received packets containing badges, plastic bags, instructions, and a checklist (also on the Web site) of what monitors should look for. Volunteers in these cars travelled to different parts of the country, where local volunteer coordinators from the various governorates were also part of the effort, to film the voting process and collect video of fraud; these images were uploaded to Web sites for viewing. Their footage was also projected in public squares onto the façades of buildings; for instance, the one housing the opposition party al-Ghad. Members of the press were provided the footage, and the organizers held press conferences. The organization Kefaya distributed CDs of the footage. The initiative was almost entirely self-funded by the shayfeen.com team, principally comprised of women.

Even before election monitoring began, the nature of complaints on the shayfeen.com Web site and those phoning in to the office made it increasingly apparent that corruption, in various forms, was one of the problems witnessed most often by ordinary Egyptians. More than 80 percent of the reports about the December 2005 elections were corruption-related. The group noted that women were the driving force behind the movement's success. They were vocal and proactive, perhaps due to their outrage and discomfort with the culture of corruption to which their children were exposed and the dissonance between the current corrupt culture and the environment in which they had grown up. Although shayfeen.com was started by highly educated individuals who put much of their own money into the initiative and were adept at utilizing new technologies to reach out to the masses, their aim ultimately was to create a dynamic in which every Egyptian feels that he or she has some role to play in fighting corruption.

Knowing Your Rights: Using Existing Tools

In spring 2006, shayfeen.com sent a letter to the head of the Election Committee, Ministries of Interior and Justice, members of the media, and the Judges Syndicate after compiling evidence of fraudulent activities by 14 (government-appointed) judges on the Election Committee from reports sent to it by NGOs and civil society monitors.[21] The Judges Syndicate began to investigate. The government charged two syndicate members with usurping authority by communicating directly with the media and interfering with the executive's authority to manage the public. The newspaper *Sawt al-Umma* was the only paper to publish shayfeen.com's letter, and it was in turn sued by one of the Election Committee judges accused of participating in the fraud. Fifty or so judges who protested in defense of the two prosecuted judges were harassed.[22] The whole series of events provoked considerable outrage and shook the public's faith in the judiciary, previously one of the last bastions of hope that people had in the establishment.

Government officials were becoming concerned by the attention shayfeen.com was receiving and the momentum that it appeared to be generating. In March 2007, security forces stormed Engi Haddad's company, ripping posters from the walls and generally trashing the office. They accused shayfeen.com of 12 infringements relating to Law 84, including incitement; corresponding with a foreign entity; possessing documents challenging government policy (one of which was the Transparency International Toolkit, a handbook of experiences gathered by civic groups to raise awareness); and propagating negative information about Egypt. Haddad exonerated herself by presenting official documents proving that shayfeen.com had been moved to another address and that the security forces had violated a private firm. She sued for damages and won.

A lawyer had meanwhile alerted shayfeen.com to the United Nations Convention Against Corruption (UNCAC), to which Egypt was a signatory.[23] The UNCAC makes every citizen a legal party, regardless of whether he or she has been directly affected by corruption; in short, it enables each person and NGO to work against corruption. Previously, human rights NGOs had been barred in Egypt from working on the corruption issue. The UNCAC stipulates that if wrongdoing, including government corruption, is witnessed, it should be reported. Thus, when Haddad, Kamel, and their colleagues were confronted by state authorities and told that they had no legal standing—because they were not themselves an "injured party"—they were able to show that the activities of shayfeen.com and Egyptians Against Corruption, spawned in September 2006 from shayfeen.com, were not only valid under the UNCAC, but were also encouraged by the legislation to which the Egyptian government had committed a year earlier. The activists and Egyptians Against Corruption filed suit, demanding publication of the UNCAC in Egypt's official legal chronicle, which was essential to render it binding in courts of law. The government subsequently published it in March 2007.

The UNCAC entered the government's Official Journal, where all major legislation is recorded, in April 2007. Prior to that point, the UNCAC was the only piece of international legislation that the Egyptian government had signed on to but that did not appear in the Official Journal; thus, for all intents and purposes, it simply did not exist; this situation of course made it difficult for the average citizen to invoke it. Haddad acknowledges that the motivation to invoke legislation such as the UNCAC and to employ it as a tool in their campaigns was probably made possible by the momentum generated by the so-called Judges' Movement the year before, in 2006.

Egyptians Against Corruption: Tapping into the Pulse of the Moment

Egyptians Against Corruption emerged from shayfeen.com in September 2006 as the natural evolution of a relatively small, successful group into a broader movement. Whereas shayfeen.com tended to be more provocative, Egyptians Against Corruption presents itself as more of a social platform with broad-based appeal. It aims ultimately to create a popular nonviolent movement, reaching out to those who previously would not have felt themselves included in Shayfeen.com's campaigns. The new organization's stance is such that even members of the ruling National Democratic Party (NDP) have wanted to become members.

Stemming as it did from shayfeen.com, which had built a good reputation for itself, people knew where Egyptians Against Corruption stood. The activists, however, set up this new organization in a Cairo location separate from shayfeen.com, so the public would correctly perceive them as two distinct entities. Bothaina Kamel, the TV presenter, became the face of Egyptians Against Corruption. She drove a car bearing the group's logo, insisted on wearing a badge on air promoting

Egyptians Against Corruption, and hosted a popular social program called "Please Understand Me." Kamel developed a huge following and emerged as a role model for a large number of women. Her association with Egyptians Against Corruption became part of her branding as a television personality.

Egyptians Against Corruption has an innovative educational Web site and platform aimed particularly at young people.[24] Mindful that educating the public is a key strategy, it launched a civic education program, "Claim Your Rights" ("Eksab Ha'ek"), to empower people to become better informed of their rights. The group tries to explain that corruption is a societal problem that must be addressed from the bottom up as well as from the top down. Via the Arab Egyptian Human Rights Organization (AEHRO), it also campaigns for the rule of law and an independent judiciary. Egyptians Against Corruption is well aware that an empowered, informed public is better able to undertake strategic civic action.

Though Egyptians Against Corruption evolved from the same need identified by shayfeen.com—to provide people with the means to oppose corruption by exerting civic pressure— its founders were determined that the organisation become distinct from Shayfeen.com.. They developed the badge with the group's prominent logo and thus far have sold many tens of thousands of them, mostly on an individual, one-to-one basis.[25] By buying and wearing the badge, each person joins thousands of others in a low-risk, mass nonviolent action. People displaying send a clear message—I am against corruption. Of the badge, Haddad said, "It is clear that a badge will not fix corruption. But by buying and wearing the pin, and the conversations that ensue, you are giving the other person a chance to enter into and generate a discussion. It is that dialogue that we are trying to achieve." Any money that Egyptians Against Corruption receives is channeled back into promoting the movement.

The group has sought to reframe the anticorruption fight in ways that resonate with ordinary Egyptians, bringing people's attention to incidents resulting in the unnecessary loss of life, such as arson, train crashes, and contaminated food.[26] Because of a lack of regulation, the turning of a blind eye (because of bribes) to mechanisms designed to ensure safety, and a lack of transparency, certain information did not reach the public domain. Often, corruption as a concept was vague, and meant different things to different people. Egyptians Against Corruption used everyday language to demonstrate to the average Egyptian that a deliberate lack of transparency and abuse of positions of authority were, among other things, all forms of corruption. The message is that every day, in every way, everyone is a victim of corruption. Egyptians Against Corruption stresses that such incidents do not occur because Egypt is poor or because of a lack of resources, but because of mismanagement and corrupt behavior. All this is underlined by the narrative that the movement is comprised of concerned Egyptians who care about and love Egypt, and who firmly believe that they are entitled to justice, equality, and a life free of the blight of corruption.

The leaders of Egyptians Against Corruption are extremely innovative. They have astutely used their contacts in television to promote their activities and have successfully pegged their messages to global events, such as International Anticorruption Day, on 9 December. Each year on this day, the group awards a prize to an "anticorruption hero," an Egyptian who confronts corruption head-on. "Corruption kills. Fight it" was the slogan to promote the campaign and competition in the press in 2006 and 2007. Government media refused to spread word of the campaign, but the independent press was cooperative. Information about it was also picked up by satellite TV.

The public is asked to vote via mobile text messaging or the group's Web site, www.nadafa.org (which means "clean"), for their preferred candidate. Prize money is donated from the movement's resources, with a prize also awarded to the Web site that through objective and non-partisan methods best succeeds in uncovering cases of corruption. The jury is composed of academics and members of the independent press. A well-known TV presenter, Mona Shazli, changed the subject of her show at short notice when she first saw the "anticorruption hero" poster and press announcement in December 2006. She now regularly covers this annual event.

Another campaign challenged President Mubarak on his record: "These are the promises President Mubarak made way back in the year. . . . Which promises have you lived up to Mr. President?" The editor in chief of *al-Ahram* rejected a paid advertisement by the group, informing its members that they could not "address the president directly," meaning in such a tone. Mindful of the context in which it operates, Egyptians Against Corruption is careful to package its discourse in a manner that makes it difficult for anybody to accuse its members or activities of being disrespectful, confrontational, or slanderous, an accusation frequently leveled at journalists, activists, and others who speak out.

Although Egyptians may not have been organized to actively confront corruption in the past, this has started to change. For example, in 2008 Golden Island, a small piece of fertile agricultural land in the Nile, was threatened with destruction when companies and officials wanted to clear it to make way for construction development. The island is often described as the green lung of Cairo. Local residents protested; they resorted to such actions as digging graves and laying in them, sending the message that they would not accept the removal of their homes and confiscation of their land. Their persistence paid off, and the project was abandoned.

Yet there are still too many who feel that they have been pushed to the sidelines—doomed to watch political events play themselves out—while their quality of life deteriorates. What Egyptians Against Corruption has tried to do is to tap into this kind of discontent and harness the huge potential that exists by providing Egyptians with a vehicle with which to make their voices heard. The government has watched in amazement at the support that Egyptians Against Corruption has received, not only from individual citizens but also from the Egyptian diaspora and NGOs that have been inspired to take up its mandate, such as the Egyptian Organization for Human Rights. Perhaps one of its biggest successes has been to make clear that postponing the fight against corruption is no longer an option.

To propagate success, Egyptians Against Corruption must continue to involve other groups (which may not necessarily think in the same way, but are fighting the same cause); reach out more extensively to regions and governorates beyond Cairo; develop consistent, sustainable actions that tap into the energy of broader civil society in the country; and break down the scepticism, suspicion, and resistance that the government has toward its work. It deserves credit for having achieved concrete successes in a country run by an authoritarian regime. Perhaps of most value, shayfeen.com and Egyptians Against Corruption have succeeded in raising awareness of the corruption issue and giving people a positive outlet for their anger and frustration. They have, via their numerous campaigns and the outcomes achieved, sent a message to the powers that be that the Egyptian people are not blind to corruption, and no longer can they remain silent.

Lessons Learned

Civil resistance can be a force for reform, accountability, and transparency in democratic and undemocratic systems by giving people the means and leverage to fight corruption, and by complementing and reinforcing conventional anticorruption strategies. The latter has included or can potentially include enacting legislation, enforcing transparency statutes (as seen by shayfeen.com invoking the UNCAC), conducting trials and judiciary investigations (as was the case in the Citizen Initiative for Constant Light campaign), creating monitoring systems, investigating judges (for example, in the shayfeen.com campaign), and defending independent institutions, such as electoral boards, as well as honest government officials and whistle-blowers. The Turkish and Egyptian cases provide valuable lessons about nonviolent struggle in general and its application to corruption in particular.[27]

Skills and Strategies

Strategic nonviolent conflict expert Peter Ackerman asserts that skills and strategies play a critical role in the success of a nonviolent movement, as they can ameliorate and in some instances overcome unfavorable or difficult situational conditions.[28] In Turkey and Egypt, political and civic space was highly restricted, street protests violently repressed; fear and apathy reigned over the population.[29] Yet, in both countries, organizers overcame these obstacles by using creative, low-risk tactics that exerted civic pressure and attracted broad participation. Organizers developed communication strategies targeting the public and various pillars of support—such as parts of the government, including political elites, officials, and the media—to challenge the corrupt status quo.

An Incorruptible Image

When it comes to fighting corruption, not surprisingly, a clean image is essential to winning support. In both cases discussed here, women constituted the face of the campaigns, either as Turkey's "anonymous aunt" or the core group behind Egypt's shayfeen.com. The lesson is that in every society, certain groups are perceived as being incorruptible and honest, and their association with anti-corruption campaigns or movements can have a galvanizing effect. In the 2006 Orange Movement against political corruption in Kuwait, it was the image of young activists organizing for electoral reform, and in the 2007 lawyers campaign against political corruption in Pakistan, it was judges rallying to preserve the independence of the judiciary.

Campaign Creativity and Tactical Innovation

There is no one formula or definitive model for civic mobilization that can be applied to all situations or causes. One constant, however, is the need for creativity. Although conditions can be unique, creativity is one of the factors that can determine the ability of civic movements or campaigns to overcome obstacles, adapt to changing circumstances, develop innovative tactics, and maximize the impact of its resources. Shayfeen.com and Egyptians Against Corruption utilized inexpensive techniques and new technologies in clever ways, such as distributing tea glasses with the shayfeen.com logo on them, which took the campaign into thousands of households, and allowing people to vote for their anticorruption hero via SMS, which gave average citizens a voice. (Mobile phones are more widespread in Egypt than is Internet access.) Creativity was also evident in almost every facet of the Citizen Initiative for Constant Light, from the organizers' communication strategies to "citizen-to-citizen" leadership to de-centralized mobilization.

Mass dispersed actions, by their nature, make government crackdowns difficult if not impossible and thus can be particularly effective under repressive conditions. The Turkish and Egyptian campaigns avoided such traditional street actions as demonstrations and marches, which can be easily suppressed. They developed instead innovative, low-risk tactics that could be undertaken by ordinary people throughout society, and in some cases, were even fun. In these cases, the actions were not technically illegal, which removed an official excuse for arrests and detention. The lesson is that anticorruption campaigns should not necessarily adopt identical tactics, but they should recognize that low-risk, mass actions are effective and can be created out of the conditions at hand. Egyptians Against Corruption also invested in training its members. Education and training, essential to building campaign and movement capacity, are important and powerful nonviolent tactics, though not often recognized as such by budding civic campaigns and movements.

Translating Rights into Everyday Realities

A common challenge for civic movements is the linkage of the oppression or injustice in an abstract form—in this case fighting corruption—to something that is everybody's personal concern. Shayfeen.com used real, even tragically fatal, examples of corruption to drive home this point. The Citizen Initiative for Constant Light tapped into national disgust and outrage over the Susurluk scandal and channeled it into a series of tangible demands.

Communication and Messaging

The Turkish and Egyptian campaigns utilized the talents of public relations professionals and media experts to design effective communications. Strategic objectives were identified and incorporated into the messaging, for example, fostering a sense of belonging, identifying the collective experience of being touched by the problem, and recognizing that everyone has a role to play and can be an agent of change.

The Need for Unity

From the outset in the Turkish case, the organizers recognized the critical importance of building unity around goals and people; this was reflected in virtually all aspects of their campaign. Core strategic objectives were to disassociate the fight against corruption from political ideology and to create a sense of campaign ownership among young and old, urban and rural, rich and poor, religious and secular. Shayfeen.com and Egyptians Against Corruption appeal to the widespread sense of injustice felt by the population at-large. The slogan "You have eyes. You can see." encouraged people to look and to report to the group what they witnessed. This simple activity, which everybody could carry out (anonymously if need be) without fear of consequences, was an effective confidence-building measure.

Strategy and Planning

The Turkish case provides an example of the difference between the spontaneous use of nonviolent action and a strategic, well-planned nonviolent campaign.

Students who impulsively demonstrated after the Susurluk scandal erupted were brutally repressed. Yet under the same conditions of political repression in the country, the Citizen Initiative for Constant Light mobilized millions and promoted civic empowerment—a necessary step in the long march toward ending systemic corruption. In a similar vein in Egypt, the behind-the-scenes work that went into the anticorruption hero campaign enabled it to be successful even when there were suspicions that its Web site had been hacked, hampering access for those who tried to log on and vote for their hero. The publicity the campaign generated and the support that it received from high-level media personalities ensured that it was still possible to save the day.

Fighting corruption is ultimately an ongoing battle. No one sector of society working on its own, whether it be the government, the private sector, or civic organizations, can ensure lasting change. In many cases, activists and others trying to bring about change already have all of the necessary tools at their doorstep. Whether the resources are human creativity or limited technologies, by being innovative and tapping into and maximizing the existing energy of their fellow countrymen and women, civic actors in every country and society need not look far afield in search of the right actions, applied at the right times and in the right way, that can change lives for the better.

Notes

The authors wish to thank Engi Haddad for her willingness to contribute her time, knowledge, and insight during the research of this chapter.

1. Narrated by Adi ibn Amirah al-Kindi, *Sahih Muslim*, http://makkah.wordpress. com/2006/11/28/ethics-and-corruption-in-muslim-countries-fact-versus-fiction.
2. Daniel Kaufmann, "Human Rights, Governance and Development: An Empirical Perspective," in *Human Rights and Development: Towards Mutual Reinforcement*, ed. Philip Alston and Mary Robinson (Oxford: Oxford University Press, 2005).
3. Arvind Ganesan, "Human Rights and Corruption: The Linkages," Human Rights Watch, http://hrw.org/english/docs/2007/07/30/global16538.htm.
4. Conversation with an Egyptian anticorruption activist, Cairo, May 2008.
5. Conversations with leading figures from the anticorruption community during travels in the Middle East and North Africa, 2006–2008.
6. Amnesty International, *Amnesty International Report 1997—Turkey*, 1 January 1997, available at: http://www.unhcr.org/refworld/docid/3ae6a9f12c.html [accessed 26 July 2009] United States Department of State, *U.S. Department of State Country Report on Human Rights Practices 1997—Turkey*, 30 January 1998, available at: http://www. unhcr.org/refworld/docid/3ae6aa7ac.html [accessed 26 July 2009]
7. This section on the Citizen Initiative for Constant Light is based on "Mass Actions for Public Participation," a presentation by Ersin Salman at the symposium "New Tactics for Human Rights," Ankara, September 29–October 2, 2004; Ezel Akay, *A Call to End Corruption: One Minute of Darkness for Constant Light*, ed. Liam Mahony (Minneapolis: New Tactics Project, Center for Victims of Torture, 2003).
8. Akay, *A Call to End Corruption*.
9. Ibid.
10. Ibid.
11. Conversations with Jack DuVall, president of the International Center on Nonviolent Conflict, 2002–2007.
12. Akay, *Call to End Corruption*.
13. Ibid.

14. Ibid.
15. "New Tactics in Human Rights: Regional Training Workshop Report," 2002, www. cvt.org/file.php?ID=1481.
16. Ibid.
17. Indeed, Egypt is the only country mentioned several times in the Quran.
18. The People's Assembly passed this measure on June 3, 2002. It provides the executive with far-reaching controls over the work of NGOs, including restricting access to foreign funding, constricting their ability to join international associations, and wielding broad powers of dissolution. The Ministry of Social Affairs can disband any association—seize its property, confiscate its papers, and freeze its assets—if it violates certain conditions (Article 42), among which are allocating resources for a purpose outside the organization's mandate, joining any institution or association outside of Egypt without permission from the authorities, accepting foreign funding without prior permission, violating any aspect of the law, and failing to hold a general assembly for two consecutive years. Dissolution is by administrative decree and is conducted without a judicial determination. From *Human Rights Features,* see www.hrdc.net.
19. There has been much comment and analysis on this issue. See for instance, Jeremy M. Sharp, *Egypt: 2005 Presidential and Parliamentary Elections,* CRS Report for Congress, September 1, 2005, http://fpc.state.gov/documents/organization/54274.pdf.
20. For further reading on the development of the group, see Robin Wright, *Dreams and Shadows: The Future of the Middle East* (New York: Penguin Press, 2008).
21. The allegations reported were confirmed by shayfeen.com in one-on-one interviews with witnesses, and in one case the documentation included video footage.
22. For additional background, see "Clashes at Egypt Judicial Protest," http://news.bbc. co.uk/1/hi/world/middle_east/4938810.stm.
23. UNCAC, a landmark convention outlining the most extensive approach to addressing corruption, obliges the state parties to implement a wide and detailed range of anticorruption measures affecting laws, institutions, and practices. These measures, like those of the Inter-American Convention against Corruption, aim to promote the prevention, detection, and eradication of corruption, as well as to increase cooperation between state parties on these matters. Compared to other conventions, the UNCAC is unique in its global coverage and the extent and detail of its provisions, including those on asset recovery. For more information, see www.unodc.org or www.unodc.org/unodc/en/corruption/index.html.
24. For more information, see Egyptians Against Corruption, www.nadafa.org.
25. The logo consists of two words—"Against Corruption"—with "Corruption" in red and "Against" superimposed in black—on a white background. The style is reminiscent of Arabic calligraphy, a classic, ornate style that contrasts with the strong red, black, and white, which are the colors of the Egyptian flag.
26. These examples are taken from a shayfeen.com flyer.
27. In the wake of the campaigns in Egypt, a judicial reform law, shelved since 1996, was passed in 2006. The judiciary had sought independence from the executive, but in the end the law only granted it autonomy over its budget and case assignments. The minister of justice retained the authority to appoint judges, so in short the executive maintained control of the judicial branch. In another development, a proposal for greater transparency in the activities of the Cairo and Alexandria stock exchanges can be traced to an anticorruption project observing these operations and documenting the anomalies found. Complaints were filed with the Cairo Capital Markets Authority for more rigorous disclosure requirements by companies and an increase in fines levied for noncompliance. Courting foreign investors, the authority proposed stronger transparency regulations for publicly listed companies. Activists have since demanded that the same type of conditions be imposed on the government's annual budget.

28. Peter Ackerman, "Skills or Conditions: What Key Factors Shape the Success or Failure of Civil Resistance?" (paper presented at "Conference on Civil Resistance and Power Politics," St. Antony's College, University of Oxford, March 15–18, 2007), www.nonviolent-conflict.org/PDF/AckermanSkillsOrConditions.pdf.

29. Human rights and civil liberties organizations confirm that political and civic repression continues on an upward trend in Egypt. See Human Rights Watch, "Egypt: Events of 2007," *World Report, 2008,* www.hrw.org/legacy/englishwr2k8/docs/2008/01/31/egypt17595.htm; Freedom House, "Egypt," Country Report, 2008, www.freedomhouse.org/template.cfm?page=22&year=2008&country=7387.

19

The Iranian Women's Movement: Repression Versus Nonviolent Resolve

Fariba Davoudi Mohajer, Roya Toloui, and Shaazka Beyerle

One of the more innovative and determined examples of grassroots organizing and civil resistance in very difficult conditions can be found in Iran, where women are channeling their grievances into a strategic nonviolent campaign to end gender subordination and to expand legal rights. Beyond its own vision of gender equality, the Iranian women's movement is expanding the frontiers of civic action. For the last decade, the movement has been treading the path laid during the country's Constitutional Revolution more than a century prior, inching toward suffrage, equal educational opportunities, and full participation in political and economic life.[1] Despite systemic obstacles and recurrent setbacks, Iranian women, with unflagging courage and determination, have continued their nonviolent struggle. They have adjusted their strategies and tactics to take into account the evolving political and cultural conditions in Iran.

Turning the Clock Back: Women's Status after the Iranian Revolution

Under the regime of Shah Mohammad Reza Pahlavi, women won voting rights—though the country did not have a democratic system—and benefited from the reform of family law codes, including an increase in the legal age of marriage to 18 years and the right to divorce.[2] Soon after the tumultuous religious and emotional upheaval of the Islamic revolution in 1979, authorities instituted a rigid system of control over women's lives through the imposition of *sharia,* Islamic law. There is no definitive version of sharia; Islamic scholars and clerics debate its interpretations and applications. Iran follows the Shiite Jaafari doctrine of sharia.[3]

Under Iranian law after the revolution, women essentially became second-class citizens. Their inheritance is half that of men. Their testimony in court and their value in "blood money"—reparations paid to a victim's family—is worth half that of a man's. Further, while men can divorce women at will, a woman must prove her husband's misconduct in a court of law. Polygamy is legal; men are permitted up to four "permanent" wives and an unlimited number of "temporary" wives.

Fathers automatically receive custody of children over the age of seven. A woman seeking to marry, acquire a passport, or travel abroad must obtain permission from a male in her family. The age of criminal responsibility for girls is nine lunar years (eight years, nine months) while for boys it is 15 lunar years (14 years, six months).[4] Although both sexes can be subjected to death by stoning as a sentence for adultery, more women than men are punished in this manner.[5] Women can no longer serve as judges.[6] A strict code mandates what women can and cannot wear.

In 1980, a few months after the ouster of the monarchy and the assumption of power by Ayatollah Ruhollah Khomeini, groups of women in Tehran launched protests against mandatory veiling. A rally on 11 March drew 20,000 demonstrators. Khomeini initially backed away from the regulation, but by 1981 the practice had become compulsory for all women, including foreign visitors.[7] The protracted Iraq-Iran War, from 1980 to 1988, created a siege mentality, as defense of the country and the problems emanating from the conflict overshadowed public discussion of other issues, such as women's rights. At the same time, the Islamic revolutionary educational system, aided by government television, propagated the ideal of an Islamic woman as obedient, religious, covered, and shameful.

In 1989, although overall repression remained harsh in the face of dissent, a small opening in civic space began to widen under the eight-year presidency of Hojjatoleslam Ali Akbar Hashemi Rafsanjani, a time known as the Rebuilding Period. A few prominent Islamist personalities close to the regime, for example, Said Hajaryan, took advantage of this opportunity to begin mildly voicing the need for reform of the revolutionary regime. At the same time, some quietly secular intellectuals and academics, such as journalist and feminist Noushin Ahmadi Khorasani, began to form discreet discussion circles. In Tehran, women joined groups debating economic development, a less controversial subject that allowed them to break out of their intellectual isolation and connect with other people, of both genders. These women forged bonds upon which they cooperated to found civic organizations and later to build a resurgent women's movement. They avoided identification with political ideologies in order to maintain their independence and prevent co-optation by political groups, for example, communists, which did not recognize women's rights as distinct from other rights.

The Reformist Era: Broken Promises, New Opportunities

During Mohammad Khatami's presidency (1997–2005), the re-emerging women's movement encountered a series of challenges and opportunities. Despite his expressions of sympathy for women's quest for equality, and their massive electoral support for him, Khatami failed to take an unequivocally favorable stand in support of any of the major demands of Iranian women, such as gender equality under the law, reform of textbooks portraying women exclusively in traditional roles, removal of the ban on women candidates for the presidency, and a meaningful increase in female government appointees. Feminists were especially disappointed by Masoumeh Ebtekar, the first woman to be appointed Vice President since the Islamic Revolution, who refused to sign any of the declarations they released. Deputy Minister of Interior Fakhrosadat Mohtashami, however, emerged as a relatively strong supporter of women's rights, trying to use her ministry to advocate for women. For example, although ultimately blocked, she attempted to approve the registration of a number of women's nongovernmental organizations.

Khatami's failures were due not only to the inflexibly patriarchal and discriminatory nature of Iran's existing constitutional structure, but also to his cavalier attitude toward women's ultimate aspirations for equality and his conviction that reforms for women would take time. By the end of his first presidential term, in 2001, disappointed Iranian feminists had came to the conclusion that it was necessary to mobilize people and create a civic force to pressure the government to enact change. They therefore broke with reformers who essentially wanted to work within the system and the Majlis (parliament).

A number of developments during Khatami's presidency indirectly provided opportunities for a new women's movement to take shape. A relaxation of controls on civic assemblies opened the door for the creation of a large number of nongovernmental organizations, including some focusing on women's issues, such as the Women's Cultural Center, founded in 1999. In spite of financial and logistical impediments, the center managed to advocate and publicize women's long-standing concerns and demands through civic action. It evolved as the key organization for bringing together professional women who became notable leaders for women's rights, including the aforementioned Noushin Ahmadi Khorasani, writer Parvin Ardalan, human rights lawyer Mehrangiz Kar, future Nobel laureate Shirin Ebadi, and journalist Shadi Sadr.

As censorship eased, the publishing sector experienced a rebirth. Several new publications employed young women on their editorial and reporting staffs. Not only did a new generation gain valuable journalistic experience and a taste of freedom of expression, they also directed the press's attention toward the views, problems, and needs of women. Ahmadi Khorasani launched *Jense Dovom* (Second Sex), Iran's first feminist journal, in 1998. The ten issues published made an impact, even in some of the smaller cities in the country. Conservatives in the judiciary hostile to the reformists closed the journal's operation in 2001. Undaunted, Khorasani skirted the ban by continuing to publish it in the form of a book, on which there were fewer restrictions.[8] In 2000, she and a number of other women, including Firouzeh Mohaher and Ardalan, founded a second journal, *Fasle Zanan* (Women's Season). These publications brought to the fore womens' experiences of gender discrimination and their demands for equality and respect. After the arid postrevolution years, the number of books and movies on feminist topics reached new heights.

At this time, female enrollment in Iranian universities steadily increased, such that by 2003 women constituted 66 percent of the total student body.[9] Higher education became one of the few outlets for young women to break through traditional familial and social constraints. As a result, young women were exposed en masse to new realms of learning and became more confident and independent. Because of the large presence of women on campuses and their involvement in university life, many student organizations expressed their support for women's demands and invited female activists—particularly those with husbands languishing in regime prisons—to air their grievances on campus.

The Internet became an important tool for women's rights organizers inside Iran. Many blogs and Web sites began to host debates on women's issues quite freely, albeit temporarily because in the post-reformist years, they would eventually be shut down. Regardless, it presented women with a new outlet through which they could write and publish without restrictions. Internet access also enabled communication among women from different parts of the country (who until then had been isolated from one another) and contact with activists from around the world.

Some activists, who still needed permission from husbands or fathers to travel, participated in a number of international conferences, some of which included workshops on women's rights. Through such gatherings, Iranian participants became more acutely aware of women's movements in other parts of the world. Exposure to the international discourse on women's rights emboldened these women to intensify their demands from Iranian political leaders. They sought in particular to stimulate public discussion about the problems faced by young girls, such as sexual abuse, and to pressure the government into instituting protective measures.

A series of discussions at the Forum of Iranian Women resulted in the draft of a report on the status of Iranian women, which was submitted to the Iranian Commission on the Rights of Women. It was based on Strategic Objectives and Actions, the 12-point platform examined at the United Nations Fourth World Conference on Women held in Beijing in 1995. The report was sent to the United Nations Commission on the Status of Women–Beijing + 10 (indicating 10 years) in 2004, but signed anonymously by "a group of women activists" in order to protect those involved from government reprisals.

A few reformists and pro-Khatami women's rights advocates assumed mid-level government positions or were elected to the parliament. They not only aired women's demands within their own political groupings, which played a role in familiarizing male colleagues with their struggle, but also took modest measures to improve women's lives. For example, Faezeh Rafsanjani, the daughter of former president Rafsanjani, worked to improve opportunities for women in sports and even created a park where women could ride bicycles, something forbidden in public.

In spite of this general awakening of dissent among women, it was not until 2003 that a new women's movement began to take shape. The impetus involved an unexpected turn of events—the awarding of the 2003 Nobel Peace Prize to Shirin Ebadi, the renowned human rights lawyer and advocate of women's and children's rights. When the prize was announced, Ebadi was on a trip to Paris. Upon her return to Tehran, thousands of people gathered to greet her at the airport, including a number of women activists. From this contact, the women decided to cooperate and launched the Forum of Women Activists in Iran, an informal group for organizing events and civic actions. Some of those who joined were affiliated with Tehran-based organizations, such as the Women's Cultural Center and the Hastia Andish Society, consisting of young women and men, mostly university students, advocating gender equality. Others, such as Khadijeh Moghaddam, a well-known environmentalist, joined independently. People attracted to the forum spanned a broad spectrum and included politically-affiliated and nonpolitical women, students, secularists, and moderate Islamists.

The women began meeting once a week. All were encouraged to present their ideas, and decisions were made collectively. They unified around two overriding objectives: outlawing stoning and achieving gender equality under the law. The ensuing two years would witness a swell in nonviolent actions, including flash protests, sit-ins, civil disobedience over dress codes and laws forbidding public gatherings, noncooperation, demonstrations, and press conferences. Young and old, mothers and daughters, men and women took part in an expanding repertoire of nonviolent activities designed to educate the public about these goals and harness civic pressure.

Soccer Protests and Other Creative Actions

To dramatize the extent of gender inequality, a number of young women—in defiance of some of the older activists—focused on an issue meaningful to all Iranians: soccer, which is a national passion, if not an obsession. Under Iranian sharia law, women are forbidden to attend live soccer matches with men in stadiums. This manifestation of inequality, while not initially supported by some of the older feminists (who thought the issue somewhat frivolous), held meaning for the younger generation. These young women staged sit-ins and protests, which attracted new blood to the movement. When they experienced police brutality, older feminists nevertheless rallied around them in solidarity, for example, publishing articles and letters, and posting statements on Web sites. Some journalists who tried to cover the women's actions had their equipment and cell phones confiscated by the authorities.

Creativity and humor became the hallmark of the soccer activists. When police confiscated their placards, they would write slogans on their headscarves. On one occasion, joined by young men, they set up a television outside a stadium and watched the game from there, cheering loudly when goals were scored. In the most daring of tactics, on June 8, 2006, a small group of youthful feminists conducted what nonviolent strategists call a dilemma action during the qualifying World Cup match between Iran and Bahrain held in Tehran and broadcast live, nationally and internationally. Storming barricades, the women managed to overtake a section of the stadium in view of television cameras. Holding signs demanding justice and equality, they boisterously watched the second half of the game.

The issue at the heart of the women's act of defiance was something most Iranians could understand—the right to support the national soccer team in a critical international match. The women's action created a dilemma for the authorities, who had two choices, neither of which was palatable: they could drag the women out of the stadium kicking and screaming, which would not only interrupt a major game, but would be witnessed by millions of people in Iran and around the world, thereby creating a negative image of the government and sympathy for the women; alternatively, they could leave the women alone, allowing them to be seen on television defying a strict prohibition. The government chose the latter. To the surprise of many, the highly conservative Ahmadinejad subsequently overturned the ban on women attending matches, arguing that "the presence of families and women will improve soccer-watching manners, and promote a healthy atmosphere."[10] Ahmadinejad's decision was then, however, blocked by the Guardian Council, the powerful, non-elected clerical body that approves all legislation and vets electoral candidates. Regardless, the women's action was a success because it pressured the president into publicly changing his position on an entrenched policy.[11]

The women's movement also devised inexpensive, low-risk methods of communication, designed to overcome censorship and to mobilize participation under conditions of repression. In 2005, on the occasion of International Women's Day, a demonstration was planned at Students Park in Tehran. The Khatami government tried to put a stop to it. Security agents summoned one of the authors of this chapter to a local office of the Ministry of the Interior, where she was ordered to call off the action on the grounds that the demonstrators had not obtained permission for the event. She asserted that the constitution allows demonstrations as long as they do not break Islamic laws, and in any case, there were no leaders in the movement and decisions were made collectively, so even if she tried to call off the event, no one would listen to her.

Because newspapers were not allowed to publish information about the demonstration, the women needed to devise creative ways to bring it to the attention of the general public and thwart the authorities' attempts to impede them. They quickly prepared small packages containing candy and a leaflet that asked questions—such as "Do you think girls should be allowed to ride a bike?"—to get people to think about how gender inequality affects daily lives. The leaflets also contained information about the demonstration. The women compiled a list of key districts in Tehran, and activists fanned out across the city to distribute the packages to people in the streets and the targeted neighborhoods. In the end, a few thousand people would take part in the demonstration.

During the run-up to the 2005 presidential elections, Iranian feminists moved into high gear. On 12 June, with the cooperation of approximately 15 NGOs, women organized a historic mass protest in front of Tehran University to demand equality in the Iranian constitution and to end discrimination in the civil and criminal codes. More than 90 local women's organizations—from the capital as well as from the major cities of Isfahan, Kermanshah, and Tabriz and from the provinces of Baluchestan, Khorasan, Kurdistan, Lorestan, and Sistan—signed a declaration released before the event. It was the largest independent coalition of women to form since the fall of the shah.[12] Some organizers were summoned to court before the event, but temporarily fled Tehran to avoid such intimidation.

Between 3,000 and 5,000 women (and men) gathered at this rally, an extraordinary number, for women's rights. There were relatively few arrests, although police harassed people on the street, and the authorities tried to prevent protestors from reaching the university. The organizers had anticipated such measures, so they chartered commercial buses to travel to the site. While pedestrians were being held back, some of the buses passed by unnoticed. In other cases, with the help of male students who reported on police whereabouts via SMS and cell phone calls, other buses avoided the authorities and were able to slip through the cordon. A number of women and men had earlier occupied bookstores near the university, pretending to be browsing. While police were busy blocking streets to the site, these protestors were already nearby or had already made it to the demonstration.

Some Islamic women were also active just prior to the 2005 elections.[13] Among the most prominent was Azam Taleghani, the daughter of Ayatollah Mahmud Taleghani, whose candidacy for president was rejected by the Council of Guardians on the basis of her gender. She and close to 100 religious and a few secular women protested outside the president's office. She engaged the police that surrounded them, a classic nonviolent tactic designed to undermine the loyalty of those carrying out the opponent's orders and to win them over to the cause. Taleghani reportedly called out to them, "Thank you brothers for allowing us to raise our voices. We will be here forever to continue our struggle and you will have to cooperate with us."[14]

Strategy, Planning, and Building Alliances

Up to this point, organizers had not conducted a systematic, strategic analysis of the struggle to define specific objectives, develop and sequence effective nonviolent tactics to achieve these objectives, and select targets for the actions. The women saw the regime itself as the overall target, and the Majlis was viewed as the principal institutional source for change. There were differences within the movement over engagement and communication with parts of the regime. Some believed that such an approach was necessary to shift support toward their demands, but others either saw this as an impossibility or took an ideological stance against interacting with the Islamic Revolutionary government, because it was considered a principal source of oppression. The members of the movement overcame their differences by compromising. Thus they agreed that those who wanted to lobby the government and parliament should do so, and they did.

The movement recognized the strategic need to create alliances with other groups in order to build their base of support. First and foremost, these feminists took a deliberate decision to encourage male participation in civic actions. They understood that it would be impossible to transform an entrenched patriarchal system without the support of men. In addition to involving male students, they established connections with a few prominent reformists (such as Mossavi Khoeini, a parliamentarian, and Mustafa Moin, former minister of culture and higher education and a presidential candidate in 2005) and intellectuals (for example, Akbar Gangi and Ali Sepasy). Their cooperation revolved around shared notions of social justice, human rights, and the economic well-being of all citizens. The latter group wrote on women's issues and gave women space to publish their views in articles and on Web sites. In turn, the women circulated pieces by the intellectuals through their fora.

Feminists also built ties with student organizations, natural allies in part because women composed the majority of the undergraduate university population. Initially, there were disagreements about whether to engage with other aggrieved groups. Some feminists argued that women should only focus on women's issues and avoid being distracted by others' causes. Others asserted that ties and solidarity with these groups would strengthen the movement by building support for women's issues. The latter view ultimately prevailed. For example, in late 2005, when Tehran bus drivers began a strike for an independent union, better pay and working conditions, and an end to corruption among managers, they found support in the women's movement.[15] Not only did the women back the strike, they also responded to the call for help from the wives of detained strikers, who were seeking the release of their husbands and were in financial distress. The feminists then went on to act in solidarity with the wives and families of other incarcerated dissenters by generating press attention, signing letters to the authorities, and meeting detainees upon their release from prison.

Women's rights activists also identified international sources of support for the movement and initiated external contacts after decades of relative isolation. This included international women's rights and human rights organizations, the UN Commission on the Status of Women, and the media. Engaging with the Iranian diaspora proved to be a point of contention, because of its disunity and strong ideological and political colorations, which could be used by the regime to divide members and supporters and accuse the movement of being externally driven. Feminists finally decided that some contact would be helpful, because the diaspora could provide an international outlet through which Iranian women could publish articles and more generally communicate with the world at large.

Beyond Tehran: Student and Kurdish Women's Movements

Although the resurgent women's movement during the reformist years was largely based in Tehran, students and Kurdish women played pivotal roles in expanding the boundaries of the struggle. Student activists from other parts of the country, including Baluchistan, Khorasan, and Khuzestan, invited feminists to university campuses to give speeches and lectures. In essence, these students constituted a rudimentary engine for activities beyond the capital, which not only expanded the movement's geographical reach but also brought them into contact with some of Iran's ethnic minorities.

Approximately 12 million, or 15 percent, of the Iranian population is comprised of ethnic Kurds, who live primarily in the northeastern province of Kurdistan.[16]

Kurdish women had long engaged in nonviolent action, but usually only in the context of minority rights. Women's issues were traditionally considered secondary to the larger struggle. It was not until around 2000 that an awakening of women's "double oppression"—as women and as a minority—began to take place. The slight opening of society under the first Khatami term and contact with the outside world led to a lessening of Kurdish women's isolation. Around 20 women intellectuals, including Negin Sheikholistami and one of the authors of this chapter, began meeting to share experiences, publish articles, and express themselves through short stories and poems in the Kurdish language. It was a critical development in laying the foundation for subsequent activities.

A nascent Kurdish women's movement parallel to and independent of their sisters' in Tehran began to take form between 2003 and 2005. One impetus came from the opportunity to publish. By 2004 one of the authors of this chapter had secured a "women's page" in a weekly magazine, a breakthrough in Kurdistan. In 2005 she and Sheikholistami launched *Rasan* ("Fist," in Kurdish), an independent women's magazine. Reformist era or not, government censors still controlled the media, and the women expended a good deal of time and energy finding ways to get around official restrictions. For the first time, women had a platform from which to report on conditions throughout the province, share experiences, debate views, and develop common approaches. A special effort was made to provide a safe and inclusive space for the voices of less privileged, less educated women. The magazine had a catalyzing effect. It demonstrated that Kurdish women wanted to play a more active role in their society. The desire for equal rights was not limited to a handful of professionals, but rather existed among a cross-section of Kurdish women, young and old, urban and rural.

During these years, activists also founded Association of Kurdish Women for the Defense of Peace and Human Rights, an unofficial group that adopted the slogan "Women's Rights, Kurdish Rights Equal Human Rights." The Iranian government refused to grant them official permission to operate. In defiance, the founders gave interviews to some overseas radio and television programs. This angered the authorities, who subsequently summoned the women to court. The group organized discussions and workshops on empowerment, journalism, and human rights, in the home of one of the authors of this chapter. Her dwelling also became an ad hoc shelter for abused women or those fleeing honor killings from as far away as Iraqi Kurdistan. These activists realized that they needed to gain support from other influential parts of society, which were of course dominated by men. Thus, they attempted to educate the Kurdish political opposition that women's rights are part of Kurdish rights, arguing that women could be one of the columns of democracy. They built ties to student groups, human rights activists, and cultural figures, sensitizing them to women's oppression. As a result, a number of young male students took part in civic actions. In 2002 Rahim Zabihi, a prominent director, made a short film about honor killings titled *Hawar*. It was shown in Kurdistan, the Tehran Short Film Festival, and in several festivals around the world. Within Kurdistan, the film brought honor killings into the public arena, generating discussion and debate.

Meaningful exchanges between Kurdish and Tehran feminists did not begin until 2003, quite by unforeseen circumstances. One of the authors of this chapter presented a paper at an international conference on Kurdish women's activism. Two members of the Women's Cultural Center in Tehran heard about it, tracked her down in Kurdistan and invited her to Tehran. Thus began the contact of the two groups.

Initially, there was some discord, as Kurdish women argued that their experience as minorities also needed to be taken into consideration. Through extensive dialogue, their Persian counterparts came to understand their perspective. Kurdish feminists published in *Fasle Zanan* and translated Persian articles into Kurdish. Tehran activists conducted workshops in Kurdistan, and their counterparts came to speak in Tehran. While Kurdish feminists continued to organize independently, the two groups shared goals, deep connections, and a complementarity of effort.

Kurdish feminists employed a number of nonviolent tactics in seeking to build their movement by educating members, raising awareness among the general public, and gaining support for their agenda. For example, they repeatedly defied regime orders and prohibitions on public assembly, a courageous form of non-cooperation. They staged civic actions designed to mobilize ordinary people and recruit new members. One of the more memorable nonviolent actions took place on March 8, 2005. Although it is not common for women to drive in Kurdistan, a female taxi agency exists to transport them. A group of drivers were enlisted to form a convoy to cruise across the capital and announce via loudspeaker the time and location of an assembly commemorating International Women's Day. Photos depicting violence against women were taped to the car windows. An hour into the action, the police moved against them, but like any good taxi driver, they knew the streets better than most and eluded their pursuers. The effect was electrifying. A standing-room crowd of 2,000 packed the hall for the assembly, including many men. The turnout was unprecedented for Kurdistan. Young male students held up placards supporting women's rights. The authorities tried to stop the proceedings by cutting the electricity, but people stayed and improvised.

The success of the Kurdish activists marked their organizers, whom the regime came to view as a threat. By the end of the year, after Ahmadinejad had assumed power, the government arrested Kurdish feminists and tortured some of them. Although these activists had not yet built deep layers of organization or a dispersed leadership, by that time, their ties to the larger women's movement in Iran had been firmly established and proved to be insoluble.

Repression and Renewal

The ascendancy of Mahmoud Ahmadinejad to the presidency in 2005 opened an era of repression reminiscent of the early post-revolutionary years. The regime began attacking civil society with the intention of decimating it. It routinely mistreats and tortures detained dissidents, workers, defenders of human rights, students, and intellectuals; it displays no tolerance for nonviolent civic action. Authorities close publications, jail media professionals, and block Web sites.[17] Women have not escaped this onslaught.

Although in 2005, even under Khatami, some nonviolent actions were met with repression, such as harassment, beatings, and arrests, the situation significantly worsened. Women's rights advocates faced threats and intimidation, such as arrests before civic actions, court summonses, sentences that do not result in incarceration but involve surveillance and forced communications and meetings with security personnel, and immediate imprisonment if a transgression were deemed to have occurred. In addition, some women were fired from their jobs, prevented from taking university entrance exams, or threatened with expulsion. Others faced family problems instigated through false accusations made to husbands about their wives by people working with the regime.[18]

On March 8, 2006, in observance of International Women's Day, feminists held a protest at Students' Park but were harshly beaten by police. They then decided to hold another demonstration on June 12, the anniversary of the landmark mobilization one year earlier. Even before the event, organizers (including one of the authors) were summoned to court and threatened with severe consequences should the demonstration go forward. Undaunted, they proceeded with the action on the chosen date. The police used massive force against demonstrators, and for the first time, deployed baton-wielding female police. Seventy people were arrested, of which 20 (including one of the authors) were sentenced to lashes or detention. The crackdown on this disciplined, nonviolent action, however, backfired against the regime, as the level of violence attracted coverage by the international media and human rights groups, which brought the world's attention to the Iranian women's movement.

After the 12 June demonstration, the women's rights organizers decided to halt conventional street actions. They recognized that they stood at an existential crossroads. To continue along the same path that they had begun down during the reformist era would surely bring their demise. They alternatively could choose to devise a new strategy that would not only enable them to survive, but would also harness the civic power necessary to grow and better challenge the system of gender inequality and discrimination. Leaders and activists began to ask themselves difficult questions: What were their strategic weaknesses? What should they do differently? How could they bridge the growing divide between the younger and older generations of feminists that was beginning to threaten the movement? Young feminists were generally more creative, brave, and willing to take part in street actions than their older counterparts, who had vivid memories of the Islamic revolution and the ensuing violent suppression of civic dissent. Older feminists tended to be more pragmatic in outlook and more amenable to hierarchical leadership.

The women reached the conclusion that they had not strategically identified targets for their actions, namely, the groups, institutions, organizations, and key figures supporting the status quo, and more broadly, society at large. Although they engaged in a range of nonviolent tactics, they nevertheless relied too heavily on traditional street actions. They also did not sufficiently set an incremental path toward their objectives, whereby each action and campaign built upon the other. Despite having developed a mutually reinforcing relationship with Kurdish feminists, the composition of the women's movement for the most part still consisted of elites based in Tehran; they were not reaching ordinary women and men to a satisfactory degree. The leadership reflected on how to better mobilize the masses and drafted a strategic plan for the movement that focused on opportunities, threats, resources, and long-term resilience. Among the challenges they examined were cultivating potential sources of support, such as moderate clerics, and sensitizing the public and the regime's leaders to the necessity of changing the unjust and discriminatory laws adversely affecting women's lives in Iran.

One Million Signatures Campaign

Following numerous deliberations over the course of several months, Iranian feminists publicly launched the One Million Signatures campaign on August 27, 2006. More than 50 activists, including young women, drafted three documents that constituted a preliminary covenant defining the reasons for and objectives of the campaign. The first document—the campaign's official statement—is a petition to the Iranian parliament, signed by individual supporters, calling for the "revision and reform of current laws which discriminate against women."[19] The second outlines the objectives of the campaign and the duties of its executive committees. The third document, a booklet titled "The Impact of the Legal Order on Women's Lives," describes the discriminatory laws and regulations and is distributed to the public.

These documents were designed to create a bond among the activists as well as to provide guidelines necessary for the campaign to incrementally move toward reaching its objectives. The women thought a petition drive would be the best means for achieving their long-term strategic goal of building an unstoppable, far-reaching, unified, grassroots movement for gender equality throughout Iran. They believe that through this manifestation of civic power, the system of discrimination can be changed, which not only includes the repeal or reform of regulations, but ultimately the transformation of Iran's political and social culture.

The campaign set out to bring about three principal outcomes—eliminating discriminatory articles pertaining to women in the Iranian civil code, ending violence against women (including honor killing, stoning, and domestic abuse), and empowering women in the public arenas of politics, the economy, and education. The basic approach would be to engage the public—ordinary citizens—through face-to-face advocacy. The campaign came to be characterized by egalitarian discourse and infused with a spirit of civic innovation. Its goals are informed by the quest for the equality of all citizens before the law, and questions not only the legal system, but the exclusive power of the ruling clerics to interpret Iran's civil and criminal codes. The campaign encourages the formation of new formal and informal nongovernmental organizations and institutions in all arenas of civic and social activities.

The movement identified five strategic objectives, which were to be addressed through a group of committees. The first objective was to raise awareness among Iranian women about their legal status, the impact of gender discrimination on their everyday lives, the constraints of social mores, and diminished economic opportunities. In order to stop passively accepting this fate, women needed to be made aware that they had rights and untapped capabilities. The second objective was to build courage among members to act despite the climate of fear and the real risk of repression. The third objective concerned building the women's movement from the bottom up. Strategists realized that grassroots involvement would be critical to increasing their numbers, mobilizing ordinary citizens, maximizing resources, offering an alternative to the grassroots network built by the clergy, and creating a sustainable, resilient movement. The fourth objective was to solidify various groups of women—for example, the secular, religious, minorities—into a unified force with shared goals better able to withstand repression and instill popular confidence in the movement. Fifth, strategists understood that countering the fears of traditionalists and winning public support required highlighting the social and economic costs for the country of oppressing women and explaining how improvements in women's rights would benefit society at large.

The idea for a petition came from a young female activist inspired by the Moroccan One Million Signatures campaign, launched in 1992 to reform the Moudouwana, Morocco's civil status code that includes family law governing women's status.[20] While political and civic space is virtually nonexistent in Iran under the current crackdown, signing a petition—a relatively low-risk tactic—does not break the law, thereby denying the regime a legal (or "legitimate") excuse for repression. Unlike street actions, this tactic can be pursued in all public and private spaces, from cafes to beauty parlors, hospitals, homes, parks, and social gatherings.

Regardless of whether an individual decides to sign the petition, this approach allows the campaign, which is ongoing, to interact with ordinary Iranians, disseminate information about the extent and effect of gender inequality, and lead more people to think about the difficulties women face in Iran. Activists compile notes on their experiences in the course of collecting signatures, including the reasons or justifications offered by those reluctant to sign. These notes will eventually be published on the campaign's Web site, a comprehensive, multilanguage tool providing documentation and news, and a means of communicating with the public. Through this site, organizers hope to increase sources of support and members inside Iran as well as get the attention of international media, and human rights and women's rights communities abroad.[21] It also posts video and presentations on YouTube, including one on the campaign itself.[22]

The campaign also focuses on internal education and capacity building. Signature collectors, who constitute the face of the campaign, are volunteers who go through training sessions before they begin work. Other volunteers engage in research or advocacy for harassed members or women in prison. The campaign has also adopted distinctive symbols, slogans, and songs, including a digitally streamed anthem, which add a compelling new dimension to its messaging and communications.[23] As digital technology rapidly evolves, it is also adeptly using social networking.

In creating the One Million Signatures campaign, organizers sought to overcome previous weaknesses while developing an overall strategic plan. The campaign firmly maintains its independence; it is not affiliated with any political party, and is free of subservience in its vision and actions to any individual, group, or ideology. The campaign's effort to build a broad-based movement involving a diversity of women—secular, religious, socialist, Islamist, conservative, reformist, and even communist—ensures that no particular sociopolitical grouping or ideology will gain an advantage.

Organizers have taken an important step toward building ties with other societal groups facing discrimination or injustice. In 2007 on the first anniversary of the 12 June attack on demonstrators noted above, women's rights advocates published a declaration expressing solidarity with and affirming the grievances of ethnic minorities, workers, trade unionists, teachers, students, and other groups. Of course, not all civic dissenters support the women. Among intellectuals, there are some who believe that they best know how to solve mounting social and political problems; others assert that formal political activity, working within the current system, is the cure for Iran's ills. After decades of revolutionary rule, many people have simply succumbed to despair and indifference and are thus unresponsive to calls for action to achieve gender equality and justice. To build unity, the campaign identified a set of common goals that are shared by different groups and that are meaningful to the average woman. Thus, the broad goal of equality under the law was translated into basic demands directly related to the daily lives and concerns of women, such as ending polygamy, freedom to marry and travel without a man's permission, and equal rights in divorce, child custody, inheritance, and so on.

The campaign's collective leadership and dispersed organization are designed to build loyalty, a sense of ownership, and resilience. Committees, such as the Mother's Committee, bring subgroups into the fold with a clear sense of purpose. No one can claim exclusive leadership of the campaign. The young generation has an equal voice with the older generation. All active members are simultaneously and collectively leaders and foot soldiers. Decision making is free of hierarchical limitations, thereby rendering the campaign more difficult to crush. The diffuse structure of the campaign also encourages local autonomy.

The One Million Signatures campaign is based on transparency. Deliberations and activities are openly reported to the public through available channels of communication. Given the crackdown on civic dissent, the women seek to reduce the risk of abuse during interrogations, forced false confessions, and harassment from intelligence forces by being open and proving that their initiative is home-grown and inclusive of the grassroots. They aim to prevent the attacks on individual activists by dispersing responsibility. They want to prevent the regime from making false accusations of external interference, which are designed to discredit the campaign and justify its suppression. Instead, organizers want to make such charges backfire by showing *their* false nature. The movement has set clear limits on engagement with the international community. It seeks only expressions of nonpolitical solidarity, including signing the international petition of "support for Iranian women in their effort to reform laws and achieve equal status within the Iranian legal system"; attention to human rights and women's rights organizations; and publicity and advocacy regarding arrests and repression.[24] It disavows support from government groups or quasi-governmental groups that "are closely linked with or are traditionally viewed as hostile to the Iranian government."[25]

Challenges and Effects

The One Million Signatures campaign faces external and internal challenges, including a multifaceted crackdown designed not simply to weaken it, but to bring it to a halt. The regime regularly blocks or filters the campaign's Web site.[26] Authorities have accused activists of undermining Iranian national security, broken up meetings and training sessions, harassed those who have lent their support (such as homeowners offering their space for meetings), and arrested activists. The charges issued against the activists are vague, such as "acting against national security through propaganda against the Order." Campaigners believe, however, that these arrests are discrediting the authorities, undermining their legitimacy among the people given that the campaign's actions are legal and transparent. More than 130 women and some men have been arrested, including Hana Abdi, Nasrin Afsali, Noushin Ahmadi Khorasani, Ronak Safarzadeh, and Amir Yaqoubali.

The campaign faces a lack of adequate financial resources, and in spite of concerted planning and training, needs to further improve its logistical preparedness. Tensions among members, in large part due to differences between older and younger activists, must continuously be managed. Ahmadi Khorasani observes in her book, *One Million Signatures Campaign*, "The campaign is the very life itself with all its challenges and contradictions. The interaction between the multitude of volunteers with different identities, backgrounds and experiences requires constantly evolving tactics and creates its own crises and problems. These constant changes and readjustments inevitably have caused a degree of frustration and confusion among some of the campaign's activists."[27] An effort is being made to keep disagreements and criticisms out in the open, through face-to-face and online discussions. Each month, organizers identify a key challenge, and members are encouraged to debate how to handle it. The intent is to reach a consensus, if at all possible.

After less than two years, the campaign counts more than 1,000 active members who have been trained in one-to-one interactions and educating the public about its issues. Local groups have been established in most parts of Iran, including in Hamedan, Isfahan, Kurdistan, Lorestan, and Qazvin. While activists face repression, they have maintained nonviolent discipline and continue attempts to make repressive actions backfire on the regime. For example, those arrested and sent to the notoriously brutal Evin prison have held workshops about women's rights for female prisoners. After being released, the activists try to assist the women whom they met during their incarceration. Parvin Ardalan, one of the campaign's founders, rallied international media attention to the cause following a particularly clumsy attempt by the regime to punish her after she had received the 2007 Olaf Palme Award for Human Rights. Officials denied her an exit visa to travel in March 2008 to Stockholm, where she was to collect the award, but rather than remaining quiet, Ardalan and other activists rallied international attention and solidarity for her plight, and taped an acceptance speech that was broadcast at the award ceremony, posted on YouTube, and can be viewed around the world.

The One Million Signatures campaign has gained the support of student groups, some of which are political and others of which are concerned about student life and freedoms. It has also cultivated a new generation of Iranian males, especially among youths. By defining themselves as feminist, these men open themselves to hateful and humiliating attacks by those who have no tolerance for the feminist cause. Nevertheless, many have enthusiastically joined the campaign, not only to express their sympathy for the situation of women in Iran, but more generally to underline their belief in the equality of human beings.

It is too early to predict the outcome of the One Million Signatures campaign; it is still under way. It should be noted, however, that in a relatively short period of time, and under harsh conditions, it has grown and extended roots throughout Iran. While the Iranian women's movement has tirelessly worked on behalf of women through the One Million Signatures campaign, it is evolving from a movement for the many into a movement of the many.

Iranian women's activism helped pave the way to the Green Movement of 2009. After Ahmadinejad was declared the winner of the June 12 2009 presidential election over popular opposition leader Mir Hossein Mousavi, evidence of widespread fraud prompted millions of Iranians, angered and insulted that their votes had been dismissed, to take to the streets in the largest demonstrations in that country since the Islamic revolution.

Iranian women, fearing that a second term for Ahmadinejad will lead to even greater erosion of their rights and roles in society, have been a galvanizing force, both in support of reformist candidates in the run-up to the election and in the Green Movement currently under way. Nobel Peace laureate Shirin Ebadi stated, "The root of the current unrest is the people's dissatisfaction and frustration at their plight going back before the election...Because women are the most dissatisfied people in society, that is why their presence is more prominent."[28]

A month prior to the vote, women formed a broad coalition, demanding legislative reform to remove gender discrimination from the constitution and for Iran to become a signatory to the international Convention of Elimination of Discrimination Against Women (CEDAW). Mousavi's wife, Zahra Rahnavard, asserted that his cabinet would adopt CEDAW and improve women's rights.[29] Mousavi promised to control Islamic vigilantes who often viciously enforce dress codes and to appoint women to important government positions.[30] Jamileh Kadivar, a female spokesperson for the candidate Mehdi Karoubi, publicly questioned the practice of mandatory head coverings for women.[31] Among the first to call for public protests in the event of fraud was Effat Hashemi, Rafsanjani's wife.[32] His daughter Faezah openly backs Mousavi and was briefly detained for her stance. One report states that it was Rahnavard who first made the call for people to chant "Allahu Akbar" from their rooftops at night.[33]

Women of all ages and walks of life, from those sporting hip headscarves to those in black chadors, have been in the vanguard of protests, displaying immense courage, facing beatings, detention and even death. If the Green Movement has a face, it is that of 26 year-old Neda Soltan, who is considered the first martyr in the struggle. Soltan was shot in the chest.[34] Young women have been standing side by side with their male counterparts braving security forces. Older women verbally confront Basij paramilitary forces or throw themselves at them to protect others.[35]

The experience of women's rights activists in organizing civic action under conditions of harsh repression, most recently the One Million Signatures campaign, has been parlayed into the Green Movement. Internet savvy, they are also using social networking and the blogosphere to mobilize people and communicate to the world in spite of government censorship.[36] To minimize attacks from security forces, women have been spotted carrying photos of the late Ayatollah Khomenei, leader of the Islamic Revolution, following clever advice from a widely circulated SMS.[37]

At the time of this writing, the outcome of the Green Movement is yet to be determined. However, the active involvement of women in the struggle is playing a catalyzing role in rousing ordinary citizens, firing up courage, developing tactical creativity and harnessing civic power, a force history has proven can be stronger than the might of oppressors.

Addendum

By Shaazka Beyerle

The Green Movement may now be moving into a more sustained phase, in which civil resistance goes beyond huge demonstrations. Nonviolent movements succeed not necessarily when there are masses on the streets, but when a large enough number of citizens withdraws its cooperation from the system, disobeys and disrupts, thereby dissolving the power of the oppressors and undermining their rule.[38]

Reports indicate that Iranians, indeed, are becoming increasingly adept and creative at engaging in low-risk mass actions that defy the regime and shake-up the status quo. Citizens are confounding authorities with multiple smaller-scale yet visible dispersed actions. Slogans are being written on money.[39] There are calls to flood the electric grid by turning on lights and appliances before the censored evening news. The homes of paramilitary Basij vigilantes are being anonymously marked by green paint or pictures of victims.[40]

Boycotts are under way, from products advertised on state television to companies selling to the regime, with information circulating through the internet, social networking and good old word of mouth. As a result, some stores have cut targeted brands and advertising has plummeted at the state broadcaster, because companies fear being blacklisted in a Facebook campaign.[41] Most egregious to people is Nokia Siemens Network, for having sold communications monitoring systems to the government, which is being used to target dissidents. One mobile phone vendor and wholesaler said that demand for Nokia cell phones has dropped by half in one month, even in the provinces.[42] In a particularly clever twist, an SMS boycott has been costing the state communications company, TCI, over $1 million a day. To stem the losses it doubled the price of an SMS. After Mousavi urged citizens to walk about the bazaars but refrain from buying, it was reported that "commerce has slowed to a trickle" in the grand bazaar, which normally would be at its busiest as Ramadan approaches.[43] There are even anecdotal indications that people are taking their money out of state banks and depositing it into private banks.[44]

Iranians are discovering what the Nobel laureate, Thomas Schelling, wrote 30 years ago, that nonviolent actions can deny oppressors what they need, including money, food, supplies and manpower. From this perspective, even attempts to demobilize the popular movement have costs. The Iranian regime cannot indefinitely cut electricity, phone links and internet without hurting its own interests. Moreover, coercion is costly. It requires huge sums to manipulate elections, feed, transport and arm security forces, as well as to maintain the loyalty of the inner circles and top commanders in the state.[45]

As in past nonviolent struggles—including Iran's 1979 Islamic Revolution that ended the brutal rule of Shah Mohammad Reza Pahlavi—a campaign to win over parts of the security forces may be pivotal. According to Iranian analyst Afshin Molavi, "the Basiji volunteer militia...[is] not monolithic."[46] There also appear to be generational divisions in the Revolutionary Guard; Iraq war veterans are aggrieved with the younger "business-oriented" generation, and believe that the mission of the forces is to guard the revolution rather than to "act as an Imperial Guard for the Supreme Leader."[47] The Revolutionary Guard's Tehran chief was detained, and 16 Guard members were apparently arrested after disobeying orders to shoot protesters.[48] If these reports are correct, they are signs of the regime's growing weakness.

Rifts are also widening in the ruling establishment. Former president, Ali Akbar Hashemi Rafsanjani, who chairs the Assembly of Experts, made a momentous speech during the Friday sermon on July 17. He accused the regime of stealing the election and said it was un-Islamic to "ignore people's votes." That he could speak in such a prominent setting in spite of Ahmadinejad's attacks on him and his family, signifies his power within clerical circles.[49] Grand Ayatollahs Yousof Sanei and Hossein-Ali Montazeri have called Ahmadinejad's government illegitimate.[50] Ayatollahs Abdollah Javadi-Amoli and Jalaluddin Taheri are challenging Khamenei's fitness to be the Supreme Leader. Ayatollah Abdul-Karim Mousavi Ardebili stated that "we do not have to pacify the protest by force" and "let the people decide who is right and who is not."[51] Iran's Parliament speaker, Ali Larijani, announced that he wants to set up a parliamentary committee to examine the recent post-election violence in an "evenhanded way."[52] Approximately one hundred parliamentarians snubbed Ahmadinejad's victory dinner.[53] If these rifts widen, the system could begin breaking apart.

Nargess Mohammadi, a journalist and human and women's rights activist, offered this hopeful assessment of the civil resistance taking place now in Iran: "The Iranian people have been working to achieve freedom, justice and democracy for one hundred years in their country and on this path they have forgone their lives and their possessions.... They continue to work toward the realization of common human ideals, and certainly they will be victors on this path."[54]

Notes

Note from Fariba Davoudi Mohajer and Roya Toloui: This chapter is based, in large part, on our firsthand experiences of life after the Iranian Revolution and our intimate involvement in the women's movement as leaders and activists.

1. The 1906 Constitutional Revolution, consisting of a number of civic protests by the religious establishment, merchants, and other classes, pressured Shah Muzaffar al-Din to issue a decree promising a constitution. An elected assembly met and drafted the document, which included restrictions on royal power, a Majlis (elected parliament), and a cabinet confirmed by the parliament. Women participated in this movement. "The Constitutional Revolution," *Iran: A Country Study,* ed. Helen Chapin Metz (Washington, DC: GPO, for the Library of Congress, 1987), http://countrystudies. us/iran/13.htm; Sanam Dolatshahi, "Timeline of Iran's Women's Movement (1800s–Present)," *Snapshots of a Movement: Public Protests of Iran's Contemporary Women's Movement, 2003–2006,* http://iml.jou.ufl.edu/projects/fall06/sanam/timeline. html.
2. Simin Royanian, "Women's Rights in Iran," May 25, 2005, http://women4peace.org/women-rights.html.
3. Shaazka Beyerle, "Courage, Creativity and Capacity in Iran," *Georgetown Journal of International Affairs* 9, no. 2 (Summer/Fall 2008).
4. Rahma Tohidi, trans., "The Effects of Laws on Women's Lives," www.change4equality. com/english/spip.php?article41.
5. Although both sexes can be subjected to this form of execution, more women than men tend to be punished in this manner. Amnesty International, "Iran: Death by Stoning. A Grotesque and Unacceptable Penalty," www.amnesty.org/en/for-media/press-releases/iran-death-stoning-grotesque-and-unacceptable-penalty-20080115.
6. "Reforming Iran: A Discussion with Shirin Ebadi, the Iranian Human Rights Lawyer Who Was Awarded the 2003 Nobel Peace Prize," *Stanford Lawyer* (Fall 2005): www. law.stanford.edu/publications/stanford_lawyer/issues/73/ReformingIran.html.
7. Homa Hoodfar, "The Women's Movement in Iran: Women at the Crossroads of Secularization and Islamization," Women Living under Muslim Laws: International Solidarity Network, Grabels-Cedex, France, 1999, www.wluml.org/english/pubs/pdf/misc/women-movement-iran-eng.pdf.
8. Elaheh Rostami Povey, "Khorasani, Nushin Ahmadi," *Biographical Encyclopedia of the Modern Middle East and North Africa* (Detroit, MI: Gale Group, 2007), 443–44, http://elahehrostamipovey.com/pdf/2_69ne.pdf.
9. Nikki Keddie, *Modern Iran: Roots and Results of Revolution* (New Haven, CT: Yale University Press, 2006); American Council on Education, Center for Policy Analysis, "Fact Sheet on Higher Education," www.immagic.com/eLibrary/ARCHIVES/GENERAL/ACE_US/FS_09.pdf.
10. "Iran To Let Women Go to Soccer Games," *USA Today,* April 24, 2006, www.usatoday. com/news/world/2006–04-24-iran-soccer_x.htm.
11. Beyerle, "Courage, Creativity and Capacity."
12. Mahsa Shekarloo, "Iranian Women Take On the Constitution," *Middle East Report Online,* July 21, 2005, www.merip.org/mero/mero072105.html.
13. "Islamic" in this context is the term used in Iran to connote the religious interpretations and practices of those people who follow the clergy related to the 1978 revolution and the present-day Islamic Republic of Iran.

14. Elaheh Rostami Povey, "Women Human Rights Defenders in Iran: Their Achievements and the Challenges That They Are Facing," presentation at the School of Oriental and African Studies, University of London, March 1, 2006, www.negotiate-peace.org/content/view/27/34.

15. Nick Cohen, "Why Striking Bus Drivers in Tehran Are the Real Defenders of Muslim Rights," *Observer*, February 12, 2006, http://observer.guardian.co.uk/comment/story/0,,1707972,00.html#article_continue.

16. Although the expression of Kurdish culture, for example, dress and music, is generally tolerated, and the Kurdish language is allowed in some publications and broadcasts, the Kurdish minority experiences systemic discrimination. According to a recent report by Amnesty International, "Kurds in Iran have their social, political and cultural rights repressed, along with their economic aspirations." "Discrimination against Kurdish Iranians Unchecked and on the Rise," July 30, 2008, www.amnesty.org/en/news-and-updates/report/discrimination-against-kurdish-iranians-unchecked-and-rise-20080730.

17. Human Rights Watch, "Iran," *World Report 2007*, www.hrw.org/en/reports/2007/01/10/world-report-2007-0.

18. These accounts of intimidation and punishment are based on the direct knowledge of one of the authors.

19. Sussan Tahmasebi, "Answers to Your Most Frequently Asked Questions about the Campaign," February 24, 2008, www.forequality.info/english/spip.php?article226.

20. Souad Eddouada, "Feminism and Politics in Moroccan Feminist Non-Governmental Organisations," paper presented at the conference "Post Colonialisms/Political Correctness" Casablanca, April 12–14, 2001, www.usp.nus.edu.sg/post/poldiscourse/casablanca/eddouada2.html.

21. See www.wechange.info or www.forequality.info.

22. See One Million Signatures Campaign, www.youtube.com/watch?v=Pdz7Ev9B9yA.

23. See Beyerle, "Courage, Creativity and Capacity." For the anthem, visit www.forequality.info/IMG/mp3/we-change.org.Sorood3.mp3.

24. "Petition: International Support for Women's Campaign," www.we-change.org/spip.php?article19. (date accessed: September 24, 2008)

25. Ali Akbar Mahdi, "A Campaign for Equality and Democratic Culture," August 6, 2007, www.wechange.info/english/spip.php?article130.

26. As of early December 2008, the Web site had been blocked 18 times. See http://learningpartnership.org/advocacy/alerts/iranwomenarrests0307. Those wishing to access the Change for Equality site inside Iran should use the following address: www.campaign4equality.info/english. From outside Iran, visit www.we-change.org.

27. This book was self-published in 2007 because the Ministry of Islamic Culture and Guidance did not grant permission for the book to be released by a state-approved publishing house.

28. Associated Press, "Iran's Women Protest: Headscarves, Rocks," June 24, 2009 http://www.msnbc.msn.com/id/31531225/

29. Elham Gheytanchi, "Iranian Women Lead the Protests," *San Francisco Chronicle*, June 29, 2009,_ http://www.sfgate.com/cgi-bin/article.cgi?f=/c/a/2009/06/28/ED8618EMUC.

30. Michael Theodoulou, "Women on Front Line of Street Protests," *The National*, June 17, 2009, http://www.thenational.ae/article/20090617/FOREIGN/706179978.

31. Gheytanchi, "Iranian Women Lead the Protests."

32. Golnaz Esfandiari, "Women at the Forefront of Iranian Protests," Radio Free Europe Radio Free Liberty, June 22, 2009, http://www.rferl.org/content/Women_At_Forefront_Of_Iranian_Protests/1760110.html/.

33. Theodoulou, "Women on Front Line of Street Protests."

34. Martin Fletcher, Video clip of student's last breath makes her martyr of Tehran, *The Times*, June 23, 2009, http://www.timesonline.co.uk/tol/news/world/middle_east/article6557858.ece/.

35. Gheytanchi, "Iranian Women Lead the Protests."

36. Theodoulou, "Women on Front Line of Street Protests."

37. Ibid.

38. Shaazka Beyerle, "Iran's Leaders Fear Their Own People Most," *Daily Star*, July 3 2009.

39. Ibid.

40. Robin Wright, "Iran's Protesters: Phase 2 of Their Feisty Campaign," *Time*, July 27, 2009.

41. Saeed Kamali Dahghan "Iranian Consumers Boycott Nokia for 'Collaboration,' " *The Guardian*, July 14, 2009.

42. Ibid.

43. Beyerle, "Iran's Leaders Fear Their Own People Most."

44. Dahghan, "Iranian Consumers Boycott Nokia."

45. Beyerle, "Iran's Leaders Fear Their Own People Most."

46. Tara Bahrampour, "Militia Adds Fear to Time of Unrest," *Washington Post*, June 19, 2009, http://www.washingtonpost.com/wp-dyn/content/article/2009/06/18/AR2009061804131.html/.

47. Michael Allen, "Iran: Regime 'Hemorrhaging' Power as Moussavi Announces Charter and New Political Front," *Democracy Digest*, July 23, 2009.

48. Ramin Ahmadi, "An Iranian Revolution That's Not Over Yet," *Forbes*, June 24, 2009, http://www.forbes.com/2009/06/24/iran-election-revolution-opinions-contributors-revolutionary-guard-coup.html/.

49. Abbas Milani, "Testimony before Committee on Foreign Affairs, U.S. House of Representatives, Hearings on: 'Iran: Recent Developments and Implications for U.S. Policy,' " July 22, 2009.

50. Pepe Escobar, "The Meaning of the Tehran Spring," *Asia Times Online*, June 16, 2009, http://www.atimes.com/atimes/Middle_East/KF16Ak02.html/. "Unjust Ruler Is Note Legitimate," Roozonline, July 13, 2009. http://www.roozonline.com/english/news/newsitem/article/////unjust-ruler-is-not-legitimate.html/.

51. Bendiz Anderson, "Ayatollah Watch," *Tehran Bureau*, July 21, 2009, http://tehranbureau.com/ayatollah-watch/.

52. Peter Beaumont, "Battle for Iran Shifts from the Streets to the Heart of Power," *The Observer*, June 28, 2009, http://www.guardian.co.uk/world/2009/jun/28/iran-mahmoud-ahmadinejad/.

53. Mir Hossein Mousavi, June 25, 2009 Report, http://www.mir-hosseinmousavi.com/news.html/.

54. Change for Equality, "Nargess Mohammadi: We Now Have to Speak of Hope and Love," July 5, 2009, http://www.we-change.org/english/spip.php?article546/.

Conclusion

Maria J. Stephan

The contributors to this volume illustrate how ordinary people in a notoriously rough geopolitical neighborhood have in numerous instances rejected docility and passivity, sometimes risking life and limb, to challenge formidable foes, situations, and conditions in the region. They have "been willing to brave death, in order to affirm life; to fight powerful overlords, in order to overcome their own powerlessness and vulnerability; and to stand up and risk repression, rather than remain on their knees," writes Rami Khoury. Rejecting violence, mostly on pragmatic, strategic grounds, the individuals, and civilian groups highlighted here decided to fight back and advance their goals using a different form of resistance. They did not always succeed, but their achievements are too many and too great to ignore, particularly for those interested in the expansion of freedom and justice in the Middle East.

Where there is repression, there is generally resistance.[1] In many of the cases examined in this book, groups turned to nonviolent struggle following years, and sometimes decades, of challenging militarily superior opponents using political violence. This shift was based, in part, on their recognition that a different, asymmetric strategy that harnessed the full power potential of the civilian population could be more effective. The questions posed at the beginning of this volume shed light on this trend.

Where Has Civil Resistance Been Used in the Middle East, by Whom, and for What Purposes? How Effective Has It Been?

As the essays and case studies in this book show, nonviolent civil resistance has been used to challenge colonial powers and foreign occupation, to resist domestic dictators and autocrats, and to promote social and political reforms, such as gender equality and an end to corruption.

Egyptians, Iranians, Israelis, Kuwaitis, Lebanese, Moroccans, Palestinians, Sahrawis, Afghans, Sudanese, Syrians, Turks, and other peoples have all embraced this method of struggle to achieve goals both reformist and revolutionary in nature, in both democracies and nondemocracies. They have done so in less developed societies (for example, in Afghanistan and Western Sahara) as well as in more economically advanced countries (such as Israel and Turkey). The targets of their nonviolent campaigns range from democracies (Britain, Israel, Turkey) to dictatorships (Mubarak's Egypt, the shah's Iran) to religious dictatorships (post-revolutionary Iran) to liberalized autocracies (Jordan, Kuwait, Morocco). These regimes have used brute force and violence as well as economic and political "carrots" to co-opt, manage, or repress opposition movements.[2]

Students, factory workers, women, intellectuals, lawyers, judges, merchants, business owners, taxi drivers, and religious leaders have been some of the "civilian mujahedeen" (in Khalid Kishtainy's words) who have challenged formidable opponents with steely determination. They've been young and old, rich and poor, urbanites and rural villagers. They were Muslims, Christians, Druze, Hindus, Jews, Sikhs, and nonreligionists. They were devoutly religious and strongly secular. Strange bedfellows, including ex-guerillas and pacifists, as well as ideological and political adversaries have joined forces in places like Afghanistan, Iran, Palestine, and Lebanon to nonviolently resist a common adversary.

Women have played a catalytic role in a number of the campaigns in the Middle East. As Tamar Hermann notes, the Israeli leaders of Arba Imahot, the Four Mothers movement, "used their maternal status as a political asset" to spearhead a grassroots campaign whose goal was to pressure the Israeli government into pulling out of the "Lebanese mud." As mothers of elite IDF soldiers who lived close to the border with Lebanon, the women had a great deal of credibility, which was further enhanced when they sought allies from across the political spectrum. Women in Iran, relegated to second-class citizenship after the 1979 Islamic revolution, have fought against difficult odds to promote gender equality in a society where power ultimately resides in the hands of a few male clerics. Palestinian women, Muslim and Christian, played a crucial role in sustaining the local community groups and popular committees that provided the organizational backbone for the first intifada. Scott Kennedy describes how Druze women peacefully confronted occupying Israeli soldiers, surrounding them and at times even going so far as to take away their weapons. Inside the occupied Western Sahara, women, including Aminatou Haidar, winner of a number of prestigious international human rights prizes, have shown steely determination while confronting Moroccan soldiers with little more than Sahrawi flags and other weapons of will, as Stephen Zunes and Salka Barca note.

Young people, the single largest constituency in the Middle East, have helped spearhead a number of civil resistance campaigns in the region and around the world. With a reputation for defying the establishment, penchant for risk-taking, savviness with technology, and a taste for challenging authority—which can be channeled violently or nonviolently—youth is a natural motor of popular struggle. Young professionals, students, and others were the driving force behind the successful Nabiha Five campaign to reform Kuwait's electoral system. In urging Kuwaitis to join in their movement, wearing orange to protest in front of the Seef Palace, these activists exhorted, "come, if you want to fight against corruption...come, if you care of your future and your children's future...come, if you love Kuwait...come."

Lebanese youth, similarly, provided the energy and organizational prowess to drive a grassroots campaign that won the backing of more than a million of their compatriots. These young people anchored the successful independence intifada with an around-the-clock sit-in in downtown Beirut and created a festive atmosphere that made protest hip and patriotic. The young leaders of the rapidly developing Egyptian April 6 movement, which grew from the earlier Kefaya movement, have used Facebook, MySpace, and other social networking Internet sites to expand the ranks of pro-democracy activists inside the country. The alliances they have forged with workers could be a critical element of their longer-term strategy of transforming Egypt's political system.

Nonviolent Islamist groups and movements have emerged as powerful actors in the Middle East during the last few decades. Yet, for reasons Shadi Hamid describes, mainstream Islamist groups in places like Egypt and Jordan have been loath to adopt more aggressive nonviolent tactics, not wishing to cause serious disruption to the political and economic status quo in those countries and wary of how their actions would be perceived by external actors. At the same time, groups like the Egyptian Muslim Brotherhood have gone out of their way to demonstrate to Western audiences their commitment to nonviolent means. Increased regime repression and the continued blockage of traditional political channels to them could lead Islamist groups to consider using more confrontational or subversive forms of civil resistance.

The nonviolent campaigns examined in *Civilian Jihad* achieved varying levels of success. Although no simple measure of "success" or "effectiveness" exists, particularly when analyzing complex social phenomena, the metric used here is whether and to what extent a campaign achieves its stated goals. Opposition goals can change over time. For instance, they may evolve from being limited in nature (e.g., passing specific legislation on corruption or gender equality) to becoming more maximalist in nature (e.g., replacing a dictatorship with a democratically elected government).

The struggles against colonialism and foreign occupation featured in this volume achieved varying levels of success. Lebanon's 2005 independence intifada brought about the withdrawal of Syrian forces from Lebanon, the resignation of a prime minister, and the holding of free and fair elections. Having achieved all three of these goals, the movement stands out as a highly effective campaign. At the same time, however, despite its successful action against foreign hegemony, the movement fell far short of transforming Lebanon's archaic, sectarian-based system of government in part because, as Rudy Jaafar and I discussed, there was no plan for sustained civic mobilization after the withdrawal of Syrian forces.

As Mary King notes, the first Palestinian intifada did more to advance Palestinian national goals in 18 months than the Palestine Liberation Organization accomplished with decades of armed struggle. This mass civilian-driven uprising eventually led to peace talks and in the process helped delegitimize the Israeli occupation in the eyes of many in Israel and the international community; it also strengthened the Israeli land-for-peace movement. It remains to be seen whether the current Palestinian-led efforts to challenge Israel's West Bank separation barrier using civil resistance will coalesce into a national strategy of nonviolent struggle to end that occupation and achieve statehood.

The Khudai Khidmatgar resistance movement posed a significant and sustained threat to British colonial rule. As Muhammad Raqib reveals, massive civil disobedience and noncooperation by the so-called Red Shirts, combined with negotiation efforts led by the Indian National Congress, imposed significant political and economic costs on the colonizing power, accelerating the process of decolonization. At the same time, the author acknowledges that the impressive nonviolent restraint shown by the Pashtun fighters eventually broke down in the face of brutal repression by the Raj. (A question worth pondering is whether and how civil resistance could be used to challenge violent extremism in today's North-west Frontier Province, where the the Taliban and al-Qaida continue to threaten regional and international peace and security. Syrian Druze embraced a policy of total noncooperation to resist Israel's attempted annexation of the Golan Heights. Although the Golan Heights remains under Israeli occupation, its Druze population has maintained its cultural and national (Syrian) identity. The Sahrawi self-determination struggle in Western Sahara has so far achieved minimal success. The Sahrawi independence movement has organized sporadic protests inside the occupied territory, despite police state conditions, and has succeeded in attracting international support. Negotiations over the territory's status between the opposition Polisario and the Moroccan government, however, remain stalled.

Popular anti-authoritarian movements also have a mixed track record. As Mohsen Sazegara and I described, the 1979 Iranian Revolution, one of the most consequential and paradoxical of nonviolent movements, successfully ousted a secular dictator in less than 100 days, but it consolidated power in the hands of a leadership that had little interest in democracy or democratic power sharing. Because those leading the anti-shah uprising were not guided by democratic principles, it is not surprising that the revolution turned into a bloodbath. Yet that mixed record did not prevent leaders of the 2009 "green movement" from associating themselves with the original goals—of justice and virtue—of that revolution. As mass protests continue in the wake of the contested June 2009 presidential elections and more erstwhile regime supporters join the side of the opposition, it is improbable that the theocratic regime will be able to persist in its current state indefinitely.

The nonviolent challenge to the Mubarak regime in Egypt has made significant advances without achieving victory. Before the Kefaya movement began launching nonviolent street actions in 2004, demonstrating in public against the regime had been considered too risky. Sherif Mansour notes that although Kefaya petered out, the movement brought civil resistance into the political mainstream, pressured the regime to hold Egypt's first multiparty elections and paved the way for new movements, including campaigns organized by judges, students, workers, and opposition parties. With parliamentary elections scheduled for November 2010 a youth and worker-led movement could play a critical role in mobilizing the population, disillusioned by the political and economic stagnation in the country, around an acceptable opposition candidate or coalition.

The reform-oriented resistance campaigns discussed in this book were relatively successful, including the Orange Movement in Kuwait, as noted above. Hamad Albloshi and Faisal al-Fahad share that the movement that succeeded in transforming Kuwait's electoral system made the calculated decision to disband after the law creating the five districts was enacted, but have left open the possibility of regrouping for pro-democracy goals in the future. In Iran, a campaign for women's rights has, according to Roya Tolouee, Fariba Davoudi, and Shaazka Beyerle, built a significant grassroots constituency in support of gender equality, but it has yet to change the country's discriminatory gender laws. The One Million Signatures campaign, the authors assert, paved the way to the massive challenge to the Ahmadinejad government in the wake of the 2009 presidential elections whose outcome hangs in the balance.

The anti-corruption movement in Egypt spearheaded by Shayfeen.com and Egyptians Against Corruption, says Arwa Hassan, has empowered ordinary citizens to record, publicize, and protest voter intimidation and electoral fraud. The campaign, which has even attracted supporters from within Egypt's ruling National

Democratic Party (NDP), led to the enactment of the Judicial Reform Law in 2006 and sent a clear message to government officials that blatant political corruption would no longer be tolerated. Shaazka Beyerle details how in Turkey the Citizen Initiative for Constant Light, launched by a group of lawyers and aided by an effective communications strategy, paved the way for a series of judicial investigations that led to the prosecution of a number of prominent officials and crime syndicate members and put corruption atop the national agenda.

The Israeli Four Mothers movement, whose single goal was the unilateral withdrawal of Israeli forces from southern Lebanon, succeeded in building a formidable grassroots movement while gaining unprecedented access to Israeli policymakers. The role played by the movement in Israel's 2000 withdrawal continues to be debated in Israel, but the campaign is held up as the paradigm of effective civic action in the country.

What Are the Main Challenges and Obstacles Faced by Advocates and Practitioners of Civil Resistance in the Region? How Have They Been Overcome?

The challenges to civil resistance in the Middle East are formidable, but not insurmountable. Conceptual barriers and misunderstandings that Philip Grant and Ralph Crow describe—that nonviolent resistance is somehow antithetical to Arab and Muslim culture and values, that it connotes weakness or capitulation, or that it cannot be effective against sophisticated armies or repressive regimes—have discouraged a serious discussion about civil resistance and its role in challenging oppressive and unjust power structures in the region. As the cases and essays in this book suggest, the credibility of those advocating civilian jihad and the ability of this form of resistance to demonstrate results are two of the most important factors in determining popular support for it. As Grant and Crow assert, "the purpose of nonviolent political struggle is to mobilize, not paralyze, oppressed and disempowered people." At the same time, local legitimacy and the ability to declare periodic victories are critical elements of success.

In addition to conceptual barriers, a number of structural and geostrategic obstacles hinder civil resistance in this part of the world. The persistence of rentier states is an obvious challenge to civil resistance and democratization, yet even petrol states depend to varying degrees on the consent and obedience of their populations to maintain their grip on political power. As Hardy Merriman notes in his overview of civil resistance, the obedience patterns and loyalties of members of key societal organizations and institutions—including expansive bureaucracies, the oil industry, state-owned media and transport sectors, and security forces—are malleable and often change in response to domestic and external action.

The shah of Iran, whose regime relied heavily on oil revenue and the backing of Western governments, was ultimately unable to maintain control over a population much of which was engaged in mass civil disobedience and noncooperation. Striking Iranian oil workers imposed severe economic costs on the shah's regime, and other "pillars of support," including students, clerics, and merchants, stubbornly defied emergency rule, making it impossible for the regime and its functionaries to immobilize society. In Kuwait, the Orange Movement demonstrated how, even in a wealthy oil state, sustained civic pressure, focused messaging, and coalition building can succeed in fundamentally altering the political status quo. Although reformist in nature, the movement's campaign illustrates that organized civil resistance can thwart oil-enriched rulers' efforts to impose their will on the population.

The Iranian Revolution and the Kuwaiti Orange Movement succeeded without any significant support from foreign governments. The mass noncooperation effort involving virtually every group in Iranian society made it impossible for the shah to maintain effective rule despite the huge economic and military support he received from Western powers. The Kuwaiti grassroots campaign succeeded in producing splits in the country's ruling elites that allowed the passage of a new electoral law. Although the Lebanese March 14 Movement received strong backing from the U.S., French, and Saudi governments, which applied significant pressure on Syria and the Syrian-backed Lebanese government, it occurred against the backdrop of a self-financed grassroots campaign that brought more than a million Lebanese into the streets in an impressive display of domestic opposition to Syrian hegemony. In this way, Lebanese mass action and external support were mutually reinforcing. It is unlikely that external pressure alone would have led to a Syrian withdrawal.

Regime repression is another major obstacle for those advocating civil resistance in the Middle East. The tactical opportunities for civil resistance in democratic countries (Lebanon, Turkey, Israel) differ from those in closed and authoritarian societies (Iran, Tunisia, Western Sahara), where freedom of speech and assembly are severely circumscribed, domestic security forces quell dissent, and prisons are filled with nonviolent oppositionists accused of undermining state security. There is a higher degree of personal risk involved in participating in nonviolent direct action in repressed societies, where publishing a critical article or participating in a street demonstration can lead to arrest, detention, torture, or death.

A number of nonviolent campaigns and movements described in this book have been able to create political space while muting the impact of regime repression, by engaging in dispersed, as opposed to concentrated, forms of nonviolent action. The wearing of common symbols (as in the Shayfeen.com and Kefaya campaigns) and the organization of boycotts and stay-aways (most notably in the Iranian Revolution and first Palestinian intifada) are two examples of dispersed actions that enable mass participation while allowing for individual anonymity. The flicking on and off of lights at 9pm each evening to protest corruption during the Constant Light campaign in Turkey was another classic example of a low-risk, high-impact tactic that proved to be very effective. The Iranian women's movement that Roya Tolouee, Fariba Davoudi, and Shaazka Beyerle examine moved from high-risk street protests to the One Million Signatures campaign, transforming a lawful activity into a form of opposition recruitment.

On the other hand, high-risk, confrontational forms of nonviolent direct action can be quite disruptive, gaining visibility for a movement, and demonstrating courage, which might influence other portions of the population to participate. It may also be the case, however, as the Iranian Revolution and Lebanese intifada seem to demonstrate, that large numbers of people are generally more inclined to take part in high-risk, confrontational forms of nonviolent direct action when they believe that large numbers of people will join them, and when they feel confident that they are part of a movement that has a chance of succeeding. Media coverage of nonviolent mass action, via traditional and Web-based sources, played a key role in demonstrating both the courage of the individual protestors and the growing strength of the opposition. The Lebanese independence intifada received strong backing from its press and the main building of the popular al-Nahar newspaper served as the operations center for the popular uprising.

Nonviolent campaigns targeting external powers, notably foreign occupations, often face the challenge of being more dependent (particularly economically) on their opponents than vice-versa. This is a significant challenge facing the Sahrawi and Palestinian populations in their struggles against the Moroccan and Israeli occupations, respectively. By combining civil resistance inside the occupied territories with traditional (judicial and legislative) and non-traditional forms of nonviolent direct action inside the opponent's society—in a sense "extending the nonviolent battlefield"[3]—Sahrawis and Palestinians could more directly target the pillars of support that Morocco and Israel rely upon to maintain their military occupations. The joint nonviolent resistance involving Palestinians and Israelis on both sides of the Green Line during the first intifada, Mary King noted, was intended to send the message that peaceful coexistence was possible, but that the occupation was debasing both peoples and needed to be ended. More recently, Palestinians whose lives and livelihoods have been negatively impacted by the West Bank separation barrier have used Israeli courts to make their case—on at least one occasion the court has ruled in their favor.

In democratic contexts, not only are there fewer restrictions on communication and mobilization than in authoritarian, semi-authoritarian, or foreign occupation situations, it is also generally easier for nonviolent oppositionists to access and wield influence inside traditional political institutions and through normal political and legal processes. This is a lesson of the Israeli Four Mothers movement, whose strategy was to move its message from the streets to the Knesset. The Kuwaiti Orange Movement and the Lebanese March 14 Movement pursued a similar inside-outside strategy, working closely with opposition political factions to advance their political goals.

At the same time, there are drawbacks to allying too closely with opposition parties, something that can limit the independent manoeuvrability of a grassroots movement, lead to accusations of partisanship and erode its broad-based appeal. In certain respects, this is what occurred with the March 14 movement after the withdrawal of Syrian forces from Lebanon. On the other hand, the strictly non-partisan nature of the Constant Light campaign in Turkey and the One Million Signatures campaign in Iran enhanced their ability to attract and maintain supporters from diverse parts of society.

Technology and Digital Activism

Technology poses an opportunity as well as a challenge for nonviolent activists. Technological advances have helped revolutionize the conduct of civil resistance.[4] Different communication technologies, from cassette tapes to Facebook, have played critical roles in the nonviolent campaigns featured in *Civilian Jihad*. In some cases, low-technology solutions were all that was needed. For example, during the Palestinian intifada, the Unified National Leadership Command of the Uprising drafted and distributed hundreds of numbered leaflets containing the goals and campaigns of the resistance. The flyers appeared "mysteriously" on street corners every couple of weeks and were read and followed religiously by Palestinians. Iranian women, in organizing a demonstration in Tehran to mark International Women's Day in 2005, overcame state control of the newspapers by preparing small packages containing candy and a leaflet, which they used to spread news about the protest around the country.

Other cases relied on analog technology. The Iranian Revolution is sometimes referred to as the "cassette revolution" because of the critical role of tapes smuggled into the country that contained speeches and instructions by Ayatollah Ruhollah Khomeini. Relying on mass, decentralized digital technology, the Lebanese independence intifada was referred to by observers as the "SMS revolution" because of its use of instant messaging to mobilize more than a million protestors from all parts of the country. Sahrawi activists inside and outside Western Sahara created Paltalk chat rooms to communicate and organize nonviolent protests. A new generation of Egyptian democratic activists has begun the so-called Facebook revolution, but now must transform virtual communication into real-time nonviolent mass action.[5]

Technology, however, can only take a nonviolent movement so far. Autocrats and occupiers have access to the same technologies as do nonviolent activists. In addition to the communications power that Middle Eastern regimes possess through their control of state-run media, they also to varying degrees have developed ways to censor, restrict, and in some cases completely halt cell phone and Internet use. It is therefore through the deliberate, strategic use of new technologies that movements have been able to leverage them to their advantage.

What Roles Have Ideology, Discourse, and Rhetoric Played in Legitimizing and Mobilizing Popular Resistance, Violent and Nonviolent?

In the Middle East marketplace of ideas, it might appear that civil resistance could never compete with armed struggle. Violent Salafi movements, such as al-Qaida, benefit from outsized media coverage and political attention due to the shocking nature of some of their attacks. The paradigm of violent jihad and the cultural significance of martyrdom in the region, as Rola el-Husseini described, combined with real-time images of civilian deaths resulting from Israeli military operations in Palestine and Lebanon and U.S. actions in Afghanistan, Iraq, and other parts of the region, have made it difficult for a discourse of nonviolent power to take root. At the same time, ideology, rhetoric, and discourse are malleable, social constructs that can be reinterpreted and adapted to changing circumstances. Hizbullah, a group that once called for the creation of an Islamic state in Lebanon, has not only abandoned that part of its original platform, it has accepted political pluralism and even embraced civil resistance as a means to advance its domestic goals. As el-Husseini noted, this acceptance of nonviolent struggle in the domestic context has not, however, extended to Hizbullah's understanding of resistance to Israel.

Culture, history, religion, and language can be reinterpreted by local actors to support civil resistance and channel militancy in nonviolent ways. Badshah Khan, who dedicated his life to the service of his community, took a Pashtun people famous for their militancy and blood feud tradition and channelled that spirit of resistance into the creation of the first nonviolent army. The pledge required of Khudai Khidmatgar members emphasized honor, duty, self-sacrifice, service, and resistance. In the years leading up to the first intifada, Palestinian "activist intellectuals" overcame significant conceptual hurdles, highlighted by decades of violent revolutionary rhetoric and PLO-led armed resistance, to build a new discourse on nonviolent resistance to Israeli occupation. Some of them built a mobile library containing some of the most important writings on civil resistance concepts and cases translated into Arabic. These ideas found their way into the intifada's famed leaflets, which articulated the goals and campaigns of nonviolent resistance during the popular uprising.

Religion and religious rhetoric is an especially powerful force for both violent and nonviolent mobilization. As Bayat writes, "Nothing intrinsic to Islam, or to any other religion, makes it inherently democratic or undemocratic, peaceful or violent. What matters are the ways in which the faithful perceive, articulate, and live through their faiths...In a sense, religious injunctions are nothing but our understanding of them; they are what we make them." Rami Khouri brings this point to life in his discussion of religion and religious discourse in inspiring principled resistance to injustice. Comparing the religious underpinnings of the U.S. civil rights movement with the "Islamist awakening" in the Middle East, Khouri shows how in both cases "religion validates and empowers political action, mobilizes communities, legitimizes protest, and gives hope, confidence, strength, and unity to citizens who otherwise feel intimidated by the more powerful ruling forces in their societies."

It remains to be seen whether cultural and religious justification of the means (violent or nonviolent) and ends (democratic rule or *sharia* or some combination) of various movements in the Middle East will lead to a battle about the interpretation of the concept of jihad itself. It seems likely, however, that a battle over this term will intensify as recourse to civil resistance becomes more widespread in the Middle East.

Beyond religious rhetoric, different forms of social and political discourse have also been used by movements in the region. One of the most powerful, not to mention highly entertaining, examples of this is the adoption of humor and satire. Whereas violent extremists often resort to hate-filled rhetoric and incitements to revenge to stir the masses, civil resistors often use humor as part of their nonviolent arsenal. Jokes, which can help people cope and survive under conditions of repression, can also be a source of popular provocation and collective dissent. Kishtainy discusses how jokes and political satire have been used in the Middle East to expose the hypocrisy, incompetence, and unjust ways of political leaders, while promoting a sense of solidarity and collective identity among citizens. As Kishtainy note, "There is no record of a regime falling because of a joke, but there is hardly any such event occurring without being preceded by a rich harvest of political jokes and satirical literature...Encouragement of the development and widespread use of political humor and satirical literature should be an essential part of any strategy of civil resistance." The spread of Internet-based and cellular communication technologies may increase the frequency of humor as a galvanizing force in the Middle East, particularly in Egypt.

In order for groups to switch from supporting violent insurrection to adopting nonviolent action, advocates of civil resistance must be able to challenge, on strategic grounds, the embrace of armed struggle. Challenges on strictly moral grounds are unlikely to hold much sway in a region where the vast majority of people feel that they are repressed or under external threat and therefore feel that aggressive resistance is morally justified. A discourse of nonviolent power could gain traction in part by comparing the costs, effectiveness, and success of armed struggle versus unarmed struggle, revealing that nonviolent action to be a viable and powerful option for resistance.[6]

How Have External Actors, Governmental and Nongovernmental, Influenced the Trajectories and Outcomes of Civil Resistance Campaigns in the Region?

The nonviolent campaigns reviewed here were homegrown, locally led, and largely bottom-up. "No foreign government or NGO," assert Saad Ibrahim and Stephen Zunes, "can recruit or mobilize the large numbers of ordinary civilians necessary to build a movement capable of effectively challenging the established political leadership, much less of toppling a government." Yet, one cannot discount the problematic roles played by external actors. Ibrahim and Zunes note that "fears surrounding terrorism and Islamist political movements have dampened even the few occasional impulses of Western leaders to stand up to Arab dictators." The terrible irony for U.S. foreign policy generally, Rami Khouri writes, "is that something akin to the civil rights movement is already taking place in the Middle East, but in the eyes of many in the region, the United States seems to be on the wrong side of the equation of justice versus oppression."

These authors go on to discuss nonmilitary tools at the disposal of foreign governments to support nonviolent pro-democratic movements in the region. The suggestions they offer include making economic and military aid conditional upon regimes' respect for minimal standards of human rights and democratic reform, supporting free and independent media, publicly condemning regime repression of nonviolent oppositionists and calling for the release of political prisoners, and abolishing antidemocratic policies and practices at home. A project launched by the Community of Democracies, the *Diplomat's Handbook for Democracy Development Support,* highlights the many practical tools and resources at the disposal of democratic embassies and diplomats to assist local nonviolent change agents in accordance with international law—and suggests ways that local activists can seek out help from embassies.

External pressure in the form of political, diplomatic, and economic sanctions, along with the threatened suspension of military aid, accompanied (but did not precede) a few of the popular nonviolent campaigns examined. The coordinated pressure on the Syrian-backed regime in Lebanon by the United States, France, and Saudi Arabia that coincided with the rise of an organized opposition in 2005 is a good example of this. As mentioned previously, however, it is unlikely that such external pressure would have been forthcoming, or that it would have forced a Syrian withdrawal in the absence of a mass, broad-based popular civic campaign demanding an end to Syrian interference in Lebanon's domestic affairs. Another example is the shift in U.S. policy toward Israel following the outbreak of the first intifada in December 1987 that included supporting UN resolutions condemning Israel's violent response to the uprising, recognizing the PLO as the official representative of the Palestinian people, and pressuring Israel to begin negotiations with the Palestinians.

External support for liberal democrats and secular political parties in the Middle East is an important way to further regional democratization, as Sherif Mansour argues. At the same time Hamid and Khouri emphasize that Western governments must engage with nonviolent Islamist groups that have already entered the political mainstream, including those that may turn to nonviolent civil resistance. Although there may be differences in opinion between these parties over the substance of democratic reform, ignoring or marginalizing Islamist groups is inconsistent with engaging with forces that challenge the Middle East's authoritarian status quo.

Ibrahim and Zunes highlight what diaspora groups and NGOs can do to support local nonviolent movements in the Middle East: these include sharing generic lessons and experiences of nonviolent activists and movements from other parts of the world, supporting the development of new technologies to allow groups to communicate past repression, and translating civil resistance books, films, videogames and training curricula into local languages.

What Lessons about Strategic Nonviolent Action Can Be Distilled from the Cases Discussed in This Book? How Does Skillful Civil Resistance Relate to Democratic Development?

As the essays in this book have demonstrated, the path of civil resistance is rarely linear or smooth. Unexpected twists and turns, frustrating set-backs and exhilarating victories make up the tableau of nonviolent struggle in the Middle East and in other parts of the world. Managing expectations, creating and taking advantage of opportunities, communicating clearly, being prepared to withstand repression, and maintaining movement momentum through adaptation, creativity, and tactical diversification are critical challenges. As with any skills-based enterprise, experience and training lead to improved performance in the conduct of civilian resistance.

A single blueprint for successful nonviolent resistance does not exist, as Hardy Merriman noted. Yet, it is possible to extract generalizeable principles of success from past campaigns and movements. Civil resistance scholars have identified three key principles of successful civil resistance. The presence of these critical ingredients may not be sufficient to guarantee success, though without all three it is unlikely that a nonviolent campaign will succeed. The three ingredients are unity, strategic planning, and nonviolent discipline,[7] which I touch on briefly. It is my hope that future researchers will examine the strategic dynamics of the campaigns and movements in this book in greater detail, and compare civil resistance in the Middle East to its applications in other parts of the world.

Unity: Creating a viable opposition requires that different groups unite around shared goals and strategies. The higher the level of unity within the opposition in the cases in this book, and the greater the diversity of groups involved in the nonviolent resistance, the more difficult it was for the opponent to suppress them and the better they performed. In many cases, unifying the opposition is more than half the battle in nonviolent struggles. The Palestinian intifada (at least during the first 18 months), the Golani Druze anti-assimilation campaign, the Lebanese independence intifada, the Kuwaiti Orange Movement, and the anti-corruption campaigns in Turkey and Egypt all developed unique strategies and tactics to promote unity and solidarity.

The strict code of conduct and rigorous training regimen that the Khudai Khidmatgar voluntarily accepted prior to joining the Pashtun-led nonviolent army, the creation of popular committees and voluntary associations in the Palestinian territories in the years leading up to the first intifada; the focus on intra-communal unity at the start of the Druze campaign that included targeting those who refused to destroy their Israeli ID cards with social ostracism; the creation of a central web-site and blog in Kuwait to unite the tech-savvy population's disparate voices of opposition around a central goal; the "anonymous aunt" who left messages for ordinary Turks to stand up to corruption; the creation of a massive tent city in downtown Beirut, complete with a huge stage for speeches and performances during the independence intifada—these were a few ways the civil resistors from this region of the world sought to bridge divides and forge a common path of struggle.

Common symbols, slogans, songs, and even jokes are used to promote unity and a sense of shared purpose in nonviolent struggles. The wearing of red uniforms and the swearing of a common oath by the Khudai Khidmatgar, the red and white scarves, the one flag policy, and the "100% Lebanese" slogan chosen by the Lebanese March 14 movement, the symbol of the eye selected by the Egyptian anti-corruption movement, and the color orange that became synonymous with the Nabiha 5 movement were only a few of the symbolic unifying elements described in the book.

There are obvious challenges to achieving unity, particularly in countries that are ethnically, culturally, and religiously diverse and where the opponent has employed the time tested stratagem of divide and rule. Until now, deep divisions between Fatah and Hamas have impeded the formation of a national Palestinian strategy to resist the Israeli occupation. The huge gulf between the March 8 and March 14 movements in Lebanon produced a stand-off that many Lebanese feared would lead to civil war after the withdrawal of Syrian forces. The ideologically ambiguous anti-shah coalition in Iran, which lacked any democratic underpinnings, quickly collapsed following the 1979 revolution and led to a bloodbath. In this sense, as Grant and Crow noted, the purely opportunistic embrace of civil resistance and/ or the belief that the two methods of struggle (violent and nonviolent) can be used interchangeably is highly problematic, particularly for those interested in institutionalizing nonviolent means of resolving societal conflicts.

More generally, the persistence of divisions between Islamists and secular democrats, some of which are founded on fundamental differences in their political visions (despite overlap on the issue of ousting the incumbent regime) have so far inhibited the emergence of broad, unified secular-Islamist fronts to challenge the Middle East's autocrats. The inability of diverse opposition groups to achieve unity, if only temporarily, and to build broad-based coalitions involving multiple sectors of society is a weakness plaguing many pro-democracy groups in the Middle East.

Strategic Planning: The second key ingredient of successful nonviolent struggles is strategic planning, or what Robert Helvey describes as "devising the basic idea of how the struggle of a specific campaign shall develop, and how its separate components shall be fitted together to contribute most advantageously to achieving its objectives"[8]. As Bayat wrote in this volume, "although structural constraints and state-sponsored repression pose challenges to effective nonviolent resistance, strategic planning can greatly empower groups to recognize and exploit opportunities by tying acts of resistance to specific sociopolitical goals."

Effective strategy involves using all available resources in the service of political goals, based on an assessment of the opportunities and constraints presented in a particular conflict environment. Core features of good strategy, outlined in chapter one, include selecting achievable objectives, concentrating opposition strengths against opponent weaknesses and eroding the opponent's pillars of support, expanding participation by building coalitions, innovating tactically, and maintaining the initiative. Movements that were able to adapt those principles and apply them to their particular situations, as in Iran, Kuwait, Israel, and Lebanon, proved to be successful.

Organizational innovations enhanced strategic planning in a few cases. The Unified National Leadership Command of the Uprising, which was responsible for drafting the leaflets outlining the goals and activities of the Palestinian intifada, played a critical role in uniting the different PLO factions while providing strategic guidance for the uprising; in Lebanon, the "chamber noire" core group of civic leaders that met in the back room of al-Nahar functioned as the planning hub of the March 14 movement and served as the bridge between the grassroots and the plural opposition; in Iran, the strategic guidance for the Islamic revolution came from the exiled Khomeini and his close advisors, though the mosque-bazaar network inside Iran facilitated the mass mobilization.

The strategic acumen demonstrated by the leaders of the Kuwaiti Orange Movement was especially noteworthy. The leaders of that movement set a realistic goal—reducing the number of electoral districts in the country—rather than calling for a more extreme goal like abolishing the monarchy. They adapted their strategy, switching from nonviolent direct action to supporting the electoral process in order to ensure the victory of Bloc 29 candidates and other opposition supporters. The Israeli Four Mothers movement, similarly, focused on a single goal—Israeli troop withdrawal from southern Lebanon—and built a broad-based coalition of supporters both inside and outside the Knesset, while using symbolic actions, like stretching a green cloth along the Israeli-Lebanese border to symbolically "re-demarcate" the international boundary between the two countries.

The sequencing of nonviolent tactics so as to maximize pressure on the opponent is a critical component of strategy. Lebanon's independence intifada, whose anchor was a tent city in downtown Beirut, at first featured peaceful marches and vigils, then ramped up pressure with larger rallies and strikes until the prime minister resigned, then meticulously planned for the demonstration on March 14 that ammassed more than a million Lebanese from all parts of the country. The mass noncooperation campaign launched by nearly every segment of Iranian society during the 1979 revolution, including a national strike that paralyzed the country, proved to be the shah's undoing. No amount of coercive force or martial law could control a population engaged in mass civil disobedience. Campaigns that rely too heavily on a single tactic, such as street demonstrations, risk losing momentum and popular support. At first this was a weakness of the Iranian women's movement until the women regrouped and developed a new strategy; in Egypt, the lack of tactical diversity was a problem that plagued Kefaya.

Nonviolent Discipline: Nonviolent discipline, the third key element of successful nonviolent struggles, gives nonviolent campaigns a strategic advantage over militarily superior adversaries. Nonviolent discipline helps delegitimize the opponent's use of violent repression, encourages loyalty shifts within the opponent's pillars of support, and encourages broad-based civilian participation. In a few cases in this volume, including Iran, Kuwait, Lebanon, the Northwest Frontier Province, Palestine, and the Syrian Golan, disciplined nonviolent resistance helped neutralize—and even co-opt the opponent's security apparatus. In these instances, fraternization with the opponent's security forces, avoiding threatening actions, and being clear about the opposition's nonviolent intentions increased the likelihood that regimes would pay a political price for violently cracking down on the nonviolent opposition.

Shifting the loyalties of the shah's army and policy was an integral part of the Iranian revolution, where special appeals were made to the security forces and flowers were placed in the barrels of soldiers' guns. Although the first Palestinian intifada was not completely nonviolent, the popular nature of the uprising, which featured masses of unarmed men, women, and children confronting Israeli soldiers, caused splits within the Israeli public and prompted an unprecedented Israeli refusenik movement. Describing the Israeli Four Mothers movement, Hermann writes, "only a firm adherence to nonviolent means could bring the masses on board, generate positive coverage by the media, and create alliances with mainstream politicians who also supported withdrawal from Lebanon."

In Kuwait, the leaders of the Nabiha 5 movement took great pains to demonstrate their commitment to nonviolent discipline even as they engaged in confrontational activities. They even informed the Minister of Interior of their planned demonstrations—not to seek permission, but to show their nonviolent intentions. During the dramatic storming of the parliament, Orange activists met with Special Forces officers and assured them that the security forces would not be targeted with violence. A bloody stand-off between the security forces and the opposition was averted.

The huge March 14 demonstration in Lebanon resulted in not a single injury or even a piece of broken glass. Extensive media coverage of the nonviolent mobilization taking place, good communication involving different parts of the movement, and a cadre of Lebanese leaders who advocated nonviolent resistance from the very beginning contributed to the extremely high level of nonviolent discipline shown by the opposition. The Lebanese opposition also made a point of fraternizing with the security forces and appealing to their sense of patriotism. Media coverage of nonviolent campaigns and movements, a topic worthy of its own book, was identified by a number of authors as being critically important to building domestic and international support for those engaged in civil resistance.

At the same time, however, there is never any guarantee that the opponent's use of violence against a nonviolent opposition will backfire, nor can nonviolent discipline compensate for the lack of effective strategic planning. The Moroccan government's use of repression against nonviolent Sahrawi activists provoked an outcry from international human rights organizations, but the Sahrawi-led resistance has not yet made Morocco sufficiently uncomfortable to bring about an act of self-determination in Western Sahara. The Palestinian intifada, which created divisions within Israeli society and prompted its military to rethink the wisdom of occupation by force, eventually succumbed to internecine violence and armed (but not especially effective) attacks against Israeli targets.

Civil Resistance and Democratization

Empirical findings linking civil resistance to durable democracy highlight the importance of studying "people power" in the least democratic region of the world.[9] As Crow and Grant assert, "the purpose of nonviolent political struggle is to mobilize, not paralyze, oppressed and disempowered people. The choice of nonviolent methods is made out of a collective conviction that only these means can ensure political change will be truly remedial rather than temporary and superficial."

The highly participatory nature of nonviolent struggles (compared to most armed campaigns), the tendency of such struggles to enjoin the support of large numbers of diverse people from different societal sectors, their emphasis on civic organization and decentralized power, and the way that sustained civic pressure encourages accountability by power holders are core attributes of functioning democracies. As Bayat writes, "civic mobilization...remains indispensable to meaningful and sustained democratic reform of the state. A shift in a society's sensibilities remains a precondition for democratic transformation."

Most, if not all of the nonviolent campaigns and movements featured in this book involved large numbers of people coming together—even if only temporarily—to challenge existing power structures and work toward common goals. An active citizenry is the bedrock of democratic development. A distinguishing aspect of the first Palestinian Intifada was the way in which local communities took matters into their own hands by organizing village-level popular committees throughout the occupied territories. These committees became the locus of nonviolent activism before and during the Intifada. The participatory local governance that characterized the first Intifada stands in stark contrast to the PA authoritarianism that followed. Similarly, participatory governance has been a key feature of the SADR refugee camps in Tindouf, Algeria, where Sahrawis have shown a penchant for nonviolently challenging the Polisario while maintaining a unified front against the Moroccan occupation.

The Kefaya movement, which united Egyptians from across the political and ideological spectrum, was a microcosm of political pluralism. However, the movement was unable to pressure the various opposition parties (secular and Islamic) in Egypt to coalesce in order to present a more unified front against the Mubarak regime. The cross-sectarian dialogue and cooperation that occurred in Lebanon during the Independence Intifada (including the youth mingling in the tent city) was a positive example of civic engagement. On the other hand, the persistent divisions between the March 8 and March 14 camps and the institutionalized sectarianism inherent in Lebanon's political system continue to pose obstacles to Lebanon's democratic development. In Kuwait, the successful effort by Nabiha 5 to put pressure on parliamentarians and ally with the Bloc 29 to advance a reform initiative was an excellent example of organized civic action contributing to more responsive governance.

The anti-corruption campaigns in Egypt and Turkey chronicled in this book are classic examples of organized civic action challenging one of the greatest obstacles to democratic governance around the world. Both campaigns helped transform frustrated and disillusioned people into watchdogs and active citizens, by providing them with the information and means to identify and report corruption. As the cases in this book have shown, civil resistance affords people the means to hold governments accountable and challenge institutions that are corrupt, incompetent, or hostile to a particular group's needs—without recourse to violence.

The examples in this book illustrate the ways in which civil resistance, when used in conjunction with traditional forms of political and legal advocacy, can strengthen democratic governance and thereby embed them more deeply in the democratic development of a society. Though there will be exceptions, such as the '79 Iranian Revolution, it can be generally argued that nonviolent movements inherently contribute to democratic development in societies, because once a population is able nonviolently to hold an authoritarian government accountable, it is reasonable to assume that that population would have a fair chance of doing so again if necessary.

The contest between civilian groups vying for democratic freedoms and self-determination in the Middle East and their regime opponents is exactly that—a contest. The success of civil resistance is not a function of destiny, it is a function of work. Yet, if the cases and trends discussed here are any indicators, civil resistance will likely play a bigger role in the months, years, and decades ahead in the Middle East, possibly making it the prime driver of a wave of democratic transitions in the region.

Notes

1. For an elaboration on this theme as it relates to the Islamic world, see Mohammed A. Hafez, *Why Muslims Rebel: Repression and Resistance in the Islamic World* (Boulder, CO: Lynne Rienner, 2003).

2. See Erica Chenoweth and Maria J. Stephan, "Mobilization and Resistance: A Framework for Analysis," in Erica Chenoweth and Adria Lawrence, eds., *Rethinking Violence: State and Non-State Actors in Conflict* (Cambridge, MA.: MIT Press, forthcoming 2010).

3. See Maria J. Stephan, "Fighting for Statehood: The Role of Civilian-based Resistance in the East Timorese, Palestinian, and Kosovo Albanian Self-Determination Struggles," *Fletcher Forum on World Affairs* 30, no. 2 (Summer 2006); M. Stephan and Jacob Mundy, "Battlefield Transformed: From Guerilla Resistance to Mass Nonviolent Struggle in the Western Sahara," *Journal of Military and Strategic Studies* 8, no. 3 (Spring 2006).

4. Regarding the latter, for example, the central mission of one nongovernmental organization, Digiactive, is to develop and disseminate to nonviolent activists worldwide knowledge about and best practices related to new technologies. This international volunteer organization has created a guide to assist nonviolent activists and movements in using Facebook as part of their struggles. The manual, translated into Arabic, has been used by April 6 activists in Egypt. See www.digiactive.org.

5. See Sherif Mansour, "Egypt Facebook Showdown," *Los Angeles Times,* June 2, 2008, www.latimes.com/news/opinion/la-oe-mansour2–2008jun02,0,323158.story; David Wolman, "Cairo Activists Use Facebook to Rattle Regime," *Wired Magazine*, October 20, 2008, www.wired.com/print/techbiz/startups/magazine/16–11/ff_facebookegypt.

6. For more information on the development of a discourse of nonviolent power, see Hardy Merriman and Jack DuVall, "Dissolving Terrorism at Its Roots," in *Nonviolence: An Alternative for Countering Global Terror(ism)*, ed. Ralph Summy and Senthil Ram (Hauppauge, NY: Nova Science, 2007).

7. For an elaboration of these three key ingredients, see Peter Ackerman and Jack DuVall, *People Power Primed: Civil Resistance and Democratization.* (Cambridge, MA: Harvard International Review Summer 2005. pp. 42–47).

8. Robert L. Helvey, *On Strategic Nonviolent Conflict: Thinking About the Fundamentals.* Boston, MA: Albert Einstein Institution, 2004. p. 151

9. Peter Ackerman and Adrian Karatnacky, eds., *How Freedom Is Won: From Civic Mobilization to Durable Democracy* (Washington, DC: Freedom House, 2005).

Contributors

HAMAD ALBLOSHI received his master's degree in International Relations at the Fletcher School of Law and Diplomacy, Tufts University. He formerly worked as a news reporter for the Kuwait News Agency (KUNA) and has been an assistant professor at Kuwait University in the Department of Political Science since 2005.

FAISAL ALFAHAD is an assistant professor at Kuwait University's School of Law. He served on the commission established by the Kuwait Transparency Society to monitor the 2008 parliamentary elections in Kuwait. Alfahad was chosen to lead a team in a joint project of the Kuwaiti Council of Ministries and the World Bank to assist the Kuwaiti government in implementing the United Nations Convention against Corruption; he was also asked by Parliamentarians Against Corruption to develop a toolkit on the convention for distribution to Arab members of parliament. Alfahad received his L.L.M. and S.J.D. degrees from the Dedman School of Law, Southern Methodist University.

SALKA BARCA, a Saharawi activist, is an outreach coordinator for the Saharawi diasporas and an advocate for nonviolent struggle through the use of technology. She also works as an independent translator and interpreter. Barca was born in al-Aaiun (el-Ayoune), Western Sahara, and grew up in refugee camps in southwestern Algeria.

ASEF BAYAT is a professor of Sociology and the Modern Middle East at Leiden University, the Netherlands. His extensive publications, including half a dozen books, cover such topics as social movements, religion and politics in everyday life, Islam and the modern world, urban space and politics, and international development. His latest book is *Making Islam Democratic: Social Movements and the Post-Islamist Turn* (2007).

SHAAZKA BEYERLE is an educator, researcher, and writer on civic empowerment and strategic nonviolent action and a senior advisor with the International Center on Nonviolent Conflict. Her areas of focus include corruption, good governance, women's rights, applications of social networking/digital technology, and citizen engagement in the Middle East. She is the recipient of a 2008 USIP Annual Grant Award.

RALPH E. CROW has spent the major part of the past forty years as faculty of the American University of Beirut and in the surrounding area, developing curriculum and teaching methods.

PHILIP GRANT lives and teaches in Santa Barbara, California, where he organizes public education programs on global issues and ecology. Earlier in his career, he taught at the American University of Beirut, where he and Ralph E. Crow conceived and coordinated "Arab Nonviolent Political Struggle," the first conference of its kind, held in Amman, Jordan. He subsequently convened forums and wrote articles on nonviolent political struggle as he traveled and taught in Polynesia, Japan, Southeast Asia, and the United States. He received his doctorate in Political Science from the University of California, Santa Barbara.

SHADI HAMID is director of research at the Washington, DC-based Project on Middle East Democracy and a Hewlett Fellow at Stanford University's Center for Democracy, Development, and the Rule of Law. In 2008 he was a fellow at the American Center for Oriental Research in Amman, where he conducted research on the relationship between the Muslim Brotherhood and the Jordanian regime. Hamid is a doctoral candidate in Politics at Oxford University; his dissertation is on Islamist political behavior in Egypt, Jordan, and Morocco.

ARWA HASSAN is currently project manager on Governance at the GTZ, the German government's international development agency. Prior to that, Arwa was at Transparency International, where she was Senior Program Coordinator for the Middle East and North Africa, working in and on the Arab World for many years. She has worked closely with civil society organizations, the private sector, and governments in the region for more than a decade. She has regularly lectured and presented at international fora on the issues of combating corruption, governance, and institutional reform. Arwa has a strong record of promoting dialogue between governments and non-governmental organizations.

TAMAR HERMANN is the dean of Academic Studies at the Open University of Israel and a senior fellow at the Israel Democracy Institute, where she heads the project on Israeli democracy and the emergence of grassroots (anti)politics. Between 1994 and 2006, she was the director of the Tami Steinmetz Center for Peace Research at Tel Aviv University.

ROLA EL-HUSSEINI is an assistant professor of Middle East Politics at the George H. W. Bush School of Government, Texas A&M University. Before joining the Bush School faculty, she was a postdoctoral associate at the Yale Center for International and Areas Studies and a lecturer in the Sociology department at Yale University in 2004 and 2005. Her most recent publications have appeared in *Comparative Studies of South Asia, Africa and the Middle East* and *The Middle East Journal.*

SAAD EDDIN IBRAHIM, an Egyptian scholar and democracy activist, is currently the Shawwaf Visiting Professor in Near Eastern Languages and Civilization at Harvard University. He has worked with countless organizations, among them the Ibn Khaldun Center for Development Studies and Voices for a Democratic Egypt, which he helped found. Ibrahim has held visiting chairs at Istanbul Kultur University and Indiana University. He has been in exile since 2007.

RUDY JAAFAR is co-founder of Nahwa al-Muwatiniya (Towards Citizenship), a Lebanese nongovernmental organization dedicated to improving governance in Lebanon and the Arab world. He is a Ph.D. candidate at the Fletcher School, Tufts University.

R. SCOTT KENNEDY is co-founder of the Resource Center for Nonviolence in Santa Cruz, California, www.rcnv.org. He can be contacted at kenncruzy@pacbell.net.

RAMI G. KHOURI is a Palestinian-Jordanian-American national, an internationally syndicated political columnist, editor-at-large for the *Daily Star* (Beirut), and director of the Issam Fares Institute for Public Policy and International Affairs at the American University of Beirut.

MARY ELIZABETH KING is professor of Peace and Conflict Studies at the University for Peace, a UN affiliate whose main campus is in Costa Rica, and distinguished scholar with the American University's Center for Global Peace, in Washington, DC. She is also a fellow with the Rothermere American Institute, University of Oxford. Her most recent book is *A Quiet Revolution: The First Palestinian Intifada and Nonviolent Resistance* (2007, 2008). In 1988 she won a Robert F. Kennedy Memorial Book Award for *Freedom Song: A Personal Story of the 1960s Civil Rights Movement*, concerning her years working in the U.S. civil rights movement. She is also the author of *Mahatma Gandhi and Martin Luther King, Jr: The Power of Nonviolent Action* (2nd ed., 2002), chronicling nine contemporary nonviolent struggles, and *The New York Times on Emerging Democracies in Eastern Europe, 1977–2005* (forthcoming 2009). With a grant from the U.S. Institute of Peace, she is completing field research in India for *Conversion as a Mechanism of Change in Nonviolent Action: The 1924–25 Vykom Satyagraha Case*.

KHALID KISHTAINY is a freelance author, journalist, and translator who has written more than a dozen works in Arabic in addition to ten books in English, including the classic *Arab Political Humour* (1985). Since 1989 he has written a daily satirical column for *al-Sharq al-Awsat* (London). Born in Baghdad, he currently lives in London.

SHERIF MANSOUR is senior program officer for Freedom House, Middle East and North Africa. He is also the Vice President of the International Quranic Center in North Virginia. Mansour has written and spoken on the use of new technologies for civil resistance in Egypt.

HARDY MERRIMAN is a senior advisor to the International Center on Nonviolent Conflict. He is co-author of *A Guide to Effective Nonviolent Struggle*, an activist-training curriculum, and has also written about the role of nonviolent action in reducing terrorism.

FARIBA DAVOUDI MOHAJER is an Iranian journalist and a lifelong human rights activist. She played a prominent role in the Women's Cultural Center, an Iranian women's rights organization, and is one of the founders of the One Million Signatures campaign for gender equality. In 2007 she received the Human Rights Award from Human Rights First.

MOHAMMAD RAQIB is a scholar and writer on the history and politics of South and Central Asia. He served as a major in the Afghan army and later worked as assistant director at the Afghan Health and Social Assistance organization in Peshawar, Pakistan. His publications include *Baluchistan: The Potential Objective of Soviet Strategy, The History and Performance of the Afghan Army* (in Pashto; 1988, published in *Khpalwaki* in 1992), and *Ghazian and Mujahidin: A Comparison of Holy Warriors from the 1800s to the Present* (in Pashto, Dari, and English; 2000). He holds a bachelor's degree from the Afghanistan Military College (1965) and a doctorate from Pacific Western University (1988).

MOHSEN SAZEGARA is president of the Research Institute for Contemporary Iran. He was a close aide to Ayatollah Ruhollah Khomeini while the ayatollah lived in exile in Paris during 1978–1979.

Maria J. Stephan is a leading expert on civil resistance and strategic nonviolent action. She currently works as a strategic planner at the U.S. Department of State, in the Office of the Coordinator for Reconstruction and Stabilization (S/CRS). Prior to that, Stephan was Senior Director, Policy and Research at the International Center on Nonviolent Conflict (ICNC), an educational foundation that studies and advocates the use of civilian-based strategies to advance rights and freedoms. She has taught at Georgetown's School of Foreign Service and American University's School of International Service.

Roya Toloui is an Iranian Kurdish women's rights activist who founded the Association of Kurdish Women for the Defense of Peace and Human Rights and was editor of *RASAN* (Fist), the first independent, Kurdish-language women's magazine in Iran. In 2006 she received the Oxfam Novib/PEN Award for writers living and working under the threat of persecution and detention.

Stephen Zunes is a professor of politics and chair of Middle Eastern Studies at the University of San Francisco. He is the principal editor of *Nonviolent Social Movements* (1999) and co-author (with Jacob Mundy) of *Western Sahara: Nationalism, Conflict and International Accountability* (2009).

Index

Note: page numbers in *italics* refer to illustrations and captions.